FOR
AYSEL

'A seder ci ponemmo ivi ambedui
volti a levante ond' eravam saliti,
che suole a riguardar giovare altrui'

And here we both sat down to face the east,
to rest, as we surveyed all we had climbed —
a backward glance can often lift the heart.

Dante: 'Purgatorio', Canto IV, 52.

B E N
N E V I S

Britain's

Highest

Mountain

Best wishes,

Ken Crocket

by

Ken Crocket

PUBLISHED BY THE SCOTTISH MOUNTAINEERING TRUST 1986

Crocket, Ken
  Ben Nevis: Britain's highest mountain.
  1. Mountaineering — Scotland — Nevis, Ben
  — History 2. Nevis, Ben (Scotland) —
  History
  I. Title
  796.5'22'0941185   GV199.44.G72N4

  ISBN 0-907521-16-9

TYPESET BY GRAY & DAWSON LTD., GLASGOW.
GRAPHIC ORIGINATION BY ARNEG, GLASGOW.
PRINTED BY THOMSON LITHO, EAST KILBRIDE.
BOUND BY HUNTER & FOULIS, EDINBURGH.

CONTENTS

ILLUSTRATIONS

ACKNOWLEDGEMENTS

Many have aided in the preparation of this book, whether in lending photographs, providing information and/or advice, or reading part or all of the MS. I am deeply grateful to all for their generosity. In no particular order they are: Ian Sykes, for pushing me into starting; Tom Weir, for providing a Foreword, for editing the MS and for encouragement; Bill Murray, for comments on Chapter 6; Jimmy Marshall, for comments on Chapter 9; John Lackie, for constructive comments on the MS; Adam Curtis, for word processing facilities; Andy Hart, for excellent work in the Dark-room; Colin Stead and Bob Lawford, Librarians of the Scottish Mountaineering Club and The Alpine Club respectively; Robin Campbell, for reading Chapter 4, and for opening my eyes to the achievements of Raeburn and Company; Graham Tiso, for trusting me once again with selections from the A.E. Robertson Photographic Collection; Karuna, for material on her husband, the late J.H.B. Bell; the late Bill Peascod, for material in Chapter 7; Miss Marjory Roy, Superintendent Meteorological Office (Edinburgh), for unpublished and other material in Chapter 3; Bill Brooker, Editor SMC Journal, for permission to borrow heavily from his Journals; Rab Carrington, for permission to use material first published in Mountain Magazine; Alan Rouse, for an extract of an essay first published in 'Cold Climbs'; the Secretaries and other office-bearers of the SMC, AC, FRCC, YRC, EUMC, GUMC, The Wayfarers' Club, The Rucksack Club and any other club who helped; Mr Alex Ross, Secretary Ben Nevis Race Association and Manager of the Ben Nevis Distillery, for his help and Highland hospitality; Nat Allen of The Rock & Ice; Julian Dow, for the analysis of Kellett's handwriting; Miss Archibald, Curator West Highland Museum, Fort William; Mr Adrian Hope, Engineer, Fort William Aluminium Smelter; Archie Hendry, for material; Hamish MacInnes and Alex Gillespie, for photographic material; The University Library of Aberdeen, for permission to use a print from the Wilson Collection in Ch.1; the Scottish Mountaineering Trust, who published this book, for financial assistance; Len Lovat, for comments on the MS; Jim MacLeod, for help with Dante's 'Purgatorio'; botanists Rose Scott and John Mitchell of the Nature Conservancy Council, for pointing out my botanical inadequacies; Graham Wylie, who designed the book; Graham Little, for the appendix on the mapping of Ben Nevis; Seonag MacDonald and Mary MacLeod, native speakers both, for help with the Gaelic appendix; W.A. Mozart & J.S. Bach, whose music helped on many a night ascent to the CIC Hut; Derek Pyper, SMC Slide Custodian; Jim Renny, for figures; Peter Hodgkiss, for information and other help, Evelyn Soutar, Alastair Walker, Ken Smith, Rab Anderson, Peter Birrell, Norrie Muir, Arthur Paul, John MacInnes, Alex Small. The debt that all climbers owe to the members of the rescue teams, civilian and R.A.F., is only too obvious.

Climbers themselves, we must be thankful that they enjoy this difficult and often hazardous aspect of the mountains. Some photographic materials have come to me by circuitous routes, but I have tried to acknowledge their source in the captions. Any photograph not so acknowledged is probably from the Author's collection. I apologise in advance for any errors or omissions and also to anyone else whom I may have overlooked.

In addition to those listed above, I gratefully acknowledge the following for permission to use copyrighted material: Macmillan & Co., for lines from 'The Last Enemy' by Richard Hillary, in Ch.2; Heinemann, for material from 'Don Whillans: Portrait of a Mountaineer' by Don Whillans and Alick Ormerod, in Ch.8; John Farquharson Limited, agents for the literary estate of the late Dougal Haston, for material from 'In High Places' by Dougal Haston, published by Cassell, in Chs. 8 & 9; Long John International, for material based on 'The Romance of Long John' by Jack House, in Ch.10; Gollancz, for lines from 'On And Off The Rocks', a collection of essays by Jim Perrin.

FOREWORD

Two important events in the late 19th century made Britain's highest summit easy for anyone possessed of time and money. The first was the building of a pony track from Glen Nevis to Britain's only mountain-top Observatory, while the second was the opening of the West Highland Railway in 1894. Before these momentous events the climbing of Ben Nevis by a casual tourist would have been regarded as something of a feat. In May 1880 a trio of climbers who came to it on hearing that the giant had not been scaled since the previous autumn decided that they would make the snow-dome theirs. They didn't expect however to meet real winter conditions when they were only half way up.

The lochan at that height was still partly covered with ice, while above the snow was almost continuous and disappearing into the clouds. Resolving to wait on the chance of the weather clearing at mid-day they amused themselves in the snow, then after two hours when nothing seemed to be happening, they took a compass bearing finding the snow getting harder and harder until they were kicking strenuously to make steps. But as they came on to the summit plateau they were floundering in deep powder snow up to the knees.

W.W. Naismith's party was keeping a sharp look out in the white-out world of the summit plateau, steering for where they thought the top must be. They knew that the flattish top sheered away in a sudden plunge of tremendous cliffs. He wrote:

". . . with appalling suddenness we found ourselves upon the brink of a yawning gulf, walking straight for it. The black rocks were capped by heavy folds of snow many feet thick, which overhung the abyss in a grand cornice festooned with colossal icicles."

The summit cairn was,

". . . almost entirely covered with only a stone or two and a pole projecting; and it was only by discovering a bottle with names inside that we felt sure we had reached the actual summit, and realised there was nothing above us nearer than Norway."

They were shortly to get another shock of surprise when they plunged down the snow for 1500 ft out of white gloom into a world of sea and mountains,

"Loch Eil with the sun shining on it; while beyond on either side, were the mountains of Morven and Knoidart, of Mull and Skye, 'unto the utmost sea' ''.

They were back in Fort William by six-o'clock discovering their feat had been daring enough to be reported in the local newspaper as the *First Ascent of Ben Nevis — without guides'*.

W.W. Naismith was an example of a new breed of adventurist tourist, mountaineers looking for challenging routes, and the great cliffs where winter lingers into mid-summer was their target. One was Professor Norman Collie, of whom you will read more. His party were able to refresh themselves inside the summit observatory after their first complete ascent of Tower Ridge in 1894. I knew nothing of the historical background to Nevis on my first heavy-pack-carrying ascent in 1931, after a cold night in a blanket on the floor of the mouldering half-way hut built in 1883. Nor did my odd companion Ritchie who was 26 and ten years older than me.

Ritchie was odd in that he liked to travel continuously over mountains carrying all his gear rather than go up and down lightly laden. His plan was to go over Nevis and on over Aonach Beag. That morning we had the top of Ben Nevis to ourselves in thick mist, and like Naismith we were on the edge of the cliffs before we expected them. Route-finding on Nevis is tricky. On finding the edge of the ground falling away rockily in front of us we should have retired. We continued down the rocks and I was soon in a state of anxiety clinging above a ferocious drop with the weight of my rucksack feeling it would unbalance me and drag me down. Far below the cliff I could see boulders, and remember letting out a wail for help.

With assistance from Ritchie I was able to work a way to safety, and keeping together we managed to traverse out. Ben Nevis had taught me a very frightening first lesson, and at the same time given me a taste of the unknown that was to draw me back to this gigantic face of cliff whose complications are so difficult to get to know, even with the help of Scottish Mountaineering Club literature. Stormy weather and obscuring mist will see to that.

On my next visit to Nevis I came to climb the Tower Ridge, and would have been a bolder seventeen year-old with a like-minded companion and a length of Alpine Club rope. As before I had slept out on the mountain and took fright as I watched with apprehension curling mists swirling round the snow-patched pinnacled crags which seemed to get bigger and bigger as I looked. Their hugeness daunted me, yet I had just come from two weeks rock climbing in Skye. Nevis looked much more savage. I turned away, feeling inadequate. I was intimidated, fearing I might lose the route, get stuck or fall off.

Third time was lucky however, when on an April day and on Army leave I set off with a member of the Scottish Mountaineering Club from Fort William to try the Observatory Ridge, which in his opinion was the most elegant of the three great Nevis ridges. Contouring into the coire he pointed out to me the main architectural features of the great cathedral of rock rising over 2000 ft above us, naming each buttress, gully, chimney and ridge. When I asked him if he thought the narrow icy blade of ridge we were intending to try was really possible in these conditions, he replied,

"It's for you to decide, for you are going to have the honour of leading it."

I did, and treasure the memory of working a way up its soaring edge, step-cutting, clearing rocks of snow to feel the friction of tricouni nails, revelling in the exposure to the increasingly big drop below our heels. Then the final arête and we were up and looking to the Cuillins of Skye and the peaks of Rum, silhouetted against the gold of the declining sun. North, south and east all the distant peaks stood clear, and we enjoyed ourselves walking within safety of the snow-cornices overhanging the big cliff edges and dropping into the depths of the Allt a'Mhuilinn over 2000 ft below.

A more chilling memory is of a January day of wet falling snow which soaked us on the northern cliffs, and as we descended our clothes froze on us and put a skin of ice on the rocks making it such slow work that I doubt if I have ever been so near being a victim of hypothermia. I was under-clad, unlike my companion. I suffered for it and had to wear a flannel round my kidneys for a year, which was another lesson from Nevis I am not likely to forget.

However my memories of Ben Nevis are slight in comparison with those of the author of this book, who puts Ben Nevis in perspective as one of the great climbing mountains of the world, with a seriousness out of all proportion to its height in metres above sea-level. Ken Crocket is a modern mountaineer who in the wintriest conditions of snow and ice has pioneered new ways on the steepest crags of the north-east face.

But it is about the whole mountain and its history he writes. Mountaineers have their own guidebooks, and climbers can find out all they need to know about routes from descriptions in the excellent works published by the Scottish Mountaineering Trust. Ken Crocket looks at every aspect of Ben Nevis. For me it has been a great privilege to go over the work with him before publication. His is an absorbing story and he tells it well.

Tom Weir, President Scottish Mountaineering Club, May 1986.

INTRODUCTION

This offering of mine on Ben Nevis concerns itself mainly with man's interaction with the mountain which is not only the highest in Britain but one of the most ferocious in Europe for weather changes. Yet on the huge cliffs of its northern face standards of climbing and technique have evolved to lead the climbing world.

I think I can claim to have run almost the full gamut of experiences good and bad that this big mountain can offer; frozen and frightened to a point of near despair, committed on an icy overhang with only two options open, climb or fall off; or soaked and shivering in a cloudburst with water foaming down the steep rocks on to which I was clinging; and the joyous good days, moving up confidently on small holds on warm rock.

The memory floods with other days on Nevis. Days when an overcast, drizzly start in Fort William gave no warning of the cloud sea visible from the summit, realised only when cutting the last steps through a gully cornice. To see only the tops of the surrounding mountains piercing a silent layer of cloud meant staying on top for the sunset — never mind that the long descent by Coire Leis was a purgatory of ice-glazed boulders.

For true suffering there is always the dreaded Allt a'Mhuilinn path, its seemingly endless inclines and elusive tracks through acres of black, quaking bog the only route not in the guidebook. The old start up the mountain lay through the Distillery and over a boggy morass known to climbers, with a grim sense of humour, as 'The Everglades'. Tales of lurking alligators helped lighten the apprehension of the dour trudge ahead. Strong men have wept on that route.

"This Mount is not like others: at the start
it is most difficult to climb, but then,
the more one climbs the easier it becomes;"

Dante: 'Purgatorio', IV, 88.

A sense of history began to creep in at the edges one night in the CIC Hut when, as a young 'lad' of about 22, I started adding up the accumulated years of mountaineering experience visible in the hut. Some three hundred years of living history was distilled there, crammed into a wooden cigar-box of a hut, itself now beyond the half-century. We were from disparate backgrounds and had travelled by different routes, but there was a common purpose, enjoyment of the mountain.

We were testing ourselves as all who come to this steep side of Ben Nevis in summer and winter do. My own pleasure was intensified by reading tales of adventure on Ben Nevis in the pages of the Scottish Mountaineering Club Journal by some of the mountain's greatest explorers. It was the genesis of this book which I hope you will enjoy.

Ken Crocket,

Glasgow 1986.

1.1 Pont's map (detail), (c.1654)

EARLY TRAVELLERS (1585 – 1865)

The origin of the name 'Nevis' is just as difficult to pin down as are early ascents. In his 'History of the Celtic Place-names of Scotland', the late Professor Watson suggests an Old Irish word 'neamhaise', meaning 'terrible', and also a Gaelic word 'ni-mhaise', meaning 'no beauty'. W.C. Mackenzie, writing in his book on Scottish Place-Names, has made an attempt to associate the Irish 'neamhaise' with the Scottish 'uamhais', or 'dread', thus drawing in the two mountains Nevis and Wyvis. The word 'neamh' in Gaelic means 'a raw and bitingly keen atmosphere', and is sometimes confused with the gaelic word 'neimh', meaning 'poison, bitterness, and malice'.

To any mountaineer who has endured a day of bad weather on the frozen north face of Nevis, or indeed to anyone who has walked to the summit in poor conditions, there will be a familiar ring to any of the above names. There is no shortage of possibilities as to the origin of the mountain's name (1-4). (see also Appendix A).

In Johan Blaeu's 'Le Grand Atlas', the map of Scotland marks a Bin Novesh, a Glen Nevish and, flowing down that Glen, the Avon Nevish. There is no Fort William of course, as that garrison was not built until 1650 and was in any case named otherwise. There is an Achiontoir, about where Achintore is sited. (5).

The year 1585 as a starting point for this history is partly conjectural, though it seems likely that it marks the beginning of a period during which a certain Timothy Pont (1565-1614) was responsible for the first topographical survey of Scotland. Pont's difficult and self-imposed task is of interest to us for two reasons. Firstly, it indicates the difficulties and dangers of travel in Scotland at the close of the 16th Century, and secondly it led to the publication in 1654 of the Scottish edition of maps by Blaeu of Amsterdam. These maps for the first time show Scotland's highest mountain as a 'Bin Novesh.' Strangely enough, although it is reasonably certain that Pont travelled through the Cairngorms, there is no recording on his maps of either Ben Macdhui, Braeriach or Cairn Toul.

Of Pont and his arduous journey over Scotland we have little first-hand information, the only original reference being found in a letter from Sir Robert Gordon of Straloch (1580-1661) to Sir John Scot of Scotstarvet (1585-1670), dated 1648. Pont, a Scot and son of the Minister at Dunnet, Caithness, graduated from St Andrews in 1583 and there exists a map of Clydesdale by him, dated 1596. He died without seeing his work published and indeed the manuscript maps would have rotted away in the royal archives of King James VI but for their rescue by Sir John Scot. It was the latter who arranged both for Robert Gordon of Aberdeenshire to revise and complete the maps, and for Blaeu of Amsterdam to print them in his monumental Atlas of The World.

About Pont's task we have the following excerpt, taken from the letter by Gordon dated 1648. (6). The translation is by C.G. Cash, utilising both Latin and French versions.

". . . For, with small means and no favouring patron, he undertook the whole of this task forty years ago; he travelled on foot right through the whole of this kingdom, as no one before him had done; he visited all the islands, occupied for the most part by inhabitants hostile and uncivilised, (and with a language different from our own); being often stripped, as he told me, by the fierce robbers, and suffering not seldom all the hardships of the dangerous journey, nevertheless at no time was he overcome by the difficulties, nor was he disheartened. But when, having returned, he prepared to publish the results of his labours, he was defeated by the greed of printers and booksellers (who refused to supply the necessary funds), and so could not reach his goal. While awaiting better times, untimely death took him away (in the flower of his age) . . ." (7).

The growth of the present town of Fort William, situated near the head of Loch Linnhe and at the southern end of the Caledonian Canal, can be said to have properly begun in 1650. It was then, during Cromwell's protectorate, that General Monk erected a fortress. Two weeks later Cameron of Lochiel attacked the fort, which was mainly built of earth, many of the garrison being either killed or drowned.

This first garrison, which had been named the Garrison of Inverlochy, was rebuilt by General MacKay in 1690, in the reign of William III. To that date, the village which had grown alongside the garrison had been known as Gordonsburgh, the land then being the property of the Gordon family. With the building of the more substantial fort in 1690 the village was renamed Maryburgh, while the garrison became Fort William.

About this time in clan history occurs one of the earliest references to Ben Nevis. Of the origins of the Camerons we know little, other than several mentions of them starting in the 11th Century, when one Angus married Marion, daughter of the Thane of Lochaber. Going forward to about 1647, Allan, the sixteenth chief, was succeeded by his grandson, Sir Ewen Dubh. When Ewen was 12 years old he was sent to the Earl of Argyll for his education. He returned to his clan when he was 18 and soon showed himself to be a strong and capable leader.

When the young chief heard that Monk was cutting down large quantities of wood for his newly built garrison he attacked, killing a large number of soldiers. Such was his character however, that he and Monk eventually settled their differences, developing a strong friendship. We have the early reference to Ben Nevis from the 'Memoirs of Sir Ewen Cameron of Locheill', (as his name was then spelled), written by John Drummond of Balhaldy in about 1737. Drummond was a Jacobite agent.

"Behind the fort there arises a huge mountain, of prodigeous hight, called Beniviss, at that time adorned with a variety of trees and bushes, and now with a beautiful green. Its ascent is pretty steep, though smooth. The top or summit is plain, covered with perpetual snow, and darkened with thick clouds." (8).

This early description of Ben Nevis would suggest that by the early 18th Century ascents of the mountains were not unheard of, but were very rare until about the mid-18th Century. Before then the prevailing attitude to mountains in general was one of repugnance and distaste, feelings very evident in the travel writings of the period. The native Highlanders had little use for the summits, cattle and game being confined mainly to the coires and lower slopes where there was grazing.

That local inhabitants visited the northern coires of the Ben before the 18th Century is very likely. An old legend, one shared with some other Scottish mountains, has it that should all the snow vanish from Ben Nevis then the land shall be forfeit. To prevent this Cameron of Lochiel, in a summer when it looked as if the last of the snow might melt away, is said to have sent locals up the mountain with straw, to protect the remaining snow patches.

Following the 1715 Rebellion Major-General George Wade was instructed by King George I to proceed to the Highlands, "to report on the situation and to suggest such *remedies as would conduce to the settlement of that part of the kingdom."* General Wade's report was presented in the autumn of 1724, and on Christmas Day of that year he was appointed 'Commander-in-Chief of all His Majesty's Forces in North Britain.' The end results of Wade's work in Scotland (and also of the much-underrated William Caulfeild, who was responsible for more miles of new road and became Inspector of Roads before retiring as a Lieutenant-Colonel) are well-enough known, being a programme of road and bridge building which radically changed communications in Scotland.

Of pertinence to our story of Ben Nevis is a certain Edward Burt, who accompanied Wade to Scotland. Captain Burt's position in Scotland, from about 1725 to 1740, was that of the receiver and collector of rents on such of the estates still remaining unsold after the 1715 Rebellion, the so-called 'Forfeited Estates'.

Edward Burt was the author of the 'Letters from a Gentleman in the North of Scotland.' This was published in 1754 (9), but the letters, some twenty-six in all, were written to a friend in London about the years 1727-1728. With the sole exception of the last letter, which was written eight years after the others, the letters were sent from Inverness at fortnightly intervals. They provide a fascinating glimpse into a world far distant from the present one — or even to the outside world at that time.

Burt himself was no lover of the hills, which he described as 'monstrous excrescences', but we are fortunate in that he left an account of an early attempt to climb Ben Nevis.

"Some English officers took it in their Fancy to go to the Top, but could not attain it for Bogs and huge Perpendicular Rocks . . . This wild Expedition, in ascending round and round the Hills; in finding accessible Places, helping one another up the Rocks, in Disappointments, and their returning to the Foot of the Mountain took them up a whole Summer's Day from five in the Morning."

The account went on to comment on how fortunate the officers were in having a cloud-free day.

A second, early description of Ben Nevis follows from the tours of Scotland made by Thomas Pennant in 1769 and 1772. Of Ben Nevis Pennant writes,

"Fort William is surrounded by vast mountains, which occasion almost torrential rain: the loftiest are on the South side; Benevish soars above the rest, and ends, as I was told, in a point, (at this time concealed in mist) whose height from the sea is said to be 1450 yards. As an ancient Briton, I lament the disgrace of Snowdon; once esteemed the highest hill in the island, but now must yield the palm to a Caledonian mountain." (10).

Pennant was a leisured and cultured English squire with an interest in natural history. His journeys were made through a land virtually unknown to the average Englishman.

The earliest recorded visits to Nevis were for scientific purposes. Professor John Hope of Edinburgh records *Veronica alpina* as having been collected on Ben Nevis in 1767, by Dr de la Roche and Fabricius, Edinburgh medical students. Twelve years later George Don of Forfar, author of 'Herbarium Britanicum' (1804), began his excursions into the Highlands. On Ben Nevis Don collected the alpine form of *Sagina maritima,* and the rare grass *Poa flexuosa.*

For five summers the botanist James Robertson collected specimens in Scotland for the College Museum in Edinburgh. In 1771, along with eight other first recorded ascents, he made an ascent of Ben Nevis. Unfortunately he left few details of the actual ascent. (11). A letter published in the Philosophical Transactions of the Royal Society in 1769 tells us a little more of Robertson's travels.

"A letter from John Hope, M.D., F.R.S., Professor of Physic and Botany in the University of Edinburgh, to William Watson, M.D., F.R.S. on a rare plant found in the Isle of Skye.

(The plant) was found, September 1768, in a small lake in the island of Skye, by James Robertson, whom I sent there in search of new or rare plants. Mr James Robertson is an élève of mine, and has been employed by the commissioners of the annexed estates to make a botanical survey of the distant parts of Scotland." (12).

Robertson subsequently went to Calcutta, gaining employment with the East India Company. (13).

Three years later, in 1774, the second recorded ascent was made by John Williams, a Welshman. The ascent on this occasion was prompted by the possibility of commercial gain, as Williams had been instructed by the Commissioners of the Forfeited Estates to *"examine the different sorts of stones particularly on the tops of high hills."* Williams later published a book on minerals, the second edition of which includes a character sketch of Williams by James Millar (Editor of 'Encyclopaedia Edinensis').

". . . he seems to have been a man of acute observation and nice discernment, of great activity, and ardour of mind; and, what is not unusual in such characters, the warmth of his enthusiasm, on the peculiar subjects of his contemplation, seems at times to have led him too far into visionary speculations."

Visionary speculations apart, Williams includes a description of Ben Nevis in Chapter 4 of his book, where he describes the 'Natural History of Mountains.'

"Ben Nevis is about a mile in perpendicular height . . . More than two thirds of the height of this mountain are composed of an elegant red granite . . . the summit of it is, nevertheless, regularly stratified with a different stone, to about one fourth of the whole height . . . the hardest rocks in this mountain are the highest . . . There is a deep gulph at the bottom of a frightful precipice, about five hundred yards on the north-east side of this mountain . . . The precipice . . . exhibits a magnificent section of the internal structure of that mountain, in which we distinctly see where the uniform mass of granite ends, and the stratified rock begins above it. We also see, that the strata of different rocks dips towards the south-east with an easy declivity." (14).

Fortunately for the following generations of mountaineers John Williams found no rocks of commercial interest on the summit of Nevis, and the mountain fell back into a brief respite, to be broken by the arrival of a new type of mountaineer — the tourist.

In 1787, some thirteen years after the ascent by Williams the Welshman, an expedition of eleven set out from Glen Nevis. The instigator of the climb was a Lieutenant Walker who was stationed at Fort William; his chief companion was the Rev. James Bailey, vicar of Otley, in Yorkshire. The party left the Glen at 6 a.m., accompanied by three Highland guides, two sergeants and three privates of the Royal Fusiliers, the soldiers acting as porters for the liquors and provisions. A Mr Kayne was also in the party.

Military training had obviously influenced the preparations for this trip, for the party was equipped with a rope and grappling iron; used on a series of rocky shelves. Throughout the ascent, which took seven hours, difficulties were encountered, and at several points combined tactics were employed. One of the soldiers collapsed just before the summit, but the strong smell of rum indicated an over enthusiastic use of the liquor supply and he soon recovered.

The successful summit party celebrated in the age-old sport of 'trundling', the reckless heaving of boulders from cliff tops, before turning their attention to the descent. This was accomplished in six hours, and though it was described as being *"rapid, though excessively fatiguing, for we were, for the most part, obliged to slide upon our haunches"*, by modern standards it was a slow descent. (15).

Another ascent in 1787 was that of a certain Thomas Wilkinson, a neighbour of the poet Wordsworth, who accompanied John Pemberton, an American Quaker, on a preaching tour of the Highlands and other parts of Scotland. Wordsworth described Wilkinson in a letter to a friend as *"An amiable inoffensive man and a little of a poet too . . ."*

Reaching Fort William, probably in late summer or early autumn, Wilkinson determined to climb Nevis, but being unable to find a willing guide he set off alone. He found himself on the wrong side of the River Nevis which he succeeded in fording, burning his boats by throwing his shoes to the far bank. His ascent details are almost non-existent, but the following extract from his account is worth quoting.

"The base of Ben Nevis is covered with soil; grass, shrubs, and trees climb up its sides to a considerable height, but its lofty summit is composed of grey rocks that seem to leave vegetation below. The north side of the mountain may be said to be hung with terrors. Perpendicular and projecting rocks, gulphy glens and awful precipices, gloomy and tremendous caverns, the vast repositories of snow from age to age; these, with blue mists gauzing the grey rocks of the mountain, and terrible cataracts thundering from Ben Nevis, made altogether a scene sublimely dreadful." (16).

Though these ascents in 1787 were the third and fourth recorded so far, there must have been others since the ore-hunting trip of Williams, for Lieutenant Walker's party found more than 30 small stone cairns on the summit plateau, erected by previous visitors.

In 1796 the Hon Mrs Murray Aust of Kensington made a thorough and energetic tour of Scotland. Arising from that tour was a descriptive guide — 'A Companion and Useful Guide to the Beauties of Scotland, and the Hebrides'. While Mrs Aust did not herself climb Ben Nevis, she did describe in her interesting book the surrounding countryside. Her tour began on May 28, and finished about October. She travelled down from Inverness about the beginning of August, describing the scene on the road from Spean Bridge to Fort William.

"Through the vast moor before me, there was nothing but the road to be seen, except a few scattered huts; some of them in such bogs, that it seemed impossible for any human being to exist in such places . . . The eight miles from High Bridge to Fort William, is the most dreary, though not the ugliest, space I had travelled in Scotland . . . The huts on this moor are very small and low, are soon erected, and must very soon fall down. They consist of four stakes of birch, forked at the top, driven into the ground; on these they lay four other birch poles, and then form a gavel at each end by putting up more birch sticks, and crossing them sufficiently to support the clods with which they plaster this skeleton of a hut all over, except a small hole in the side for a window, a small door to creep in and and (sic) out at, and a hole in the roof, stuck round with sticks, patched up with turf, for a vent, as they call a chimney . . .

In these huts they make a fire upon the ground . . . At night they rake out the fire, and put their beds of heath and blankets (which they have in abundance) on the ground, where the fire had been, and thus keep themselves warm during the night."

Continuing on to Fort William, Mrs Aust was lucky enough to gain a view of the mountain.

"In its shape there is beauty, mixed with the sublime and terrific. In front a soft verdant sloping hill; behind which is a hollow, and a lofty crescent rising from it, with its high pointed horns; joining to one of which are towers of huge rocks, furrowed by continual torrents; with hollows and chasms filled with snow, forming a rare contrast in summer, with the black and grey rocks of the crescent, and other huge masses adjoining . . . The summit, however, of Ben Nivis, I am told, is a bed of white pebbles, some of them beautiful."

1.2   Ben Nevis from Corpach, (c.1880)

Finally, Mrs Aust retold an amusing story connected with Ben Nevis.

"I learnt, in those parts, another instance of the great love a Highland man has for whisky. A lady of fashion, having conquered that ascent, before she quitted it, left on purpose a bottle of whisky on the summit: when she returned to the fort, she laughingly mentioned that circumstance before some Highland men, as a piece of carelessness; one of whom slipped away, and mounted to the pinnacle of 4,370 feet, above the level of the fort, to gain the prize of the bottle of whisky, and brought it down in triumph." (17).

The poet John Keats made a grand tour of Scotland with his friend Charles Brown, in 1818. On August 2 he made an ascent of Nevis with Brown and a local guide. The ascent was described in a four-page letter to his brother Tom, which also included an imaginary dialogue between a Mrs Cameron and Ben Nevis; running to 74 lines. It seems that this Mrs Cameron had the dubious honour of being the fattest woman in all Inverness-shire, who at the age of 50 had nonetheless succeeded in climbing Nevis, some years before Keats. The Keats party set out at 5 a.m. and soon arrived at the first slopes,

". . . after much fag and tug and a rest and a glass of whiskey apiece we gained the top of the first rise."

Before long, the party entered a mist, in which they walked to the very top.

"The whole immense head of the Mountain is composed of large loose stones — thousands of acres — Before we had got half way up we passed large patches of snow and near the top there is a chasm some hundred feet deep completely glutted with it — Talking of chasms they are the finest wonder of the whole — they appear great rents in the very heart of the mountain though they are not, being at the side of it, but other huge crags arising round it give the appearance to Nevis of a shattered heart or core in itself."

Keats went on to describe the cloud effects and glimpses of other mountains through "cloudy loop holes", before climbing a cairn built by some climbers. "It was not so cold as I expected — yet cold enough for a glass of whiskey now and then." The descent was not to his liking. "I felt it horribly. 'Twas the most vile descent — shook me all to pieces."

In the letter to his brother was a Sonnet Keats wrote at the summit of Nevis:

> "Read me a Lesson, muse, and speak it loud
> Upon the top of Nevis blind in Mist!
> I look into the Chasms and a Shroud
> Vaprous doth hide them; just so much I wist
> Mankind do know of Hell: I look o'erhead
> And there is a sullen mist; even so much
> Mankind can tell of Heaven: Mist is spread
> Before the Earth beneath me — even such
> Even so vague is Man's sight of himself.
> Here are the craggy Stones beneath my feet;
> Thus much I know, that a poor witless elf
> I tread on them; that all my eye doth meet
> Is mist and Crag — not only on this height,
> But in the world of thought and mental might." (18).

Several factors help explain the rapid growth of tourism in Scotland at the end of the 18th and beginning of the 19th centuries. The improved road networks of Wade and Caulfeild made travel easier. Also the Napoleonic Wars, by cutting off the Continent, redirected adventurous tourists north to Scotland. Many of these early travellers were inspired by recently written travel books; of a type containing a new enthusiasm for the countryside. It should be borne in mind that that great catalyst of travel, the railway, did not reach Fort William until the autumn of 1894, an absence which greatly delayed the exploration of Ben Nevis.

Sir John Carr described a tour through Scotland undertaken in 1807; his description of Fort William as it was then is probably a fair and accurate one.

"Fort William is situate on Lochaber, bordering on the Western Ocean, yet within the shire of Inverness . . . the town was erected into a borough in honour of Queen Mary: it is a long street of indifferent houses, stuccoed white, and is chiefly inhabited by fishermen, who carry on a considerable fishery in the lake. The inn is rather destitute of accommodation. Nothing can be shabbier, as a fortification, than Fort William; it has neither strength, space, nor neatness . . . The farce of shutting the gate at the hour usual in fortified towns is still preserved in this travesty of a fortification.

I was now in the region of rain, which descended with little intermission, during my stay at Maryborough, with a copiousness which I have not often beheld. Rain, which continues in this neighbourhood for nine or ten weeks together, is called by the natives by the gentle name of a shower.

When I first saw (Ben Nevis), the atmosphere was tolerably clear, and it then appeared to be as ugly in shape as it is in size. In some of its chasms in its northern side, the whiteness of eternal snows singularly contrasted with its vast masses of black and grey rocks." (19).

Another travel book written at that time was 'The Highlands and Western Isles of Scotland', by John Macculloch. Published in 1824 this described an ascent of Ben Nevis, in which Macculloch only too clearly turns out to be the hero. It also describes a summit blizzard and the shortcomings of the professional guides then available.

". . . on the 20th of August, as I looked out of the window of the inn at Balahulish, at six o'clock in the morning, it was a fine day . . . I stole my own horse, saddled him, roused the ferryman, launched the ferry-boat, rode off to Fort William, breakfasted, and by one o'clock was on top of the mountain . . .

From the rarity of fine weather and a cloudless sky at Fort William, and because the distance to the top of Ben Nevis is considerable, and the ascent laborious, it is not often visited. Measuring it as well as I could by pacing, I found it about eight miles; the path on the mountain, which is very circuitous, amounting to about six, out of which there are two of a very steep and laborious ascent . . .

Doubtless, the ascent of Ben Nevis is considered a mighty deed; and, in consequence, there are various names inscribed on the cairn within the plain; while some had been written on scraps of paper, and enclosed in bottles which had been drained of their whisky by the valiant who had reached this perilous point of honour. Such is the love of fame, 'that the clear spirit doth raise', to carve its aspiring initials on desks, and to scratch them on the windows of inns . . . But we must not enquire too curiously into this folly; and when we are inclined to sneer at those who are now inscribing their unheard-of names on the tombs or barracks of Pompeii, we must remember how grateful we are to those, who, probably with no other greater ambition, scratched their own, two thousand years ago, on the statue of Memnon . . .

But the summit itself is utterly bare, and presents a most extraordinary and unexpected sight . . . It is an extensive & flat plain, strewed with loose rocks, tumbled together in fragments of all sizes, and, generally, covering the solid foundation to a considerable depth . . . I had not time, however, to walk round the whole plain before there came on as dense & bitter a storm of snow as I ever experienced . . . I was not, however, alone, since I had with me what is commonly called a guide; a lad who had volunteered his services . . . I had gained too much experience in guides not to know that . . . they were, generally, either useless or mischievous . . . when my guide found himself in a whirlwind of fog and snow, so thick we could scarcely see each other . . . he began to cry . . . the unhappy animal . . . vowed that if he ever lived to get home, he would never guide a gentleman again. He would even surrender his five shillings, if I would show him the way down the hill . . . There was but one way down from this wide plain . . . I had observed the bearing of this path at first, and therefore, taking out the compass, walked boldly on.

By the time his kilt was thoroughly cooled, and that he had vowed never to wear one again, the storm cleared away, and we returned by the road of Glen Nevis. The descent from Ben Nevis by the glen is not inconvenient, and it is wild and romantic. It is said that Cameron of Glen Nevis holds his lands by the tenure of an unfailing snow-ball when demanded." (20).

From the early 1830's until the late 1860's a small salmon-curing factory used a storeroom belonging to the Caledonian Canal. This cured salmon caught locally in Loch Eil and Loch Linnhe, the cured fish then being taken south in sailing smacks. At Corpach was an ice-house, used for storing the fish before they were processed. The ice was usually taken from a nearby millpond during winter cold spells, but there is a reference to the collection of snow from the north face of Ben Nevis in two seasons when the supply of ice must have run out, probably in the summer or autumn. The following account was written in 1835 by the parish minister.

"The deep clefts on the north-east side of Ben Nevis are never without snow. For two seasons when ice failed, the snow gathered and condensed into ice in these clefts and was of great service to the salmon curers. The country peasants with their small hardy horses carried it down in panniers on horseback." (21).

As to the actual site of ice collection there is no description, though a study of the mountain in early summer shows that one possible site accessible to horses is the gorge lying below the Secondary Tower Ridge. Failing this, ice collectors would probably have had to climb up to one of the large snow patches which linger on to mid or late summer, such as the one below Zero Gully.

Mountaineering for the sake of Science continued on into the 19th century, the geologists following upon the heels of the botanists. Born in 1809 of an ancient Scots family, James David Forbes was elected (in competition against Sir David Brewster) to the Professorship of Natural Philosophy in the University of Edinburgh in 1833. He was then not quite 24 years of age. This early ability was despite, or perhaps because of, an absence of formal schooling. Though primarily a physicist, his keen powers of observation coupled with a love of the mountains led him naturally to a secondary interest in geology, culminating in his classic study on glaciation, 'Travels Through The Alps'. (22).

Scottish professors at this time had the option of giving all of their annual lectures in any space of six consecutive months; allowing much time for research or holidays. Forbes made several extended rambles across Scotland during his long holidays, and in 1847 climbed Schiehallion and visited Ben Nevis, *"hoping to write a book on the group"*. In 1848 he made a survey of Ben Nevis, walking round the mountain in three days with a guide, but carrying his own provisions. In 1851 his health broke down and his climbing days were over. Despite this

1.3   Portrait of James Forbes, (c.1833)

in 1855 he wrote that he was *"still crazy about the Alps"*, and *"loved the Scottish hills the better for their snow."*

During the 1848 trip of Forbes we have the first record of step-cutting on Ben Nevis (though not in Scotland, for in 1812 a Colonel Peter Hawker cut steps on Ben Lomond).

"As we approached the head of the glen, we got only glimpses of snow fields and broken rocks above us; and at length we were immersed in the fog, which fortunately was not very deep. We kept on the rocks as long as we could, and at length found that there only intervened between us and the ridge a short steep ascent of drifted snow, most truly Alpine. It was too late to think of receding, and it was not far; so assuming my new mahogany tripod as an Alpine stock, I proceeded foremost to make steps in the most approved Swiss fashion, to the no small edification of my companion, who had never seen such an operation before. The upper few yards were so steep that I actually could not get one foot stuck into the snow before the other, and had to get along sideways." (23).

After the scientists came the measurers, the Ordnance Survey. There is an amusing reference to these map-makers in a book by John Hill Burton, published in 1864. (Burton was an advocate. In 1867 he was appointed H.M. Historiographer for Scotland). Climbing Ben Nevis by the tourist route, Burton gained the summit plateau, where slowly thinning mist revealed a strange sight,

"It was neither more nor less than a crowd of soldiers, occupying nearly the whole table-land of the summit! Yes, there they were, British troops, with their red coats, dark-grey trousers, and fatigue caps . . . The party were occupied in erecting a sort of dwelling for themselves-half tent, half hut." (24).

It seemed, as Burton soon learned, that the Survey had already conducted some surveys on Ben Macdhui and were now beginning to do the same work on Ben Nevis, so as to decide which of these two mountains had the honour of being the highest in the United Kingdom. At this time, Burton was told, the Cairngorm mountain was 'leading' by some 20 feet, subsequently he was informed that Ben Nevis had it by a few feet.

With slow, timid steps, one individual at a time, a new direction towards the hills was beginning to take shape — the climbing of mountains for fun. Ben Nevis had a few years respite left in the middle of the 19th century, but the day of the climber was approaching.

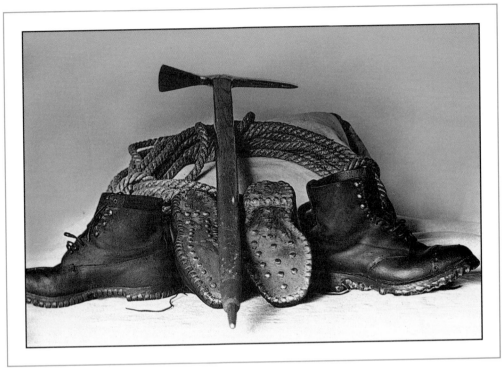

2.1 Ice Axe, Rope, and Boots

THE FIRST CLIMBERS (1866 – 1896)

The middle of the 19th century saw a new phenomenon — the outdoor club. Originally social and walking groups, they gradually evolved into something like the climbing clubs we know today. One of the earliest Scottish clubs to show a specialisation towards climbing was the Cobbler Club, formed in Glasgow in 1866. For the main part, however, the Scottish hills were still regarded as a training ground for the Alps. There was a nucleus of Alpine Club members living and working in Scotland. These climbers, some of whom began exploring in Scotland, were to function as a catalyst, in bringing about an awareness of what Scotland could provide as a climbing ground in its own right.

Though further south than the Isle of Skye, Ben Nevis in the 1880's was less accessible. From 1870 a train from Inverness could meet the Skye ferry at Strome. By contrast, when travelling from the south the Oban Line stopped at Tyndrum, leaving a wild stretch of rough road to Glencoe and Fort William. It was probably not only on picturesque grounds that Glencoe was often approached by boat up Loch Etive; it was easier to travel by water. The old road to Glencoe took a higher route than the modern route and was often blocked in winter by drifting snow. So it was that as late as 1880, an ascent of Nevis by the tourist path could excite the national newspapers to print an account.

The sixteen years beginning in 1880 saw the development of Ben Nevis as a climbing ground. More than that, it saw Scottish mountaineering develop as an entity, distinct in character and style from Alpinism. It is perhaps appropriate to begin with an account of the first ascent of the season of Ben Nevis, in 1880, by a man who stands amongst the giants of Scottish mountaineering pioneers — William Wilson Naismith (1856-1935).

Born to parents who were fond of the hills, Willie Naismith received his schooling at Gilbertfield House School, Hamilton, where he had Andrew Bonar Law as an almost exact contemporary. Hamiltonians remembered Naismith, to put it mildly, as a rather careless, pleasure loving young man. He became, however, as his obituary in a local newspaper stated, *"a conspicuous example of the transforming power of the Gospel"*, and was, as his tribute from the pulpit read, *"one of the 'twice born' "*.

Naismith began walking from an early age, and remembers being taken up a hill of over 1,000 feet when six or seven, and Ben Lomond when about nine. (1). Always a prodigious walker, in 1879 at the age of 23 he walked from his home in Hamilton to the summit of Tinto and back — a distance of 56 miles. At the age of 60, in July 1916, he walked from Glasgow to the summit of Ben Lomond and back again; 62 miles in 20 hours, including stops. When asked by his young nephew John Fergus what food he carried on this expedition, Naismith replied that he found a bag of raisins in his pocket quite good. His favourite low-level hills seemed to have been the Campsies; the boggy, basaltic hills which protect Glasgow from the worst of the northerly winds. In his small pocket note-book from 1873 to 1919 he kept a brief record of his ascents; including a note of 313 visits to the Campsies, reaching Crichton's Cairn 139 times, and Earl's Seat on 85 occasions. (2).

On leaving school Naismith took classes at Glasgow University, eventually qualifying as a chartered accountant. In 1872 George Ramsay, Professor of Humanity at Glasgow University and a member of the Alpine Club, gave his Junior Latin Class a lecture on Alpine Climbing, along with a demonstration on the use of an ice axe. Naismith was fascinated, and when he came across a copy of Whymper's 'Scrambles in The Alps' he devoured it with the most intense delight.

Growing up as he did into a man of deep religious convictions, Naismith eventually avoided Sunday climbing, though never passing judgment on those whose love of the hills surpassed their desire for a hard bench and a long sermon. For 27 years he was an elder in Kelvinside (Botanic Gardens) Church, Glasgow. Professionally busy as a chartered accountant and insurance manager, he found time for activities in addition to mountaineering. These included skating; once on a frozen Loch Lomond as far as Rowardennan (during the great freeze of 1895), and a balloon ascent over Glasgow on September 2, 1901, reaching an altitude of 5,350 feet.

Lord Mackay (a Court of Session Judge, member of the SMC and the AC) described Naismith as,

". . . a human being of the finest steel, modest and self-effacing. He was physically compact and of small build, with corresponding small hands and feet, which seemed made to go into or on the tiniest holds." (3).

Naismith's friends considered him to be a confirmed bachelor, but at the age of 70 he surprised them by marrying the daughter of an Aberdeenshire minister. He died in Strathpeffer aged 79 and is buried in Bent Cemetery, Hamilton.

Other than eponymous routes, Naismith will be remembered for his formulation of 'Naismith's Rule', first described by him in the SMC Journal of September 1892. This was, in his own words,

". . . a simple formula, that may be found useful in estimating what time men in fair condition should allow for easy expeditions, namely, an hour for every three miles on the map, with an additional hour for every 2,000 feet of ascent." (4).

On the evening of May 1, 1880, Naismith and two clerical friends arrived in Fort William, after a tedious if charming voyage down the Caledonian Canal in the ancient steamtub 'Plover'. There they learned that Ben Nevis had not been climbed since the previous autumn, and the next day, despite a layer of cloud covering the summit, they set off after nine a.m. to attempt the hill.

After gaining the north ridge of Meall an t-Suidhe and passing the lochan, the party climbed above the snowline and into the cloud. Hoping for a clearing, they amused themselves for two hours attempting to glissade; sliding upright down the snow with the aid of stout walking sticks. This almost ended in tragedy when one of the party began to accelerate down a gully packed with hard snow, but fortunately a rock stopped the descent in time.

Finally they decided to recommence the ascent, mist or not, floundering along on the broad summit plateau up to their knees in deep snow. After finding themselves at one point walking straight towards the cliff edge, they corrected their course and continued to the top using a compass bearing. The summit cairn was almost completely covered, and it was only by discovering a bottle with names inside that they were sure of their ascent. A hasty lunch during a sleet shower and an uneventful descent saw them back at Fort William at 6 p.m.

On their return they were interviewed by the local newspaper reporter (probably, Naismith thought, at the instigation of the landlord of the 'Alexandra Hotel'), with the result that a report headlined 'First Ascent of Ben Nevis — Without Guides' was published in the national press. They had in fact attempted to find a guide that morning, but were provided instead with a compass and an *"indifferent map"*. (5). To help put this period into perspective, a glance through the 'Glasgow Herald' for May 12, 1880 would find such current matters as the Afghan War, the continuing Inquest into the Tay Bridge Disaster, and a note that, *"last night, St.Enoch Railway Station was lit by electric light."*

This ascent was three years before the summit observatory and its good bridle path were built, and the year before Clement Wragge began his daily summer ascents; making meteorological observations at the summit and at intermediate points. (The story of the Observatory is told in Chapter 3.) Surprisingly, it was to be another 12 years before the first rock climb on the north face of Ben Nevis was put up, and then by a team from the north of England. There is good evidence, however, that at least one of the easy snow gullies received an ascent during the 1880's.

The Summit Meterological Observatory was built in 1883, and from a book written by W.T. Kilgour, who was an observer for a period at the Observatory, we have the following interesting account of what must have been one of the first climbs.

"One bracing afternoon in winter, not long after the Observatory had been opened, a member of staff who had gone out for a walk on the snow was more than amazed on looking over a precipice to see, about 1500 feet down, two dark objects laboriously scaling the ice-covered and snow-clad face of the declivity . . . Roped together, and cutting foot and handholds with their ice axes, slowly but surely those two venturesome climbers made the top by a route which had never, within mortal ken, been previously attempted." (6).

This description, written round about the mid-1880's, is of one of the earliest snow and ice routes put up in Scotland, and most likely refers to an ascent of No.3 or No.4 gully, by climbers unnamed. Unfortunately, there is no reference to this ascent in the Observatory Logbook. From the floor of Coire na Ciste, the upper section of No.4 Gully is concealed, while No.3 Gully is plainly visible directly above, making it likely that No.3 would have received early attention. In his 1902 Ben Nevis Guide, W. Inglis Clark notes that,

"there can be no doubt that this gully (No.3) was one of the earliest climbed, the writer's knowledge of it going back to 1870." (7).

This statement might be taken as indicating an ascent, in which case it dates the first known ascent back to that date.

In March 1884, a solo ascent of a very icy Ben More, equipped only with an alpenstock (a long, metal-tipped pole), convinced Naismith that in winter and spring the higher Scottish mountains ought to be treated as seriously as Alpine peaks — using the same equipment; axes and a rope. The chief difficulty, as Naismith admitted, and other individuals were experiencing, was in finding someone else with whom to climb.

Although Scotland in the late 1880's had a growing number of mountaineers, contact between them was almost nonexistent, and consequently information about mountains, routes, techniques and so on difficult to come by. On January 10, 1889, a letter appeared in the 'Glasgow Herald', proposing a 'Scottish Alpine Club'. The writer was Naismith, and in spirited tones he described mountain climbing as *"one of the most manly as well as healthful and fascinating forms of exercise."* Naismith also described that it was —

". . . almost a disgrace to any Scotsman whose heart and lungs are in proper order if he is not more or less of a mountaineer, seeing that he belongs to one of the most mountainous countries in the world."

Naismith's letter was answered on January 14 by 'Cairn', the pen-name, as it turned out, of Gilbert Thomson and D.A. Archie. These two, while in favour of the formation of a club, objected to any Alpine reference, pointing out that height was no test of difficulty. Naismith replied favourably on January 18, and the following day Ernest Maylard wrote suggesting the name 'Scottish Mountaineering Club'.

In 1866 Professor George Ramsay, along with Professor Veitch and Mr Campbell Colquhoun of Clathick had founded the 'Cobbler Club'. Since then, wrote Ramsay in a journal article,

"with the notable exception of (Professor Veitch) I had never, outside the limits of my own family, met with a single Scotsman who cared seriously to practise the art of mountaineering". (8).

Consequently, on a gloomy, foggy morning in the last week of January 1889, Ramsay was delighted to receive a visit from Maylard and a friend, who wished to discuss the formation of a club. As a result of that meeting, Maylard organised a meeting for any gentleman (and, as a point of fact, lady), who might be interested.

The first meeting took place in the Christian Institute, Bath Street, Glasgow, on February 11, 1889, with Professor Ramsay in the chair. About 40 were present and a provisional committee was formed to set up a constitution. The Scottish Mountaineering Club was

2.2   Founders of the SMC

formally set up one month later, on March 11, 1889, with a membership of 94. Of these original members, 14 were already members of the Alpine Club, 17 came from Edinburgh, 13 from various other areas in the east and 12 from England; the remainder living in and around Glasgow. It would seem that no ladies were present at this first meeting; they were soon to found The Ladies' Scottish Climbing Club.

Although the Cairngorm Club had been founded shortly before the SMC, the latter was immediately the driving force in Scottish mountaineering; the first journal appearing in January 1890, with Stott as Editor. (Stott was responsible for the SMC Club Song, sung once a year at the Annual Dinner. Work duties took him first to New Zealand, then Australia. His letters to Douglas are full of nostalgia and the desire to return to Scotland, but he married and settled in Australia). The first full committee included: Maylard, who was then a Demonstrator in Medicine at Glasgow University, as Secretary, Thomson as Librarian, Naismith, characteristically refusing all attempts to elect him President, became Treasurer, while Ramsay became the first President.

With the publication of the SMC Journal, originally thrice yearly, and a succession of mountain guidebooks, the SMC became a mine of information; many of its members already being experienced Alpinists able to pass on knowledge and techniques. Ben Nevis and Glencoe were still difficult of access, but the golden age of Scottish mountaineering was about to unfold.

In 1894 Edward Whymper wrote of the north face of Ben Nevis —

"This great face is one of the finest pieces of crag in our country, and it has never been climbed, though every now and then adventurous ones go and look at it with wistful eyes." (9).

Unfortunately Whymper, in common it seems with everyone else, had no knowledge of the highly successful visit in September 1892 by a family from the north of England — the Hopkinsons, three brothers and a son. Ironically, Whymper himself had spent a week ascending Nevis — not to put up any climbs — but to conduct experiments with aneroids for a manufacturer, comparing readings taken top and bottom. This was just one month before the visit by the Hopkinsons (10).

The Hopkinson family from Manchester was a Victorian example of progress through hard work. The father began as a mill mechanic and later rose to become Mayor of Manchester. All five of his sons were academically gifted and became experienced alpinists. The noted alpinist W.C. Slingsby was a cousin. The eldest son and natural leader was John (1849-1898). John's son Bertram (1874-1918) joined his father for the trip to Ben Nevis. The other brothers were Alfred (1851-1939), Charles (1854-1920), Edward (1859-1921) and

Albert (1863-1949). Following a climbing disaster in the Alps in 1898 in which John, two daughters and his son Jack were killed on a traverse of the Petit Dent de Veisivi, the surviving brothers ceased climbing completely.

On Saturday September 3, 1892, John, Edward, and the eighteen year old Bertram walked up under the north face of Ben Nevis. They were confronted with a bewildering succession of steep arêtes, ridges, pinnacles and gullies; extending for a total frontage of two miles of cliffs. Three immense rock features formed prominent landmarks; North-East Buttress and Carn Dearg Buttress on the left and right flanks, and the central feature of Tower Ridge. None had been climbed or named.

That day the barometer was rising briskly; there were squally N and NE winds with showers of snow throughout the day. It would have been excusable had the Hopkinsons been content with a lesser route — instead they chose the major feature of Tower Ridge. Starting at an elevation of about 2,400 feet, Tower Ridge rises boldly to form a shapely pinnacle 700 feet high. A climb in its own right, this is the Douglas Boulder. Crossing the

2.3   Tower Ridge, Summer (c.1902)

Douglas Gap behind the Boulder, the ridge narrows and leads, at a moderate angle, to a rock step in the ridge called the Little Tower, which presents the first real difficulties of the ridge.

Above the Little Tower the ridge leads without complication to the uncompromising bulk of the Great Tower, leading steeply in a 100-foot rise to its cairn at 4,216 feet. As far as the Great Tower the route is straightforward but here the climber is obliged to find a way up the tower. On that Saturday in 1892, Edward, John and his son Bertram climbed the ridge as far as the Great Tower. We have little details of the ascent; they almost certainly avoided the Douglas Boulder and started instead up the gully to the east. On reaching the Great Tower they traversed rightward on to the west face and climbed a narrow chimney. They were then defeated by a steep pitch. Presumably they then reversed back down to their starting point and so down to Fort William.

The weather was poor for the next two days, being very cold on the Sunday as the Hopkinsons returned. Charles joined the original three in walking to the top. There was mist or fog around until 4 p.m., after which the summit was frequently clear. The temperature remained low all day, with slight showers of snow falling in the forenoon. This time the four Hopkinsons descended from the summit plateau to gain the Great Tower from above. They then reversed this by a route on the west face, probably by a Very Difficult variation now known as the Recess Route. After an exposed traverse, they regained their high point of Saturday and completed the descent, thus completing the first rock climb on Ben Nevis.

On Tuesday September 6, the Hopkinsons returned for further exploration. Again there was mist or fog until the afternoon, followed by occasional sunny intervals. The three brothers and Bertram walked further up the Allt a'Mhuilinn to the biggest challenge visible on the skyline — the North-East Buttress, the eastern of the three ridges. They described the climbing on this as interesting, but much easier than on the central ridge. Finally, on Thursday September 8, they climbed the introductory pinnacle at the foot of Tower Ridge, now known as the Douglas Boulder. Their route cannot be identified with any certainty, though they *"descended it on the north face"*.

The Hopkinsons had enjoyed exciting and doubtless satisfying climbing on two of the major features on Ben Nevis — and for the first time at that — but despite this they chose not to report their ascents until August 1895, when a short note appeared in the Alpine Journal under the title 'Alpine Notes — Ben Nevis.' (11). In all probability they regarded their ascents as training for the Alps, and had little or no conception of their significance in the early days of Scottish climbing. In the interim, the growing activity of the recently formed SMC was soon to provide its own impetus. The interest of that club, and one of its members in particular, was about to switch its focus to Ben Nevis. That member was Doctor, later Professor, Collie.

John Norman Collie (1859-1942) was born on September 10, 1859 at Alderley Edge, Manchester. *"It might be fairly claimed that he was a Scot"*, stated his obituary notice (12), for his grandfather was tenant of an Aberdeenshire farm, and his father lived for several years at Glassel on Deeside, before moving to Bristol. It was at Glassel that Collie ascended his first hill, the modest Hill of Fare, at the age of eight. In a long scientific career which spanned over 40 years, his original researches in Chemistry won him many honours, as did his outstanding endeavours as an explorer and mountaineer. He took the first X-ray of a human subject for medical purposes, and he claimed (though this is controversial) to have discovered the rare gas Neon.

Collie joined the SMC in 1891 and the Alpine Club two years later, serving on the committees of both clubs and becoming President of the Alpine Club in 1920. His travels and climbs were widespread; from the Alps and the Canadian Rockies, to the Himalayas, and the Isle of Skye, which eventually became his chosen home and final resting place. His long partnership, and

2.4 *Norman Collie, oil portrait*

indeed deep friendship with the local guide John Mackenzie was responsible for many successful ascents on that island. When Mackenzie died in 1933, Collie made a lone ascent of Am Bhasteir, stating that it was his last climb — and so it was, though six years later he was to leave London and settle down at Sligachan Hotel, facing out over the moors to his beloved Cuillin.

There is a poignant reference to Collie's last years at Sligachan, when a trainee fighter pilot, Richard Hillary, and his companion decided to spend their four days of leave on Skye. This was in the spring of 1940. A bus advert prompted them to seek out the Sligachan Hotel.

"We were alone in the inn save for one old man who had returned there to die. His hair was white, but his face and bearing were still those of a mountaineer, though he must have been of great age. He never spoke, but appeared regularly at meals to take his place at a table tight-pressed against the window, alone with his wine and his memories. We thought him rather fine."

The next day the two pilots set off early to climb Bruach na Frithe. After a successful ascent they decided to follow a stream which led back to the hotel, a rather cold and wet decision, as it turned out. Over dinner they described their exploits to the landlord.

"His sole comment was 'Humph', but the old man at the window turned and smiled at us. I think he approved."

Hillary returned to the Battle of Britain in which he was shot down and badly burned. During a long period of convalescence he wrote 'The Last Enemy' (13), containing the above description of Collie. He was killed in active service in 1943. Collie died in November 1942, from a short illness following a fall and a soaking while fishing in Loch Storr. He was buried according to his wish beside his old companion and friend John Mackenzie, in the little graveyard at Struan.

The SMC had early begun to organise club meets at several centres, notably at Inveroran Inn at the west end of Loch Tulla. At this time the nearest railway station was ten miles south, at Tyndrum. On the first of January, 1894, Collie wrote to Willie Douglas, the Editor of the SMC Journal.

"If I possibly can allure a few friends I shall be up in Glencoe next Easter so we may meet there, there is a splendid climb straight up Aonach Dhu on Stob Corrie an Lochan from Loch Triochtan about 2400 feet of precipice which I once did years ago — and which I should'nt mind doing again. I have been away from Scotland too long." (14).

Collie attended the Easter Meet of 1894, based at Inveroran. He had with him two guests from the Lakes; Godfrey Solly (1858-1942), a solicitor, and Joseph Collier (1855-1905), a Manchester surgeon. After a night in the crowded inn the three moved on to Glencoe, where they recorded several new routes before moving on again, this time to Fort William.

On Friday, March 30, Collie and his two friends decided to attempt Tower Ridge. There is no evidence that they were aware of the Hopkinson descent 18 months earlier, and it is certain that there was no knowledge of the ascent of North-East Buttress as late as May, 1895

2.5   *SMC Meet at Inveroran (1894)*

— even by W.C. Slingsby, a cousin of the Hopkinsons. Ben Nevis was in full winter condition as they bypassed the Douglas Boulder on its eastern flank to gain the ridge just above the Douglas Gap. That fruitful combination of the right party, route and conditions was about to culminate in a magnificent ascent.

Those seeking details of the first ascent of Tower Ridge will be disappointed, for the account which Collie left in the SMC Journal of September 1894 is in a somewhat unusual form. In a letter to Douglas, dated June 27, 1894, and accompanying his account, Collie wrote that,

"I send an attempt — written largely of experiment — laborious I fear — a pseudo Rabelaisian alchemistic etc attempts — which I commend to your Editorial clemency. Deal gently with it — but don't scruple to say if you don't want it — I go to Switzerland to be dragged over the mountains by Mummery and Hastings in about a month. Yours in haste, Norman Collie." (15).

Douglas of course accepted Collie's article, and with great efficiency had it ready for publication shortly after, as a letter from Collie confirms.

"Kensington W. 11 July, 1894. Dear Douglas. I return the proof sheets corrected — + hope that when they appear in the S.M.J. the select band you mention may find some interest in their perusal — but 'I hae ma doots.' I have put my signature in the form of an anagram at the end of the paper. P.S. would'nt the title look better in italics?". (16).

Collie's article for the SMC Journal was signed by Orlamon Linecus, the expedition setting out from a Castrum Guillelmi.

"Nor did they issue forth unprepared, for they bore with them the proper, peculiar, fit, exact, and lawful insignia of the brotherhood, a flaxen rope coiled even as the mystic serpent, likewise staves curiously shapen did they take in their hands . . ."

Very early on in the ascent, Collie's party came across the nail scratches left by the Hopkinsons, for having gained the ridge the party pressed on,

2.6   Norman Collie, (c.1894)

". . . and by inspection were they aware how others had travelled on the same way, for on the stones and rocks were there certain petrographical scrapings and curious markings deeply graven, and very evident."

The Little Tower does not receive a mention by Collie, the climbers continuing on up the ridge until they came,

". . . to a great rock, a majestic tower; here were they perforce compelled to depart to the right hand, placing themselves in steep and perilous positions on slopes of ice."

Today, this way of climbing the Great Tower in winter, by the West face, is rarely attempted. One competent team who climbed this way in the 1970's described it later as "desperate". Of the climb Collie wrote —

"Still all things have an end at last, — good Wine, Pinnacles, Spires, cabalistic Emblems, and oromaniacal Wanderings . . . So did the three find the perilous passage across the headlong steep finish. Then did they pass onwards to the Labyrinth, the rocky Chaos, and greatly did they marvel at the exceeding steepness thereof; so that only by great perseverance, turning now to the right and now to the left, were they able to break themselves free from the bonds and entanglements, and climb sagaciously upwards to the summit of the great tower."

Looking down from its top the party saw —

"Behind, and far below, imprinted in the snow were the steps by which they had mounted upwards, winding now this way now that, looking like scarce seen veins in finest marble."

Now the party of three had to negotiate the Tower Gap to reach the final slope leading to the summit plateau and the safe haven of the Observatory.

"Thither therefore did their footsteps trend. First did they pass along the narrow Way, treading with exceeding care and exactness, for there was but foothold for one alone, the path being no broader than a man's hand. Next did they descend into the Cleft . . .But now before them stretched the white Slope, which lay beneath the topmost summit, and steeper became the path, going upwards with a great steepness."

2.7   Looking down on The Great Tower (c. 1960)

Collie's party was beginning to feel despair, as the top part of the Ridge does indeed look very steep from below, when —

". . . lo! from out of the clouds a rope descended, and a voice was heard:– 'Fear not, now have ye attained to the Consummation, enter into the mystagorical, quintessential, and delectable pleasure-house of devout Oromaniacs.' And what joy, think ye, did they feel after the exceedingly long and troublous ascent? — after scrambling, slipping, pulling, pushing, lifting, gasping, looking, hoping, despairing, climbing, holding on, falling off, trying, puffing, loosing, gathering, talking, stepping, grumbling, anathematising, scraping, hacking, bumping, jogging, overturning, hunting, straddling, — for know you that by these methods alone are the most divine mysteries of the Quest reached." (17).

The three happy climbers had taken five hours for the first complete, and first winter ascent of a major route, climbing in nailed boots with long, wooden-shafted ice axes and short lengths of manilla rope. Their time would be regarded as good by a modern party of three, on a long route whose difficulties increase with height and which in most winters sees benighted parties. The Observatory logbook for March 30, 1894 reads,

"Today Mr McIntyre postmaster Fort William and Mr Wallace Post Office surveyor visited the observatory. Three other gentlemen also came up; climbing the cliff up the buttress at point beyond second gorge and having to cut steps almost the whole way in the ice."

Collie thought that it *"resembled the Italian side of the Matterhorn, and was the best climb he had ever had in Scotland."* He certainly must have been very pleased with the route, for the Observatory log for the next day stated,

"Today two strangers climbed Ben Nevis and the cliff the same way as before, one of them being one of the previous party".

Collie's partner on this second ascent was Geoffrey Hastings.
On hearing of Collie's ascent Naismith sent a rueful letter to Douglas —

March 30

Faint aurora seen at 3½ and Bright aurora at 2½ and all night after that accompanied with strong earth currents in telegraph cable - The currents were in both directions but continued for several minutes in each direction at a time - at 2½ the Aurora was all over the sky in the form of bands stretching from WSW to ENE with a very dark belt to S° the centre of which was about 30° above horizon - There were also thinner dark bands to N°

Today Mr McIntyre postmaster Fort William and Mr Wallace Post Office surveyor visited the Observatory - Three other gentlemen also came up, climbing the cliff up the buttress at point beyond second gorge and having to cut steps almost the whole way in the ice -

2.8 Observatory Logbook for March 30, 1894

"Hamilton, Saturday night. My Dear Douglas, Just got yours enclosing Collie's which I return with many thanks. The Sassenachs have indeed taken the wind out of our sails maist notoriously I *wull* say that. However I suppose we must make a virtue of necessity & try to look pleasant about it. Those beggars were more wide-awake than we — in skimming the cream off Glencoe & Ben Nevis the year *before* the railway opened, while we in our innocence were still planning what we should do *after* that event.

Collie no doubt is 'a pure Scotsman' (tho' perhaps in a Gladstonian sense) *[Gladstone then being an Englishman resident at Fasque, near Lettercairn — KVC]* but his 3 pals tho' all very nice chaps are undoubted undiluted specimens of the genus pock-pudden. This is truly a sad day for auld Scotland. Let us hope that the hotel keepers at Ft. Wm. took a good few bawbees off the Englishers. Flodden or even Culloden was nothing to this . . ." (18).

Always the gentleman however, Naismith wrote to Collie congratulating him on his ascent, as a letter from Collie to Douglas confirms —

"16 Campdengrove, Kensington W., 20.4.94. . . . I had a letter the other day from Naismith in which he congratulated me in the most delightful manner on my Easter climbs. After I had read your letter I felt as if I had rather been poaching on your ground on Ben Nevis, but I assure you it is many years ago since I made up my mind that on the first possible opportunity when I could get another man I would have a try at the old Ben . . ." (19).

For the next decade or so the defences of the ridge, particularly around the Great Tower, were probed and tested, and variations and escape routes recorded. The ridge had its third ascent on September 27, 1894, by Willie Naismith and Gilbert Thomson. Informing Douglas by letter from Fort William, Naismith suggested the name Tower Ridge, and so it has been ever since. Naismith's letter is interesting in showing the standard of proficiency so early gained by those pioneers.

"Fort William, Friday morning. My dear Douglas, As my telegram y'day would announce Thomson and I got up the North face of B. Nevis all right. We followed Collie's route exactly except I think that while we got on the rocks of the ridge near the foot Collie seems to have kept up a gully to the left (E) for some distance & joined the ridge higher up.

The climb at present is quite easy — the only bit that requires care being 10 feet 'a.p.' [absolutely perpendicular — KVC] on the side of the big tower, but when the first man is up there is no difficulty for those following . . . Excepting the tower and the cleft the only places where one would like to be roped are one or two short chimneys in the lower portion of the ridge . . . The whole N. face is bare rock and snow and very grand. There are several easy gullies most of them still full of snow so one had better take an axe even in Sept. unless he means to stick to 'the Tower Ridge'. How w? that name do for Collie's climb?

The climb I want to look at when I come back is by the great eastern ridge or buttress due E of the Observatory and next to Collie's ridge on the left as you face the Ben. On most views of the hill from Banavie or Corpach this Eastern buttress is seen on the skyline. It is a.p. at the end but might I think be reached higher up." (20).

In the autumn of 1894 the West Highland Railway finally opened, and the SMC switched their 1895 Easter Meet to Fort William. That April, some 27 members and their guests assembled at the 'Alexandra Hotel', Fort William. Norman Collie was present, as were other figures such as Douglas, Maclay, Maylard, Munro (of Munro's Tables fame), Naismith, and the Rev. A.E. Robertson, first person to complete all the Munro's. Several gullies were climbed by the 'Axe-men', while a new ridge leading to the top of Carn Dearg was climbed by three parties; the first being composed of Collie, Naismith, Thomson and M.W. Travers. The new ridge was christened the Castle Ridge, after the huge castellated rock mass which towers over it. The two great ridges however, Tower Ridge and the North-East Buttress, were pronounced impracticable, due to the thick plastering of snow and ice which hung in great white blossoms from the rocks.

The 1892 ascent of the North-East Buttress by the Hopkinsons was still completely unknown to Scottish climbers in May, 1895. During the Easter Meet of 1895, the buttress became —

". . . the object of ambition to a large circle of climbers, the chief topic of the smokeroom at nights, and the focus of many critical glances during the day. It would also have been climbed had the ice upon the rocks not forbade the attempt."

So William Brown began his delightful account of a later successful ascent of the buttress, along with his friend William Tough (pronounced 'Tooch').

The new railway was to be used in approaching Fort William, with the Queen's Birthday as the date, but the two could not find a suitable train. They accordingly worked out an original 'programme' which, as Tough remarked, *"would have been utterly repulsive as applied to anything else but the N.E. Buttress."* They therefore arranged to travel to Kingussie by the night express on Friday, May 24, cycle to Fort William, climb their route on arrival, cycle back to Kingussie the same day, and return to Edinburgh by train, reaching the city on the Sunday evening. There was, wrote Brown,

"a certain gloomy satisfaction that we were doing something quite out of the common, which deepened in gloom as our arrangements waxed in originality."

It was, predictably enough, very grey and miserable when Kingussie was reached at 3.50 a.m. on Saturday morning.

"Rain was falling dismally, and underwheel the roads were a fell compound of mud and newly-laid metal."

Cycling past Laggan Bridge, the two intrepid travellers had just topped a stiff brae when

". . . a sudden report, resembling the simultaneous opening of six bottles of 'Bouvier', was followed by Tough's despairing cry, 'Your tyre's punctured'."

Pushing the cycle three miles to the Laggan Hotel, in the expectation of finding a horse and trap, they found nothing zoological other than midges, and were then faced with a thirteen mile walk to Inverlair.

"Tough mounted the remaining bicycle, with a pyramid of ropes, axes, and rucksacks piled up on his shoulders, while his fellow-traveller half-walked, half-trotted alongside. In this order, with an occasional change of parts, when the pedestrian became (or said he was) exhausted, we straggled to Inverlair, and completed the rest of the journey comfortably by train."

The weather had remained fairly clear if dull, until the two climbers swung past Meall an t-Suidhe and descended into the valley of the Allt a'Mhuilinn. Then,

". . . the blackness that had been lying on the horizon rose high towards the zenith and threatened to cover it. The Red Mountains were still clear & sunny, but round the flanks of Carn Dearg the mist came stealing, — at first in mere wisps of vapour, then in great smoke-like masses, which mounted to the topmost crag, and blotted out nearly the whole mountain. In ten minutes there was scarce anything to be seen but the scree slope on which we stood, and a black swirling mass straight ahead, where the storm clouds were eddying round the crags of the four great ridges."

The well-travelled pair eventually reached the foot of the buttress at 5.30 p.m. As to the weather,

"Even a native might have praised it. For ten minutes the rain descended with a straightness that would have been creditable in furrows at a ploughing match . . . Crouching behind a stone we saw our visible world fade away into a murky circumference of twenty feet broad . . . Early in the day there had been some awful penalties laid upon the man who should breathe even the word 'retreat' but now we shamelessly discussed it in all its bearings."

Suddenly it cleared as they approached the rocks from the east. There was by now a respectable waterfall coming off the ridge, with innumerable smaller ones. They gained the first platform and roped up at 6.15 p.m. Following a succession of small chimneys and gullies they gained a tiny platform, more of a small cup scooped out of the ridge. This they called the second platform, above which they found the really interesting work began.

"There are little towers up which the leader had to scramble with such gentle impetus as could be derived from the pressure of his hobnails upon his companion's head . . . A sloping slab we found too, where the union of porphyry and Harris tweed interposed the most slender obstacle to an airy slide into the valley."

The climb then went steadily until they reached a point when they judged they were within a few hundred feet of the top. In the thickening mist, they had come up against a small problem, made difficult by water. Then they tried the slabby rocks on the left, but these turned out to be *"the man-trap of the ridge."* Tough amused himself for three- quarters of an hour there but,

"Judging by the movements of the rope, and the vigorous adjectives that reached my ears, the game was more energetic than amusing."

Tough admitted defeat and came back to join Brown. By this time — it was 9.45 p.m. — daylight was almost gone, and the two climbers were facing a bivouac.

"Over the gaunt grey rocks the darkness of night had settled down, rendering our position inexpressibly weird and eerie. To me it seemed that the only alternative was to bivouac where we stood; but the chief guide, while frankly admitting that two inches of nose represented his own limit of vision, drove me at the point of his axe to explore the rocks on the right. They 'went' quite easily. Up a short gully we raced and panted to the foot of a steep smooth corner about 40 feet high, formed by the junction of two rock slabs. Here, when I mildly suggested the absence of reliable holds, the inexorable guide gave me the choice of going up at the point of his ice-axe, or by pure traction at the end of the rope, along with the luggage. I chose the former." (21).

The hard-pressed pair reached the Observatory at 10.05 p.m., and were welcomed by the staff there. After an hour of sleep they began the descent and the weary journey back to Edinburgh; regaining that city early on Sunday evening, after 45 hours of continuous travelling. They were met at the station by the Club Editor Willie Douglas. A telegraph sent from the Ben Nevis office at 9.05 a.m. on Sunday to Douglas read: *"Climbed our ridge reaching top 10.5 Saturday extremely difficult and sensational Brown."*

After Brown had written his account the Alpine Journal came out with the short note of the Hopkinson ascents. These came as a complete surprise to the members of the SMC, and in an appended note to his article, Brown is at pains to make it clear that they knew nothing of the earlier ascent. A letter from Gilbert Thomson to Douglas shows some of the nationalistic spirit that was running high then.

"75 Bath St. Glasgow, 27th May, 1895. Brown and Tough will be prood prood men over their buttress. I have studied its photograph pretty much, and W.W.N. and I thought it looked as if it might go. Next to the pleasure of being one of the pioneering party, at the loss of which I must confess a little disappointment, there is the satisfaction of having it done by two men who are so thoroughly identified with the S.M.C. and not by what N. would call glaikit Englishers." (22).

●   ●   ●

"A Meet of the Club will take place at the Alexandra Hotel, Fort-William, from Thursday 2nd April, to Tuesday 7th . . . *A special Saloon Carriage,* reserved for Club members & their friends, will leave Queen St (High Level), Glasgow, at 3.50 p.m. on Thursday, 2nd April and Fort-William on Tuesday, at 7.35 a.m." (23).

2.9   SMC group, Easter Meet, Fort William, (1896)

36

2.10   North-East Buttress (c.1970)

Thus was the SMC Easter Meet of 1896 advertised, the second to take place at Fort William. The 1896 meet was beset by wet weather, but despite this, Tower Ridge received five ascents; one before the actual meet, and four during it. Of the 32 members and guests present perhaps the most infamous name was that of Aleister Crowley, while amongst the guests there appeared a name destined to take Scottish mountaineering to levels of ability and skill which remained unmatched for over a quarter of a century. The name was Raeburn, of whom more later, but the 1896 Easter Meet is now to be remembered for one of Naismith's finest climbs — the first winter ascent of North-East Buttress.

As regards information on the winter ascent, Naismith's modesty is again a major obstacle, as it was not until 1925, in a retrospective article on early winter climbing, that he gave a few lines of detail of the ascent. In the contemporary report of that 1896 Meet by William Brown, only passing mention is made of this major ascent.

". . . another party of five made the ascent by the North East Buttress . . . only climbed once previously, but since, frequently undertaken and successfully accomplished." (24).

The party of five consisted of; Naismith, then 40 years of age; W. Brunskill; A.B.W. Kennedy; William Wickham King (1862-1959); and Frances Conradi Squance. The date was Friday, April 3. Naismith wrote of the ascent —

"This was a long day, for we were on the buttress for nearly seven hours. The party was a jolly one, but rather large for speed. The rocks were plastered with snow and ice and distinctly difficult. At one or two places the route followed by the first climbers was impossible, and had to be varied. [Here Naismith seems to be referring to Brown and Tough, though by April 1896 he must have known of the Hopkinson's ascent — KVC]. Until we actually reached the summit, there was a slight doubt as to whether the top would 'go' or not, for a pitch that Brown had climbed with difficulty was now found to be iced and hopeless; but by crossing to the left side of the buttress, we followed a narrow gully, at first hard ice but afterwards good snow, which led us past the last obstacle. It was pitch dark long before we arrived at the Alexandra Hotel." (1).

North-East Buttress in winter is now a classic Grade III. Like Tower Ridge the major difficulties are high on the mountain and in most winters both routes see their share of epic ascents, with retreats, benightments (the Man-Trap!) and other character-building occasions.

Elsewhere on the mountain other climbers on this Meet were busy. Both of the easy, if avalanche prone, Castle Gullies were climbed. Naismith climbed the Original Route on The Castle, now a Grade III, along with Brown, Maclay and Thomson. Late on Good Friday morning, William Cecil Slingsby, Geoffrey Hastings and Dr. Collier left for the north face of Nevis. After some indecision they decided to attempt a steep and narrow snow gully visible high above, even though it was by now after 3.30 p.m. The top of the gully, now named No. 2 Gully, was invisible to the climbers as they broke steps in the soft snow leading towards the gully. At the foot of the gully was a frozen mass of ice, a useful landmark in misty conditions.

The three climbers proceeded up the gully; its average angle of about 40 degrees increased to about 60 degrees nearer the top. To the great dismay of Slingsby, the finish of the gully was blocked by a cornice some 10 or 12 feet in height, overhanging in places, with its lower half of ice. It was now 5.30 p.m., and the party had partly frost-bitten fingers and toes. Collier volunteered to attempt an escape on the left; traversing to where the snow seemed to abut on to a snow ridge. Reaching the foot of the cornice again, Collier belayed on to a cone of hard-frozen snow (a belay known as a snow bollard, which when correctly applied is much superior to an ice axe belay) and decided to bring up Slingsby. With the backing of Slingsby now, Collier was able to overcome the final few feet, and soon Hastings was able to join them, puffing up behind with his 14-pound camera and two rucksacks. On gaining the summit plateau they found two men in kilts, not climbers, one of whom complained that he had eaten all his food, half of his companion's, and had drunk all of his flask of whisky, and that he was still dying for want of food. The three climbers fled. (25).

It seems fitting somehow to end this section with a preliminary glimpse of a major character in the story of Ben Nevis. Harold Raeburn was a guest at this 1896 Easter Meet of the SMC in Fort William. During the meet he began his list of climbs on Nevis with an ascent of Direct Route on the Douglas Boulder. The other three on the climb were William Brown, who led the crux, Lionel Hinxman and Willie Douglas, the affable Editor of the SMC Journal. All 700 feet of the 'Boulder' was irreverently named after Douglas. Presently graded Very Difficult, the Direct Route was climbed with hail showers and a cutting wind.

As early as 1896, with routes such as these and a core of skilled and energetic mountaineers, Ben Nevis had been established in no uncertain terms as a major British climbing ground. It was also, no less significantly, the major winter climbing area. And as we will shortly see, Raeburn et al were about to usher in new standards of climbing, standards which would take mountaineering on the rocks and winter slopes of Nevis to new heights.

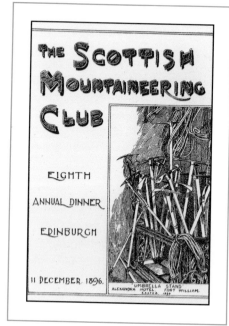

2.11   SMC Dinner Menu showing Umbrella Stand at The Alexandra Hotel, (1896)

3.1   Portrait of Alexander Buchan (c.1890)

THE BEN NEVIS OBSERVATORY (1883 – 1904)

To the walker or climber who gains the summit plateau of Ben Nevis on a summer's day, the two most prominent features will be the cairn and trigonometrical point at the actual summit, and the spartan emergency shelter; both raised to stay above the level of the winter snows. But the emergency shelter partially conceals a third feature, as it is built upon the remains of a much older structure. Stretching away from the shelter will be seen the disintegrating but still distinctly rectangular shapes of what was once home for several hardy Victorian gentlemen scientists — amateur meteorologists who conceived and built a remarkable observatory on Britain's highest summit — and manned it continuously for 21 years.

The English and Scottish Meteorological Societies were founded in 1850 and 1855 respectively. These Societies were run by enthusiastic amateur meteorologists who maintained their own weather stations and collected and analysed data on rainfall, hours of sunshine, cloud cover, wind speed and direction and so on. The unpaid observers, as they were known, were for the main part schoolteachers, ministers, doctors and those of a curious bent who had both the time and facility for such work. The Secretary of the Scottish Meteorological Society from 1860 to 1907 was Alexander Buchan, and in filling this salaried position he played a leading role in the development of meteorology both nationally and internationally. Buchan (1829-1907) was also Librarian of the Royal Society of Edinburgh. In 1867 he identified six cold spells and three warm spells for that year in Scotland. His first cold spell occurred from February 7-14. Examining data over a number of years he concluded that these spells happened from year to year, with very rare exceptions. In 1928 a Parliamentary Bill fixing the date of Easter foundered, because the proposed date, April 11-14, coincided with Buchan's Second Cold Spell. This latter term became fixed in weather lore.

Society members may have been meteorological amateurs, but they had some very talented members in their lists, including many professors from the Scottish Universities such as Tait, Crum Brown, Chrystal, Geikie the geologist, McKendrick, and Lord Kelvin. The Honorary Secretary of the Scottish Society in 1877 was Thomas Stevenson, father of Robert Louis and designer of lighthouses and inventor of the Stevenson thermometer screen. They were therefore quick to rise to the challenge laid down in the summer of 1877, when the President of their English counterpart suggested the establishment of *"mountain observatories on isolated peaks."*

The opinion of the Scottish Society was that Ben Nevis was the obvious candidate for such an observatory; being the highest summit and lying close to the main track of incoming Atlantic depressions. Any observations which could be made at the summit, it was thought, would be of prime importance in the preparation of weather forecasts and, more importantly perhaps, in the accumulation of useful data which could then lead to a better understanding of weather processes in the Atlantic Seaboard area. At this time the mechanism of frontal systems was not understood; had it been, it would have been seen that the logic behind such an observatory was flawed. A similar observatory placed on one of the Outer Hebrides could have been just as useful at indicating fronts, but the observations have special value as a detailed record of mountain weather.

The fund raising by the Scottish public, the building of the bridle path, the erection of the summit observatory, and its continuous manning for 21 years was nothing short of a magnificent achievement of the Scottish Meteorological Society and generosity of the Scottish public.

Stevenson drew up plans in 1879 and following on his calculations the Society ascertained that a sum of £1,000 would be sufficient to build an observatory and that annual maintenance, including the salaries of the observers, would come to about £300. The Society felt that if using money gathered from individuals and Scottish firms they could build the summit station, then it would not be asking too much from the Government to take on the annual running costs. On approaching the Government for funding however, they were disappointed to learn that no money could be made available, and there the plans for the observatory halted.

At this point an interesting character popped up. His name was Clement Lindley Wragge who hearing of the Society's plans volunteered his services for a preliminary series of observations. In a letter to Alexander Buchan, the Secretary of the Scottish Meteorological Society, he offered to climb Ben Nevis daily during the summer of 1881, making observations along the way and at the summit. The Society would pay Wragge's expenses. Wragge himself was a *"tall, lanky, gawky, red-headed man with big feet always encased in Blucher boots."* (1).

From June 1 until October 14, 1881, Wragge made the daily ascent of Nevis, accompanied by his faithful, though no doubt occasionally bemused New-foundland dog Robin Renzo. Wragge was additionally assisted by William Whyte. The route Wragge took is now redundent, though it was the way often taken by the first climbers. Wragge used a pony as far as 2,100 feet. Starting from Banavie at an unearthly 4.40 a.m., his route was by the north flank of Meall an t-Suidhe, to reach its lochan in time for a 7 a.m. set of readings. His observations included the obvious ones such as temperature, humidity and barometric

3.2   Portrait of Clement Wragge (c.1883)

pressure, as well as the wind direction and strength and comments on clouds and any other phenomenon he found of interest. Buchan's Well; a spring at a height of 3,375 feet was the site of the next halt at 8.30 a.m., followed by the summit itself, where readings were taken every half-hour from 9.00 to 11.00 a.m. Readings were again taken on the descent, sea level being regained at 3.30 p.m. Mrs Wragge meanwhile was making simultaneous observations at sea level, 20 in all, between 5 a.m. and 6 p.m. All of these times, naturally, were at the mercy of the weather.

On numerous occasions Wragge, quickly nicknamed 'the inclement rag', was so cold and stiff on reaching the summit that he was unable to unlock the instrument cage there until a small fire was lit to thaw out his fingers, all the while crouching under a miserable shelter of stone walls and tarpaulin. In late August of that year, a reporter from the 'London Times' was unlucky enough to accompany Wragge on one of his trips. Sleet was falling in a Force 11 gale, and the journey across the plateau had to be made on all fours. The reporter was suitably impressed both by conditions and Wragge's work and a glowing article followed.

The Society presented a gold medal to Wragge on March 22, 1882; for his great services of the previous summer. The summer of 1882 again saw Wragge making the daily climb, this time assisted by Angus Rankin and John McDougall; making additional observations at six intermediate stations. Angus Rankin stayed on to work at the observatory for the entire duration; he ended up in the post of Superintendent. For the two summers' work, Wragge and his assistants received £450. The distance from Wragge's home at Achintore to the summit of Nevis was 7.3 miles. Assuming that Wragge shared out the £450 equally over the two summers, which is unlikely, the reward per trip to each man would have been about 60 pence, a reasonable day's wage for manual work though hardly enough to support a wife and a home.

Clement Wragge did not stay to work on at the observatory; there are suggestions that he was not a popular figure, and significantly perhaps, he was not present at the opening. He went on to other, even higher offices, becoming Government Meteorologist in Queensland, Australia. His efforts over the two summers however were the subject of great public interest, and stimulated by this an appeal for funds was launched early in 1883. At a meeting of the Directors of the Ben Nevis Observatory held on September 6, 1883, the post of Superintendent was discussed. An advertisement placed in 'The Scotsman', 'Glasgow Herald', and the scientific journal 'Nature', attracted 19 applicants including Wragge and Robert Traill Omond, both of whom had written in earlier. Omond had worked in Professor Tait's laboratory, and though not a graduate he had attended classes at Edinburgh University. In the end, Omond, who obtained the position, turned out to be an ideal choice.

The appeal was a great success, £4,000 plus being raised within a few months, most of the donations coming from the Scottish public, though there were some donations from further afield, including one from Queen Victoria for £50. For some reason, the Worshipful Company of Fishmongers, London, also made a donation, of some 25 guineas. Work began almost immediately both on the summit stonework and on the construction of the bridle path. The designer of this path was the local schoolmaster, Colin Livingstone. He was one of the last of the old parochial schoolmasters, dying in Fort William on Jan 10, 1916, at the grand age of 89.

Modern ascenders now follow the route taken by the path; from the farm of Achintee in Glen Nevis across the south flank of Meall an t-Suidhe, up through Coire na-h-Urchairean to the lochan, and then by long zig-zags up a tiresome slope to gain the plateau. The bridle path was built by local labour in an amazing four months, and nowhere in its five-mile length does it exceed a gradient of one in five. Many years were to pass before major repairs were deemed necessary, raging burns having long since washed away portion of the track. A more direct start is often taken now, beginning from the Youth Hostel in Glen Nevis, though the original start from Achintee Farm is well-maintained and more pleasant.

As the path was steadily nearing the summit the observatory was taking shape, the contractor being a James McLean of Fort William. (McLean is now remembered by the last steep rise on the summit plateau — known as McLean's Steep). The local masons employed were, naturally enough, using the rock at hand — the dark volcanic rock known as andesite. At first the observatory consisted of one room about 13 feet square, off which opened three small sleeping bunks at one end, and a coal-cellar and storeroom at the other. The building was built following the double skin practice; an interior wooden core consisting of a double wall of wood filled with felt, the inner wall being further covered with linoleum, and an outer shell of stone walls, built to withstand the shrieking violence of a sou'wester.

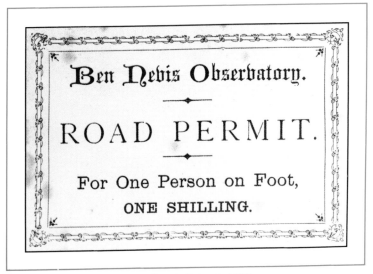

Ben Nevis Obserbatory.

ROAD PERMIT.

For One Person on Foot,
ONE SHILLING.

3.3   Permit Ticket (c.1913)

The stone walls at their bases varied from four feet to ten feet thick, this last below the tower. The roof was sheeted in lead covered by snow boarding, and the windows were double-glazed. The architect was a Mr Sydney Mitchell. To provide the observatory with communications, an armoured telegraph cable, originally a marine cable, was laid from Fort William to the observatory, the Post Office collecting an annual fee of £357. The telegraph was replaced by a telephone in July 1897.

The cost of construction for the summit observatory, including equipment, came to £1237.15s.2d., while the bridle path costs amounted to £793.6s.3d. To help defray the cost of maintaining the path a permit system was brought into use. Those going up the mountain on foot bought a ticket for one shilling, while three shillings, later raised to five, was charged for those going up by pony. A small guidebook, priced one shilling, was also available. However, as one commentator stated later, many of those reaching the summit must have by-passed the toll-gate, as takings never matched the number of tourists.

The formal opening of the Ben Nevis Observatory took place on Wednesday, October 17, 1883. A reporter from 'The Scotsman' was there to record the ascent by the opening party (2). At 7 a.m. the rain was descending in torrents, but by 8 a.m. it had miraculously stopped. The procession met at the 'Alexandra Hotel' and punctually at 9 a.m. set off, headed by a piper playing the march 'Lochiel's away to France'. Mrs Cameron Campbell of Monzie, on whose ground the observatory had been built, had agreed to perform the opening ceremony.

The path, from its newness and the amount of rain which had recently fallen was a perfect quagmire, and most of the party, which included nine ladies, took to the slopes to the side of the path for the first part. Higher up, the snow gradually thickened, being eventually about a foot in depth. For the last thousand feet the ascent was particularly tedious on account of the snow, and the party was much refreshed when the pipes struck up with 'The Campbells are coming'. The leaders of the party reached the observatory just past noon, and were met by Mitchell (the architect), R.T. Omond, Mr Omond (of Oxford), W.M. Whyte (the current observer) and Mr Haig, the Inspector of Works, these gentlemen having ascended the hill earlier in the morning.

3.4   A.N.O., R.T. Omond & A. Rankin at Observatory (c.1885)

Mr Mitchell handed the key of the doorway to Mrs Cameron Campbell and the party wasted no time in entering the 'living room'. A fire was blazing, around which the ladies speedily clustered, and in a few minutes cups of coffee and tea were being gratefully received, along with sandwiches. Only then did the official opening ceremony take place. John Murray (later Sir John Murray of the 'Challenger' expedition office) was present on behalf of the

Scottish Meteorological Society, and in a speech in reply to Mrs Cameron Campbell, he prophesied that in future years thousands would ascend Ben Nevis.

The observatory was not complete that first winter; the observing tower being deliberately left until the following year. The first winter's observations, taken by Omond and his assistant Angus Rankin, were intended to be mainly eye observations, after which the Council would have a good idea of what instruments the observatory should be equipped with. Observations did not start from the summit station until November; until then readings were taken in the same fashion as had Wragge. Angus Rankin experienced no little difficulty the day after the observatory had been officially opened, as the following extract from the Logbook indicates.

"Fort William 4 a.m. (A.R.) 2,000 ft., 6.15 a.m. Did not reach the top! Reached about 200 ft. above Buchan's Well at about 8.30 a.m. But could not untie my coat to make a note or look at my watch (hail drift) all along from 2,500 ft. but at Buchan's Well it became so thick and blinding that I could not see anything. I stood for some time (I could not sit, nor walk easily, my clothes were one solid mass) but the drift and hail became worse and worse, till it became quite impossible to ascend, and almost so to descend — my own tracks being filled up. Reached the lake at 9.30 a.m." (3).

Regular observation commenced on November 28, 1883, the observatory being manned by a crew of three; two observers and a cook. On occasion there would be an extra observer or scientist in residence, and in summer a telegraphist was provided by the telegraph office in Fort William. For the first seven years, the observers stayed at the observatory for ten months; when the low-level observatory was built in Fort William this was changed to a duty spell of three months, observers rotating between stations.

Hourly readings of instruments had to be made manually, due to the often hostile conditions, and so a shift system was devised; eight hours at night and four hours during the day. The first heavy snows of the winter soon highlighted design flaws, as drifting snows quickly enveloped the observatory. As snow accumulated, the observers had to tunnel their way through to the surface, and eventually the tunnel extended to over 30 feet in length, with a rise in level of some 12 feet. Thereafter, the entrance became very difficult to keep clear, and although the observers were very snug while inside their cocooned shelter under snow, readings were becoming more and more difficult to make.

The summer of 1884 saw modifications to the summit observatory, including a slightly larger extra room for use as an office and laboratory, two more bedrooms, a visitor's room and, to overcome the snow problems, the 30-foot high tower, the final effect reminiscent of a conning tower of an old submarine.

The wooden frame of the new tower was put together in Edinburgh, dismantled, and brought to Fort William. It vibrated in a strong wind but its construction was sound and it performed sterling duty every winter; acting as a high level door when snow was covering the

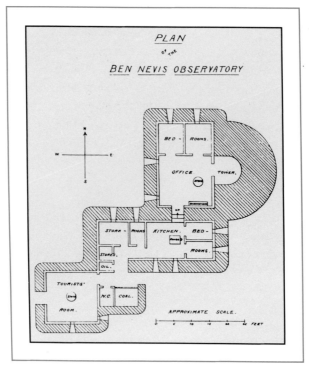

3.5   Plan of Summit Observatory (c.1890)

main structure. Windows in the tower permitted a view of conditions, before venturing outside to read instruments, and in addition anemometers were attached.

As may be imagined, life on the summit of Ben Nevis was one of extremes, from the indescribable fury of a winter storm, to the paradisical beauty of a temperature inversion, when only the highest peaks rose out of a flat sea of cloud, the summit basking in calm sunshine. The observatory was provisioned by pony, and as a precaution against bad weather preventing the roadman reaching the observers, stores for nine months were kept. Tinned food in the larder included; beef, mutton, tongue, salmon, turnips, peas, peaches, prunes, tomatoes, milk. Other food included bread, potatoes, rice, tea etc.

Observers at the summit accepted the poor working conditions simply because they came to appreciate the strange and beautiful isolation of the summit. The log books are crammed with descriptions of sunrises, sunsets, haloes, aurorae and electrical phenomenae such as St. Elmo's fire, when all projecting objects including the observer's hair emitted a hissing sound, a glow being visible if at night. R.T. Omond, the first Superintendent received £100 per annum.

W.T. Kilgour, author of a book on the observatory, seems to have worked at the summit for two holidays as a relief observer, probably for a month at a time. He graphically described typical winter weather.

"Here, in the day-time there was always the same blank whiteness. Above, below and around, with not a single particle the eye could rest on, and at night an awful pitch darkness which might be felt. There was the terrible boom of the gale on the sides of the hill, the rattle and groaning of the chimney pipes, the constant vibration of the tower and the ever-present feeling that the rest of the universe was tearing past at double the speed of an express train." (4).

High wind was one of the most difficult conditions the observers had to contend with, and on many occasions they were knocked off their feet while attempting the hourly readings. In the worst gales they roped together, and found that crawling on all fours was the easiest and safest method of progression. For the very worst of weather, an emergency system was employed, using thermometers whose bulbs projected through holes in a screen attached to the tower. The system of grading the wind strength had as its unofficial top grade, the disappearance of the observatory. Fortunately this was never realised — though a remarkably accurate method of estimation of wind force employed the angle at which an observer had to lean into the wind.

Another part-time observer, Alexander Drysdale, later presented lectures illustrating life at the summit. He describes the readings made during a typical storm, which, perhaps surprisingly, were almost welcomed by the observers, as being a relief from days of dull, misty weather.

"Soon the main door . . . was blocked with drift, and the use of the tower door was necessary. The one appalling moment was when the tower door was opened and the 100 mile per hour gale roared past, sucking the air from the building . . . Out, nevertheless, on to the roof he went closing the snow-choked door with difficulty behind him, steadied himself against the gale and waited for a lull to tack over to the guiding rope to the thermometers. The rope attained he slipped his arm round it, and struggled blindly forward, with lantern carefully shielded . . . Last hour, perhaps, the snow lay level with the roof, now a broad channel had been swept out by the wind. Into that he stumbled. A yard or two further on an immense snowdrift had been formed. Into that he next blindly dived, and so on until at last after a much longer 30 yards than you would imagine . . . the thermometer screen was reached." (5).

The thermometer screen was fixed to a vertical ladder, up which it would be raised step by step as the depth of snow increased. The luckless observer on a bad night would find his lantern blown out at the wrong moment, necessitating a retreat to the observatory and a start all over again. To read the rain gauge in such weather was, of course, nonsensical. A few days of such weather was more than enough to alleviate the observers' boredom, then they were ready to welcome back the formerly hated monotonous, calm foggy weather.

3.6   Ponies at Observatory (c.1903)

In summer ponies made three or four journeys a week with a load of 2 cwt (102 kg) each towards the winter supplies. In winter the roadman, as mail carrier, climbed the Ben nominally once a week. This obviously depended upon the weather, and up to six weeks elapsed between visits to the observatory. This six weeks isolation is alluded to in an article by the alpinist C.D. Cunningham. On February 11, 1884, Cunningham made an ascent of the Ben by the tourist route in company with Emile Rey, the Courmayeur guide, and John Cameron, a local guide from Fort William. They were the third party of visitors to climb the mountain since the observatory opened.

"The three observers had had no communications for about six weeks apart from telegraph, so we offered to bring fresh fruit and milk, newspapers, mail etc. The snow on the ground was hard and crisp & much sooner than we expected we reached the final slopes before gaining the summit."

Cunningham noted that,

"there is no physical reason why the observers should not go down to Fort William whenever they feel disposed to do so, if for no other reason than for health and exercise. 'Had you come here on the Lord's Day', said the head observer, 'you would not have gained admittance.' This gentleman's dread of Sabbath breaking was evidently greater than his fear of alcoholic 'steemulants', as he accepted, with apparent satisfaction, a quart bottle of whisky which we brought." (6).

On the descent Cunningham and Rey were able to glissade for some distance, a mode of descent which Cameron evidently saw for the first time. Cameron showed his appreciation of an ice axe v. cromack by taking Cunningham's axe to the local blacksmith's to be copied.

Recreation for the observatory staff during off-duty hours was not difficult to improvise; in winter tobogganing was a great favourite, and it seems a miracle that no serious accident took place, considering the proximity of the great cliffs. Skating and curling was also possible on a frozen Lochan Meall an t-Suidhe. The ability to play a musical instrument was valued, and on one occasion they arranged a gramophone recital by telephone from Fort William. Playing 'ping-pong' on a prepared table of hard snow was another unique form of recreation.

Summer tourists provided another form of amusement. Many of these made use of the telegraph office to send messages to relatives and friends, though, as Kilgour noted rather wearily, most of the messages were of a mediocre standard, about 75% being along the lines of "Missed the view but viewed the mist." Climbing visitors, particularly during the winter months, were made very welcome, and many a late night knock at the observatory door was the result of a hard ascent under poor conditions. The observers themselves had little opportunity or perhaps inclination to climb, though a note in the log for September 8, 1889 records an ascent of No.3 or No.4 Gully by observers Turnbull, Gray and Miller, the party having first descended via the Carn Mor Dearg arête.

Animal life on Ben Nevis, as recorded by the observers, seems little different from the present; bird life commonly included the raven and snow bunting, with lower down the mountain ptarmigan. Eagles were a rare sight. On a smaller scale insects were often found in large numbers, particularly following autumn storms, when they would be carried up by wind. A family of stoats was usually present, taking up residence near or in the observatory stable. These were often chased but seldom caught, two which were caught, suffered the fate of being stuffed. Weasels and field voles, rats and mice were also seen, while a fox made its presence known only by its prints in the snow. Plant life at the summit was virtually absent amongst the volcanic rocks.

At Edinburgh University, those who had graduated with Honours in Mathematics and Natural Philosophy were given the opportunity to work at the summit for one of the summer months, in order to allow the regular observers to take a holiday. In September 1896, two students availed themselves of this chance, one of them being a John S. Begg. He was so taken with his month at the summit station that he volunteered to return again in the middle of October, taking up an ordinary observer's duties until Christmas.

Fortunately, Begg kept a diary of his experiences, to be published in the Cairngorm Club Journal in 1897. The latter half of Begg's article is taken up with his personal observations, and paints some of the details of observatory life and the scenes that they witnessed while working there.

The middle fortnight of November 1896, wrote Begg,

"was one of the most disagreeable, as regards weather, one could imagine. With the exception of one day throughout that fortnight we never saw more than ten yards in front of us; thick, soaking mist; with the temperature mostly above freezing point; heavy showers of rain and sleet, and occasional gales from the S.E. reaching one day a velocity of 100 miles per hour. The house too leaked badly and the floors both of office and kitchen were pretty much covered with basins, pails, etc, to catch the water . . . However, about the 23rd, the mist rolled away, and once more we revelled in the sunshine. Such a revolution, in fact, did this delightful change in the weather work in our spirits that we got quite excited, threw sea boots at each other, and ended by dancing on the roof the Highland Fling."

The two weeks' bad weather ended with that most beautiful of mountain weather phenomena; a temperature inversion or cloud sea, when only the tops of hills rise above the clouds. These conditions, as Begg experienced, sometimes last for several days, and while an observer at sea level is experiencing raw, cold and overcast conditions with occasional drizzle, the summits above the cloud are in brilliant sunshine, with air so dry that any snow would sublime, or pass into water vapour without first turning into water. Begg described one particular scene during November 1896.

"I had just taken the 7 p.m. observation and the air was so delightful that I took a constitutional up and down the observatory roof. The lightest of southerly airs blew gently and caressingly, and prevented the stillness of the whole scene from becoming oppressive. Above, the sky was cloudless; below, the clouds were sinking like great white lakes into the hollows between the hills. From the bosom of one of these lakes to eastward rose the moon, and while it was rising the upper half was as gold, while the half still in the cloud was red as blood. But not till it had risen quite above its white bed and shone with all its pale splendour in the opal sky did one feel the full charm of the scene. Over all the clear blue island mountain tops around it seemed to cast a fairy-like shimmer; and in that calm and impressive stillness, far, far above the noise and feverishness, the sin and misery of man, cut off from it all by those white sheets of cloud, amid the everlasting hills, bathed in the soft ethereal moonlight, one's spirit felt linked to the eternal and at rest.

ON BEN NEVIS: A MEMORY
My heart the beauties of the night enthral,
A dream of tenderness and pure delight;
Round me below the fog-lakes slowly fall,
Yet linger in the valleys, pure and white.

Calmly the moon in her pale splendour shines,
And casts o'er all her opalescent shroud;
Mountain and hill stand forth in softest lines,
Peeping like myriad islands through the cloud.

Blest is my soul to know this tranquil hour,
Earth with its sin and strife is far away;
Love seems the essence of the eternal power,
Life is no riddle but a harmony."

On the morning of Sunday, November 29, Begg was startled by a tap at the window. He went out to find two men shivering in the pre-dawn chill; they had been drinking in Fort William the previous evening, and while in their cups had laid a wager with their cronies that they would climb the Ben.

"The unfortunate narrator had frequently to break off his story and leave the room as his drinking, combined with the excessive exercise of climbing, had sadly upset him, otherwise I have no doubt he would have fallen asleep too like his now snoring companion."

In April, 1897, Begg returned to the summit for a few weeks, and while there witnessed the first ascent of Tower Gully, on the 25th.

"Up this, with ropes, ice axes, and all the other paraphernalia of the Alpine climber, came three members of the English Alpine Club. It certainly seemed a rash and foolhardy experiment, but their coolness and courage were rewarded after six hours hard work by their reaching the summit in safety, when the four of us greeted them with a hearty cheer and all-round hand-shaking, and finished up with a merry meal in the observatory kitchen. The most intrepid members of the Scottish Mountaineering Club had declared this feat to be impossible, so it must have been with considerable chagrin that they read in the papers next day of the success of their English friends." (7).

The three climbers were Geoffrey Hastings and the two Haskett-Smiths; on the 26th they made the first ascent of Gardyloo Gully. The ascent of Tower Gully had been complicated by a huge cornice overhanging the finish; through which the party had had to tunnel. The SMC Easter Meet in 1897 was at Tyndrum, and also from a yacht; some of the SMC must have felt some emotion at the snatching of two obvious routes in their absence.

3.7 Wragge's Well (c.1895)

In summer the water supply was Wragge's Well near the observatory, as well as roof drainage, though before the erection of a large water tank at Wragge's Well — a relic of Wolseley's campaign in the Sudan apparently — a drought necessitated a pony lift of water from the Red Burn. The other necessary routine at the summit station was bucket drill, the dumping of the accumulated rubbish etc over the cliff edge. The gully into which much of the rubbish accumulated was originally named 'Tin-can Gully'; it is now known as Gardyloo Gully, from the old Edinburgh cry as rubbish was about to be heaved out of a householder's window into the street below.

The dumping of rubbish in winter was made more exciting by the weather and the occasionally overhanging snow edge of the cliff; accordingly we find an interesting early reference to a prototype snow anchor or belay. The disposal party would be roped to a log fixed under a pile of stones. In one incident the observers discovered how difficult it was to pull a man over a snow cornice, when an observer had been lowered to recover a snow-shoe. His companions were beginning to despair of getting him up when reinforcements arrived in a party of mountaineers.

The building was warmed by an open cooking stove in the kitchen and also by a closed stove in the office. The usual fuel was paraffin coke; light to transport and burning with a clear hot flame and little ash. Only during the worst of storms did the temperature of the office fall much below 16°C. Fires then had to be kept low, as the flow of air up the chimneys heated them to red-heat. The coldest conditions were obtained indoors during storms in late autumn or early winter, before snow had a chance to build up an insulating cover. Temperatures then could fall below freezing point inside the observatory. Another necessary duty of the observers was to adjust the chimney when a change of wind began to blow back smoke and fumes into the office. Drysdale gives an account of this perilous operation; usually required during bad weather.

3.8   Bucket Drill (c.1885)

"The roof was gained by means of a narrow outside ladder whose rungs had to be cleared of ice . . . The top attained, the adventurer made a grab at the lightning rod, dropped on his knees; hacked off the masses of ice encrusting what was now by a change of wind the lee side of the chimney cowl; and then proceeded to tie the canvas firmly round the windward side; — shielding his face the while from the icy chunks that pervaded the air and giving an occasional shake to his half-frozen fingers; whilst not forgetting to keep his head clear of the rotating anemometer or the wildly-swinging wind-vane." (5).

With living conditions such as described, it is perhaps hardly surprising that the observers felt no need to add mountaineering to their already exciting and periodically uncomfortable lives.

Another hazard of the weather was that of electrical storm. These were rare but unpleasant, as an observer was occasionally knocked down when near the office stove. On June 19, 1895 a lightning strike caused some damage. Two of the observers were eating in the small hotel annex adjacent to the observatory, while a third was in the office. Shortly before 3 p.m. a great flash filled the hotel, accompanied by a terrific crash. In the observatory there was an even more vivid flash and deafening report. The telegraph apparatus emitted a cloud of smoke as did the stove, the office being soon filled with dense smoke. Kitchen items were hurled across the room while parts of the telegraph were fused. The casing which screwed on and retained the bone button of the electric bell in the visitors' room was burst and with the button was also thrown across the room. Smoke and flame appeared from behind the wainscot between the kitchen and office doors, but was soon under control. No one was injured during this strike, which was the closest call the observatory suffered.

3.9   Interior of Observatory (c.1903)

Each hour the office barometer was read. The observer on watch then made the outside readings of the thermometers in the screen, changed the raingauge, and made cloud and wind notes. At certain other times other observations were made; depth of snow, atmospheric dust, ozone, rainband, earth currents, duration of sunshine, earthquake records. Interestingly, one effect of the wind was to create a partial vacuum in the building, an effect well known to the staff.

The sunshine recorder used an ingenious system still in use today and based on a crystal ball; as the sun's rays were focussed through the glass they burned a line on a prepared strip of card. The observers had a problem with a certain class of tourist who enjoyed showing how the recorder could also light a pipe. For measuring the wind speed a Robinson hemispherical cup anemometer was mounted above the tower. This could, however, only be used when the temperature was above freezing point as ice built up rapidly during conditions of freezing fog. Throughout the year the direction and force of the wind was recorded by the observers, standing on the observatory roof. This estimate was then compared with the anemometer readings made during the summer months.

It seems that the original intention of the observers was to use the Beaufort force scale, but on calibrating wind force with the anemometer readings, it was found that on the Ben Nevis scale a given wind force had a considerably higher mean wind speed equivalent. For example, Force 8 on the Beaufort scale normally meant a mean wind speed of 37 knots; on the Ben Nevis scale it was 63 knots. A gale is defined as having a mean wind speed of 34 knots or over.

In a 1903 paper Angus Rankin provided statistics on the number of gales with mean speeds over 43 knots observed in the 13 year period 1884-1896. Rankin's data show, not surprisingly, that January was the worst month for gales, with a total for the 13 year period of 640 hours of gales, 6.6% of the possible time. This was in comparison with the 'quietest' month July, which had only 48 hours of gales. The frequency maxima occurred around midnight and 9 a.m., and most of the gales were from the southern half of the compass, with the strongest being from the south-east. The observers noted that northerly winds struck the cliffs and were then deflected upwards, passing over the top of the observatory without attaining high mean speeds at observatory level. This is a feature of micro-climate well known to most mountaineers. (8).

A comparison of the wind frequencies at Ben Nevis made with later data from Stornoway radiosonde ascents show significant differences. Assuming that wind directions are fairly similar to those from observatory years, the conclusion is that the wind speed and directions on Ben Nevis are very site-specific. It is likely, for example, that winds from the west or north-west are deflected around Carn Dearg and appear as very gusty northerlies at the summit. South-westerly winds may be backed to a more southerly direction, while south-easterlies are accelerated up the relatively gradual slope. (9).

The average annual temperature for the summit of Ben Nevis was 0.3°C for the period 1884-1903. At Fort William it was 8.4°C over the period 1891-1903. An interesting feature of the temperature averages was the low value for March, reflecting the strongly maritime influence on temperature. The average temperature differences between the Fort William and Ben Nevis Observatories (difference in height 1331m) was at a maximum in April and at a minimum in December, the average difference for the whole year being 8.5°C. This is equal to 0.64°C per 100m height difference.

Temperature inversions were associated with anticyclones centred close to the area, and were often accompanied by very low humidities at the summit. Frequently the top of the inversion lay between Fort William and the summit, the temperature increasing with height between the top of the inversion and the observatory. The largest negative temperature difference observed was 9.8°C at 9 a.m. on February 19, 1895; i.e. the summit of Ben Nevis was 9.8°C warmer than Fort William.

The lowest air temperature observed on Nevis is surprisingly high to those unfamiliar with the data, the lowest temperature actually observed being — 17.4°C on January 6, 1894. Weather conditions which give very low temperatures at valley sites in Scotland are those in

3.10   Observatory in summer (c.1903)

which a marked inversion is likely to occur. The mean daily variation of temperature is also surprising, being very small. For July it is 2.2°C, while in winter it was only 0.3°C.

The staff frequently noted the rapid changes in temperature, pressure, wind speed and direction, and precipitation which occurred. These rapid changes are of obvious importance to mountaineers. The mean temperature ranged from about −5°C in February, to 5°C in July, being below freezing point from the beginning of October to early May. These figures apply to the summit, however, and conditions at the foot of the cliffs can be quite different, as some climbers have found to their cost.

During the 21 years of summit observations, Ben Nevis was in sunshine for about only one-sixth of the possible time; the summit was clear for about one hour in five in December to one hour in two in June. The diurnal variation in the occurrence of mist or fog was small; it rarely pays, therefore, to wait in the hope of a clearing.

The sunniest month was June 1888, with an average of 8.3 hours per day, while December 1893 will probably go down on record as one of the gloomiest, with a total of 1.1 hours of sunshine for the entire month. (See end of book for more weather data).

3.11   Observatory in winter (c.1903)

Since temperatures on Nevis are close to freezing point for most of the year, the additional factors of saturated conditions and moderate to high wind speeds combined with a temperature of slightly below freezing point often give a rapid build-up of rime ice, whiskery crystals of ice building up on any projecting features, including a climber's beard, eyebrows, eyelashes, and the rocks of the cliffs. The log book describes a post of cross-section four inches square which in less than a week grew a crystalline growth of about five feet by one foot.

The observers had, as has been alluded to above, great difficulty in measuring precipitation. The rain gauge would often be filled with drifting snow, for example, even although no snow was falling. On average the late spring and early summer gives the driest parts of the year, like the rest of Scotland. The wettest year was 1898, which had just over twice the rainfall of 1895, the driest year. The nature of the rainfall on Nevis is indicated by the data for 1898, when daily falls of 25mm or over accounted for 58% of the total rainfall, and falls of less than 12.5mm accounted for only 18%. The mean annual rainfall of Ben Nevis was 4.08 metres.

Much of the snow which falls on the summit plateau of Nevis is subsequently thawed or is blown elsewhere. The depth of snow was measured at a post on a flat part of the plateau, over 20 yards from any obstruction. Maximum snow depths were normally reached in April, but in 1903 the maximum depth of 3.17 metres occurred on May 18. The greatest depth recorded was 3.61 metres on April 3, 1885.

Somewhat ironically, although weather was the prime area of research at the Ben Nevis Observatory, perhaps one of its most outstanding, if indirect contributions to science was to come from the realms of particle physics. During the summer months, young physicists sometimes acted as relief observers. One of these was Charles Thomson Rees Wilson, who at the age of 25, two years after taking his degree at Cambridge, spent a fortnight at the summit in September, 1894. Wilson (1869-1959), was a Scot, born in Glencorse. During his stay at the observatory, the various cloud and optical effects, along with later experiences of electrical storms on Nevis, all made a great impression on Wilson. The next year he began experiments at the Cavendish Laboratory which led to his development of the Wilson Cloud Chamber.

Wilson's original intent was to study experimentally the optical phenomena of coronas and glories and Brocken Spectres. These are the rainbow-like coloured rings and human-shaped shadows that you can see thrown on to a bank of mist by strong, low sunlight. Almost immediately however, he found that his apparatus would allow him to make visible the tracks made by individual ions and to study their behaviour.

"In September 1894 I had spent the fortnight working at the Observatory on Ben Nevis which was to lead both to my cloud chamber work and to my lifelong interest in atmospheric electricity. Now I began to make experiments on clouds, made by the expansion of moist air, attempting to reproduce the beautiful optical phenomenon of the coronas and glories I had seen on the mountain top . . . I found that within a certain range of expansion there was rain-like condensation at each expansion showing the existence of nuclei of a particular kind always being reproduced. With greater expansions the condensation became cloud-like, the number of droplets increasing at an enormous rate with increasing expansion. By May 1895 these experiments were sufficiently advanced for me to read a paper before the Cambridge Philosophical Society." (10).

By a happy coincidence in the autumn of that year (1895) Röntgen discovered X-rays, and in 1911 Wilson finally succeeded in producing the first photographs of the tracks of ionizing particles. For this he was awarded the Nobel Prize in 1927.

On July 27, 1969, Miss Rosamund Wilson, the daughter of Professor C.T.R.Wilson, unveiled a commemorative plaque on the summit of Ben Nevis. The plaque, affixed to the south-east wall of the observatory ruins, indentifies the ruins and tells briefly of the connection between Professor Wilson and the observatory.

Other scientific and well-known personages visited and worked at the observatory in its time. In July 1885, Professor Vernon and his assistant performed experiments on the intensity of light from flames at low pressure. During 1890-1891, John Aitken tested his dust counter at the observatory. Captain Scott received permission to test equipment for his Antarctic expedition but was unable to go himself, two of his officers spending the winter of 1900 instead; Michael Barne for magnetic observations and Charles Rawson Royds for meteorology. The cook of the 'Discovery' also stayed at the observatory.

W.S.Bruce, who had been temporary superintendent of the observatory from 1895-1896 was later to mount the 'Scotia' voyage to the South Orkney islands and Weddell Sea. Two of the 'Scotia' scientific staff, D.W.Wilton and R.C.Mossman had also worked on Nevis.

By the end of the 19th Century, the running costs of the observatory were about £1,000 per annum. Many private individuals were exceptionally generous in supporting the cause, but could hardly be expected to continue thus for much longer. In 1902 the Meteorological Council announced that the annual grant of £250 for the low-level observatory would cease after that year. The Prime Minister was led to appoint a Committee of Enquiry, before which eminent scientists gave evidence, some of which, unfortunately, was conflicting.

Lord Kelvin, on the Committee, was supportive, whereas Professor, later Sir Arthur, Schuster, felt that it had served its purpose. The Treasury offered an annual grant of £350, the same total as before, as the summit observatory was then receiving an annual grant of £100. As the necessary income was £950 per annum the outcome was inevitable, and the Directors of the Management Committee had no real choice but to close down the observatory.

The last entry in the log was that of October 1, 1904. Snow was falling and mist enveloped the summit. A week later, the equipment having been dismantled and removed, the staff turned the key to lock the door and went down the mountain for the last time. The sum cost of the entire venture during its remarkable 21 years life had been just over £30,000. The Government had contributed a little over £5,000 of that amount.

One of the rooms at the summit observatory was opened during the summer months for the refreshment of visitors. This continued until 1916, with a previous observer, James Miller, acting as keeper. Miller had served at the observatory from 1884 until its closure, and when the possibility of a reopening was examined in 1930, in conjunction with an International Polar Year Commission, he immediately volunteered, though he must have been about 70 years of age. The observatory was never reopened however, and the ravages of time, weather and careless visitors to the summit all took their inevitable toll. An accidental fire in 1932 caused some damage, and the attentions of climbers seeking shelter did little to help matters.

Perhaps the final nail in the coffin occurred just before Easter 1950, when a party of climbers was seen stripping the valuable roof lead with the skill of practised craftsmen, the booty of coiled lead being rolled down the mountain for removal by lorry.

3.12   Breakfast in Summit Hotel (c.1902)

The observations made at the Ben Nevis and Fort William observatories were extensively studied at the time, notably by Alexander Buchan, Robert Omond, Angus Rankin and R.C. Mossman, and many papers were published. The actual data were published *in extenso* in the Proceedings of the Royal Society of Edinburgh; there they are available to all for further study. Summary tables were also published. (11).

One hundred years after the opening of the observatory and its weather records, the heavy tomes of the Proceedings of the Royal Society of Edinburgh were taken off their shelves, and a beginning made on the transfer of data to computer data sets. This transfer was made possible due to a Manpower Services Commission Community Project; beginning at Edinburgh University in June 1983. During the six months of the project approximately eight non-consecutive years of data were transferred, and it is hoped to extend the project to cover all 20 years of the observatory's records. The use of electronic techniques in data handling will permit further analytical work on this valuable mass of data.

This chapter cannot close without brief mention of another act of private enterprise — the small 'hotel' on the summit, close to the observatory — a small annex built by a Fort William hotelier some time after the building of the observatory. It was open during the summer months right through to the end of World War I, and was run by two young ladies, who were frequently indignant at being awakened at all hours by visitors coming up to view the sunrise. Board and lodgings, of a rough sort, were available; lunch for three shillings, or tea, bed and breakfast for ten shillings, there being four small bedrooms. As will be seen shortly, this hotel helped in some explorations on Ben Nevis.

4.1 Portrait of Harold Raeburn (1905)

RAEBURN AND COMPANY (1897 – 1926)

Each year, usually on the first Saturday in December, the Scottish Mountaineering Club holds its Dinner. Every second year the retiring President steps down and without ceremony, indeed it goes unnoticed by some, hands over to the incoming President his seals of office. The first is a club badge in gold, to distinguish it from the usual bronze, but the second pays a singular honour to one of Britain's most accomplished mountaineers of the past. It is a long, wooden-shafted ice axe once owned by Harold Raeburn (1865-1926).

An all-round mountaineer, Raeburn had both a burning passion for the mountains and the natural ability that sets apart so many of the great. A native of Edinburgh and, (other than a short spell in Partick, Glasgow) resident there for most of his life, Raeburn belonged not to the professional classes which continued to dominate climbing at the turn of the century, but to the new fast-expanding middle class, his early career being that of a brewer. A bachelor all his life, Raeburn devoted his considerable energies to mountaineering, with yachting and ornithology as secondary recreations. His diaries on the Birds of Shetland are lodged in the National Library of Scotland.

A measure of Raeburn's climbing activity can be judged by the fact that of the thirty new routes on Nevis from 1896 to 1921, his name appears on exactly half. In 1902, he made the second ascent of Crowberry Ridge Direct on the Buachaille Etive Mor, at that time dismissed by the Scottish establishment as unjustifiable. Of more significance perhaps were his ascents of Raeburn's Arête on Nevis, that same year, and his earlier lead, in July 1898, of Flake Route, Very Difficult, on Church Door Buttress of Bidean nam Bian.

A contemporary described Raeburn thus,

"Few have had a wider knowledge, or a more intense love of Nature in all its aspects — birds and beasts, flowers and rocks, the natural features of the countryside — all attracted his keen observation, and to a nature such as his the call of the mountain was irresistible . . . Light, wiry and active, with supple limbs and a beautiful balance, he added to his physical gifts an indomitable will, a sound judgment as to routes and possibilities, and a fearless self-reliance." (1).

Lord Mackay, a keen judge of men, made a terse description of Raeburn.

"Physically and mentally hard as nails, trained by solitary sea-cliff climbing after birds' haunts, he was certain, unyielding and concise in every movement, both mental and physical."

It seemed that Raeburn had his own peculiar climbing style, one borne out by photographs of him climbing.

"He could keep his lithe body closer to, and in almost complete contact with any rock he had to deal with. And he had a capacity of grip that was astonishing. He was possessed of strong muscular fingers that could press firmly and in a straight downward contact upon the very smallest hold."

Of Raeburn's character, Mackay makes what is clearly an honest appraisal.

"In controversies as to routes or as to times required, he was a stern opponent. His notes of recorded times in every climb achieved, and his constant comparisons by small seconds with the time of to-day, were often anathema to me, who preferred to enjoy the hopes and the passing incidents at large, without being checked by the watch . . . Something, I sometimes thought, of Stalin was in his make-up. Even you could see his mind, acting as Molotov's, as it came back and back to his original assertions. And yet he was ultimately fair in debate."

Lord Mackay finished his portrait of Raeburn with an anecdote. Raeburn, Lawson and Mackay had had a long, tiring but successful day on Arran, and were descending Glen Rosa. Raeburn hated being forced to a pace that was beyond his liking and Lawson walked at a tremendous pace.

"Harold suddenly sat down and refused to go another inch unless the pace moderated. Lawson did not agree. So he said, 'Just go on, I'll wait.' Lawson went on and, if anything, increased his pace. I (torn between) lengthened my step and kept up with Lawson. In due time and in complete darkness we arrived in the square of light before the door of Corrie Inn. We turned to one another to wonder what had become of Raeburn, and looked round casually. There he was, just at our backs, on the edge of the same square of light from the inn door. That again, I think, is a bit typical of his pertinacity and endurance." (2).

In the autumn of 1896 Raeburn applied to join the SMC, proposed by Willie Douglas and seconded by Naismith. On December 2 his application was passed. Within the club hierarchy, he rose to become Vice-President from 1909-1911, ultimately turning down the Presidency itself, just as Naismith had done before him, through modesty. Indeed, as a letter from Naismith to Douglas in 1896 indicates, Naismith also refused the post of Secretary, writing that,

"I have no ambition whatever for any more important post in the Club — Indeed I should prefer either now or soon to retire into private membership . . . ". (3).

The first climbers on the Ben had quickly reached a high standard in mixed climbing in winter — snow, ice and rock — on routes such as Tower Ridge and the North-East Buttress. Raeburn was to push back the known frontiers of possibility and extend this expertise into the pure snow and ice of the gullies, in addition to which he brought to Scotland the rock climbing standards already in vogue further south.

A prominent Edinburgh man had joined the SMC the year before Raeburn. The two would make ascents together in the coming years. William Inglis Clark (1856-1932) was born in Bombay, where his father was minister of the Scots Church. His mother died of cholera when he was about a year old, when he and his elder brother came to Edinburgh. When he was nine the two brothers made a night ascent of Goatfell on Arran, to watch the sunrise.

4.2   Portrait of William Inglis Clark (c.1900)

Clark's interest in Ben Nevis was probably kindled by an uncle, Charles Simson Clark, who had climbed the mountain some 45 times. When one day William made an ascent of Nevis with a friend, by way of Glen Nevis and the Carn Mor Dearg arête, he was fortunate to find a temperature inversion at the level of the arête. There he also met Professor Heddle and Colin Philip.

Foster Heddle, Professor of Chemistry at St Andrews, held that chair for 23 years. His great interest in geology is marked now by the Heddle Collection of Scottish minerals. Heddle was one of the first Honorary Members of the SMC and attended the opening ceremony of the Ben Nevis Observatory. Colin Philip was a watercolour artist and member of the SMC, designing and drawing at least one of that club's early dinner menus. Both Heddle and Philip accompanied Clark and his friend to the summit of Nevis.

Clark, who later went on to become President of the SMC, was just as interesting a personage outside of mountaineering. At Edinburgh University, studying chemistry, he became assistant to Professor Crum Brown, gaining his D.Sc. before he was 21. He had to wait until that age to be formally capped. In order to be independent he then went to work in the lab of Messrs Duncan Flockhart & Co, where he later became a partner.

While in that firm Clark was the first to have the idea of putting unpleasant tasting drugs into capsules, inventing and designing the necessary machinery for the entire process. Becoming a wealthy Edinburgh chemist, he owned that city's first car, with the registration S1. Passing this on to Lord Kingsburgh (First President of the Automobile Association), he kept the registration S2 for his own use, running an Arrol-Johnston 'dog-cart'. The Clarks were early advocates of the use of the car for mountaineering transport. As one of the first car drivers in Switzerland, they were stopped and fined for driving at the alarming velocity of 9 m.p.h. He was also an enthusiastic and expert photographer, in the days when a camera was built of mahogany and brass and could weigh over 14 pounds. His early experiments in colour photography were published in the SMC Journal for 1909. (4).

For the next two years the easier gullies were explored, April 1897 seeing ascents of Tower Gully, Grade I, and Gardyloo Gully, Grade II, by Hastings and the Haskett-Smiths.

4.3   Portrait of Rev.A.E. Robertson (c.1906)

4.4 *Aysel Crocket on Tunnel Route, Eastern Traverse, Tower Ridge (1976)*

4.5 *Bill Young on Eastern Traverse, winter (c.1960)*

Moonlight Gully, next to No.5 Gully, was climbed on January 3, 1898 by William Inglis Clark and Tom Gibson. Moonlight Gully, as the name would suggest, was finished under the light of the moon, and gave the party nine hours of constant step cutting. Staircase Climb, Very Difficult, was climbed on July 12, 1898, by J.H. Bell. J. Maclay and Willie Naismith. On September 11 of that year, Raeburn and Gibson made the first summer ascent of the Original Route on The Castle, a Very Difficult rock climb.

Until 1900, any climber going up or down Tower Ridge climbed the Great Tower by any of the variations to the west; none of which were particularly easy in summer, and all of them serious undertakings under snow or ice. On September 6 of that year Naismith and the Rev. Archibald Aeneas Robertson discovered a narrow ledge leading out on to the eastern face of the Great Tower. This exposed traverse led through a tunnel formed by a fallen block, then climbed directly up to the summit of the Great Tower. As it was much easier than the western variations it almost immediately became the favoured route, and is now followed by virtually every climber doing Tower Ridge. (5).

During Easter 1901, a very strong team consisting of Raeburn, Douglas, Rennie and Willie Ling attempted Observatory Buttress, the wall-like buttress facing Tower Ridge across Observatory Gully. Snow was pouring down over ice-sheeted rocks, and after a gain in height of between 2-300 feet they decided to retreat. As Ling wrote later,

"The steepness was such that in places handholds as well as footholds had to be cut in the ice. Such climbing may not be very difficult, but it becomes a question of time and endurance, and the party decided that neither commodity would hold out." (6).

As it was, the party ran into a blizzard crossing the plateau, reaching Fort William just before midnight.

That Ling should remark on the climbing in such terms is indicative of their abilities, as Observatory Buttress in winter is now Grade V. [Raeburn climbed guideless in the Alps from 1902 onwards. With his closest friend Willie Ling, he climbed the North face of the Disgrazia in 1910, now graded at TD.] During the retreat that day, the party's eyes, and those of Raeburn in particular, must have rested often on the next ridge to the east, Observatory Ridge, which was to be the scene of a remarkable solo ascent two months later.

Dr Inglis Clark and his wife Jane decided to spend several nights in the small summit hotel on Nevis, and on June 21, 1901 walked up to the summit, having first sent a wire to Raeburn in Edinburgh. Raeburn caught the 4.30 a.m. train the next day, arriving in Fort William by 10 a.m., but unable to form a rope at such short notice he continued alone, walking up through a cloud burst to gain the foot of Observatory Ridge.

Of the solo ascent Raeburn wrote,

"I remember three distinctly good bits on it. First the slabby rocks near the foot. Then a few hundred feet up an excellent hand traverse presents itself. It is begun by getting the hand into a first-rate crack on the left, then toe-scraping along a wall till the body can be hoisted on to a narrow overhung ledge above. This does not permit of standing up, but a short crawl to the right finished the difficulty . . . The third difficulty, and the one which cost the most time, is rather more than half-way up, where a very steep tower spans the ridge. I tried directly up the face, but judged it somewhat risky, and prospecting to the right, discovered a route which after a little pressure 'went'." (7).

Raeburn's solo ascent had taken three hours. Sitting in the sun at the top of the route, Raeburn heard for the first time in summer a snow bunting (usually, though not always, a winter visitor), and he finished his account of the climb by admitting that if asked to choose between the climb and the song, he would be tempted to choose the latter; fortunately, he concluded , the snow bunting's song was a bonus to a most enjoyable scramble. The next day, with the Inglis Clarks, he again attempted Observatory Buttress, but heavy rain forced them down and they finished up North-East Buttress. Climbing just left of Slingsby's Chimney, they gained the First Platform by a new route, Raeburn's 18-Minute Route.

One year later Dr Inglis Clark was convalescing from an illness. Toward the end of June he decided to climb on Nevis, and stay at the summit hotel. In company with his wife and

4.6 Mrs Inglis Clark, Crowberry Direct, (c.1904)

G.T. Glover a start was made on Thursday, June 25 with the second ascent of Staircase Climb, a Very Difficult route on the west flank of Carn Dearg Buttress.

"What a spot for middle-aged folks to be in!" wrote Clark, having gained the crux, an overhung recess in an exposed position.

"No thought of business or secretarial duties . . . but a steay stand with muscles braced and a side hold in the crack, were the prelude to the contact of fierce hobnailers with but lightly protected shoulder blades." (8).

The Clarks had arranged a rendezvous with Raeburn, who was in a yachting race in the Firth of Forth; due to poor winds Raeburn would arrive later on the Saturday, and meet the party at 2 p.m. at the foot of Observatory Buttress. The Clarks, with Glover, now turned their attention to the west flank of Tower Ridge, and Friday evening saw a successful summer ascent of Glover's Chimney, a wet Very Difficult now rather neglected in summer, but popular as a winter route.

Saturday morning dawned as clear as the previous days, and Clark and Glover decided to tackle another line while waiting for Raeburn. They chose the Pinnacle Buttress of The Tower, which lies immediately left of Glover's Chimney. A late start, due to the midnight finish of the previous day, saw them gaining the Great Tower at 4.15 p.m. from where, wrote Dr Clark,

". . . eagerly looking down we espied a moving speck on the rocks of the Observatory Buttress. It was that solitary climber, who amid the great immensities of the place seemed to traverse invisible ledges, and to climb where foot and hand holds could not be seen. Our chance of a share in his great enterprise was gone, and the reproachful glance of my wife who had waited for us two and a half hours at the 'Gap' was such as to make us hasten aloft . . ."

That 'solitary climber' was of course Raeburn, who had given up the wait and decided to solo the buttress. In a remarkably understated essay by Raeburn the climbing is confined to just four lines.

"Below, was the fast flowing shadowtide; above, the blaze of sunlight, and oh, blessed thought, perhaps afternoon tea. It was enough, I went up, and, fifteen hours from the Sea, stood upon the Summit." (9).

Observatory Buttress, Original Route, is a 700 foot Very Difficult, steeper and more compact than earlier routes. Drinking his afternoon tea on the summit, Raeburn described the climbing to his friends, telling them of the 'pulling in holds' which made the steep climbing possible. It was Raeburn's third attempt on the route and the fourth day of a heatwave, the shade temperature at the summit on that day reaching a record 66.4°F. (22.7°C).

4.7   *Pinnacle Buttress (South Trident),(c.1902)*

Glover now left the party, leaving Raeburn and the Clarks. On the Sunday, the fourth day of the Clark's stay, they climbed the South Trident Buttress, called by them Pinnacle Buttress. The difficult pitch on this was the steepest ever experienced by Clark, and at several points, he noticed, the rope hung parallel to the rocks. The 1902 team avoided the lowest tier of the Buttress, which seemed impossibly steep; indeed, it was not climbed until 1934, by G. Graham Macphee.

Not content with one route, Raeburn and the Clarks now turned their attention to the Comb, the fierce buttress which is the most prominent feature in Coire na Ciste between the Tower Ridge and No.3 Gully. They succeeded in climbing the easy sloping ledges at the foot of the buttress and the rightward slanting rakes; these led to the buttress edge overlooking a gully (Green Gully). Here Raeburn declined to try the 'rotten chimney', but instead traversed rightward into the gully, which they then followed for 100 feet.

As they had been forced off the Comb proper, Raeburn's party, not liking the look of the rest of the gully came back some distance and traversed rightward across the face. They eventually found a way up the cliffs overlooking No.3 Gully, following ledges and rocks of what is now known as No.3 Gully Buttress, a popular winter route. This was on the fourth day of the week and was the fifth first ascent.

The first successful and complete ascent of the Comb was not to be made until 1921, when A.S. Pigott and J. Wilding, leading climbers from the south, succeeded in finding a way through the band of steep rock above the slanting rakes. They followed the sloping ledges — which are of rotten and loose rock in many places — much as had Raeburn 19 years earlier, and then forced the 'rotten chimney' rejected by Raeburn. The chimney proved to be the crux of the route, graded Severe.

But if Raeburn had failed on the Comb that sunny Sunday, he succeeded brilliantly on the Monday with his best and hardest route of the week — the futuristic Raeburn's Arête on the First Platform, North-East Buttress. This excellent Severe lies on the same buttress as Raeburn's 18-Minute Route, recorded the previous June. The arête looks down the Allt a'Mhuilinn, and consists of a parallel series of steep, narrow ramps. Raeburn gave no details of his ascent with the Clarks, beyond a straight route description, though he did comment that —

"From a climbing point of view this ranks among the steepest on Ben Nevis, and would be impossible but for the magnificent nature of the rock." (10).

There is a mention of Raeburn's Arête elsewhere by Clark, which describes Raeburn soloing besides the Clarks, but it is not clear whether this was on the first ascent or on one made later.

Outside of that week's climbing, the only other new route on Nevis that year was a Very Difficult climb by W.C. Newbigging and a Swiss companion, on August 21. This was Newbigging's 80-Minute Route, some distance left of Raeburn's Arête, and from its name we might detect a little poke at Raeburn's serious regard to time-keeping for ascents. After that superb week of climbing, Ben Nevis was not to see another such burst of concentrated activity by one party for more than half a century.

No first ascents were recorded in 1903; the SMC held their Easter Meet at Inveroran and on Skye, Raeburn attending the latter. On the first day of 1904, however, a strong party climbed the North Trident Buttress. The rope of four was Maclay, Raeburn, and two cousins from Dundee, Harry and Charles Walker. The route is now graded a IV. On the first ascent the

Ben was in a not untypical January condition, with little snow, and thin ice lining the cracks and chimneys.

Raeburn returned to the Trident Buttresses in April 1904, when with Jane Inglis Clark and her son Charles he completed his trilogy of ascents here with the Central Trident Buttress, more of a gully than a buttress on this snowy ascent. Elsewhere on the mountain, the Walkers found a buttress climb on the North Wall of Carn Dearg—Cousins' Buttress, climbed on June 11, while an easy route was found up the south-west ridge of the Douglas Boulder.

The first thundering wave of exploration on Nevis had broken. There were to be no routes in 1905. Raeburn *et al* had untouched rocks to explore on other mountains. He was fast approaching the peak of his form however, and recorded two outstanding routes before the Great War broke out. The first of these was to be the only route recorded in 1906. It was a winter ascent which stretched both Raeburn and his meagre equipment to the limit — Green Gully.

Raeburn had attempted to climb the Comb during the heatwave of 1902. His party then had gone a little way up the gully on the right of the Comb, but had not perserved and had retreated. Raeburn was unstoppable however and on Sunday, April 22 of 1906 he met the Rev. Archibald Aeneas Robertson in Fort William, for another attempt on the Comb. Gales had been hammering Nevis for several weeks, and Raeburn reached Fort William in rain and snow to find that Robertson was unable to climb, due to a slight indisposition.

Raeburn was saved from the necessity of soloing, fortunately, as Robertson introduced him to a gentleman from Geneva, a member of the Swiss Alpine Club, Monsieur Eberhard Phildius, who was staying in Fort William. As the two climbers passed Carn Dearg Buttress, the wind, which had changed overnight from a wet southwest to a cold northeast, blew flurries of powder snow about the ice-covered rocks.

Raeburn's plan was to climb Green Gully until it was possible to gain access to the buttress rocks on the left, but the climbers found even the approach difficult, with one or two feet of soft snow covering harder, icy stuff. These potential avalanche conditions prompted them to clear the soft snow away and cut steps in the hard layer underneath. Raeburn described the ascent in a now classic essay.

"Now we found ourselves looking up, so far as the mist and the descending cataracts of snow dust would permit, the steep gully which should give access to the ridge. Then began the real struggle. Keen frost reigned, and a biting wind moaned among the icy battlements . . . we two, stormers of one of the salient towers, felt the blast strike us now and again as it swept round the angle of the Comb."

4.8   The Comb/Green Gully (March, 1984)

A great problem, then, as now, was the choking clouds of spindrift, the seemingly innocuous, tiny crystals of snow blown by the wind.

"From above one could, to a certain extent, take cover beneath the shield of our cone-pointed, brim-turned-down felt hats, but occasionally the snow that fell mixed with the seldom ceasing stream that poured down the gully, was caught by the powerful ascending eddy and rushed up, thus taking us behind our defences. The pain of a stream of icy snow in the face is so great that work must stop, and the face covered till breath is regained."

Raeburn and Phildius found the gully rising, initially, in two steep sections; with an average angle of probably 70 to 75 degrees, small portions approaching 90 degrees. While climbing ice, as many a leader has discovered to his dismay, an angle of 75 degrees feels like 90 degrees, or vertical, with anything steeper feeling overhanging. The conditions underfoot that day in the gully were fortunately excellent, snow-ice allowing Raeburn to cut firm handholds as well as footholds.

"Ice work of this kind". continued Raeburn, "is, however, particularly cramping and exhausting, and progress was slow. To hang on with one hand, while that long two-handed weapon, the modern ice axe, is wielded in the other, is calculated to produce severe cramps in course of time, and did so now . . . I suggest for climbs such as this our going back to the original Swiss icemens' tools, the iron-shod straight 'baton', and the light tomahawk-like hatchet stuck in the belt when not in use."

In advocating the use of a shorter ice tool Raeburn was decades ahead of his time. He seems to have retreated somewhat from this point of view a few years later, though, as in his book, published in 1920 he criticises the fashion for very short axes.

The two introductory ice pitches were led by Raeburn, the second pitch taking three attempts before a tired leader cut his way up to an easier section of the gully. Here Phildius took over, the two deciding to continue up the gully, as the buttress to the left, now accessible, was fringed and crowned with unstable-looking cornices of ice and snow.

The finish to the gully was blocked by a huge cornice, more than 12 feet high. This is fairly large by Nevis standards, the gales of the previous weeks obviously having built it up. The climbers decided that their only chance at this point was to traverse out right, where a rib of ice-covered rock ran up to meet the cornice, reducing its height by half. At this point also, the cornice was only slightly overhanging. Raeburn described the hair-raising finish.

"This way eventually 'went', but the 'Comb' was game to the last, and I must confess to a feeling of helplessness for a moment as I stood on my ice-axe, driven horizontally into the vertical snow wall, some hundreds of feet of little less than vertical ice-plastered rocks stretching away down into the depths of the mist beneath, while my fingers slid helplessly from the glassy surface of the cornice névé, in the vain endeavour to find or make a hold by which I might haul myself up. The problem was solved by a retreat, until Phildius was able to pass me up his axe. Then the ice-plating was quickly shattered, and with fingers well crooked in the tough névé, a steady drag landed the body over the cornice lip, and Phildius soon followed." (11).

Ironically, Raeburn himself may have helped to consign this fine climb to a period of obscurity. In his essay he apologised for the climb, admitting that they were never once on the exact arête. But he was defiant in stating that this did not matter, as he and Phildius went out for a climb and got one, both of them being pleased by the ascent, in as icy conditions as Raeburn had ever seen Ben Nevis.

In the 1919 edition of the Nevis Guide, an updated edition of the 1902 publication, the gully is dismissed in a few sparse lines.

"Raeburn made an icy ascent on 22nd April, 1906, which, although not on the arête, yet led to the summit of the Comb. The climb was, however, almost entirely on snow and ice." (12).

Raeburn's ascent of Green Gully rapidly faded between the pages of the SMC Journal, as no one seemed willing or able to follow such a masterly lead. The route suffered the exact same fate as another classic route of Raeburn's — Crowberry Gully in Glencoe — a later party making what they thought was a first ascent. On April 4, 1937, 31 years later, J.H.B. Bell recorded a winter ascent of the Nevis gully, naming it Green Gully. Raeburn's ascent was still unrecognised on the publication dates of subsequent climbing guides to Ben Nevis — in 1936 (13), and 1969 (14), and it has taken until the 1970's for a growing awareness of Raeburn's achievements to surface.. (15).

Not all ascents made during this period went smoothly, though fatalities were, for a long time unknown, because leader falls were likewise unknown. The consequences of a leader fall were so obviously serious, given the minimal equipment used then, that no leader fell. But poor conditions and lack of experience were just as awkward then as they are now, and the following account was not the last epic to be experienced on Nevis.

The 1907 New Year Meet of the SMC was based at the Alexandra Hotel, Fort William. The first three arrivals on the Friday, December 27, were J.H.A. MacIntyre, T.E. Goodeve, and Charles Inglis Clark, the 18-year old son of Dr and Mrs Inglis Clark. On the Saturday the trio decided to attempt Tower Ridge, a first for all three, as the ridge did not seem to have as much snow on it as the North-East Buttress. They had with them two ropes; one 80-foot and one 60-foot. They tied on to the 60-foot rope, their first error, as the necessary short pitches inevitably meant great delays.

The party started up the West Gully of the Douglas Gap at 10 a.m., Goodeve leading, as he did throughout the entire episode. Considerable effort was needed to gain the ridge itself by noon, which should have warned the party of the limited daylight remaining, but they pressed on, their second error, and reached the Great Tower at 4 p.m. Darkness was now setting in and they decided to take the escape route off the Ridge, by the way now known as the Eastern Traverse. Unfortunately, as Clark wrote later,

"We had a hazy impression that an easy ledge ran round the west side, enabling one to reach the Gap, without climbing the Tower itself."

So Goodeve's party began to traverse the Great Tower on its western face, encountering difficult route finding. After several hours they reached a snow gully, which they could follow visually about halfway down to Coire na Ciste. This they began descending, easily at first, then with step cutting, and finally, after lowering the last man down an ice step, the other two joining him using steps, they found themselves at the top of an overhanging pitch. The gully, they finally realised to their horror, was Glover's Chimney, first climbed in summer by G.T. Glover and Charles's father. Further descent was impossible. Abseil slings were not used then, even given a belay, ropes were of inadequate length, and the foot of the pitch an unknown distance away in the dark, hidden by an overhang.

The three were now fairly exhausted, but began to climb up to the ridge again, using the rocks on the right of the gully. By 8 p.m. they had regained their former level, opposite the western traverse under the Great Tower. To this point there had been a little starlight, but now clouds rolled in, and with no lanterns, their visibility was very limited. This fact may have been an advantage, as their position would have been a frightening one in daylight.

Not far below the summit cornice, a twenty foot rib of steep rock was encountered. Goodeve and Clark succeeded in climbing it, though not without difficulty, and then it was MacIntyre's turn.

"As my frantic struggles had effectually removed every trace of snow for the last man to get a foothold on, there was nothing for it but to lift him bodily by the rope. Goodeve and I sat stridelegs on the ice-arête . . . and at a shout from below, with all the speed our tired muscles would allow, brought MacIntyre up, struggling and kicking like a fish . . . Half an hour of step-cutting up a terribly steep ice-slope brought us to the cornice." (16).

Fortunately the cornice was straightforward, and some time after midnight the plateau was gained. As they were unable to take a compass bearing, a gale blowing out their light, they wandered off route into Glen Nevis, missing the search parties organised by the rest of the Meet. One party, however, found their steps on top.

Finally, Raeburn found them at 9 a.m. on Sunday morning, and led them back to Fort William, thirty hours after they had set out. Two of them had frostbitten hands, and Goodeve a head cut from a slip during the descent, but otherwise their remarkable display of endurance says much for their general level of fitness.

MacIntyre, in his report of the Meet in the SMC Journal, ended with the following.

"Some of the members present offered an opinion which might profitably be enlarged to the following:– It is a courtesy due from every party to their fellow-members to make sure before leaving the hotel, either that some one connected with the hotel, or that some of their fellow-members, then resident, are conversant with their intentions for the day." (17).

As a post-script to this episode, a route was recorded in the winter of 1971, on the right side of Glover's Chimney. Graded at III, a careful reading of Clark's account ties in with this later ascent, and the route is now called Goodeve's Route, a fitting memorial to the climbers of 1907.

The pace of exploration had slowed by 1905 and was about to cease completely. On September 28, 1908, Raeburn climbed the fine buttress which now bears his name, in Castle Coire. His companions were H. MacRobert and D.S. Arthur, and the Very Difficult route was finished despite heavy rain. Raeburn's Buttress is now a fine winter route, though its arête section is enjoyable in summer. Raeburn did little new in the next few years, due to an accident, though on September 28, 1911, he climbed Raeburn's Easy Route, an elegantly easy way up the cliffs left of the Comb.

4.9   Goodeve (c.1914)

The First World War broke out, almost completely putting a halt to climbing. Those not away fighting were working to near exhaustion on the home front, while economic measures in any case reinforced a voluntary ban on luxuries such as unnecessary travelling. The strictures of war also hit publishing, delaying the second edition of the Nevis Guide and preventing Raeburn from publishing his book, then in MS form.

Raeburn, now 49, was too old to be accepted for the Royal Flying Corps despite all his efforts. Instead he threw himself into 15 and 16 hour days in an aeroplane factory. Younger men enlisted and some of them died in the fighting, including Charles Inglis Clark. By 1920 however, conditions had eased somewhat, and in April of that year Raeburn made a return visit to Nevis for his last major ascent on that mountain — the first winter ascent of one of his own routes, Observatory Ridge.

The Easter, 1920 Meet of the SMC at Fort William was the first to be held there since 1914. On Tuesday morning of the Meet, Raeburn, W.A. Mounsey and Frank Sidney Goggs set off from Achintee. A small amount of new snow had fallen overnight and the party decided to try Observatory Ridge, a first winter ascent being especially tempting. A 100-foot rope was shared between the three, Raeburn leading, Goggs second and Mounsey, the heaviest, being third man. This was a conscious decision, belays being somewhat nebulous during this period.

The good memory of the leader facilitated the route-finding in the lower, steep section. Higher up, stamina and experience were to be demanded, as snow began to fall again and conditions became steadily worse. High up the ridge, steep, glazed rocks formed a barrier, as Raeburn attempted a traverse to gain an easier gully line. Goggs described the ascent —

"Once again Raeburn went to the left, saying, 'It's got to go.' I stood at the rock spike with Mounsey a yard or two away, Raeburn disappeared round the corner, and for the next quarter of an hour we saw nothing of him, but heard and saw hard snow and ice hurtling down. The rope went out very slowly, but it went, and that was the chief thing."

Raeburn's party now found themselves in a broad, open, snow gully. The snow was hard, and at two small ice falls steps were cut; but otherwise Raeburn scraped and kicked footholds in order to save time.

"Raeburn ran out length after length of rope, only one man moved at a time, and rarely was our leader able to say that he had his ice axe well in. Our conversation seemed to consist in the following repetition :- Goggs to Raeburn, 'Last six feet.' Raeburn to Goggs, 'You must come: I have no hitch.'"

In his article Goggs conveys the epic nature of such ascents, with the physical and mental discomforts accepted by the climbers as being intrinsic to a good day on the hill.

"The only thing I feared was cramp: the steps were perforce small, the angle steep, the ice axe could rarely be depended on to give a satisfying sense of security, the leader had to take his time, and occasionally we had to wait, not at the most convenient stances, but just where we happened to be at the moment: the strain on our leg muscles (after five war years) was therefore considerable. As under the conditions described, physical failure on the part of any of us would have been distinctly unpleasant, I eased my position as much as possible, but from start to finish, the climb was remarkable for its lack of comfortable stopping places." (18).

Finally, just under six hours from the foot of the ridge, the successful party gained the plateau. The sun, which had been threatening to break through the scurrying clouds, bathed them in a triumphant glow as they finished the climb. It had been a remarkable exhibition of sustained, mixed climbing. Raeburn, who had led the entire route, was 55. The second edition of the Ben Nevis Guide, edited by Harry MacRobert and published in December 1919, had been put out of date by Raeburn's ascent of Observatory Ridge. One thousand copies were published, some 600 selling in the first year, most of them to non-members of the SMC.

During the same Easter Meet an unnamed SMC party made a winter ascent of Raeburn's Easy Route, the pleasant, zig-zagging line weaving up through the cliffs at the head of Coire na Ciste. On September, 1920, a Dr E. Lüscher on holiday in Scotland soloed both the North-East Buttress, and a new route on the North Wall of Carn Dearg. Subsequent parties and guide book authors however have found it impossible to define the latter line with any certainty.

Most parties of climbers from the south were at this time heading for the Cuillins of Skye, but in September 1921 A.S. Pigott and J. Wilding spent two days exploring Ben Nevis. On the 23rd they put up a variation on the Great Tower, a Very Difficult corner and slab rising up from the start of the Eastern Traverse. The next day they succeeded in climbing the steep rocks of the Comb, following the path of Raeburn for the initial section of slabby rocks, then climbing a Severe and loose flake-chimney which Raeburn had declined to attempt in 1903.

4.10   Raeburn in action, (c. 1906)

"This crack proved loose and rotten, and after ascending for about fifteen feet the leader was glad to traverse to the left on small and sound holds". (19).

In 1920 Raeburn's "Mountaineering Art" was published (20), dedicated to his friend Willie Ling, *"climbing colleague in the solution of some severe problems of mountaineering art."* Raeburn was on an expedition to Kanchenjunga in 1920, and in 1921 he was made leader of a mountaineering party on the Everest Reconnaissance. Overwork while ill with influenza, and a bad bout of dysentery in Tibet put him into hospital for two months. On recovering he set off cross-country to rejoin the expedition, eventually reaching 22,000 feet by sheer will-power. Returning home he suffered a complete breakdown of his health and gradually weakened, dying four years later, on December 21, 1926.

With Raeburn's death, the art of Scottish winter climbing went into a decline. During the next decade winter ascents of Castle Ridge and the easy gullies would be made, but little else, for there was no one of Raeburn's stature to continue the exploration. These few routes made after Observatory Ridge were ripples in the otherwise still waters following the maelstrom of the Great War. Raeburn himself had been an anomaly; a prodigy even in age, while the next generation was still learning to walk.

5.1   Inspection at Hut site, (1927)

A NEW HUT, NEW CLUBS (1924 – 1933)

The summit observatory had closed in 1904; the small hotel was to follow suit towards the end of the 1914-1918 War. Both had afforded shelter and hospitality to many climbers and walkers reaching the wind-swept summit, perhaps fatigued after an arduous winter ascent. In 1925, most climbing on the Ben was undertaken, as before, on a daily basis from a Fort William Hotel, a strenuous exercise at the best of times, more so if for several days in a row.

Two SMC members attending the Club's Easter Meet in 1925, A.J. Rusk and R.N. Rutherford,

"... disdained the flesh pots of Fort William, and camped out in the palatial Rest House, halfway up the Ben, the comforts of which they shared together with a number of unusually active rats." (1).

The 'palatial Rest House' was the refuge on the bridle path; the old half-way station of the observatory, now falling into disrepair. As chance would have it, also attending the Meet was A.E. Maylard, one of the original members of the SMC, and indeed one of its founders. Alfred Ernest Maylard (1855-1947) was a physically tall man, the proud owner of a beard which, wrote an observer, *"was so carefully tended that it seemed as if he couldn't be the man himself if you took and shaved him."* (2). He was somewhat reserved in character, a consultant surgeon at the Victoria Hospital, Glasgow. He died at his home in Peebles, in his 93rd year.

5.2   *Charles Inglis Clark (1918)*

Wandering up the old path to the summit Maylard came up to the refuge.

"On arriving at the half-way refuge I found it occupied by two junior members of the Club who were away at the time, but had left all their belongings for a day and a night's lodgings. The rotten wooden building was in a wretched condition, absolutely unfit to be occupied by any human beings. As a medical man I could not but admire the enthusiasm of these two junior mountaineers, that they were willing to undergo such discomforts in the pursuit of their pleasures; but at the same time I recognised the risk they were running in damaging their health for future days by sleeping in such a hovel with wet and wind creeping through innumerable crevices." (3).

During dinner in Fort William, at the Alexandra Hotel, Maylard spoke to those seated nearby about the need for a properly constructed hut. Sang, the Club Secretary, was also present, and seated next to him was his guest, the factor for the Ben Nevis Estates. The factor was amenable to the idea of a hut and promised to give as much assistance as possible. The next problem was in financing the project. Maylard thought that the hut should be built as a war memorial, and recollected the loss of one of the Club's most popular younger members, Charles Inglis Clark, son of William and Jane Inglis Clark. Maylard then wrote to Clark explaining his idea, and to his great joy Clark replied almost at once that he and his wife would gladly erect a hut to the memory of their son.

5.3   Hut under construction (1928)

Negotiations commenced regarding the lease, Sang playing a major role. Permission to go ahead was received on July 28, 1927. (Negotiations were greatly delayed because the Club's application for a site coincided with the transference of ground around Ben Nevis from the Abinger Trustees to the North British Aluminium Co. Ltd).

That year, a small group consisting of Sang, Alexander (Sandy) Harrison, owners, architect and builder walked up the Allt a'Mhuilinn, and after some deliberation chose the site for the hut. These worthies have often been (unfairly) the object of much nocturnal abuse, as tired climbers stagger up through the energy-sapping and demoralising bogs of the Allt a'Mhuilinn path on dark, stormy nights. In fact the hut, at a height of 2,200 feet, is placed on a small spur just above the spot where one turns up from the Allt a'Mhuilinn to enter Coire na Ciste. In all probability its position could not be bettered.

The architects were Mears and Carns-Wilson of Edinburgh, and the builders W.T. Gibson & Co. of Glasgow. Initially, plans were drawn up for a hut built to accommodate 20, but the cost would have been excessive and the hut was scaled down to sleep eight, in the comparatively luxurious comfort and spacing then employed. The builder, W.T. Gibson, was a member of the SMC, and lived at the site for six weeks as foreman. The first load of materials went up by pony on May 7, 1928, and by June the massive stone foundations had been laid and most of the woodwork delivered to the site. The workers were meanwhile living in bothies at the construction site. The building was finished by October 8, attention then switching to the interior furnishings.

The dimensions of the hut, in its original form, were 26 by 24 feet, with a 9-foot- 6-inch ceiling. The walls are two and a half feet thick, of local stone. An inspection will show both andesite and granite in the walls; the hut actually sitting on andesite, with granite boulders having tumbled down from Carn Mor Dearg, the boundary between the two rock types being nearby, approximately following the course of the Allt a'Mhuilinn burn which runs just behind the hut.

As was the summit Observatory the hut is really a double; a wooden hut sitting inside a stone shell, separated by an air space. There is a small attic reached by ladder, used for storing hut spares. The original entrance door faced the cliffs, and opened into a tiny hallway with an inner door beyond. Excess snow could then be shaken off before entering the hut itself, though in winter the floor never really dried out. Since then, a small annexe has been added, allowing storage of rucksacks outside of the main living and sleeping area. There is a drying-room off this. The Charles Inglis Clark Memorial Hut, to give its full name, is unique in Britain.

Originally eight teak bunks with wire mattresses were installed; each bunk having bedding, air-pillow, and a fold-down front. The original stove was for cooking as well as heat, and of course used coal. The possibility of delivering the coal by air was looked into at first, this being the age of the aeroplane, but it was quickly deemed inpracticable. Instead, coal was brought up by pony.

Since then the hut has been converted to propane gas for lighting and heating; and the gas cylinders are replaced every two years with the aid of a helicopter, though for a number of years tracked vehicles managed to carry cylinders to a site just below the hut, from where they completed their journey by stretcher. The helicopter lift affords an exciting hour or two of hard work, as empty and full gas cylinders are swung in a cargo net above the hut site.

Original furniture still present in the hut includes a wooden table, made and presented by the Rev. A.E. Robertson, a small bookcase from the Ladies Scottish Climbing Club, a barometer from the JMCS, and a Bible from W.W. Naismith, signed by him and the Inglis Clarks. On the walls are a bronze memorial plaque, and a photograph of Charles Inglis Clark in uniform.

The opening ceremony was set for Monday, April 1, 1929, at 3 p.m., and in preparation for this the Inglis Clarks went up by pony on the Sunday. As the occupants were finishing dinner on Sunday evening, the inner door of the hut was violently thrust open and two climbers lurched in, covered in snow and near exhaustion. In a story all too familiar, it transpired that they had fallen down Gardyloo Gully, and had gone down 600 feet or more. After rest and refreshment they were able to continue down the hill. So even before its official opening, the CIC hut had justified its presence as an emergency shelter — given that someone is in residence. (4).

5.4   Original interior CIC Hut (Sept., 1929)

The opening party at the hut included the President — Col. G.T. Glover, Vice-Presidents A.E. Robertson and Harry MacRobert, past Presidents Ling and Goggs, the first Custodian of the hut — Robert Elton, and of course the Clarks. With a healthy and typical irreverence, there had been pre-opening visitors, *"members of the baser sort,"* whose names on the first page of the Visitor's Book were pointedly ignored, *"in the hope that the Hon. Custodian would thereafter cut it [the page] out and consign it to the Allt a'Mhuilinn."* (5).

At 2.55 p.m. punctually the hut was emptied and the door locked. The President, Glover, opened the proceedings with a few words about the steps leading to the building of the hut. This was followed by a prayer of Dedication by the Rev. Robertson. Dr. Inglis Clark formally presented the hut to the SMC and amid cheers and *"the ticking of amateur cinemas,"* Mrs Inglis Clark unlocked the hut. All then entered for tea — at one point nearly 100 were actually inside, a record which even subsequent University Club Meets have failed to surpass. Some 400 cups of tea were consumed. The afternoon's proceedings were followed by a Dinner in Fort William.

Fifty years on, in 1979, the CIC hut celebrated its Jubilee. Obviously there had been changes since 1929, including the building of the annexe in 1974. Inside, the coal stove and

THE
SCOTTISH MOUNTAINEERING CLUB

SPECIAL HUT DINNER
Palace Hotel, FORT WILLIAM
MONDAY   ∅   1st APRIL 1929
∅   ∅   ∅   ∅   ∅

GEORGE T. GLOVER, PRESIDENT
In the Chair   ∅   ∅   ∅   ∅   ∅

5.5   Dinner Menu for opening of Hut

paraffin lamps have gone, as have the old bunks. Now the hut uses gas for lighting and heating, and rebuilt sleeping accommodation (mostly under the supervision of the then custodian, Ian Clough) along the lines used in Alpine huts allows sleeping space for 18, though now and again some unfortunate on the outside berth of a top bunk crashes to the floor while turning over in mid-sleep.

For the Jubilee celebrations on may 12, 1979, the SMC used modern transport and engaged a helicopter to fly up several of the non-mountaineering guests. These included Charles F. Inglis Clark, the son of Charles Inglis Clark, and some of the Jeffrey family, related to Mabel Inglis Jeffrey, daughter of the Clarks. Robert Elton, the first custodian, was also present. A plaque was unveiled by Mr Clark, between 60 and 70 visitors being present, despite poor weather. As in 1929, a dinner in Fort William followed the opening. (6).

As with any other hut privately built, owned and run, the CIC Hut has come in for its share of abuse over the years; both verbal and physical. The hut was built for the use of the SMC and their guests. This was fine when climbers were much fewer in number and perhaps less aggressive in character than now. With an annual usage of over 2,000 bed nights, it is now difficult for non-members to gain access without booking well in advance. To be as fair as possible, bookings with the custodian are not accepted more than a year in advance.

On a busy day on Nevis at the peak of the winter climbing season, several hundred climbers may pass the hut, many with expectations of being able to use its facilities as a casual shelter, a demand impossible to accept. Additionally, there is the sad fact of a tiny criminal element who now roam the hills with an eye to stealing any valuable equipment left unattended. Ironically, one victim who lost a rope from the unlocked hut had been an advocate of the 'open hut philosophy'. Any genuinely needy persons, of course, can expect help from the hut and its occupants, who, it should be remembered, are climbers themselves, and being in the 'front line', have on very many occasions effected rescues from the hut. A stretcher is kept in an unlocked shack along with the police radio for just such events.

5.6   Gas lift at CIC Hut, (June, 1985)

Members of the SMC work hard on several work parties every year, as do other clubs on their own huts. The CIC hut suffers because of its isolated, and valued position. Most of the climbing on Nevis is done by day visitors who walk up from the road, and when one reads some entries in the CIC Log Book, it is debatable whether on some occasions the hut has been an advantage or a liability.

"24th November, 1973. People without the key arrived at 3.15 a.m. after a really foul walk-in . . . found hut locked and empty. Party of seven spent night in radio shack. Party with key failed to find hut . . . spent night on some God-forsaken scree slope in poly bag (100 yards from hut)."

"Dec. 1973. We hereby claim a record. Distillery to CIC in 22 hours — one bivouac."

This last unfortunate, indeed, could not find the hut during his second day's wanderings in the Allt a'Mhuilinn Glen, and was about to settle down for a second bivouac when he was found by another party going up to the hut. (7).

The opening of the CIC Hut in 1929 acted as a powerful stimulus to exploration on Nevis. The increasing numbers of younger, active and less wealthy mountaineers had little in common with their elders; many of them couldn't afford the cost of hotels. Hotels in any case were less enthusiastic, and less well staffed after the 1914-1918 War, with the days of the *"call at 5.30 for breakfast at 6"* fast disappearing.

In July 1924, R.N. Rutherford, Archie Hutchison and Arthur Rusk, all SMC members, enjoyed a climbing holiday in the Bernese Oberland. Rusk told the others of his idea for a new mountaineering club — one in which younger, inexperienced climbers could learn the basics of mountaineering with kindred spirits. The SMC at this juncture was, to be quite straightforward, in some danger of becoming a fossil institution; the 1914-1918 War, a generation gap, and the SMC's self-limiting qualification rules, modest though they were, all conspired to prevent a growth in membership.

In 1924 the three main Scottish clubs were the SMC, the Cairngorm Club, and the Ladies Scottish Climbing Club. The SMC held two meets a year, based at hotels, and no indoor meets other than its Annual dinner. There were no slide shows or other informal meetings outside these venues, at which information and advice could be gleaned, and partnerships struck up. The growing numbers of new climbers were becoming frustrated. (8).

During a stormbound day in the Mutthorn Hut in the Lauterbrunnan Valley, the three climbers mentioned above worked out a constitution and penned a name for the new club — The Junior Mountaineering Club of Scotland. The first meet of the JMCS was held at the Narnain Boulder below The Cobbler, Arrochar. The weather was bad, and Rusk was still in his sleeping bag under the boulder when the first section of the Club, the Glasgow section, was officially inaugurated. There were 13 present; five of whom were already members of the SMC. Shortly after, the Edinburgh section was begun. (9).

Qualifications for entry to the JMCS were refreshingly minimal; one had to be at least 17 years of age. The constitution further stated that its intentions were to provide a training ground for men taking up mountaineering and a source of new members for the SMC. Within ten years the Glasgow section alone numbered 72; in later years it would grow to over 200. During these ten years, its members helped to re-establish rock climbing standards; winter climbing, all but neglected since the First World War, was about to recommence, thanks to inspiring examples from a handful of SMC members.

A now classic article exists describing the early JMCS Bus Meets. This was written anonymously in the form of a letter to the Editor of the SMC Journal. The letter describes in hilarious and obviously scathingly accurate detail many of the characters and activities of the 1950's — but the atmosphere was little different then than it was in the early days and a few short excerpts will paint the picture.

"Youth Hostels we never liked much; they were like trains but slower and wanted their wardens sweeping out. Ritchie's loud genealogical salute to the four-eyed one at Crianlarich who liked dancing still warms up Old Men . . . Marshall was there, a wee laddie and polite; Haig, Hood, Cole, Rodgie, Scott, Millar, Bulbous and more, sundry musicians on mouth-organs, combs, jugs and alimentary tracts, a varied horde, and when all these were emptied on to a stricken landscape together they drained into the night at once, like swill down a gutter, tentless ones trotting helpful and effusive and friendly, gloomy grubhunters like Dutton furtive behind, undeterred by stones; these parasites, clutching dogsbowls for alms, wandered from tent to tent suitably undernourished, then crawled into dubious heaps of their own for the night. And all this time the driver was backing his 32 seats alone in the dark down a 10 ft. Highland waterway with no lights and 32 dead lemonade bottles clanking behind him." (10).

The JMCS was not the only club to be formed during this period of social change, though as regards climbing on Nevis its influence was, initially, to be the most important. Between 1920 and 1933 at least six other Scottish clubs were formed; Dundee University Rucksack Club (1923); the Grampian Club (1927); the Ptarmigan Club (1929); the Tricouni M.C. (1930); the Creagh Dhu Club (1930); the Lomond M.C. (1933). These were to be followed shortly by several University clubs, whose more liberal outlook allowed women easier access to the hills.

There was now a hut on Ben Nevis, and new clubs with young, enthusiastic climbers. Conditions were suitable, given a catalyst, for the next wave of exploration on the mountain.

6.1 G.G. Macphee and A. McNicol at CIC Hut (c.1951)

THE 1930's (1930 — 1939)

The 1920's in Scotland found the hills at their quietest and mountaineering on them at a low ebb; the 1914-1918 War had caused many changes. But a new régime was about to emerge, not from the SMC, though it was to provide some leadership, but from a host of new and energetic young club members —

". . . those vagrant hordes unwashed, unshaven and chip-eating, sleepers in howffs and travellers in fish-lorries, those who — in their unselfconscious days — are the salt of the sport" (1).

They were to play a major role in the coming revolution in Scottish mountaineering.

If those *"vagrant hordes"*, mostly belonging to the fast-expanding ranks of the JMCS, were the foot-soldiers of the revolution (at least as regards Nevis), then the SMC provided two senior generals in the shapes of Bell and Macphee. These two were very different characters, and of great influence in the exploration of Nevis during the 1930's.

James Horst Brunnemann Bell (1896-1975) was born in Auchtermuchty, Fife. The son of a Scottish minister and a German mother, he began his mountain adventures when he was about 14, setting out for the hills by bicycle with his sister Ilse. He walked up Nevis when he was 16, having cycled the 47 miles from Newtonmore in the teeth of a gale. This was in 1913, when the summit hotel was still open and one shilling was charged for the use of the track. Bell joined the SMC in 1922, and his steady development as a mountaineer, both in the Alps and at home, was to establish him finally as one of the most able and influential of Scottish mountaineers between 1930 and 1950.

By profession he was an industrial chemist specialising in papermaking, gaining a D.Sc. from Edinburgh in 1932. Like most of the employed in the 1930's, he usually had to work on Saturdays, and had only a few week's annual leave, and yet his output of routes was steady for 20 years or so, apart from three war years. Not only did he inspire young climbers by example, he made a point of finding and climbing with the most active of those around, male or female, his generosity of mind and spirit encompassing all.

His well-documented enthusiasm, or at least tolerance of bad rock,

"any fool can climb good rock. It takes craft and cunning to get up vegetatious schist and granite", led to some routes which are now rarely climbed, such as Hesperides Ledge on The Comb.

"It is a steeply inclined, curving shelf and is a perfect garden of mossy and lush vegetation . . . there are several exceedingly delicate corners to negotiate with a most precipitous drop on the right. The vegetation is loosely anchored, the rocks are rather loose, and there are practically no positive holds . . . ".

In this description by Bell the obvious enthusiasm rings through loudly.
Alex Small later recalled how,

". . . often in the company of Sandy Wedderburn we would, after attending a concert by the Scottish Orchestra, compress ourselves into the redoubtable Austin Seven and head out for Glencoe, Jim driving with his legs wrapped in a travelling rug against the cold and invariably taking his logically direct route over the Anniesland roundabout, discoursing the while, — Marx, dialectical materialism, Engels, Russell, Mozart, the Aonach Dubh buttresses, hand-made pitons, Forfar bridies, civil rights, Cambridge, and more supporting proof of his theory that there had to be three concurrent factors to induce a major accident. Kingshouse would appear out of the dark; and stiffly we entered." (2).

Bell's most significant new routes on Ben Nevis were to be the series of seven routes on the west face of the North-East Buttress. These lay below and above The Basin, midway between Zero and Minus One Gullies. Their pattern, when traced out, led the cliff to be named The Orion Face, after the winter constellation in the northern skies. As the editor of the SMC Journal for a record 24 years (1936-1959), he was influential in a wider sense. W.H. Murray wrote of this aspect,

"His editorship of the Journal coincided most fortunately with a period of revolution in Scotland. He made the various new climbing forces known to each other, and linked them by airing their ideas. He kept all abreast of events, at the time presenting articles that related Scottish conditions and practice to those of the world's greatest ranges. In short, he tried to keep us all in balance, and succeeded." (3).

Of very different appearance to Bell was George Graham Macphee (1898-1963). Born and educated in Glasgow, Macphee graduated in Medicine then moved to Dentistry. Settling finally in Liverpool he had two lucrative private practices and a University post. As President of the University Club, Macphee was conscientious, helping young climbers find their feet in the sport. Where Bell was small and sturdy, with a broad Fife accent, Macphee was big and broad. Bell's lack of concern over his weekend dress was obvious, whereas Macphee's greater sartorial elegance was accompanied by an upper-class drawl. In the Lake District he made the first descent of Moss Ghyll Grooves, ostensibly so as to be able to write in the hut book, "M.G.G.G.G.M."

A very real antipathy arose between the two, a situation not unknown in a sport which has its fair share of strong personalities. This situation began during a visit to the Alps, when Bell, Frank Smythe, Macphee and a fourth set out to do a route. It seems that the fourth man, who was climbing with Macphee, dropped his axe and was obliged to retreat. Macphee should have gone down with him but instead left it to Bell. On Nevis in particular a great rivalry existed between them; they climbed together at least once there but thereafter they had to go their own ways. Occasionally this rivalry spilled over on to the pages of the CIC Hut Log Book, as the following exchange of entries indicate.

"April 14th, 1938. G. Graham Macphee. Arrived from Liverpool (Glasgow-Fort William 2 hrs 29 mins) Left Hut 4.30 p.m. Up Tower Gully, Down No.3 Gully.

This book is for *climbs* — Time of reaching first hairpin, first bog — time taken to boil kettle etc are equally irrelevant!

April 6th, 1939. G. Graham Macphee. Arrived from Liverpool; Glasgow-Fort William 2 hrs 28 and a half minutes." (4).

On New Year's Day, 1929, Bell made a solo first ascent of No.4 Gully Buttress, on easy ground just right of No.4 Gully. Though not in itself a particularly worthy route, it was the first new route on the Ben since Pigott's visit in 1921. The route was recorded as having been climbed in company with Robert Elton, first custodian of the CIC Hut, but Bell's personal logbook makes it quite clear that Elton had gone down the hill, leaving Bell to solo the route. Four other first ascents followed that year; one by Bell, a Very Difficult variation on the north face of the Great Tower.

In 1931 Macphee, who had first reached the summit of Nevis at the tender age of eight, returned as a climber to spend a June holiday in the CIC Hut, along with his guests A.T. Hargreaves and H.V. Hughes, both excellent climbers in the Fell & Rock C.C. Hargreaves especially was an active climber on gritstone and sandstone outcrops, and was to write the 1936 Climbing Guide to Scafell. In 1930 Hargreaves and Macphee had climbed The Crack on Deer Bield Crag in the Lake District, still graded at Hard Very Severe, and a route capable of defeating strong parties. Hargreaves had a reputation of being an impatient man, probably born of a desire to fill every available minute of the day on the hills. His idea of a day's climbing was an early walk to the crags, a good day on the rocks, and a good walk home — whatever the weather.

On June 14 the three climbers were joined by Mrs Mabel Inglis Jeffrey, the daughter of William Inglis Clark, for a wet and miserable ascent of the Douglas Boulder Direct. Two days later Hargreaves, Hughes and Macphee made the second ascent of a direct variation to Observatory Ridge. This had first been done in August 1930, by G.C. Williams, J.L. Aikman, A.R. Lillie and A.N. Rutherford. The first ascent party had needed to use combined tactics and considered the climb a magnificent expedition at a grade of Severe. Macphee's party recorded their ascent with the short comment that *"combined tactics were not employed"*.

From the hut door however, they had spotted an unclimbed line on the Great Buttress of Carn Dearg. This magnificent 600-foot buttress presents rock architecture on a scale unique in Britain; its great series of overlapping slabs, steep corners and chimneys offer many of the longest and finest routes in the country. By 1931 no route had attacked the steep face of the buttress, though several had taken the easier, broken rocks on its northern flanks. On the left flank of Carn Dearg Buttress, as it is now called, Macphee's party noticed a smaller, curving buttress, up which Hargreaves forced a route.

The rocks were wet from morning rain, and vegetation gave the pioneers some extra work. The crux was an exposed slab just over halfway up the route. Small holds on the slab had to be dug out from beneath turf and slimy earth moistened by incessant drips from the overhanging right wall. This pitch gave the party no little difficulty. But the buttress had been breached, even if by a flanking route. The route was finished in rain, snow and mist, and when the trio arrived at the top of No.3 Gully, then a favourite descent route, it looked too fearsome to tackle without axes. They then made a long trudge over the summit and back to the hut via the Carn Mor Dearg arête. This probably pleased Macphee, as one more ascent to add to the tally he kept of summit visits to Nevis throughout his climbing career.

To this date new climbs had usually been named after the leader. Fashions were changing however, and Hargreaves gave this route the logical if dull name of Route I. The grade was Severe and the date was June 17. The following day it rained heavily and they rested, *"and even Hargreaves was quite resigned to a day's inactivity."* (5). On the next day, having read in the Climbs Book of an attempt on Observatory Buttress by George Williams and Logan Aikman in September 1930, they set off to *"have a look at it"*.

The climb they were to succeed on was to the left of Raeburn's Original Route and took a more direct line. The leader was again Hargreaves, and it is interesting to note that rope techniques had not changed much from the previous decade, 80 feet of rope for the leader, pitches no more than 60 feet in length, rope being required both for attachment round the climber's waist and for belaying. When Bill Murray began climbing in 1935, the only authority he had to go on was the General Guide published by the SMC, and a section therein by Raeburn. The article by Raeburn recommended 80 feet of rope between three climbers. It was immediately obvious to Murray that this was insufficient, and they began climbing using first 60 feet between climbers, then 80 feet. By 1936 they were using 100 feet for the leader, and 120 feet for the longer winter leads. During the 1930's, a gradual change was made from the full-weight hemp rope to a thinner line; one-inch or one-and-a-quarter inch circumference. This permitted a longer rope to be carried and longer run-outs by the leader, especially in winter. Nailed boots were commonly used, though the use of plimsolls or rubbers for the harder rock climbs was on the increase.

High on Observatory Buttress a snow shower halted proceedings, Macphee's party reversing a pitch to wait it out at a safe belay. After lunch the snow stopped and the route was continued. An early example of a chockstone belay on a Scottish climb is mentioned here, when Macphee described a *"removeable chockstone found in a hole, which was used as a belay."*

The difficulties on Route I had been graded at Severe, mainly due to the first ascent problems of vegetation and wet. Route I is now a Very Difficult, as is Macphee's Direct Route on Observatory Buttress. Standards on Ben Nevis had not yet risen above those of Raeburn, but a whiff of exploration was in the air. On Sunday, June 20, Hargreaves had to leave, but first they rose early and made an ascent of Raeburn's Arête. This was probably the third or fourth ascent, and certainly a very early one, Macphee finding the route to be one of the finest on Nevis. (Pigott & Wilding had made one in September, 1921).

"This climb must be one of the finest on Nevis. We were fortunate to get it done on the only occasion during a whole week when the weather conditions made it justifiable. The rain held off until we were past the difficult parts. Reasonably good conditions are essential. 120 feet of rope was found inadequate between 2 climbers if satisfactory belays were to be used. Shortage of rope occasioned much loss of time on the climb." (5).

In fact Hargreaves inadvertently made a variation; being forced on one pitch to make a run-out of 130 feet to gain a belay. There was still no use of intermediate runners for protection, though on rare occasions a leader had been known to untie and thread his end of the rope behind a chockstone, before tying on again and continuing.

The lack of an-up-to date Guide Book told on the Monday, as they made what they thought was a new route on the Comb. In fact, as they discovered later, they had followed Pigott's Route of 1921. Later that year, 1931, Macphee was given the task of editing a new edition of the Ben Nevis Guide, the last edition being the 1919 revision by MacRobert. In writing his guidebook Macphee had taken on quite a task. He was living in Liverpool, which meant a round trip of about 640 miles, and the holiday allowance of that period was not generous. However he owned a Bentley, in which he would drive to Glasgow on a Friday evening and pick up a climbing partner, who would then drive the remaining miles to Fort William.

At this point it should be recalled that the new Glencoe road was still four years in the future. The old road, now forming a section of the West Highland Way, had been made after the 1745 Rebellion, and was virtually unchanged from that period. The part over the Black Mount was particularly prone to drifting snow in winter, while the road surface was usually noticeable by its absence; potholes being numerous. Most climbers had no car; the members of the new clubs especially being unable to afford such a luxury. This, and the long working hours, or unemployment with a corresponding real poverty, helped explain the continuing domination of Nevis climbing by the SMC, JMCS, and a handful of visiting English climbers.

The rising tide of young people enjoying the countryside did not go unnoticed. At the SMC Dinner in Glasgow in 1931, an impromptu speaker told,

". . . of a rising movement in his parish of young men who had not the opportunity of the gentlemen present, but who satisfied a genuine craving for beauty by 'hiking'. This desire, he was convinced, could be extended into a proper appreciation of mountains, if guided in the proper way." (6).

The nation, of course, was then enduring an economic depression.

On September 13, 1933, Alan Hargreaves returned to make another first ascent on Observatory Buttress. Rubicon Wall, as it was named, lay on the left flank of the buttress, and we may deduce from its name that the party found it a difficult and committing climb. Hargreaves' companions were Frank and Ruth Heap. Belays were difficult to find on the climb's slabby rocks, and the party wore plimsolls due to the delicate climbing encountered. The route became known as the hardest rock climb on Ben Nevis, being graded as a Very Severe. It is now a Severe.

6.2   Murray, MacAlpine & MacKenzie after 2nd SA. Rubicon Wall, (August 1937)

The second ascent was probably in September 1936, by Bell, Colin Allan and E.A.M. (Sandy) Wedderburn. Bell described the climb as being sound, steep and difficult, but also recommended it highly to a strong party, noting in passing that there must be considerable scope for variations. On August 1, 1937, a strong JMCS party assembled below Observatory Buttress in a heat-wave. The climbers were Bill MacKenzie, Bill Murray, Archie MacAlpine and Douglas Scott, and they were intent on climbing Rubicon Wall. Like Hargreaves' party, MacKenzie's team changed into plimsolls, stowing their heavy, nailed boots in their rucksacks. At one point the JMCS party attempted to climb more directly a short traverse which Hargreaves had been obliged to make; they failed, and MacKenzie had to retreat by abseil.

The lack of good protective equipment such as artificial chockstones, which modern climbers take for granted, was becoming a serious limiting factor by the 1930's. Climbs such as Rubicon Wall highlighted this shortage, as MacKenzie's party found only two good natural rock belays during the entire 400-foot climb. But a new style of climbing was beginning to emerge; by balance and the occasional friction move, and with the ascent of Rubicon Wall by Hargreaves in 1933, standards on Ben Nevis were again on the rise.

The JMCS were active elsewhere on Nevis in 1933, as M.S. Cumming, E.J.A. Leslie and Pat Baird (JMCS and President of the Cambridge University M.C.) made the first ascent of Green Hollow Route, a Very Difficult line just right of Raeburn's Arête, on April 6. Baird, who died in Ottawa on New Year's Day, 1984, went on to complete 50 years membership of the SMC. He was also one of the leaders of the winter climbing renaissance that was about to unfold in Scotland, making the first winter ascent of S.C. Gully in Glencoe in 1934.

By 1934, Macphee was deeply engaged with research for the Ben Nevis Guide. His task could be compared to running on a treadmill, for as fast as he climbed one route, a new one would rise up to taunt him. His old rival Bell was active in this respect, though as Bell's climbing was geographically more widespread than Macphee's (who through necessity had to concentrate on Ben Nevis), the latter made more first ascents on Nevis.

A rare winter route was recorded in March 1934, when H.W. Turnbull and J.Y. Macdonald climbed North Gully, Grade II. This was the first route to find a way up Creag Coire na Ciste, left of No.4 Gully, and it opened the door for several other short but enjoyable winter lines. The description of the first ascent indicates the state of winter climbing in the early 1930's.

"The difficulties were encountered in the lower pitch . . . This pitch required a full run out of 80 feet rope up a steep ice wall, over an ice bulge at the narrowest point, & thereafter up a further steep ice wall where the gully widens. This pitch was not overcome until 2 hours had been spent in clearing loose sloshy snow (one foot thick) and in step cutting . . . four attempts were made on the lower slope before the bulge was reached and successfully climbed . . . Crampons were used by one of the party." (4).

Easter 1934 marked the date of a fatal accident on Nevis, one which robbed Britain of one of its most promising climbers. Maurice Linnell and Colin Fletcher Kirkus left Kendal on Linnells's motor bike, just after midnight on Good Friday. They camped on the slopes of the mountain and at 8 a.m. on the Saturday, March 31, set off to climb The Castle, the slabby buttress lying between the two Castle Gullies.

At 1 p.m. that same day, Kirkus was found wandering alone on the shoulder of the Ben. His face was badly damaged and covered in blood, but he managed to gasp out *"He's in Castle Gully. I think he's dead. He's hanging from the rope by the neck."* The three climbers who had come upon him, Alistair Borthwick, Bill Thomson and Colin Petrie, covered Kirkus with all spare clothing, while a fourth climber descended to Fort William for medical help. Borthwick and his friends retraced Kirkus's steps, having no trouble deciding which steps to follow as bloodstains had pattered a gruesome trail to the cornice edge.

The bloodstains led to the top of the South Castle Gully, up which they could see erratic steps. For 500 feet the gully was bounded by the impressive walls of the Castles. It was from a point round an edge below the Castles that the steps had come. Using a 100-foot length of rope Borthwick was lowered over the cornice to look. He found the surface to be very dangerous — soft snow on top of ice. At the slightest touch this snow would slip away, revealing the bare ice.

It seems that Kirkus had slipped when only a few hundred feet from the finish of the route. Linnell was belayed 100 feet below on an ice axe driven into the snow. Kirkus accelerated down in a cloud of falling snow, passing Linnell. The axe snapped, Linnell was dragged from his stance and both climbers fell several hundred feet, falling over small rock cliffs. Somehow the rope snagged, bringing the two climbers to a halt. Kirkus hung unconscious, while Linnell, his neck broken in the fall, was dead. When Kirkus came to he dragged himself over to his friend and tried to carry him down the 45 degrees slope. When this proved impossible he tried to drag him upwards.

Finding that he was unable to move Linnell's body, Kirkus set off up the gully, bleeding badly and concussed, using a broken ice axe to cut steps. The slope steepened above to an angle of 70 degrees, blocked at the top by an overhanging cornice. Ben Nevis this Easter of 1934 was in exceptionally heavy snow condition. The cornice overhung by 3 feet and was 4 feet thick. Borthwick described the finish of Kirkus's ordeal.

"Three feet below it were two steps chipped in the ice. They were about 3 inches deep by 4 inches wide. On these two tiny ledges, Kirkus must have stood for close on an hour while he hacked his way through the cornice. And he did it all with only half an ice axe . . . Kirkus's climb is one of the finest mountaineering feats I know." (7).

More climbers were enlisted into the rescue effort, Kirkus being put into the small tent he had shared with Linnell for one night. Over a dozen mountaineers eventually gathered at the cornice edge. Four of the most experienced were lowered on 500 feet of rope, tied together from several climbing lengths. They cut their way down the other Castle Gully, finding that the gully Kirkus had climbed was too dangerous. At 8 p.m. the four had run out all the rope and were still 300 feet short of Linnell. His body lay at the same level but separating them were 300 feet of icy slope. The four unroped and began cutting their way across. After 150 feet however clouds obscured the moon, making their already dangerous task virtually impossible. They then descended to the CIC Hut using two torches, reaching that haven at midnight.

The next morning a party from the Hut cut their way up to Linnell. He was, as they feared, dead. They brought him down, a party of 30 taking turns to carry the stretcher. Kirkus himself had endured the often bumpy descent without a murmur.

Kirkus recovered and climbed again, later writing an instructional climbing book. He was never to regain his full powers as a climber however. He was killed in action during the Second World War. Linnell is buried in the small graveyard in Glen Nevis. Their accident is only one of a series of fatal episodes in this area of Ben Nevis, parties being avalanched either while approaching or while climbing The Castle or the Castle Gullies. The slabby rocks hereabouts can only just hold snow, an avalanche being easily triggered by the unwary or unlucky climber. Borthwick made the following comment on the accident.

"The outside risk in this case was soft snow on top of ice. The snow had a hard crust on it. Even to the expert eye it looked as if it would hold. It did not. It gave when weight was put on it." (7).

In September of that year, two visiting Jugoslavian climbers were introduced to Sandy Wedderburn, who arranged to accompany them on some climbs. The visitors were Edo Derzaj and Marko Debelak, and as they were accustomed to climbing on the steep limestone of the Eastern Alps, they accepted the use of pegs for protection and belays as being normal.

Wedderburn approached Bell and asked him to suggest a line, as *"none of the known routes were difficult enough to give them a due impression of the majesty of the Ben."* (8). Zero Gully was suggested, but on arriving at its foot on September 16, it was neither dry nor filled with snow, so they took to the rocks on the left,

Wedderburn described the first ascent of what was to be called Slav Route, made on September 16.

"The fun began at once. After a lead out of over 50 feet up a delicate slab the rock provided no belay. A sound as of hammering came from above, but . . . I held my peace. Then Marko climbed the pitch. In the various articles which have been written about her climbs she has been likened — or rather her method of climbing has — to a squirrel and to a spider. Clad as she was in someone else's trousers, her movements were as striking as they were skilled . . ."

After a further two pitches the rain started and the fourth pitch, an easy chimney ending at an overhang with no belay, demanded another peg. Starting up the fifth pitch heavy rain began washing rocks down on the unprotected climbers, who were forced to retreat some distance to find shelter.

"At last the rain slackened and the eye of faith was able to discern a diminution in the water supply. The pitch above was climbed again. 'What would you like most now?' Edo called down. I shivered: 'A hot bath.' 'All right.' A movement to the right, and before I could even pull at the rope Edo was plunging through a large waterfall which joined the main gully just below."

The climbing after the waterfall was interesting but not difficult, and the three soon reached the summit to meet up with Bell. Slav Route is now graded Severe, intermediate in difficulty between Rubicon Wall and Raeburn's Arête. Wedderburn was aware of the current antagonism against the use of pegs, and he finished his account of the ascent with an explanatory note.

"On our first pitch we had a choice of three courses: we could have descended and abandoned our route; we could have continued up the difficult and unknown rock without any belay for the second man; we could drive in a piton to be used as a belay. One must distinguish between two entirely separate ways of using pitons: as direct aids to climbing . . . or as safeguards where the natural rock provides no belay . . . I have been able to satisfy myself that the use of pitons . . . purely to safeguard, is, on new climbs at least, unexceptionable." (9).

As for Jim Bell, he was delighted that the party had used pegs — probably because he knew that it would annoy Macphee. The second ascent, under mixed conditions, was that by Bell and Colin Allan on April 5, 1936. (See later this chapter).

In the early 1930's winter climbing in Scotland was still moribund. Nothing of great import had been climbed in the 14 years since Observatory Ridge: that route itself was still awaiting a second ascent. There were tentative moves towards some of the gullies, but with rare exceptions the peak of difficulty on Nevis at this time seems to have been the short ice pitch in Gardyloo Gully. The ten winters that had followed 1920, it must be admitted, had been lean ones for snow, even had there been climbers willing and able enough to extend the known limits of difficulty. By 1935 Raeburn's thoughts and deeds had, as if with the snows, all but disappeared; dusty notes in journals held by old men, unread or misunderstood by young climbers. A demonstration of the Scottish winter potential was badly needed, and there was none better to provide it than Macphee.

He was reaching the peak of work on his Nevis guide, visiting the mountain at least monthly. Despite bad weather he was repeating old routes and putting up new ones. In March 1935 he was rewarded with better weather, staying at the CIC Hut with his frequent companions, George Williams, and Drummond Henderson (JMCS). The intention was a winter ascent of the Tower Gap West Chimney, better known as Glover's Chimney, which descends into Coire na Ciste from the Tower Gap. It was this gully that Goodeve's party had partly descended on their epic night out. The route is now a Grade III.

Macphee's party was slow to start on March 17, reaching the foot of the gully after midday. The first pitch, in typical good condition, was a steep icefall, some 120 feet in length and overhanging at one point. The three climbers tied on to a 200-foot length of line as Macphee set off up the big pitch. Williams described the climbing later in what was to be for some an inspirational journal article.

"After a preliminary reconnaissance, Macphee started cutting up the wall. Owing to the excessive inclination of the pitch, handholds had also to be cut, and all the cutting had to be done with one hand, whilst the other preserved the balance. It was obviously extremely exhausting work, and after 40 feet or so the leader descended for a short rest."

Macphee set off again and ran out 100 feet of rope, at which point Williams had to unrope to give the leader more rope. After two hour's step-cutting and a 135-feet runout he gained a stance and brought up the other two. They then traversed left over iced slabs to enter the gully proper, continuing up over two smaller ice-falls. Stopping for lunch, the tension was temporarily released when it was discovered that Macphee had packed away the hut firelighters in place of the sandwiches.

They continued up the gully in worsening snow conditions. Macphee had to clear away 18 inches of loose snow to cut steps in the underlying ice, with the other two in the direct line of fire below. this was years before crampons became common-place of course, and although nailed boots could work well with small steps, they did need these steps. By the time Macphee reached the foot of the final chimney it was 8 p.m. and virtually dark. He continued up the chimney, climbing a chockstone pitch which proved almost impossible.

"I could now but dimly see him as he moved slowly and steadily upwards. Now and then, when in cleaning holds of ice his ice-axe struck the bare rock, I could see sparks fly out. Above the chockstone the conditions, instead of easing off, became harder. The entire

6.3 Macphee, FWA Glover's Chimney

chimney was sheeted with ice and there was no place where the leader could take a proper rest, much less to which he could bring me up. It was a thrilling experience for the second and third, straining their eyes in the darkness watching the leader's figure dimly silhouetted against the sky as he got nearer to the Tower Gap. By superb climbing he reached the Gap and announced his arrival there in no uncertain manner." (10).

Ice sheeted the rocks on the last 30 feet of the chimney, the second and third man using a loop of rope let down by Macphee to facilitate their ascent. Even then difficulties continued, with more than a hundred steps having to be cut before the summit plateau was reached. Macphee and his two companions finished up on the plateau at 10 p.m., where Macphee with his characteristic thoroughness walked across to tick off another visit to the summit cairn. His companions considered that they were quite satisfied with the exertions of the day, however, and coiled the rope instead. Later that night, Macphee made an uncharacteristic confession in the Hut Log,

"Under the existing conditions, this magnificent climb was one of the most arduous & exacting expeditions the present leader has ever accomplished." (4).

Williams' article on the ascent was published in November 1935. It was the long-overdue seed crystal; from then on a growing number of climbers began to regard any route as a winter possibility, given a good coating of snow and ice. Continuously steep or overhanging ice would have to wait until new techniques made these accessible to a greater number of climbers, but a new impetus had been gained.

In April 1935 Macphee, Williams and G.F. Todd made an icy ascent on Cousins' Buttress, the rounded pinnacle just left of Raeburn's Buttress. From the description by Williams, there seems little doubt that they made the first winter ascent, in thawing conditions, of at least the lower section of the Ordinary Route. Macphee chose not to record this ascent however and it is now credited to C.H.C. Brunton and Jim Clarkson, on February 14, 1957. At a standard of Grade III, the route includes a spectacular traverse over the chimney of Harrison's Climb.

1935 might safely be called 'Macphee's Year,' for he climbed no less than eleven first ascents, summer and winter. Among these were: Glover's Chimney, now Grade III, the unrecorded Cousins' Buttress, also Grade III, a Direct Start to the North Trident Buttress, Severe, a Very Difficult on the Central Trident Buttress (Jubilee Climb), two Very Difficults on the First Platform to the right of Raeburn's Arête (Bayonet Route and Ruddy Rocks), and a

Severe on the east face of the North-East Buttress. (The Eastern Climb). Perhaps the greatest impact of Macphee's routes lay in their acting as an example; encouraging young climbers to follow his lead and find their own way on the under-utilised rocks and icy gullies of Ben Nevis.

Jim Bell, meanwhile, was plotting an audacious project, one that would take him five years to complete. The steepest large rock feature on Nevis is Carn Dearg Buttress, but the largest by far and easily the longest is the west face of North-East Buttress, now known as the Orion Face. This huge slabby face overlooks Observatory Ridge, and dominates the view up the Allt a'Mhuilinn Glen. Just below the centre of the face is the Basin, a depression where snow lingers late in the season, and a good landmark.

6.4   Macphee & A.N.O., Gardyloo Gully

In June 1932 Bell was at the CIC Hut in poor weather with his friend Frank Smythe. They formulated a plan to make an ascent of the face, starting at the bottom right near the foot of Zero Gully and climbing to the Basin. From here, Bell was confident that he could find a finish to the plateau. Over two years passed, and in September 1934 Bell pointed Wedderburn and his two Jugoslavian guests to the general area, resulting in Slav Route. But the face was still inviolate. Wedderburn advised Bell that access to the Basin from the lower part of Slav Route looked impracticable, and in July 1935 Bell attacked the face from a point further left.

The rock structure determined the general line of Bell's route. Seen from a distance, the face consists of huge ribs, running up and leftwards at an angle of about 20 degrees from the vertical. Bell and his companion, Miss Violet Roy of the Grampian Club, decided to follow the rib which passes to the left of the Basin. The features of the face, as Bell discovered, were seen clearly on rare occasions; either very early or late on a mid-summer's day, when the glancing rays of the sun threw up highlights and shadows.

Bell realised that plimsolls, especially the tatty, aged pair that he possessed, were of no use on the smooth, slabby ribs — socks were used instead. The two climbers found the lower section of the climb to be the hardest, with very few belays on a slabby rib of excellent rock. A little higher up difficulties eased somewhat and nailed boots were donned. From the Basin two well-defined routes seemed possible; the left and right-hand rims of the Basin, with the right appearing the more broken and the left developing into a true arête, finally terminating in a very short ridge abutting on to the crest of the North-East Buttress.

Bell and Violet Roy decided to continue up the left rib, which gave easy climbing until it steepened into an overhanging nose. To climb this on the left seemed impossible, so Bell moved rightward on very small holds then back left and up. It had been a hard section, and to lessen the risk of Roy hurting herself in a swinging fall she climbed up more directly. Violet Roy, who had been unhappy on the lower section using the unfamiliar technique of climbing in socks, came on the rope at one point, but this was at the last difficult part of the route and the climb was soon successfully completed.

The face had been opened up, though to Bell it had many unsolved problems. He was still intent on climbing a direct route from the Basin to the summit of the North-East Buttress, though that particular wish had to wait until 1940 for fulfillment.

Two small but interesting events occurred in 1935: on June 23, a large block in the Tower Gap became very unstable and finally crashed down Glover's Chimney, fortunately with injuries to no one. The block had been stepped on by hundreds of climbers crossing the Gap; with its disappearance the Gap was now safer, if a little more difficult. A note in the Hut Log for June 18 by Macphee noted its instability. On June 23 Macphee and Williams aided the erosions of time and sent the block crashing into Coire na Ciste.

The second event was the complete absence of snow on Ben Nevis for only the second time in living memory; or at least within the memory of a deceased local resident who had been born in 1840. On September 28, Macphee visited the places on Nevis where patches of snow were usually to be found, and there were none. The one other occasion when a complete absence of snow was recorded was in 1933.

In 1936 J.H.B. Bell began his 24-year reign as Editor of the SMC Journal, a position in which he had considerable influence on the course of Scottish mountaineering. In the same year Bell's old rival Macphee had his Nevis Guide published, containing 110 pages of text and 35 illustrations (11). The Guide was reviewed generously by Bell, though not without one or two errors being highlighted, one of which was a premature summer ascent of Green Gully, wrongly attributed in the Guide to Bell. As with most guidebooks, its compilation had promoted an increase in exploration on Nevis; admittedly much of it by Macphee.

The two great gullies which flank Observatory Ridge — Zero and Point Five — had interested Bell since 1925. They were so prone to avalanche, and so often inundated by continuous spindrift, however, that Bell doubted their feasibility, though Zero looked the more possible of the two. Its name had been suggested by Bell, who admitted that though it was not a good name, they had yet to hear of a better one. The principal gullies on Nevis were numbered. Starting at the right of the cliffs and counting down, what is now called Tower Gully should in fact be Number 1 Gully. The next one to be named, logically enough, was Zero Gully, running up the left side of Observatory Ridge.

Zero Gully received a partial ascent on April 5, 1936, by Bell and Colin Allan. It was a partial ascent in the sense that the gully was abandoned after 100 feet when they ran out of good snow, the rocks of Slav Route on the left then being followed for several pitches before re-entering the gully and cutting steps the remainder of the way. The two climbers left the hut complete with ice axes, a couple of pitons and a hatchet. Their plan was to attempt the gully and if the lower part proved impossible, to traverse right under Observatory Ridge and attempt the gully right of that (Point Five!). This second gully, Bell remarked, was shorter but looked pretty awful with a cascade of ice halfway up.

The day was a glorious one as Bell and Allan worked their way up the snow at the foot of Zero Gully. All went well up to the bergschrund below the almost vertical section of the gully. On the right side was a cascade of icicles while ahead were waterworn and frozen moss-covered slabs, quite impossible. Bell and Allan took to the rocks on the left, bypassing this section by some difficult slabby climbing. Finally they gained the easier ground in the snow-filled gully and cut steps to the summit plateau. Descending by No.3 Gully, Bell suffered what could have easily been a fatal fall.

"Then it came to me by carelessness. Allan said that I started down with a grin on my face. I myself don't remember just where it struck me that things were not just right. He said I slipped into an avalanche runnel of polished ice. In any case all my efforts at braking were useless. I shot off with extreme rapidity, was flung onto my back and continued accelerating. I was past the portals of No.3 now. There was a little cleft below, an embryo bergschrund of which I struck the lower lip and was promptly tossed up into the air. Then I rattled down on to a pile of hard avalanche debris, was tossed into the air again and came down with another bump still on my back."

Bell had almost come to a halt when he began to pick up speed again. He finally came to rest about 200 feet above Lochan Coire na Ciste. It had been an amazing escape for Bell, who suffered only scratches and a strained ankle.

"In any case Allan and I both declared that never had we enjoyed such a magnificent, hard winter climb . . . The old Ben is a grand opponent but even No.3 Gully in such circumstances exacts *respect*." (12).

Of interest are the various angles of slope as measured by Bell's clinometer. The gradient of the gully for a long way above the steepest section was 55 degrees, higher up it continued at a uniform 51 degrees (13). The weather remained fine for a week after Bell and Allan's ascent, and on April 11 Macphee and Williams followed Bell's footsteps. Macphee made it clear in the Hut Climbs Book that he considered the ascent to have followed Slav Route for the main part.

"Set out to do the climb described by Bell . . . We found traces of Bell's steps leading up to the highest part of the snow cone at the foot of the gully. Here the steps led on to the rocks on the left, and from Bell's description and the recent scratches on the rock it was clear that he followed the Slav Route . . . We saw where the footsteps re-entered the gully, after climbing the Slav Route for about 700 feet. The two icefalls mentioned by Bell were surmounted just before a blizzard suddenly started to blow. In a short time new snow began to pour down the gully, and the final and fortunately now short portion was negotiated with difficulty to reach the summit at a late hour." (4).

Bell considered the ascent the hardest winter climb that he and Allan had ever done, though he admitted that it was not a 100% pure ascent. His partial ascent of Zero Gully, like all other winter climbing to this date in Scotland, had been done in nailed boots. Ten point crampons, with no front points, were available, though very rarely used. On iced rocks, nails retained a definite advantage, allowing for delicate climbing. This often suited the terrain found, say, in the Southern Highlands and in Glencoe, but most of the major winter climbs on Nevis contain a high proportion of snow and ice, and the lack of suitable crampons was a block to further developments. The ice axe was becoming shorter, though at some 32 inches long it remained heavy and clumsy, particularly for the overhead, one-armed cutting which steep bulges required. Despite this, winter climbing was slowly emerging from the dark ages.

On April 10, 1936, Macphee soloed South Gully, Creag Coire na Ciste. This very enjoyable if short Grade III begins with an exposed traverse out from the foot of Number 3 Gully then climbs up steeply via a narrow gully. Macphee experienced great difficulty at the cornice. This was a bold ascent to make in 1936, given the equipment of the day. The only other routes of note in 1936 were both by Bell. The North-West Face Route on the Douglas Boulder, climbed on May 10 with W.G. McClymont, is a Difficult climb with good rock and climbing. A far tougher proposition was made on September 13, when Bell was joined by Allan and Wedderburn for an ascent of Left Edge Route, a Severe on Observatory Buttress. This climb starts up the right-bounding rib of Point Five Gully.

At first the three climbers attempted the wall on the left of Point Five Gully, but it proved impossible, with holdless slabs and sections of overhanging rock. They then turned their attentions to the edge of rock at the extreme left of Observatory Buttress.

"The first 100ft. were easy, then we roped up, Wedderburn being on the lead. There followed 60 feet of pretty severe stuff, slabby, finally trending a bit to the right to a good stance."

The whole climb was on good rock, wet in places, taking four and a half hours climbing time. The leaders, Wedderburn and Allan, thought the route Severe.

If one were to analyse ascents on Nevis in the mid-30's, the prevalence of the SMC and JMCS would continue to be apparent. The newer clubs such as the Creagh Dhu, partly by choice and partly by circumstances, concentrated on hills nearer to home — the Arrochar hills and latterly Glencoe. By 1936 the JMCS was about 200 strong and growing. For an annual fee of 7s.6d., wrote one Club historian,

". . . each member obtains the joy of attending Club Meets (often including a lift to the hills), comradeship on the hills, and, where necessary, the advice and leadership of experienced members (JMCS or SMC), two issues of the SMC Journal (which would cost 2s.6d. each if bought in a shop), the privilege of using the CIC Hut at reduced terms, the right to attend six winter lectures (with a free tea thrown in) . . .", and so on.

In 1936 the SMC membership numbered 303, and of 11 applications for membership, six were declined, having insufficient mountaineering qualifications. The official qualification deemed necessary then was 40 ascents (an increase over the original 1896 necessity of a minimum of 12 climbs, at least six of them in Scotland) with each ascent either a 3,000 foot mountain or a climb involving some little difficulty. There were signs of friction developing between the two clubs, as the top climbers in the junior club climbed steeper and smoother walls while the old guard in the SMC stayed firmly and happily in the past (Bell, Macphee, Williams and a handful of others excepted). The JMCS, however, were supplying the SMC with about two-thirds of their new members, and an uneasy truce ruled, one perhaps best exemplified by the following extract from the CIC Log.

"April 4th, 1937. W.M. MacKenzie, W.H. Murray, A.M. MacAlpine. Gardyloo Gully + arête to Carn mor Dearg. The gully was found to be ridiculously easy and is not at present recommended to other than complete novices in snow-climbing.

(This party should try the climb again when there is *less* or, better still, *no* snow in the gully. GGM). (The above party has every intention of climbing the gully again under better conditions. They are not unaware that gully climbs vary enormously in winter. On 4/4/37 Gardyloo Gully was easy. WHM)." (4).

Bell was again active in 1937, and on April 4 made what he assumed was the first ascent of Green Gully. Raeburn's ascent in 1906 had been lost in the mists of modesty and buried in the pages of old journals — besides which, ran current thought, no one could possibly have climbed such a route in 1906. Bell's companions were a good team from England. Dick

Morsley, heavily bearded and the spokesman, Jack Henson, tall and quieter, and Percy Small, the expert rock climber. Bill Murray later described the breakfast scene in the CIC Hut, providing further insights into Bell's character.

"I watched Bell make breakfast for his own party. Porridge, sausage, and kippers were all stirred into the one pot. As a practical chemist, he was imbued with the truth that a meal was a fuel-intake, therefore its separation into 'courses' was an auld wife's nicety, and not for climbers. He later persuaded me to share his burnt toast, on the grounds that charcoal was a bodily need. He expounded equations of chemical change, and showed how charcoal absorbed the troublesome gases of stomach and gut, to our mutual benefit. Bell when cook could talk one into eating almost anything. But not even that toughest of characters, Dick Morsley, had a palate tough enough for Bell's porridge. After one spoonful, he strode to the door and flung his plateful out onto the snow. The hut for me was a school of further education." (14).

Bell's opinion of this breakfast was of course slightly partisan,

"We arose at 8 a.m. & cooking commenced. Our first course was a magnificent collation of porridge, tomato soup, peas & beans. One had to acquire the taste . . . Sausages were partaken alongside & then smokies & finally tea, cheese etc." (12).

The four climbers were soon to need the energy devoured at breakfast, as Bell began soloing the first easy section of Green Gully. On reaching the first severe pitch they roped up.

"The pitch started from the lower right hand corner & led obliquely upwards to the left over a bulge of very hard ice which took much hard cutting to fashion steps. Twenty feet up there was a prospect of rock holds, but when I got there the first big rock came away . . . "

Bell stayed on and finished the first pitch, bringing up Morsley to the belay. Above was another bulge of ice which Bell had to climb directly. This was dangerous as the ice was wet and none too compact. Bell found it necessary to drive in the pick of the axe well above his head, using the wooden shaft as a steadying hold. Bell continued leading above this pitch, several pitches taking them to the upper basin of the route and the second big pitch. This pitch gave the four climbers as severe a test as any they had experienced on a mountain.

6.5   2nd WA Green Gully, Bell leading, (April, 1937)

"The ice wall was nearly vertical. In the right hand corner & straight up was a possibility as some rocks with tiny ledges promised a way up. But that was about vertical too at the start and the falling drops of water from the overhanging right wall fell out in a most discouraging manner. I should have realised that I was getting tired . . . "

Bell was defeated on the steep ice and came down to discuss the situation with his friends. They decided to try the arête on the right, first Henson and then Bell failing before the best rock climber in the group, Percy Small, had a try.

"We all fixed ourselves securely with our ice axes in the somewhat loose snow & let him start. With a magnificent effort using the smallest hold he got on to the arête & turned the corner. We cheered, but there was no heartening reply."

Small had got himself into a desperate position. Rock holds were very poor or non-existent and his balance was precarious. He decided to reverse the pitch before he became tired.

"Soon he reappeared on the edge. He had to descend quickly as his strength was ebbing away. With a final warning that he might come off any minute he started to descend, imploring us for advice where to put his feet. About a quarter of the way he held on, then he came off & fell clear of rock into the gully bed. I felt a tremendous strain on my axe & it was jerked right out. But the second axe held tight & he was brought up on the snow unhurt but a little shaken. A party of two could not have taken this risk."

It was now almost 5 p.m. with the climbers in a perilous situation. The mist had descended, shuttering them into the icy confines of the gully. The wind gusted down coldly, swirling the mist about and hurling down loose snow to fill up their hard-won steps below. The prospect of a night out was not inviting and in any case would solve nothing. There were about two hours of light remaining and a descent, sacrificing an axe as a belay above the first big pitch, would take longer than that. Even climbing the pitch above would guarantee nothing.

They finally agreed to allow Henson another attempt, this time trying the inside right route. They gave him exactly an hour, by which time he must have shown reasonable grounds for ultimate success. Henson soon attacked the pitch in the corner and after a retreat for a rest got lodged on some rock footholds.

"At intervals we shouted up enquiries. Henson was a tall, quiet fellow. His replies were always quiet and deliberate — 'I think it ought to go' — 'I think I can do it' — and then after a long period of hacking with little apparent progress — 'I know I can make it go!'. Morsley turned to me in triumph. 'You leave it to Henson. He doesn't say much, but he means what he says . . . " (12).

At last Henson reached snow above and straightened up to his full height. The relieved climbers below gave out a loud cheer as he disappeared over the top of the pitch. A uniform slope of hard snow lay above, leading into the gloomy twilight. The cornice was reached and Henson took the lead again. A careful break in the last snow wall and he was on the plateau in the last glimmer of daylight.

Bell said farewell to his new friends at Achintee, with mutual expressions of friendship and respect and the promise to climb together again. He had first met them two days earlier. As a footnote to this meeting, they did climb together again, meeting in Glencoe a few months after their epic ascent of Green Gully.

Bell's summer route of 1937 was with J.F. ("Hamish") Hamilton, who a year before had led the first ascent of Agag's Groove on Glencoe's Buachaille Etive Mor. In the autumn of 1936 the same two had made an abortive attempt on the slabby rocks left of Point Five Gully, in bad weather. On July 11, 1937, a repeat attempt found the slabs to be too difficult, so they chose to go some distance left. The route taken followed the left edge of the slabs by an intricately weaving line round overhangs and up grooves. After climbing for several hundred feet, Bell and Hamilton were faced with a vertical wall, broken by a steep chimney. Bell described this difficult section.

"The entry into the chimney involved difficult progress up smooth, sloping ledges. From a niche in the chimney it was quite obvious that direct upward progress was hopeless, as the chimney was roofed by steep, holdless slabs. An escape seemed to be possible on the left, but the position was so precarious that the leader was compelled to drive in a ring-spike and pass the rope through a spring-hook before moving upwards to the left on to a small jutting corner of rock. For the next 4 feet of traverse boots and socks were removed, and a delicate friction glide on a smooth slab led to assured safety." (15).

Bell's route, now named the West Face, Upper Route, was graded at Severe. Although not of high quality, it was yet again the opening up of a new face by the old master. This face is now taken by several excellent winter routes, while the difficult slabs further right were not to be climbed until the two Marshall brothers effected a Very Severe up them in 1966.

Membership of the JMCS by 1938 had risen to almost 400, a piece of news ill-received by the SMC. Bill Murray, who was Secretary of the younger club at that time remembers having to pass on this news — "*A brass hat fixed me with a steely eye and barked, 'We don't want climbing gorillas in* this *club!'* ". Murray told this senior member of the Club why he (and others) were not particularly enthusiastic about joining the SMC. The main points of the argument by Murray and his contemporaries were the lack of monthly meets and indoor meets such as slide shows. However a possibly awkward situation between the two clubs was soon to be averted, with the onset of another World War in a year's time. Since then, relations between the clubs have been amicable.

The different generations of climbers were also going their own way as regards equipment. In a 1936 article on Snow and Ice, Macphee advised that the modern tendency to have a very short ice axe was, like many modern tendencies, carried to absurd extremes. "*A shaft about the length of an ordinary walking-stick is probably best,*" he wrote, though he did recommend longer ropes, moving away at last from the 80-foot length of Raeburn's time (16).

Meanwhile, Douglas Scott in 1936 had had a very short axe made for him by a blacksmith. This short axe facilitated the third winter ascent of Crowberry Gully that same year (Raeburn, of course, had made the first ascent, while Bill MacKenzie, using a long axe, had made the second a week before Scott). On hearing of Scott's axe, Murray immediately went to an ironmonger's shop and bought a 14-inch slater's hammer. With a side-claw removed this ultra-short ice tool allowed steep pitches to be cut with greater ease, reducing route times dramatically. Tricouni-nailed boots were still worn, however.

Learning from a hard lesson on the Buachaille at the end of 1936, Murray and his friends also took to carrying battery head-torches, to enable them to climb up or down after dark and reduce the fear of benightment. Archie MacAlpine, who was a dentist, used a dental head-torch to great effect. This ability was soon to be needed when, in February 1938, the second winter ascent of Observatory Ridge was made.

When MacKenzie, Murray and MacAlpine stepped on to the start of Observatory Ridge at 9.30 a.m., they soon discovered that conditions were not good; two inches of wind-slab covering sugar-like snow. The steep, bottom section of the ridge took more than four hours, with even worse snow and the most dangerous section of the day's climbing. Finally, Zero Gully was gained, only to find loose snow covering hard ice. By now it was dark, head-torches were donned and steps were cut all the way. Fortunately the weather was good, with a star-studded sky above as the party thankfully gained the plateau and hurried to shelter in the old observatory. It was just before midnight, 14 hours from the start, and 18 years after Raeburn's ascent. (17).

The winter discovery of 1938 was Comb Gully, running up the left flank of The Comb. This fell to a strong party from England, F. Gardner Stangle, Dick Morsley and Percy Small, the latter two having been on the second ascent of Green Gully with Bell the previous year. On April 12 they headed towards Comb Gully, with the climbers' intention of 'having a look at it.' Stangle was the acknowledged leader of what was probably the hardest gully at that time on Nevis, Green Gully being the only other contender.

Owing to a period of very mild weather and a wet March, the gully contained much ice and little snow. Normally a section of steep snow leads up towards a rock outcrop, where the gully narrows and becomes more chimney-like. Typical of Nevis, it is difficult to find a good rock belay here, as hopeful-looking cracks turn out to be disappointing. On the first ascent Stangle found the short length of his modified slater's hammer invaluable on the steep ice and he used the pick of this tool on all the ice pitches. The ice cave at the foot of the crux ice pitch was eventually gained, and again no rock belay was found, but as the snow was good and hard an axe belay was taken.

Stangle set off up the ice.

"The gully now curled to the right . . . Water falling over a chockstone had frozen into a solid column for 20 feet, the upper reaches of which had partially thawed suggesting a stance under the chockstone. There was no possible way of continuing save up this pillar. After much cutting, hand-holds were made through the column and after several descents for rest, the diminishing thickness of the ice contained natural holds less satisfying. The lip made a good stance and much demolition of icicles hanging from the rock roof revealed a thread belay. A lot of ice had to be removed before a landing on the right wall could be effected. This was disconcertingly free from ice or footholds." (18).

6.6 Comb Gully (March, 1978)

The crux ice pitch leads on to steep snow, with perhaps a tiny bulge to overcome before the final snow slope. The climb had taken Stangle and his rope over eight hours, most of which had been spent on the ice pitches. Today, Comb Gully is a fine and justly popular route, a Grade III/IV like its companion gully on the other side of the Comb, Green Gully. Both routes are about 450 feet in length. Comb Gully will often provide a steeper crux section and perhaps more technical climbing, while Green Gully is usually more sustained. But to directly compare two such good routes is a fruitless exercise.

The summer of 1938 produced several rock climbs. Two were on the First Platform and other than a few remaining variations they completed the obvious routes on this face of the North-East Buttress. The first of these was by Leslie and Baird on June 19. Lying between Newbigging's 80-Minute Route and Raeburn's Arête this new Severe was christened with the clumsy title of Newbigging's 80-Minute Route (Right-Hand Variation). Three weeks later, four members of the Ladies Scottish Climbing Club arrived to tackle Raeburn's Arête. Nancy Ridyard and Annette Smith formed the first rope, with Nancy Forsyth and Janet Smith as the second.

The four ladies started about 30 feet too far to the left; a fortuitous mistake, as they ended up doing a fine, independent line. Their Very Difficult route followed grooves parallel to Raeburn's Arête and finished close to the original line of Newbigging, thereby being tagged with the name of Newbigging's 80-Minute Route (Far Right Variation). (Sadly, Forsyth, an excellent climber, was to be killed six years later elsewhere on the mountain).

Pat Baird and Leslie found another route in June, 1938, with the pleasant Baird's Buttress, Difficult, just left of Raeburn's Buttress. The last route to be recorded in 1938 was a short Difficult in June, by a team who had figured prominently during this period — Leslie, Murray, Wedderburn and Bell. Their route, the North-West Face, lay on the right-hand side of Observatory Buttress.

Meanwhile, Macphee had finished his Nevis Guide in 1936, and perhaps understandably had reduced the frequency of his tedious 640-mile drives from Liverpool. But he returned to make one more ascent before war broke out in 1939. On April 7, 1939, Good Friday, Macphee and three others traversed left from the foot of Gardyloo Buttress under the steep rocks of Indicator Wall. This compact face — the highest on Nevis, and consequently in Britain, is named after a viewpoint indicator which the SMC erected on the plateau above, in 1927. The indicator was destroyed by vandals in 1942.

Macphee, R.W. Lovel, H.R. Shepherd and D. Edwards completed their exposed traverse and reached the end of Indicator Wall, where a gully leads upwards. This gully gave what Macphee described as "a magnificent climb," a 500-foot Grade III, and often a fairly hard one at that, depending, as always, on the conditions prevailing. The traverse out from Observatory Gully to gain the foot of the climb is exciting in poor conditions, while the climb itself — Good Friday Climb — is a short but interesting route, twisting up a series of short gullies and through rocky steps to gain the plateau. The best belay at the top is often the summit trigonometrical point, as the climb finishes opposite the highest point in the land.

With the winter ascent of Good Friday Climb, the inter-war exploration of Ben Nevis was at an end. Unlike the First World War however, climbing did not come to such a grinding halt, but continued, albeit at a reduced level, throughout most of the war years. The leaders were to be J.H.B. Bell and G.G. Macphee as before, with the addition of a new name on Nevis — Brian Kellett.

7.1   Laidlaw, Murray & Bell, CIC Hut, (June 1940)

A CONSTELLATION OF CLIMBS (1940 – 1949)

The effects of the Second World War on Scottish climbing were less severe than those of the 1914-1918 war. Although travelling was restricted, the island of Skye and areas north of the Great Glen being out of bounds to most, more servicemen were stationed in Britain. It was possible, with much determination, to climb during leave periods. The summer of 1940 was to be remembered throughout Britain as one of the best for weather and by the end of May even Nevis was sweltering under a blue sky.

In July 1935 Bell and Violet Roy had opened up the possibilities of the great face left of Zero Gully, climbing the rib system left of the Basin. But Bell had ambitions of a direct ascent from the Basin to the summit of the North-East Buttress. He expressed surprise in 1940 that nothing had been done here during the intervening years, and certainly it seems a strange neglect, as there were by now many fine young climbers doing great things elsewhere — The Rannoch Wall, Raven's Gully and Clachaig Gully were all climbed during that period.

On June 10 a JMCS/SMC group assembled at the CIC Hut. W.H. Murray, Douglas Laidlaw and W. Redman of the JMCS, and J.H.B. Bell and J.E. MacEwen of the SMC. Bell's log book described the day's activities.

"McEwen & I went up Slav Route to the final easy terrace, where he photographed Murray posed at the foot of the great slab rib on the Basin route. Actually Murray & Co did not climb this rib, although it was part of the 1935 route. I could not, at the time, positively say to him whether this was so, or not, so his party climbed up the open slab corner on the other side of it (from us) & reemerged above it . . . He got good photos of Murray on Rib Slab below Basin."

Murray had been climbing with Laidlaw and Redman. Laidlaw was then 18. Two years later Laidlaw was killed over Germany when his bomber was shot down, the rest of the crew having bailed out at his command.

On June 14, Bell returned with John Wilson of the Perth JMCS and at last succeeded in making his direct route from the Basin. They left their boots at the foot of the rocks and followed the original route to the Basin, climbing in plimsolls and, for the main part, in socks. (The best plimsolls for this task apparently were sold by Woolworth's, who stocked the thinnest.) Five hundred feet or so of climbing took them to the Basin, where Bell stopped for lunch.

Bell described the crucial, upper stretch of his direct route.

"After lunch we ascended a moderate buttress for 120 feet to an easy terrace. Then the difficulties recommenced and continued for about 600 feet. The crux is at and just above a remarkable, prominent, steep slab overhung by a wall on the right. This main feature is well seen from the Hut

7.2   W.H. Murray at foot of Great Slab Rib

and so is the second great slab. One follows an oblique, upward line to the left towards this double slab, which is about 200 feet in height. There is a short, bad traverse above it, some easier rocks, and then a final steep wall with knobs of quartzite for holds. Above the difficulty we gained the crest of the N.E. Buttress above the Mantrap and reached the cairn on the top of the Buttress after 215 feet of easier climbing . . . We are both convinced that this 'Long Climb' of 1,480 feet is the longest and finest route of sustained difficulty on the Ben." (1).

There were now two problems remaining on the face, Bell thought. One was to climb the original route more directly up the inclined rib of rock above the Basin. Murray and Laidlaw had climbed the rib by a more difficult way, Redman having climbed up first by the original route, but they had included a right traverse and the truly direct line was still waiting. In August 1940, George Dwyer arrived, fresh from hard exploits on Clogwyn du'r Arddu, Wales. On the 4th they launched themselves at the rib of the original route. Proceeding up the left rocky rim of the Basin they reached the overhang where the route traversed to the right. Here they took to a tenuous groove just left of the crest instead, negotiated a severe pitch, then broke through the difficulties by entering a smooth scoop. The holds in this were just sufficient, easier rocks being gained above.

The second problem Bell wished to solve was an entry to the Basin from the large ledge low down on Slav Route, known as the First Platform of Slav Route. An easy traverse into the Basin from higher up Slav Route had been made in July 1938 by Alex Small, J. Wood and A. Anderson, but Bell wanted a more direct entry. Again Dwyer and Bell left their boots behind and climbed in socks, Dwyer leading the crux pitch. Even with the rope above for comfort and in socks, Bell found the first few moves to be about at the limit of faith and friction. A short traverse above to avoid an overhang then allowed access to the Basin.

From the Basin, Bell and Dwyer made a relatively easy traverse leftward, finally emerging on to the crest of the N.E. Buttress at the Second Platform. This traverse gives access to the Basin from N.E. Buttress, starting at a conspicuous V-notch. Bell was to use this knowledge in his plan for a complete Girdle Traverse of the cliffs.

There now remained the difficulty in naming the routes. The climber or climbers who first climb a route have the privilege of giving it a name, and until about the mid-1930's route names tended to be rather dry; Central Buttress, Route 1, and so on. With the influx of new clubs and young climbers on to the scene, and latterly with the sometimes heated imaginations of climbing students, route names became more interesting. Perhaps the ideal course, as Bell was eventually to take, was to find some feature of the climb or crag, and find a name which was in accord with the feature.

After Wilson and Bell had finished the direct or "Long Climb", they had long discussions as to its name. Wilson suggested calling it the "Fall of Paris" climb, not realising (according to Bell's log) on that perfect climbing day how tragically appropriate that casual suggestion was, soldiers of the Third Reich occupying Paris that very day, June 14.

7.3   Bell, FA The Long Climb (June, 1940)

That winter Bell went on a solitary ramble on some low hills and came up with the solution to his route-naming problem. No doubt the sky was clear and starry as he walked home that night, with the winter constellation Orion rising before him. He would name the route based on the principal starts of that constellation — Orion the Hunter, whose fancied similarity to the figure of a man with upraised arm, belt and sword was described in antiquity.

The Basin would occupy the position of the three stars of the Belt, while from each of these rose one of the upper routes. The straightened out original climb led to the giant red star Betelgeuse, forming the right arm of Orion. This was the brightest star in the constellation and was accordingly given by astronomers

7.4   *The Constellation Orion*

the Greek letter Alpha, and so that climb was Alpha Route. The original route above the Basin would be Zeta; in the middle would be Epsilon Chimney; while to the right would be Delta Route, forming the upper half of the Long Climb, and leading to Orion's head.

Below the Belt of Orion is a vertical line of stars representing his sword. This agreed with the Great Slab Rib of the original route. The bright star Rigel was at the start of both Slav Route and the direct entry to the Basin, hence Beta Route. Through the passage of time and the rise and fall of favoured routes, Bell's 'Long Climb' has, ironically, been firmly fixed as the title of his best route, a long climb indeed at 1,400 feet, and a classic and popular Severe. The variations Alpha, Zeta, Beta, and the Epsilon Chimney retain his original names.

Bell had looked leftward across this giant of a face — now known to climbers across the world as the Orion Face — and pronounced that it seemed very unlikely that any climb could be done between Platforms Rib on the left and Bell's Alpha Route. Most of the great ribs of rock on this section, he noticed, were severely undercut in their lowest sections. As will be seen shortly, Bell was soon to be proved wrong; this area of the face was breached in 1944 by two routes.

Elsewhere on Nevis that fine June in 1940, other routes were being discovered, no less than five by one man — Henry Iain Ogilvy. A Scot who was President of the Cambridge University M.C. from 1939-1940, Ogilvy was one of the new breed of rock climbers, shaking the established groups with his ascents of the first Very Severe wall routes on the Rannoch

Wall of Buachaille Etive Mor — Red Slab Route and Satan's Slit, climbed in 1939. The history of Scottish mountaineering would almost certainly have looked very different had Ogilvy not been killed in a climbing accident in September 1940 along with his girl-friend, Lucy Robson, in the Cairngorms.

Ogilvy's June on the Ben began on the 19th, climbing with C.F. Rolland and making an ascent of the big, right-hand wall of Carn Dearg Buttress. Evening Wall, a 700-foot Very Difficult, overlooks Waterfall Gully, its name suggested by the pleasing exposure to the setting sun. Two days later they climbed Compression Crack, a 400-foot Very Difficult on the right flank of Raeburn's Buttress. The latter route starts up a clean water-worn chimney corner, providing strenuous and progressively more difficult climbing. On June 22, Ogilvy and Rolland, along with J.R. Hewit, climbed the Tower Face of The Comb, a Very Difficult line taking in some dubious rock. In fact, as Ogilvy commented in the CIC Log, *"Owing to the nature of the rock & moss encountered we suggest 'Quisling Wall' as a name."* (2).

Two variations on either side of the Great Tower completed Ogilvy's list of first ascents on Nevis, climbed in one busy week. But this was not his last visit to Ben Nevis during his tragically short climbing career. On July 25 he attempted Gardyloo Buttress with N.P. Piercy. This steep little buttress stands imperiously at the head of Observatory Gully. Its name is by association with Gardyloo Gully on the left, into which the Observatory staff used to dump refuse.

(The word Gardyloo is probably a corruption of the French 'gardez l'eau', from the warning cry of Edinburgh householders as they were about to pitch domestic refuse and worse, into the public street below. This was usually done at 10 p.m. each evening to the beat of the town drum; woe betide any passerby who was not either nimble of foot or quick to shout "Haud yer han!".) The buttress has two edges. Ogilvy attempted to follow the clean-cut left edge, and wearing socks made considerable progress before the rain came on. He then abseiled into Gardyloo Gully, leaving behind three rope slings and two karabiners.

Another attempted route was that of the complete girdle traverse of the Ben Nevis cliffs, a Bell inspiration. Girdles, the climbing of a cliff across its width, rather than the more normal bottom to top, were in fashion at this time. Although seldom repeated in later years, they certainly provided the pioneers with much entertainment at the time, often landing them in positions and situations otherwise never reached. In August, 1940, Bell and Dwyer made a start on the grand girdle, beginning on the valley side of Castle Ridge. Their attempt fizzled out four hours later, in dense mist on The Comb, the two climbers finishing up Pigott's Route to complete their holiday.

Bell was back on September 21, 1941, with J.D.B. Wilson. Starting at the Carn Mor Dearg arête, they roped up on reaching the N.E. Buttress and reversed the V-traverse to gain the Basin. Exciting times were had crossing the great, and then unclimbed gully of Point Five and also on a section of rock right of Glover's Chimney. They crossed The Comb on their grand tour by means of Hesperides Ledge, first climbed by Bell and Wilson the previous June. At this point Wilson made it quite clear that he,

"hated the very sight of the beautiful plants on Hesperides Ledge, and considered that he had done enough for the day." (1).

Bell continued alone, taking less than an hour to go from No.4 Gully to South Castle Gully.

". . . an easy rise took me to the Carn Dearg Buttress Cairn . . . There I halloed and danced a wardance, seen by Wilson from the corrie below."

The Girdle Traverse was complete.

June 1941 on Nevis saw attacks, both by climbers on Gardyloo Buttress, and by a German bomber on the vital installation that was so valuable a target - the Fort William aluminium factory. The Dundonian team of Syd Scroggie, John S. Ferguson and Graham S. Ritchie were in residence at the CIC Hut; Ritchie described both of these attacks in an entertaining essay. At two o'clock in the morning the hut residents heard the drone of an aircraft.

"Steaming mugs of tea in hand, we moved out into the night where the great cliffs of the Ben towered jet-black against a dark sky. No sound came to us save a soft rustle of wind. Yet we lingered expectantly. Then lazily, so lazily, converging streams of red tracer-shells rose from behind Carn Dearg and mounted the sky. Two great flashes lit the horizon and the hills stood revealed for an instant. But not a sound was heard. It was all rather eerie and exciting, yet peaceful and strangely beautiful."

The audacious German bombing run came to nothing strategically; one bomb exploded in a tinker's encampment, but of the two bombs which were direct hits neither went off. One landed next to the waterpipe where it comes out of Meall an t-Suidhe, while the other crashed through the roof to land in the very centre of the factory floor, surprising the workers at their benches. Later that day the climbers left the CIC Hut and approached Gardyloo Buttress. By the time the first rocks were gained it was 6 p.m. (Double Summer Time would then be in force).

"Sydney led off from the bergschrund below the rocks, leaving John and myself contemplating a litter of Observatory rubbish, prominent among which were unmistakeable portions of a certain china article which caused quite disproportionate mirth, as such things do on such occasions. Our leader meantime was not on difficult *looking* rock; yet, after a paltry 30 feet, there he was calling for ironmongery, and in particular for a variety referred to as 'wee beauties'. 'John,' I said, 'nip up and give Syd a hand; he's off form.' After 'nipping up' some 10 feet he descended precipitately upon me, lit a cigarette and commented shortly, 'Syd's doing O.K.' Thereafter we both sobered up considerably."

At the top of the slabby first section, all three removed boots and continued in socks. The buttress had little in the way of natural belays and only two rock belays were found by the climbers. Eventually they gathered on a ledge below two thin chimneys, at the top of which were some insecure-looking blocks. They decided that the gully wall offered the best chance for future advance, and after placing a piton roped down and returned to the Hut via Tower Ridge, first leaving an ice axe high up on the Little Tower, *"just to ensure that we did return on the morrow."*

The next day saw the three back on the buttress at their previous high point. From there Scroggie set out to climb on the gully wall. After some 40 feet he moved back on to the true ridge throwing down a huge unstable block. This weaved its way down the snow in Observatory Gully, finally coming to rest by the Allt a'Mhuilinn. Another 30 feet of steep but delightful rock led to a small ledge, and there all three perched, *"feet dangling in the void, for all the world like the Three Wise Monkeys."*

Ritchie was to spend hours on this ledge, while the other two attempted what was plainly the crux of the route.

"Time passed swiftly and inexorably. The evening shadows began to lengthen in the corrie. Then a glorious light flooded down Gardyloo Gully, suffusing the rocks with an unbelievable purple glow which slowly paled and suddenly was gone . . . An hour fled by while the ropes moved spasmodically upwards, never more than a few feet at a time. The tension never relaxed, but rather grew . . . No verbal communication was possible . . . and when, at length, the ropes began to swing down like the cables of a lift I could only assume that our attempt had failed." (3).

The two leaders told of steep holdless grooves and ribs and continuous exposure and had continued until further direct progress was doubtful and a traverse right to the central snow patch out of the question. A deeply rusted karabiner and a weather-faded belay loop were produced — evidence that they had passed Ogilvy's high point of July 1940. Scroggie and Ferguson were convinced that the only chink of weakness in the buttress lay further right, a good prediction, as it turned out.

The line attempted by Ogilvy and Piercey and by the Dundonians in 1940 and 1941 respectively, was finally climbed in June 1962, by the brothers Marshall and George Ritchie. At a good, solid grade of Very Severe, it is described in the current guide book as a superb route with fine situations — Left Edge Route.

Speaking in 1984 of the attempt by the Dundee team, Jimmy Marshall was of the opinion that had they traversed right then the route would have fallen and the buttress would have been climbed, but climbing is a sport permeated with such fascinating 'ifs', and to the climbers on the spot at the time an outcome is often not visible and sometimes highly risky. By 1941 then, Gardyloo Buttress was both unclimbed, and growing in reputation.

Other than Bell's Girdle of the North Face, there were three new climbs and a variation in 1941. The first route to breach the steep Indicator Wall was climbed by J.F. Scott, J.T. Austin and W. Moore, on July 11. A Very Difficult, it climbs grooves and a wall near the left end. The previous day, M.W. Erlebach and Edward Pyatt had climbed a Difficult on Creag Coire na Ciste — Central Rib, while on September 23, S. and B.P. Thompson climbed the Difficult Thompson's Route on 3 Gully Buttress. All three of these routes now provide excellent winter climbing. Finally, on the last day of August, Route I received a Direct Start by Robin Plackett and W.W. Campbell, at a standard of Very Difficult.

By 1942, the setbacks of the war in Europe and the consequent economic stringencies were beginning to tell; very little climbing was done, and on Ben Nevis only one new climb was recorded. That sole route however saw a new name on the mountain, a climber whose short-lived but intense climbing career was to fascinate later generations of climbers — Brian Pinder Kellett (1914-1944).

The lone route of 1942 was the first summer ascent of Number 2 Gully. Several prominent climbers had previously failed on this. In September 1911 Raeburn attempted a relatively snow-free ascent, but high in the gully there was a considerable quantity of fresh snow. At one wet and slimy pitch not far from the top a large amount of snow came down upon the leader and retreat seemed sensible. Twenty-four years later Macphee had a try at climbing the gully; he too was stopped, this time by the great volume of water coming down the major difficulty — the Great Pitch.

On August 30, Kellett and J.A. Dunster entered the gully. It had been dry for a week, though this often makes little difference in a wet gully. The scree in the upper parts was so unstable that Dunster unroped and sheltered at the foot of a subsidiary gully. Kellett graphically described the crux section, a 35-foot stretch of very thin climbing —

"There was a good spike belay very high up on the right wall, over which the rope was thrown. But the small holds on the right wall were rotten and worthless and the ascent was finally effected by the back on this wall with the side pressure of the foot on small vertical holds in the gully bed. These latter holds sloped badly and were water-worn and wet, so great difficulty was experienced. Near the top one could face inwards and reach good holds at the top of the steep part . . . " (4).

With the possible exception of Point Five, No.2 Gully remains the hardest of the summer gullies on the north face of Nevis, being at least Very Severe. Kellett however was not to commence the main thrust of his Nevis explorations until 1943, when he arrived in Torlundy below the Ben to work in the Forestry Commission. He was a pacifist who had determined not to fight; after a spell in prison he volunteered for the Forestry, hoping at first to work on Skye, then settling for Torlundy and Ben Nevis.

Kellett's brief but illuminating period on Ben Nevis lasted two years, essentially the summers of 1943 and 1944. As regards first ascents in 1943, Kellett's climbing began on May 22 and finished on August 11. His climbing on Ben Nevis took a systematic approach, with a view to climbing and checking all the known routes. We are very fortunate indeed that he kept a series of three personal notebooks, into which were entered detailed notes on the routes. Into these small, maroon-coloured books, entries were made in a neat and concise hand, dark blue ink for descriptions, red for route names. A handwriting expert, analysing Kellett's writing, has made the comment that by nature the writer was,

"methodical rather than brilliant, a highly controlled and physically strong individual who was nonetheless occasionally prone to making mistakes. " (5).

In the April 1944 number of the SMC Journal was an article by Kellett titled, 'Recent Rock Climbs on Ben Nevis' (6), stating that the article was intended to serve as a supplement to the 1936 Macphee edition of the Ben Nevis Guide. At the end of his article, which contains descriptions of many routes, was a classified list of climbs, including routes graded as Very Severe. To help give an impression of Kellett's activity in the summer of 1943, he climbed 91 routes or variations on Nevis, out of the existing total given of 106. Many of these he was obliged to solo, sometimes climbing midweek after a hard day's Forestry work. He would also take the odd day off when the weather was settled, to the annoyance of his employers. For training, Kellett would hire a bike and climb on the Polldubh crags in the evenings.

Where Kellett's notebook mentioned photographs for illustrating cliff features, he often gave Cartesian coordinates; e.g., (Photo. J. 22, 327, 3.8, 3.3); the last two numbers given being horizontal and vertical coordinates in inches, measured from the bottom left-hand corner of the photograph. The first two numbers were, of course, the source and page number.

Over Kellett himself there hovers an almost inevitable air of mystery. At school he was competent in several sports and an excellent chess player. (He played chess after work with the blacksmith at Torlundy, and was probably of county champion standard.) Powerfully built, he had begun to solo routes while working in the Lake District — though not in accountancy, in which he had qualified — but in the Forestry in Ennerdale.

Of the 91 routes climbed by Kellett in 1943, 17 were first ascents, 14 of them solo. From these bare statistics we have to picture a solitary climber steadily working his way through the lines on

7.5   Brian Kellett (1942)

Ben Nevis, existing or future, with a methodical determination. Not that his days on the hill were without incident; on Nevis he suffered three falls, before the one that ended his life. In January 1943, while on a solo ascent of the Secondary Tower Ridge, he fell while crossing the Tower Gap, shooting down the entire length of Glover's Chimney and over the ice pitch at the foot of the route to land in snow. When he got back down to the hut after this fall, miraculously unhurt, he pinned a note on the door asking for help in recovering his axe, lost during the fall.

But Kellett's standing as a climber, in a technical sense at least, should be judged by the routes he left. On May 22 he made a Severe variation to Bayonet Route, climbing alone above the overhang bypassed by Macphee on the first ascent. Repeating Bayonet Route in 1985 using modern equipment, the author declined to take Kellett's route at the overhang, instead moving up the overhang at its left end. To follow Kellett's variation involves a bold and committing move using a friction hold, with no certainty of the outcome.

Two weeks later on June 9 Kellett made a lone examination of the upper reaches of a line to the right of Route I. There was a St. Andrews University Club meet in the CIC Hut that day when Kellett appeared looking for a partner. Arnot Russell agreed to go along with him. The two made the first ascent of Route II, a Severe which started up Route I then broke out right to traverse across the great buttress below the overhangs. It is a remarkably fine climb with breathtaking situations, climbed on the first ascent in socks, in order to overcome damp and vegetation. Kellett's note in the CIC Log makes the following comment on Route II.

"Conditions good as far as Green Ledge, where light rain started. This gives a good face climb mainly on rough slabs with good, small holds. It is very exposed, but not unduly difficult in rubbers. Severe . . . " (2).

Following the ascent Russell and Kellett descended via Route I then to round off a good day climbed the Direct Start to the North Trident Buttress.

On July 2, Kellett escaped death for the second time, on a solo ascent of Route A on the North Wall of Carn Dearg. While attempting to identify this old route he fell on a chimney pitch, possibly due to loose rock. Kellett gave the route a grade of Very Severe, the hardest of the routes he climbed that year.

A slightly easier solo climb that month was the first ascent of The Italian Climb at Severe. This is the chimney-gully line on the west flank of Tower Ridge, now a popular Grade III in winter, and was climbed on the eighth day of perfect weather. The initial chimney proved to be the hardest pitch, mossy and still wet. Above this Kellett made a strange discovery. Moving up the next section he reached a small cave at the back of the cleft.

". . . a walk then led to the cave . . . where a piton and a sort of ladder, formed by a strong pole, with nails on both sides was found." (2).

Higher up The Italian Climb Kellett inspected the overhanging Left-Hand Branch, but judged it impossible. The ownership of the home-made ladder found in the cave will probably never come to light. In March 1940 J.Y. Macdonald and H.W. Turnbull had attempted the route, but found the second pitch to be in bad condition. No doubt other parties attempted the route as well.

The following day, Sunday, July 25, Kellett made no less than three new routes, two at Very Difficult and one at Severe, the last a solo ascent of 1943 Route on the bottom tier of the South Trident Buttress. Climbing with E.M. Hanlon and Gordon Scott, Kellett made an ascent of Evening Wall, possibly the second, then made the first descent of Route II. Scott took up the position of last man, the most responsible position on descent. The original finish of Route II was up the right-hand of two grooves mentioned by Ogilvy. In order to give Route II a separate finish from Evening Wall, Kellett descended the left-hand groove. The green ledge on Route II, visible from the hut,

". . . was carpeted with yellow, white, and pink flowers. Those who wish to perfect their turf technique are recommended to visit this airy garden." (2).

The second ascent of Route II was that by Kellett and B.P. Thompson on April 10, 1944. The two were almost benighted on this occasion, descending by Ledge Route. Of the last pitch of 1943 Route Macphee, in his 1936 Guide, stated that the final groove was the obvious route but that it looked almost impossible. Kellett was now beginning to look unstoppable.

Route B, on August 11, was the scene of a near tragedy. Kellett was climbing with Jim Bell and Nancy Forsyth on the North Wall of Carn Dearg. There are several explanations for the attraction this face seems to have held for Kellett. Firstly there were several vague routes, the clarification of which had eluded Macphee. Secondly, this area of impressively steep walls was one of the lowest on Nevis, a point of some convenience to Kellett who on occasion climbed in the evening.

Bell gives an account of this third fall by Kellett, taken from his climbing log.

"K. started off, N.F. belayed round belay near foot of chimney. I was unroped as I was coiling up the 100-ft line which was no longer necessary. A rumble from above & I just caught sight of Kellett flying downward past me. At the same time I felt a blow on the head, not sharp but dull & my head began to feel all warm — with flowing blood. Nancy shouted to me to grasp & try to stop the rope. It was, of course, utterly impossible. The thing was running down fast & jerking about. Then it stopped, Nancy was drawn up sharp against the belay in a strained position & there was silence. The rope to Kellett was taut. It held."

Bell looked down to the edge where the rope disappeared, about 70 or 80 feet below. Then he heard Kellett shouting. He was unhurt apart from numb hands, hanging with just a faint pressure on the rocks and no real hand holds. After some time Bell succeeded in getting the end of the 100-foot line to Kellett, who then tied on to that. With both Bell and Forsyth pulling, Kellett appeared above the edge, shaken. After a rest he climbed up until level with the other two but 30 feet to the right. As he had doubts about making the traverse, the other two climbed over to join him. Bell had a profusely bleeding scalp wound, while Forsyth, who had belayed Kellett with the rope running behind her body, suffered from a badly lacerated hand, a result of braking Kellett's fall with her bare hands.

Kellett admitted that Forsyth had been very successful in slowing his fall; she had probably saved his life. Slowly, the shaken but grateful trio made their way down easy terraces leading to the usual staircase-gully approach to Raeburn's Buttress. This was very wet. Bell was last, with Kellett letting Forsyth down on the rope. Bell missed what happened next, but a hold broke off while Kellett was descending, pitching him down about 5 feet or so. Ironically, this tiny fall severely damaged his left knee and his right hand. As he insisted that he could make his way down the other two soon drew ahead, reaching the hut just before 7 p.m. An hour later, with supper ready, Kellett was still not in sight, so Bell went up to look for him.

"I soon met him going very slowly but past the worst of the descent. He had to keep the injured leg & knee joint straight all the time. For this he had arranged a loop on a bit of line, the loop under the instep & rope in his hand."

The next day, Kellett's knee had swelled to twice normal size. The fall had taken place on the Wednesday; on the following Monday Kellett slowly hobbled down to Fort William, using a broom as a crutch. There it was found that he had fractured a patella and a finger. Bell also went down on the Monday, soloing up Tower Ridge and returning to Fort William via Glen Nevis. As to the cause of the fall, it seems that Kellett had been relying on a chockstone placed by him on a previous ascent. When pulling up on this it came out and Kellett fell with it.

By the time Kellett recovered fully, summer had finished, the first of the two summers he lived to the full climbing on Nevis. Route B (a Severe) along with a Direct Start climbed by the Placketts the following June, an introductory chimney pitch, and Route A, are now climbed in combination, fittingly called Kellett's North Wall Route, a 550-foot Severe.

Bell climbed with Kellett on one occasion only, described above. Following Kellett's last and fatal fall, he remarked that it had come as no surprise to him. This remark may well have been coloured by the frightening experience on Route B, and it was no help that Bell, who was a personal friend of Nancy Forsyth, had introduced her to Kellett. After that fall on Route B, Bell warned Forsyth about climbing with Kellett. However, she did climb with him again. The point remains nonetheless, that the sensible codes of the day decreed that the leader must not fall.

Apart from Kellett on Nevis, no other climber was making first ascents in 1943. Over a third of those using the CIC Hut were troops, a party of whom climbed Tower Ridge fully equipped, including rifles. The army group comprised one officer and 14 other ranks of the Lincolnshire regiment, who climbed the Ridge in full battle order, carrying rifles and wearing army boots (excepting the C.O.). The party moved in five ropes of three and despite wind and rain climbed the ridge in under six hours. All but the leader were virtual novices with only scrambling experience.

One wet day some soldiers staggered into the CIC Hut where they accepted the hospitality of the climbers resident there, who included Bell. The soldiers began complaining about their C.O., referring to him as a "bloody mountain goat". When Bell enquired as to his name, he was highly amused on learning that it was Sandy Wedderburn.

Bill Murray was now a prisoner of war, as were several others. If the war was to bring any benefits to mountaineering, it would be in the form of better equipment — nylon ropes, better karabiners, vibram-soled boots — though the majority of climbers had to wait several years to see any of these. On October 25, the JMCS approved Kellett's membership application, thus allowing him easier access to the CIC Hut.

The summer of 1944 was to see another one-man campaign by Kellett, a total of 15 first ascents; 11 solo. He opened his last summer with a variation to Bell's Beta Route on the Orion Face, climbing wet and mossy slabs in socks to gain the Basin by a more direct line. This was on June 17, but perhaps of more interest was his climb of June 20, one of his best discoveries on Ben Nevis — the Left-Hand Route on the Minus Face.

East of the Orion Face the rock has a leftward tilt and is seamed by a series of buttresses and gullies, three of the latter being particularly prominent. Bell had already named the steep gully on the left flank of Observatory Ridge Zero Gully, the broad and easy Tower Gully to the left of Tower Ridge originally being No. 1 Gully. This nomenclature overlooked the narrow rift full of overhung pitches, lying between Observatory Buttress and the steep slabby rocks on the right-hand edge of the west face of Observatory Ridge. This steep gully, Kellett decided, should be called Point Five Gully, while the three gullies left of Zero, again by analogy, he named Minus One, Two and Three Gullies respectively. (7).

The narrow buttress between Minus One and Two Gullies was named Minus One Buttress, while the broad buttress between Minus Two and Three Gullies became Minus Two Buttress. It was on this last buttress that Kellett was to record two routes, the Left- and Right-Hand Routes, both Very Severe. The first to be climbed was the Left-Hand Route, climbed on June 20 in company with Robin and Carol Plackett. Three days earlier, Kellett had spent three or four hours examining this face, deciding that there were at least three routes to be found.

The route followed cracked slabs to a stance below and right of the prominent overhanging nose on this face, then took to a steep bulging slab on the left. The slab was the crux of the route. Each of the three climbers took their own line on the crux pitch, the leader wearing socks for a wet slimy crack, traversed above a bulge. Thereafter plimsolls were worn, with 120 feet of rope found to be just adequate.

The second ascent of Kellett's Left-Hand Route was on July 9, 1949 by J.H. Swallow and Arnot Russell. Ten years after the first ascent, a strong team from Cambridge University made the first of a series of summer raids on Scotland. Two ropes approached the foot of Minus Two Buttress in the summer of 1954, the first composed of Mike O'Hara and Eric Langmuir, the second of John Peacock and Arthur Muirhead. Conditions were wet and greasy and a late start ensured that it was the afternoon before the rocks were gained. O'Hara set off and at the top of the first pitch, a smooth and greasy slab, belayed to a peg. Langmuir described the second, crux pitch, in an essay written for his club journal.

"Mike was overflowing with confidence and could hardly be restrained from dashing off before I was properly belayed. When he was unleashed he disappeared over the edge with a grin. 'Hold tight.' I gave what I hoped was a reassuring 'Aye'. I still retain a vivid picture of his massive form moving slowly upwards on invisible holds and can recall the prickly sensation at the back of my neck as I caught a glimpse of daylight between the uppers and vibram sole of one boot. A fierce looking mantelshelf on to a tiny ledge on the edge of space came as a fitting climax to this splendid pitch." (8).

Today, Left-Hand Route is a deservedly popular climb, only just Very Severe and taking in a fine series of steep slabs and corners. It takes a few days to dry out, as do most of the routes on this face.

The day following the first ascent of Left-Hand Route, June 21, 1944, Kellett made an unsuccessful attempt on a major line on Carn Dearg Buttress. The line he had been thinking of since the previous summer was the long, conspicuous chimney near the right-hand edge of the buttress — now the classic route Sassenach. The chimney does not reach to the ground and is seemingly impossible to reach from directly below, but like other climbers who were to follow, and possibly even earlier climbers unknown, Kellett hoped to gain the foot of the chimney by traversing in from the left.

To gain this traverse Kellett climbed a steep 50-foot wall on a little subsidiary buttress. This deceptive pitch is now the start of another great classic route — Centurion. Kellett and Robin Plackett gained the ledge left of the start of the impressive Centurion corner and decided that the gangway traverse looked feasible. A direct entry to the gangway was prevented by a serious-looking steep and smooth mantelshelf and an attempt was then made to traverse right at a higher level by climbing the chimney of Centurion. This was successfully followed for 30 or 40 feet to a spike belay where an old rope sling was found. Some anonymous party, it seems, had attempted the formidable line of Centurion some time ago.

Further upward progress, noted Kellett.

". . . was not inviting, nor was the projected traverse right across a very smooth slab, so we had to come down." (2).

Frustrated, that same evening Kellett soloed an easy route on the Douglas Boulder, the Left-Hand Chimney, recording it as a poor climb. Sassenach was to have several other attempts made on it before finally succumbing to the power climbing of Whillans and Brown in 1954.

The good weather of June 1944 left, being replaced by a familiarly wet July. Kellett was indefatigable however and on the first day of July attempted the prominent gully which drains the lower part of the Secondary Tower Ridge. This last feature is a curious slanting shelf, running parallel to the main Tower Ridge, and some feet below its crest on the west side. Secondary Tower Ridge had first been climbed in the early 1930's by J.Y. Macdonald and H.W. Turnbull. The prominent gully attempted by Kellett was one of two mentioned by

Macdonald and Turnbull, who climbed the left-hand one. Kellett climbed the lower shallow section of the gully, but half-way up ran into a formidably steep pitch of 60 to 70 feet. This was also wet and Kellett descended slightly before escaping by a rightward traverse.

The gully was named Vanishing Gully by Kellett, no doubt due to the fact that as it nears the ground it narrows to a crack and finally vanishes altogether. Macdonald and Turnbull had rather diffidently named it as being a 'Trouser-Leg Gully', and it was known by this name when Archie Hendry climbed the gully in the summer of 1943. Kellett, however, had no knowledge of this ascent. Vanishing Gully is now a superb winter route, a Grade V climb high on any climber's list.

One week later in the afternoon and evening of July 8, Kellett explored the west face of Observatory Ridge, where Bell and Hamilton had already pioneered a route in 1937. The Very Difficult line Kellett found lies to the left of Bell's route and he suggested that it be called the Lower Route to distinguish it from the original (upper) route. Like Vanishing Gully, Kellett's Lower Route is now a winter classic, graced with the less clumsy title of Hadrian's Wall. These winter ascents, however, were some years in the future and had to wait for the changes that were still to affect Scottish winter climbing, changes that were going to see difficulties increase by an order of magnitude.

The last two weeks of July 1944 were to be Kellett's finest, climbing alone on another seven routes. On July 20 he made use of the fourth day of a spell of dry weather and climbed Minus Two Buttress by the Right-Hand Route, Very Severe. We will never have full knowledge of such ascents — there were so few climbers about during the war years especially that there was rarely anyone who could witness such events — but from descriptions of contemporaries, we know that Kellett was very methodical in his explorations; carefully examining a possible route from as many angles as possible before deciding whether to attempt it or not. As to his climbing technique when soloing we again have little knowledge, though in addition to his powerful physique we know that he had the high degree of self-control necessary when soloing routes of a high calibre in uncharted areas. His climbing style has been described by a contemporary as excellent, a pleasure to watch.

When Kellet considered a route of sufficient difficulty, he carried a rope. Equipment then was very limited and unless good spikes and blocks were evident on the route then protection would always have been minimal. Once started on his lone ascent of the Right-Hand Route, Kellett was, to all practical purposes, committed to finding a way up the cliff.

Right-Hand Route is 350 feet in length;, giving delicate and exposed climbing with more sustained difficulties than its companion route. Kellett noted the absence of belays, remarking that very long run-outs would probably be necessary. Following the difficult lower section, 550 feet of easier climbing leads to the Second Platform on North-East Buttress. The ascent of Right-Hand Route owes itself to a strange quirk of fate. On the walk up the weather was so hot that Kellett decided to shed his shorts and other unnecessary clothing, placing these garments

7 6   Kellett, South Trident Buttress (c.1944)

on top of his rucksack. On gaining the Hut he found the clothing missing, having fallen off somewhere on the path. His intended route that day was Gardyloo Buttress, but he thought that the sight of him arriving at the summit almost naked would not have amused the tourists on top, so instead he chose to attempt the line on Minus Three Buttress. Right-Hand Route then became perhaps the sole route on Nevis to be climbed trouserless.

The second ascent was in June 1955, by the Cambridge team of Langmuir, O'Hara and Downes. They considered it to be a route of high quality, *"another daring performance by Kellett."* (8). Comparing the two routes of Kellett's on Minus Two Buttress is invidious, but Left-Hand Route, though easier, is the more interesting route.

But Kellett's eyes were returning again and again to the little buttress which dominates the head of Observatory Gully — Gardyloo Buttress. On Sunday, July 16, he made a reconnaissance of the buttress, climbing the short, Moderate crack up slabs on the Tower Face of the buttress. Gardyloo Buttress had been attempted at least twice in the past; by Ogilvy in 1940, and by Scroggie in 1941. Both of these failures had been on the clean-cut, left edge of the steep buttress face, looking down the full length of Observatory Gully. Kellett, with his highly developed instinct for a line spotted an alternative on the right wall of the left edge.

July 22 was to see Kellett's boldest lead yet, as he started up the band of easy angled rocks at the foot of Gardyloo Buttress. Serious climbing started for Kellett as he climbed up twin cracks on the steep wall above, traversing right beneath an overhang then directly over a smaller overhang to gain a very small stance in a recess. Kellett recommended that it would be better not to bring up a second to this point, as the only belays were small, insecure-looking blocks on the floor of the recess. The 15-foot corner that followed was to prove to be the crux of the route and in some ways Kellett's finest moment on Nevis.

Kellett, significantly, described this section of the route in great detail, as he spent almost an hour in a strenuous position, cleaning holds and working out a solution, all the while conscious of a horrible and very final drop to the gully boulders below.

"The left wall is perpendicular, the right wall slightly overhanging; handholds on the left wall, though well placed for climbing straight up it, are not well adapted for preventing the body being pushed off to the left by the overhanging right wall. The key to the pitch is the large spike handhold facing horizontally left; this was used by the left hand and had to take most of the weight of the body, while the mossy holds above were cleaned and tidied with the right hand. The higher holds had to be groped for as they could not be seen from below . . . Once preparations were completed the right hand was shifted from a flat press hold to a much higher hold (rather unsatisfactory) and then the left hand unwillingly left the beautiful spike for another hold, also much higher. This was really the hardest movement as both feet were on very poor holds and the body was being pushed off left all the time by the overhang." (7).

Once Kellett had gained the upper handholds he was able to step up on to his previous right hand hold and finish the corner. Some strenuous yet delicate climbing remained to be overcome before the wet and mossy final gully was gained. The route had been climbed solo in three hours, wearing plimsolls, with the crux alone taking one hour. It was, obviously enough, a Very Severe.

The second ascent of Kellett's Route was made in damp conditions in June 1955, by the ubiquitous Downes and O'Hara. There was snow at the top of the buttress, which is at a height of about 4,350 feet, with melt water trickling down the rocks. The two Cambridge climbers found the 15-foot corner reminiscent of the corner on Pigott's Climb on Clogwyn du'r Arddu, though steeper and more exposed. Kellett's 'beautiful spike', so necessary at the crux, was found to be unsound, wet rock additionally precluding the required pull-up. The corner was eventually climbed with the aid of a foot-loop hung delicately from the 'flat press-hold', no apology being felt necessary, considering conditions. (9).

Several other routes fell to Kellett during the remainder of July, including a Very Severe on the bottom tier of the South Trident Buttress and a Very Difficult on the middle tier of the

7.7   Kellett's notebook for July, 1944, describing Gardyloo Buttress

same buttress. The Very Severe is now graded at Severe, giving what the current guide describes as a *"superb climb"*. (10). This 1944 Route, as it is called, climbs the right-hand of four large and conspicuous grooves. The rock was very wet when climbed by Kellett, which may account for his uncharacteristic overgrading.

On August 20 Kellett recorded his last route on Nevis — a direct ascent of Cousins' Buttress, the subsidiary buttress abutting the North Wall of Carn Dearg Buttress. This Severe route took the buttress directly, Kellett in his description referring several times to loose rock, noting that it required careful treatment throughout. This particular area of Ben Nevis, as has been noted above, was one of Kellett's favourites; he was to return here for one last ascent.

The weekend of September 1 was a holiday weekend and Nancy Forsyth travelled from Dumfries to Fort William to spend a weekend climbing with Kellett, based at the CIC Hut. When Forsyth had not returned home by the Monday evening her sister contacted the Fort William police. They sent a man up to the hut on Tuesday afternoon. He reported that their belongings were in the hut, but that there was no note of their whereabouts. A search party numbering 18 was organised to go up on Wednesday. By 9 p.m. on Wednesday Bell heard that nothing had been found.

The weather on the Saturday had been showery and much worse on the Sunday. Bell arranged to join Miss Forsyth on the Thursday, meeting her on the Oban train at Dunblane. At Fort William they picked up Nancy Ridyard, all three walking up through heavy rain to reach the CIC Hut at 7 p.m. Just after midnight they were joined by Archie Hendry's party, and G.C. Curtis and G.H. Townend who arrived independently. The search was organised for Friday by Bell and Hendry, the latter and four others going up to Castle Coire.

The likeliest location, Bell argued, would be the base of Cousins' Buttress, as (a) Kellett had just done a new route there and (b) Kellett was unhappy with Macphee's guide description of the original route. Hendry decided to climb the Castle himself. A recall signal had been arranged, beating an empty oil drum with ice axe shafts. Bell and Ridyard were in No.2 Gully when the dull booming of the oil drum was heard. Hendry had spotted the two bodies from below the rocky base of the Castle and had shouted the news to his party. Everyone now gathered at the hut, joined by Harrison and Fletcher who had come up from Fort William with the SMC stretcher. Twelve men went up to the site of the accident.

The two bodies were severely injured, particularly Kellett's. Forsyth was lower down, near the foot of the stepped gully between Cousins' Buttress pinnacle and the foot of Raeburn's Buttress. Kellett was some 15 feet higher up the gully. Above them was the almost 200-foot high pinnacle of Cousins' Buttress. Forsyth had most of Kellett's full-weight climbing rope coiled regularly over her left shoulder and lying over her right hip. She lay on her left side and was wearing an oilskin hood. Both climbers were tied on by waist loops in the usual fashion. The stretcher party took Forsyth down first then after a rest and some food went up again for Kellett. Thereafter a party consisting of naval and police personnel took over, carrying the bodies down to Fort William.

Bell was wary of arriving at a cause of the accident given the flimsy evidence available. He thought that it had probably occurred on Saturday, September 2, as they had been up in the hut on the Friday evening. Forsyth had left her oilskin cape in the hut and the Sunday had been wet all day. To judge from the arrangement of the rope, the two had probably been on easy ground, with Kellett leading. Bell thought also that it had not been a slip by Forsyth, as the top coil of rope carried by her had not been drawn up tight. It was perfectly possible, of course, that Kellett had been struck by a rock and had then pulled Forsyth off. Whatever the cause, death was obviously instantaneous.

"A brilliant rock climber", wrote Bell of Kellett, "He seemed to be devoid of fear on the rocks. Hence, it may be that his margin of safety was really smaller than if he had a touch of fear in his constitution . . . I had a sub-conscious feeling since 11/8/43 that K. was not altogether safe. Also, I warned him by mouth & letter later on. On the other hand K. had given up the idea of 2 desperate new climbs which he had formerly contemplated [Sassenach and Point Five Gully — KVC]. Also K. was meticulous about his belays." (11).

That Friday night Bell and Hendry stayed at the hut. Understandably, it was not a pleasant evening and the two slept but little. Also present were J.A. Dunster and B.P. Taylor who were up for a week's holiday. They were, according to Hendry, not very competent, and did not propose to climb anything exceeding Very Difficult in standard. (This was the same Dunster who had seconded Kellett on the first summer ascent of No.2 Gully.) Taylor spoke little and Dunster discussed routes with Bell and Hendry. Bell remembered warning Dunster that Observatory Buttress, though not especially difficult if on the correct line, was likely to give problems if one went off route. Two days later Taylor was killed on Observatory Buttress, the two climbers being unroped at the time.

Dunster and Taylor had completed Observatory Buttress as far as the start of the 300 feet of easy scrambling which leads to the summit. The two set off up this unroped. After about 200 feet Taylor traversed below a small buttress which Dunster tackled direct. When Dunster was about 50 feet up this he heard a considerable rockfall and could get no reply from his friend. He descended and traversed to where rock scars were evident. Only a coil of rope was visible in a small gully below. Taylor was lying dead at the foot of the buttress.

The next day, Saturday, Hendry went down to Fort William. The weather was now glorious, and Bell wished to leave the mountain with some of his gloom dissipated.

"So I left early & alone with my pack & reached Tower Ridge below first steep bit beyond the Douglas Boulder Gap. There was a good deal of new snow higher up & not a little verglas in places, I remember difficulty at a place on Little Tower, little or none at Eastern Traverse Great Tower, some considerable trouble at Tower Gap & at final exit above. But what was more impressive was the glorious aspect of Gardy Loo Buttress, a stupendous fairy castle, glistening white in the sun which had just pierced the mists on the crest of the Ben . . . " (11).

Kellett had gone, killed while doing what he loved the best. It would be difficult, if not impossible, to suppose where Kellett's climbing might have led. In more normal times — with no war, regular climbing partners and improved footwear and equipment — it is difficult to imagine many routes on Nevis proving too difficult for a climber of Kellett's abilities. At the time of his death he was 30 years of age. In his two summers on Ben Nevis he had lived on a wave of exploration never seen before or since. He was buried in Glen Nevis, looking over to the southern slopes of the mountain he made the last two years of his life. His other monuments remain on the north face of Nevis, including the fairy castle that is Gardyloo Buttress, first climbed by him to give Kellett's Route, and as seen by Bell, "glistening white in the sun . . ."

Kellett's death left a vacuum in climbing on Ben Nevis which was not to be filled until activity picked up again in the 1950's. By the mid-1940's, members of the established clubs were too involved with the war effort. The membership of the SMC, some 307 at the outbreak of war, was down to 276 in 1944. Of 310 CIC bed-nights that year, four SMC members accounted for 17. Between the wars the number of small clubs had risen amazingly, especially in Glasgow, Dundee and Aberdeen. That the SMC was not yet aware of this latent force was still evident in 1945, when a review of Scottish Climbing Clubs referred to a Dundee club as a *"training Club for the SMC."* (12).

The University clubs in Scotland had been active to varying degrees since about 1920 but it was only following the Second World War that their contributions to mountaineering became more tangible. The Scottish clubs for a long time never approached the size and activity of the Oxbridge clubs; almost certainly the chronically impecunious condition of the average Scottish undergraduate was a major cause.

The Ptarmigan Club founded by Jock Nimlin and W.C. Dougan in 1929 was no longer active as a club. There had been 16 original members and no others were admitted, a certain way towards corporate suicide. The Creagh Dhu were 22 strong at December 1945, the club's limit on membership being 30. This limitation, along with a six month's 'apprenticeship', maintained a friendly and close-knit atmosphere in the years following the war, even if it did lead to an ironic elitism, a state normally tacked on to the established clubs. It also led to a fierce standard of climbing, and the Creagh Dhu, especially in Arrochar and Glencoe, were soon to be responsible for some remarkable ascents.

The Lomond Mountaineering Club had been founded by John Harvey in 1933. From the start it was a well-organised mixed club, having around 70 members at the end of the war. The exploits of the Lomond Bus which carted members round all the major climbing centres — and twice to Switzerland — have gone down into history.

Other clubs were now hiring buses, and with a flood of cheaper and better equipment — thanks to the war — an increase in the number of climbers was not far off. Unfortunately this also meant an increase in the number of accidents on Scottish hills. Between 1925 and 1945 there were 45 deaths, eight on Ben Nevis. In the pre-war years, a call for help following an accident usually meant organising a rescue party put together by the SMC in Glasgow and Edinburgh. An accident would invariably be followed by letters of censure in the press, condemning climbing as too dangerous, suggesting that Ben Nevis be put off limits during the winter. Following the war, a more rational argument began to be heard, especially as statistics showed that a healthy, fit and properly equipped careful climber was much safer on a mountain than while crossing a busy road.

By 1945 the number of climbers living in and around Fort William prompted the formation of the Lochaber section of the JMCS. This club was later to become independent; its contributions to mountaineering and mountain rescue on Ben Nevis have always been high. In particular Dr Donald Duff, who settled at the Belford Hospital, Fort William, became deeply involved in the treatment of accident victims.

On February 22, 1946, the Himalayan climber and explorer H.W. Tilman of the Alpine Club and J. Cortlandt-Simpson of the JMCS were involved in an accident. They had finished a route, arriving at the summit in mist. From there they chose to descend via the Carn Mor Dearg arête, taking a compass bearing in order to find the correct line of descent. Unfortunately the two were soon heading as have many others too far leftwards, towards the line of cliffs known as the Little Brenva Face.

Seeing a gully, Tilman started to descend, but slipping on powder snow covering ice he fell several hundred feet, injuring though not breaking a leg. Cortlandt-Simpson, seeing so experienced a leader apparently descending under control, leapt after him, to discover to his horror that he too was falling. By some miracle no major injuries were incurred, the two continuing their descent to the hut rather shakily. This incident prompted the often-quoted remark that if a man could climb safely on Ben Nevis, he could climb safely anywhere. It also brought about the story that Nevis had something against members of the Alpine Club.

Climbing on Nevis following the war had to wait until those in the armed forces were released to civilian life, though before 1950 there were some isolated but significant ascents. June 16, 1946 saw one such route when The Crack, a 600-foot Very Severe on Raeburn's Buttress was climbed. The party on this occasion were H.A. Carsten of the Climber's Club and T. McGuinness of the Lomond M.C. The crack taken by this fine, if neglected route is the most striking feature on the slender pinnacle that is the upper part of the buttress. The Crack is about 300 feet long and strenuous, with a series of overhangs.

At Whitsuntide Carsten and Macphee went up to the CIC Hut. On the walk up Carsten's attention was fixed by a feature not mentioned in any of the books he had read. It was also, Macphee assured him, unclimbed. The feature was the straight and vertical crack cleaving Raeburn's Buttress. That evening the two climbed Tower Ridge, but the next evening, following an ascent on the North Wall of Carn Dearg, Carsten made a short visual inspection of the line, while Macphee went down to the hut to prepare dinner.

The upper section of the crack, Carsten knew, had been climbed by Raeburn on the first ascent of the buttress, gaining it from the gully on the left. Remaining unclimbed was the steep lower section. Carsten thought that the approach rocks looked practicable, with the crack itself a formidable problem. In a slight drizzle and in the rapidly deepening dusk he went down to the hut, the line now a major objective for his holiday.

Three days went by before Carsten could approach the buttress again. After a solo ascent of Route II he decided that there was just enough time to attempt the approach rocks. The result, as Carsten put it,

"... was one of those dogged fights into which a climber can plunge quite unintentionally, and which he has no desire to repeat."

Carsten found that the approach rocks made a staircase of about half a dozen steps. The steps were, however, deceptive. Each step concealed a rounded top and overhang. At 30 feet he found a crack and banged in a peg, resting from a sling while he recovered his nerves. He was trailing a length of line behind him and fed this through the peg and sling as a purely psychological running belay. Finally his curiosity got the better of him again and he moved on, finding the next moves to be harder still, with little chance of reversal.

"The next few feet had to go and I gave them no chance of standing upon the order of their going, so they went. With a strange feeling, a blend of triumph, respect and some surprise I reached and stood on the ledge beneath the crack itself."

Carsten realised that it was quite out of the question to continue alone. Looking around the ledge for a belay he found it to be loose and rotten, but a traverse found some perched blocks, suitable for an abseil anchor. The abseil was the most awkward he had ever done, as to go straight down would have left him suspended in space and he was obliged to make a diagonal descent, hoping he would neither swing off the line of descent, nor bring down the perched blocks and fall to the bottom. As luck would have it he made it to the precise spot as planned. Tucking away the free end of the rope under an overhang he descended to the hut to join Macphee.

It was to be another three days before Carsten could return to his route. Macphee went down the hill pleading a sore leg, leaving Carsten alone in his tent, awaiting Dr Duff who had promised to come up the hill and help recover the rope. Until then Carsten soloed several routes, and on his last day on the hill he was pleased to see Duff, with Tommy McGuinness, a competent member of the Lomond Club. Carsten's spirits rose as saw another chance at attempting the Crack. Duff stayed at the bottom to watch the battle.

Repeating the first pitch, Carsten was surprised how difficult it was, despite his prior knowledge and the presence of the fixed rope as a safety factor. On the ledge below the crack the two were soon sorting out the 270 feet of line, their sum total of rope. The drizzle had now started as Carsten launched himself at the crack. At first it was wide enough to admit his entire body, narrowing and forcing him partly on to the face. Fifty feet above the ledge he abandoned the crack and took to an overhang. The holds were good, allowing him to reach a ledge on the right, not visible from below. Here a peg belay permitted him to bring up McGuinness.

The two climbers were now assembled below the biggest bulge on the face, the crack, little more than a few inches wide, and the crux of the route. As the rest of the face was smooth, it was the only way up.

"However, a chockstone immediately below the overhang provided encouragement. I went up to examine its stability and returned temporarily exhausted by the effort. After a short rest I again ascended and before my strength faded away I managed to whip a sling round it and clip in a karabiner. Then down I went like a sack of potatoes. After a short rest my strength again returned and with it came determination. I tackled the third ascent with some energy, pulled up to the chockstone, jammed arms and fists into the Crack and stepped up minute holds on the left wall, hoping my feet would stay put as the tricounis in my boots were worn down to the plates.

Carsten had hoped that there would be a ledge at the level of the overhang, but it turned out to be sloping. His arms were beginning to weaken as he was forced to continue jamming up the crack.

"This proved a little too wide for secure jamming but the closeness of the goal provided power for a few more energetic movements until I found myself firmly wedged in the now widening Crack, gasping for breath. The bulge had gone."

The Crack had been climbed, though there was still one good, steep pitch remaining above the climbers' heads. A third ledge below this provided a good belay for the pair, as the drizzle hardened into a steady rain. Despite the rain, the climbers and the rock remained dry, thanks to the overhang above. Good holds on this made it enjoyable though, and Carsten could look down past his feet to savour the rock scenery below.

"The rain beat into our faces but we hardly felt it. Our spirits were above the clouds for we had won the day and made a climb which promised to be comparable in quality with the other good routes of Ben Nevis and was possibly harder than any of them." (13).

Commenting on the crux pitch, Carsten thought that it had not been excessively severe, merely strenuous and a problem similar to the Holly Tree Wall, the whole beautifully clean and reasonably safe. McGuinness had thought that the first pitch was the worst.

Ten years later The Crack had an eventful ascent when in September 1956 an 18-year old student from Edinburgh University decided to attempt the route. The student's name was Robin Smith, who was to feature largely in the near future, but on this ascent events were not to go smoothly. Smith succeeded in gaining the ledge above the crux, and was bringing up his second, whose,

". . . hands were above the bulge, one hand in the crack, and one hand on the slab, he was very nearly there with only one more move to make, but there he came off. He was on a tight rope, but with the stretch of the nylon he went down about 2 ft and swung away from the overhang. His fingers were too tired to pull him back, he was hanging on the rope, slowly spinning, with nothing below him for about 150 ft."

There was no other option but to lower his swinging second to the ground. Smith was now marooned at the foot of the last crack pitch in the fast gathering darkness, the very stuff of epics. He decided to attempt a solo ascent, thinking he could hide inside the crack and wiggle his way up with some security. Unfortunately, just before the end of the overhang the recess was blocked by a roof.

"So from under the roof I had to wriggle sideways to the edge of the Crack, and leaning out, fumble for the guidebook's good holds over the overhang, then swing out of the Crack, and swarm over the top. . . I set off on the wriggle, at first facing the recess, but I went too high and my head got stuck, so I came back and I thought, if I face the recess then I can't see where I'm going. I set off again, facing space, and I got to the end of the wriggle and finished up leaning out of the Crack. From here I began to fumble and before long I found the good holds, but I thought, rot the guidebook, these are obviously poor. I had no qualms about the swing, it was just that having swung I might not make the swarm, and I might not manage to swing back." (14).

Smith somehow managed to reverse back to the ledge, where he spent a miserable night. At dawn, as his would-be rescuers were pounding up the hill, he noticed a line of weakness crossing the face to the right. This traverse turned out to lead fairly easily to easy ground above the bulge, and so to the terrace below the final arête.

There were only two new routes in 1947: No.2 Gully Buttress, Very Difficult, on August 2 by J.D.B. Wilson and G.A. Collie, and Surgeon's Gully. The former climb is now a pleasant winter route, lying just left of No.2 Gully at the head of Coire na Ciste. Surgeon's Gully, originally called the Strawberry Chasm, is of a very different nature from any of the routes normally climbed on Ben Nevis: it is formed, not from the usual dark volcanic rock which forms the summit mass and cliffs of Nevis, but from the reddish Outer Granite; on the Glen Nevis flank of the mountain.

There are seven main gullies facing Glen Nevis, most of which were explored by 1946 and 1947. Perhaps the one person most closely involved in these explorations was Dr Donald G. Duff, after whom Surgeon's Gully was named. A Very Severe route of some 1500 feet, this is one of the major gullies in Scotland; as late as the 1970's it still awaited a complete ascent of the introductory, middle and upper central branch. It was first climbed by D.H. Haworth and

G.J. Ritchie on August 15, 1947. The guide book describes 21 pitches of varying lengths, taking a climber as far as the finishing point of the original ascent. Above lie the final three branches of the gully, only the leftmost, easy branch having been recorded.

The winter of 1947-48 went down as being one of the coldest of the century, with a major pandemic of influenza scything through the population. The previous eight years of clothes rationing were not helping to equip enthusiastic climbers wanting to tackle winter routes; food was rationed to about 4 oz of meat per week, with an ounce or two of cheese as additional protein. All this helped explain the quiet note with which the 1940's were ending; no routes in 1948, two variations and one route in 1949.

The route in 1949 was a winter ascent of Tower Cleft; the unusual deeply-cut chimney at the right-hand side of the small crag lying under Tower Gully. On January 22, J. Francis and G. Pratt attempted what they thought was Gardyloo Gully, but owing to bad visibility they in fact had entered the deeply-cut chimney. They retreated in the face of a 30-foot ice pitch. Francis and Pratt returned on February 13; on this occasion they turned back on coming up to a 20-foot ice wall. Finally, on February 19, their determination paid off with a successful ascent. As they emerged on to the snow slope below Tower Gully they discovered that a sudden thaw had made snow conditions very dangerous. Rather than continue upwards or traverse left under Gardyloo Buttress they abseiled back down their new route.

In the summer of 1949 Bill Peascod made his first trip to Nevis. He had been climbing with Macphee since 1945, putting up several first ascents with Macphee in the Lakes. Peascod's first impressions of the cliffs of Ben Nevis was a fairly typical one — amazement at the size and scope of the great north face. He recognised almost immediately that the normal Lake District pitch-by-pitch route description was not easily applied on Nevis, which had a more Alpine atmosphere.

Macphee and Peascod climbed, in addition to other routes, Rubicon Wall and The Long Climb in order that these routes be checked out for a new edition of the guide, by Macphee. Rubicon Wall was climbed without much difficulty, though it was found to be delicate. The Long Climb, however, provided a problem at one point, due to a lack of suitable belays.

Macphee at this time was climbing with 200 feet of lightweight rope, known as abseil line, and of about 8 mm in diameter. This long rope saved the day, as Peascod found himself almost a hundred feet up with no belay, the climbers using the rope doubled. His two slings had already fallen off small spikes lower down. With difficulty, hanging on to handholds, he managed to retie the rope into one long length, and with this rather doubtful security just gained a niche higher up where he fastened a belay round a dubious spike.

When Macphee gained the belay, he frightened the life out of Peascod by putting his full weight on to the spike belay — an "all or nothing test". Nine hours after starting the route, and still maintaining the full length of Macphee's abseil line between them, the two climbers reached the top. Peascod, who died of natural causes at the foot of Clogwyn d'ur Arddu in

May 1985, tells of his long and interesting climbing life in his autobiography, published just before his death at the age of 65. (15).

The relatively slow pace of climbing at the end of the 1940's was to be much shorter-lived than that following the First World War. Clothing and equipment were improving, as ex-W.D. gear became available. Jim Bell was delighted with his first pair of rubber soled boots, bought in 1948 and first tried out in Skye, in May of that year.

"I was highly delighted with my boots shod with Itshide moulded rubber soles & heels. They proved excellent for Cuillin rock dry, wet or even with hail on it. They were perfectly good on trap. They did wear down a bit at the toes in the course of a week involving quite a number of descents on sharp scree."

A small flood of mountaineering books was entering the bookshops: Bill Murray's 'Mountaineering in Scotland', published in 1947 (16) was especially to have a significant influence on young climbers, as did Bell's 'A Progress in Mountaineering', published in 1950 (17). There were other good books of the time of course, but these two included chapters on climbing on Ben Nevis. Another milestone had been reached in the course of mountaineering.

8.1 *R. Marshall, R. Smith, D. Haston, G. Tiso & J. Stenhouse (sitting), (c. 1959)*

RENAISSANCE (1950 – 1958)

Between the start of 1950 and the end of 1955 just ten routes were recorded on Ben Nevis. Several of these, however, were of great significance. Macphee's guide to Ben Nevis had been published in 1936 and was due for revision. It's format was in any case unsuited for a climber's breeches pocket — it measured an unwieldy 220mm x 145mm in the familiar SMC red cloth binding.

Towards the end of August 1950 Macphee arranged a week's climbing based at the CIC Hut. Bill Peascod and Brian Dodson hitched their way up from the Lakes to join him. On August 28, Peascod spotted a likely-looking buttress route just left of No. 3 Gully, which they were descending at the time. Macphee, C.H. Peckett and J. Renwick had been climbing Observatory Ridge, and they followed Peascod and Dodson up the new buttress route. It was raining during their ascent, which probably accounts for their grading of Severe, Very Severe in bad weather. They named the route Gargoyle Wall, after a projecting rock seen on the skyline of the buttress. It is now graded Very Difficult, one of the hardest routes of that standard on Nevis.

When the Lakes climbers had arrived at the CIC Hut, Macphee had explained his method of maximising the amount of climbing. This included minimising the amount of time spent in washing up after a meal. Instead, each climber would stick to his own set of cutlery and would save half a slice of bread for the end of each meal. With the bread, cutlery could be cleaned as its owner saw fit.

The day after Gargoyle Wall, Macphee, Peascod and Dodson set off to attempt Minus Two Gully. At this time, 1950, none of the Minus Gullies had been climbed, summer or winter. They roped up with Peascod in the lead and Macphee as third man. Peascod climbed the first hundred feet or so fairly easily in one run-out then brought up Dodson before continuing up the second pitch of 80 feet to a cave belay. While taking in the slack rope between him and Dodson a small stone was dislodged, and aimed for Macphee, nearly 200 feet below, bouncing off the rocks to strike Macphee on the side of his head.

No safety helmets were used by British climbers at this time. Macphee collapsed on the stance, blood streaming from his wound. Peascod and Dodson prepared to descend when to their great relief Macphee slowly levered himself upright. After a few moments, and holding a handkerchief to his head, Macphee decided that he was fit enough to descend to the Hut; the other two must continue. As he seemed perfectly coherent, they reluctantly carried on, noting Macphee's deliberate descent to the CIC Hut.

In the prevailing damp and greasy conditions the gully proved awkward at several points, with the crux on pitch five involving a hard move round a bulging edge. With Macphee's accident and these conditions, it took the climbers seven hours in total to climb the route. Minus Two Gully, like its two sister gullies, is now a much sought-after winter climb, while in summer it rates as one of the hardest Severes. On their return to the Hut, Macphee was found to be fully recovered, the remainder of the week's holiday continuing as enjoyably as the start.

The sole discovery of 1951 on Ben Nevis was the Severe Continuation Wall, climbed on October 7 by Tom Weir and the brothers Ian and Allan McNicol. This route took the "repulsive wall" left of Raeburn's Buttress. The day was a wet one and Weir (later a well-known writer and television personality) was obliged to climb in socks. The wall was also very loose, and is perhaps a safer route in winter, following its ascent by Brian Dunn and Davy Gardner in February 1977. It then provides an icy Grade IV in this quiet corner of Nevis.

The early 1950's saw the fast growth of the University Mountaineering Clubs, with Cambridge and Edinburgh prominent on Nevis from about 1954 onwards. Astonishingly, since Comb Gully in 1938, there had been only one winter first ascent on Nevis until March 23, 1952, a spell of 14 years. That day marked the first winter ascent of Observatory Buttress, when Dan Stewart and W.H. Foster of Edinburgh University climbed the Direct Route. On their ascent, which took just under six hours, they encountered a considerable quantity of ice.

Direct Route is a rarely-repeated Grade IV which despite its name is not as direct a winter line as the Ordinary Route to its right, which it crosses. Nonetheless, Direct Route was a fine piece of climbing and a harbinger of the new age soon to arrive on Nevis; an age already arrived further south, where the Creagh Dhu and others were busy climbing the rough lava walls and icy chimneys and gullies of Glencoe.

The two ascents recorded in 1953 — one route and one variation — introduced several names that were to influence Scottish climbing for more than 20 years to come. On an Edinburgh JMCS meet in September of that year were Jimmy Marshall and Charles Donaldson, staying at the CIC Hut. It had been wet for days when on September 23 the two climbers recorded Fives Wall, a Severe on the south face of No.5 Gully Buttress. The climb was wet and socks were worn. The following day, as the hut log book cryptically records, the weather was good, and a line was attempted on Carn Dearg Buttress, 90 feet being climbed before descending. The two climbers then made a damp ascent of The Long Climb.

The line attempted by Marshall is now the great chimney of Sassenach. On the first 'look' at the line, Marshall worked out a traverse line, crossing the slabs right of the corner, before retiring to the hut. The next day, in company with George Ritchie, a serious attempt was made, but the lack of protection on the overlaps became only too obvious. They then decided to try the huge corner above, known to them as the 'great book corner'. Marshall stepped right from the belay ledge and followed the corner to take a belay where it steepened. Ritchie for some reason had a very awkward time entering the corner, and with his confidence seeping away down the rope persuaded Marshall to give up the attempt. A great opportunity had been lost to the Scots. That summer in the Alps, Marshall met Brown and Whillans in Chamonix and mentioned the chimneys and corners waiting to be climbed on the right of the great buttress. *"There was no great sense of urgency regarding lines"*, remembers Marshall.

1953 saw another notable failure on Sassenach, when on October 7 the lure of its dank chimneys attracted a strong Aberdonian team. Over on one of their rare forays to Nevis were Tom Patey, Mike Taylor and Bill Brooker, then students at Aberdeen University. They followed previous attempts and tried an entry from the left; starting up the small, subsidiary buttress taken by the first pitch of Centurion.

Brooker recollects that with a youthful romanticism they had already named the big buttress the "Wall of the Winds". So far apart were they in technique from events further south, he also confessed, that it never entered their heads for a moment that a direct entry to the Sassenach chimney might be possible. They started up the first pitch in what was their usual order of climbing — Patey first, Taylor in the middle, and Brooker as third man. Patey had just that summer in the Alps bought his first pair of vibram-soled boots, an over-tight pair of 'Frendo' boots. It seems from a photograph of this attempt, however, that Patey was wearing plimsolls while trying the difficult traverse. Reaching the first stance he brought up Taylor.

8.2   Philip 'Bish' McAra on The Bat traverse (1982)

Belayed by Taylor, Patey crossed the overlapping slabs right of the great corner of the future Centurion, placing a peg runner halfway. He was unable to turn the edge, however, handicapped by his footwear. When it became obvious that they had no hope of gaining the chimney system from the left they retreated by abseil, just as Kellett had been obliged to do nine years earlier. Undaunted, the three climbers moved to the right flank of Carn Dearg Buttress and attacked the rocks at a new point.

The Aberdonians gained the foot of the prominent chimney by a 150-foot traverse from the right, from the grass section above the lower part of Evening Wall. The traverse itself was not without interest, starting with a 40-foot abseil and continuing with a very hard move across an overhanging wall to gain some exposed ledges on the very edge of the buttress. This point was some 100 feet above the ground. A 60-foot Severe traverse then led round to the foot of the chimney.

Patey led up the chimney, coming up hard against a massive chockstone at 40 feet. This rock, he realised, could not be dislodged without wiping out his second. The chockstone moved when touched, unnerving Patey. There was just over an hour of light left, thanks to the earlier manoevrings of the day, so a tactical withdrawal was decided on. The overhang below was so great that their 100-foot abseil rope hung free without reaching the ground, forcing the tired climbers to reverse the last part of their traverse. In the general rush to get off the rocks before night fell three pegs were left behind. To add to the gloom of the party, their first abseil rope remained firmly jammed, though the thrifty trio returned two days later to recover that item.

Before any Scottish party could return to the chimney line on Carn Dearg Buttress the long and wet autumn nights had arrived, to be followed by winter. Scottish climbers then, and until very recently, did next to no rock climbing through the winter, waiting instead until about late April before putting down the axe and taking to rock again.

One impressive day's climbing was the April 1954 outing by Len Lovat and Tom Weir, during which they climbed all three major ridges on the north face of Ben Nevis in winter condition. From their tent in Glen Nevis they made an early start, reaching the CIC Hut before its occupants were up. Their first route was Observatory Ridge. Descending Tower Ridge, they passed a party from Inverness, about half way up the climb. Crossing the foot of Observatory Gully, they went up Slingsby's Chimney and climbed the North-East Buttress, crossing the summit to greet an astonished Inverness party who had just finished their climb.

The ascent of Sassenach in April 1954 came as a bad surprise for Scottish climbers. The successful party was the Mancunian team of Joe Brown and Don Whillans. Joe Brown has been described as the greatest household name in British climbing since Whymper and certainly his productive rock climbing career, often in partnership with Don Whillans, was responsible for advances in techniques and standards during the 1950's. For six winters of that decade Brown and his fellow members of the Manchester-based Rock and Ice Club climbed on Ben Nevis. At this time, Point Five Gully was unclimbed in either summer or winter, Brown joining the select group of climbers who had, or were, attempting it.

At Christmas 1954 Brown visited the Ben with his girlfriend Val. Nat Allen remembers seeing her for the first time on the platform at Fort William. *"Who the hell's that?"* he said to Brown, *"Hi!"* Val said. *"Well, she can't stay in the Hut, its men only"* Allen stated. So Nip Underwood and Allen stayed in the CIC Hut while Val and Joe camped outside for five days until the tent collapsed, forcing them into the hut to join the rest of the party. In fact, while the SMC continues to be all-male, it does not exclude mixed parties from the CIC Hut, which indeed used to have a small corner set aside by a curtain as the 'married quarters'. Allen's misapprehension may have arisen from the situation at Lagangarbh, the SMC hut in Glencoe, where a condition of the original lease excluded mixed parties.

In April 1954 the Rock and Ice were again on Nevis. Brown and Ron Moseley were planning another attempt on Point Five, having gone as far as having Moseley's mother make a two-man bivouac tent out of old barrage balloon material. The tent was to be pitched close to the foot of the gully so as to ensure an early start. The mountain, oblivious to such human follies produced a gale. Point Five Gully was also in uncompromising mood, waves of loose powder snow pouring down its narrow confines. After two days of fruitless gully watching Brown and Moseley gave up. On Saturday, April 17, Brown went over to Carn Dearg Buttress, where Don Whillans was working on a new route.

Donald Desbrow Whillans (1933-1985) would be rated by most climbers as one of the best mountaineers Britain has produced, with ascents of many classic rock climbs in Britain and in the Alps. Later in his bold climbing career he took part in a series of expeditions to the bigger ranges, including Everest and the successful ascent of the South Face of Annapurna in 1970. His name continues to live not only in his routes, but through the Whillans climbing harness and Whillans Box, the latter a metal-framed rectangular tent for expedition work. He died of heart failure in the summer of 1985.

8.3   Joe Brown & Joe 'Morty' Smith, (c.1961)

Whillans had been working on a direct entry to the great chimney system on the buttress, trying to find a way through the steep lower band of rock which defends the chimney. Nat Allen had been his second throughout these attempts. On Good Friday Whillans and Allen had attempted one steep groove then climbed the first pitch before abseiling down. On Saturday they were back on the route with Brown, who suggested an alternative line. Traversing right, Brown came across an old sling, left, thought Whillans, by John Cunningham on an earlier attempt. Whillans joined him at the stance from which they surveyed the next section; a vertical wall leading to a massive overhang. About ten feet up a crack was a smaller overhang, above which was the base of the main roof.

Brown jammed a couple of stones into the crack and using slings on these pulled up to the big roof. A large chockstone loomed out above. Moving slowly, Brown managed to reach this and place a sling on it. Whillans was certain the pitch was now secure, but to his surprise Brown began to retreat, saying he had nearly fallen off, that it was too strenuous. It had taken an incredible amount of strength to thread the sling in freezing conditions. It was growing dark, so they agreed to return next day. Brown thought that the overhang was too strenuous for one man to climb in one go so they decided that Whillans would replace the slings removed by Brown during his retreat.

On the Sunday morning Whillans led direct from the ground to the belay beneath the overhang. Continuing on up to the chockstone, he found that through careful climbing he still had plenty of strength, so Brown suggested that he continue. Whillans later described the crux section.

"I moved out and round the edge of the overhang. Straight away I knew why Joe had said it wouldn't go . . . the only holds were small, slanting grooves leaning awkwardly to the left. I got my right foot jammed in the crack, foot tapping against the chockstone and levered myself so that I could see the rock above. Stretching my right hand, I gripped the top of a V-shaped block. I was just preparing to put my full weight on it, when I felt it move. Like lightning, I jammed my leg even further into the crack. Carefully I tested the block again. It was either that or nothing. I decided it probably wouldn't pull out any further and, before I could have any second thoughts, I put my weight on it. A couple of moves to the left on the sloping holds and the pitch was finished." (1).

The barrier pitch to the chimneys above had finally capitulated. The chimney itself gave 200 feet of classic climbing, followed by grooves for 300 feet. The route had been snatched.

Nat Allen had left the attempt to Brown and Whillans on the Sunday, watching Whillans powering over the roof. Allen then joined up with Don Cowan and climbed The Castle, descending Carn Dearg Buttress to the top of the difficult climbing carrying the nailed boots belonging to the successful pair (who were climbing in pumps). The party then descended No.5 Gully, to be shouted at by George Ritchie who was soloing Jubilee Gully with his weekend sack. The Scottish climbing fraternity, or in reality its West, East and North-East cells, received this ascent as they would a national disaster. "English Bastards!" was the immediate reaction by Ritchie. This unorthodox message of congratulations immediately suggested the route name Sassenach to Whillans and Brown.

Any thoughts the Rock and Ice may have had for celebration were rudely interrupted that evening, when a climber rushed into the encampment with the news that a woman had fallen from the Great Tower and was hanging on the rope. A rescue party set out into the night, formed of Rock and Ice, Creagh Dhu, who were camping nearby, and SMC members from the hut. Brown and Whillans reached the Great Tower from above, and reversing the line of Eastern Traverse reached the tied-off rope to which the victim was attached. The two climbers pulled on the thin, icy rope until their hands were bloody, but it remained firmly fixed. The woman had fallen about 40 feet while climbing the Great Tower and though held by her woman companion, had hit her head during the fall.

Archie Hendry of the SMC and Allen pulled the stretcher up Observatory Gully. Hope, who had been arguing with Hendry all evening about some missing coal had the First-aid sack, so he went on with Cowan and Greenall to join Whillans and Brown. With all five pulling on the rope it remained stubbornly fixed. Although there was little doubt in the climbers' minds that the woman was dead, Brown was lowered down to her. By now it was about 1 a.m. Her rope had frozen to the rock where it made contact, explaining its immobility.

8.4   Don Whillans, Cwm Glas, (1983)

The woman was dead. Even had she survived the head injuries and the cold, the rope would have slowly asphyxiated her; climbing harnesses were a long way in the future and 30 to 40 minute's pressure from a simple waist attachment would kill. The exhausted climbers had risked their own lives on a dangerous rescue attempt. The climbers waiting on the summit plateau were also in danger, from exposure to the biting wind. All were much cheered by the arrival of the RAF Mountain Rescue team just before dawn.

Sassenach set a new pattern in Nevis climbing, being both long, at over 600 feet, as well as difficult and steep — the first of the modern 'classics'. Kellett's ascent of Gardyloo Buttress had been difficult if short, while Bell's Orion Face routes were long but not difficult. The route is now graded as a Hard Very Severe (E2 if climbed free), technically straightforward for the modern top grade of climber, though in nature a grand mountaineering route of character.

The following summer Len Lovat and Tom Patey arrived, armed with a letter from Brown describing the route. The first pitch went easily for Lovat and he brought up Patey to look at the second pitch. Patey's eyes opened wide as he examined the overhangs and realised that he would never be able to hang on, let alone climb the pitch. The two climbers doffed their hats and retreated.

Some of the character of the route may be gleaned from the account of the second ascent on June 13, 1956, by Bob Downes and Mike O'Hara, two very competent climbers of the Cambridge University MC. Downes and O'Hara were wearing PA's by 1956, the rock climbing boots designed by Pierre Allain in France. These enabled another leap in rock climbing standards. Manufactured nuts, or chockstones, were still some years away however, jammed knots or slings being used on Sassenach for protection.

On the crux second pitch noted the Cambridge climbers, some of the rock required delicate handling, while the leftward grooves above the overhang were found to be more technical and strenuous than the roof itself. This pitch occupied the team for four hours.

"The chimney itself is very strenuous, characterised by loose chocks and green slime. The security itself is sufficient, but owing to the width of the chimney it is a mistake to carry a rucksack . . . The pitches above are not easy . . . it's difficult to think of a route which has the character of Sassenach, or its *grande envergure*. Although the hard pitch is only half the length of Cenotaph Corner, to this party at least, it seemed more tiring, more precarious, certainly more baffling than that climb." (2).

In describing their eleven-hour battle on Sassenach, Downes was demonstrating a characteristic modesty, as his remarkable determination had been tested by a prolonged hailstorm during their ascent, causing some delay. Mike O'Hara, later Professor of Geology at Aberystwyth, remembers,

". . . coming off with a whole ledge while leading up to the base of the big chimney, and being stopped on the lip of the overhang. Also a fantastic moment having followed Bob up the first pitch of the chimney, carefully avoiding the huge jammed (loose) flakes and putting my knee onto the jammed boulder stance which Bob had been using — which promptly exited downwards and cleared the loose flakes from the chimney, and swept the whole area. Heard all over the mountain!" (3).

In 1954 then, Sassenach was one of the greatest mountaineering routes in Britain — continuously difficult and strenuous for 600 feet, an Alpine line. Its ascent stunned the Scots; complacency had been revealed. All that could be found elsewhere on Nevis that year was a

Difficult by Malcolm Slesser and party, a short route right of and parallel to the upper part of Glover's Chimney. The Gutter, as it was christened, was climbed in heavy rain. Even that route may have been in part a summer ascent of the winter line taken by Goodeve's party in 1907, on their epic 30-hour travail on Tower Ridge.

As if to add insult to injury, the first new route the following year was by the energetic Cambridge Club, on their second summer visit to Nevis. Downes and O'Hara spent five perfect days in June 1955, camping under the cliffs. Included in the list of routes by the Cambridge team were second ascents of Kellett's Route on Gardyloo Buttress, and Right Hand Route on the Minus Face. New ground was also broken, with the first ascent of North Eastern Grooves, a possibility of which they had first noticed during a visit the previous New Year.

North Eastern Grooves climbs Minus One Buttress — that *"elegant court companion"* to the Orion Face, which it defines on the left. The Buttress starts off as little more than a broad rib, its foot often masked by the last of the winter's snow. It then swells to its maximum breadth at half height before tapering spectacularly to a finish at a giant flake, reluctantly connected to the main mass of the North-East Buttress by a rickety arête.

The original intention of Downes and O'Hara had been to follow a crack line on the buttress, running from bottom right to top left. However, at just over one third height a belt of overhangs crosses the face, forcing the two Cambridge climbers off to the left on the fourth pitch. After an excursion across Minus Two Gully and up by its left edge, a right traverse allowed Minus One Buttress to be regained. The continuation of the lower crack line, in the form of a deep groove, was then followed for a short distance to reach the buttress crest at a spacious terrace. A giant 40-foot flake, the crest of the ridge and the final arête saw the finish of the route, abutting on to the North-East Buttress.

Downes and O'Hara had pioneered the first part of the route on June 17; on June 21 they finished the climb, joined by Eric Langmuir. It was, they admitted, artifical in its upper section, though the climbing was good and the position excellent.

There were two other first ascents in 1955 — both made in the same weekend on a rare visitation by the Creagh Dhu. Perhaps one of the most succinct descriptions of that renowned Glasgow club comes from the pen of Jimmy Marshall, often associated with the Creagh Dhu, though not a member. Writing in a retrospective journal article Marshall describes a youthful summer ascent of Raven's Gully, when he and his friend had been 'taken' by Willie Smith [i.e. taken up, and taken in!]

"... it came to me that we had partaken of the height and depth of experience, but more significantly, had been shown the way and the light by Glasgow's Ullyssean crew, to a new and vital life style waiting to be enjoyed in our Scottish mountains." (4).

It must be left to some other place and time to tell the story of the Creagh Dhu. Suffice it to say that in life they are as large as the legend. One point which must be examined is their neglect of Ben Nevis during the 1950's. Most of the Club could and did have weekends in the Lakes and in Wales, travelling by motor bike. One of their members, Charlie Vigano, has explained this neglect of Nevis.

"The Ben was too far for even a club bus at the week-ends because you had to get back to Glasgow early enough on a Sunday night to allow people who lived out of town to catch their last buses home. This meant leaving Fort William at 5.00 p.m. Motor-bikes in winter were alright occasionally for Glencoe because you made for and left from proper huts. A couple of wasted and wet trips to the Ben would soon kill the urge: it really needed four-wheeled transport." (5).

Had the Creagh Dhu been as active on Ben Nevis during the 1950's as they were in Glencoe, the guidebook would read very differently.

On Saturday August 27, 1955, Zero Gully received its first ascent. The three Creagh Dhu climbers were Willie Smith, G. McIntosh and Mick Noon. Wearing vibrams they soloed the first 200 feet or so before roping up. Then followed 300 to 400 feet of climbing with poor belays. The crux was about half-way up the gully, requiring a run-out of about 140 feet. The route was graded a Hard Severe and had occupied them for three and a half hours.

On the Sunday Noon and McIntosh entered Point Five Gully, switching to nailed boots. This is harder than Zero Gully, summer or winter, and provided eleven pitches of climbing before easing off higher up. The grading of Point Five Gully is Very Severe. Neither gully is likely to receive many summer ascents. Indeed, both gullies had been the object of a winter ascent since at least the 1930's, the only factor preventing a strong attempt on them by MacKenzie and Murray's group being the snow and ice conditions of that decade.

Marshall, who has climbed Point Five in summer, probably making the second ascent, rates it as a good worthwhile climb, though some care has to be taken over the rock, the typical small flakes found in Nevis gullies being on occasion suspect.

The increasing use of the comfortable and light rubber-soled boots with Vibram or Commando soles was being paralled by the number of winter accidents. These were usually caused by a slip on hard snow or ice, or by a loss of control when glissading. It was not yet fully understood, particularly by impecunious young climbers, that vibrams in winter could be lethal unless used in conjunction with crampons. This was in contrast to nailed boots, which in effect carried their own built-in crampons.

In the May 1954 issue of the SMCJ there was published a note by Dr Donald Duff, containing a warning about icy conditions on Ben Nevis and inadequate footwear. This warning was to be highlighted by a shocking accident on December 19 of that year, when five naval cadets lost their lives by sliding off the descent slope towards the Carn Mor Dearg arête, falling on to the rocks of Coire Leis.

A climber reaching the summit plateau of Nevis in winter has three common routes of descent to choose from. If returning to Glen Nevis then the route used is the tourist path. If descending to the Allt a'Mhuilinn then the choice is either via the Carn Mor Dearg arête to the south-east, or by No.3 or No.4 Gully, usually the latter. This gully is just over one mile from the summit as a climber would have to walk, avoiding the cliff edge and the potential threat of cornices above the gullies en route. In bad weather at an altitude of over 4,000 feet, one mile can be an impossible distance to cover, particularly as a south-west gale would be forcing one directly towards the cliffs.

The alternative descent route should a climber reject No.4 Gully lies south-east, down the relatively short slopes to gain the start of the Carn Mor Dearg arête and the head of Coire Leis. This route has two great dangers, however, and its deceptively easy slope has been the site of several tragic accidents, including that of the unfortunate naval cadets mentioned above. In clear weather the descent is a pleasant one with super views over the surrounding hills. In wintry conditions, two factors can combine to make this route a death-trap to the inexperienced or unready.

On either side of the descent is a steep slope; that to the north-east drops 1,250 feet into Coire Leis, that to the south-west drops 1,500 feet to Coire Eoghainn. The descent route receives any sunlight direct. After many cycles of alternate thawing and freezing a particularly hard surface of ice can build up, coating the slope and any projecting boulders with a smooth and dangerous surface. This is the first factor in the equation. The second factor follows from the subtle topography of the descent. In going down from the summit the general direction for the arête is to the south-east, but the plateau leads one in a more easterly direction, towards the finish of the North-East Buttress. If a climber continues to be drawn this way for too long, a deceptive, convex slope will be reached. This leads, imperceptibly at first, into a gently sloping scoop, followed by a slide into the top of a gully and the last drop into Coire Leis.

Lower down the descent slope the angle eases and the descending climber must face in a more southerly direction. A slip here can land one on the boulders of Coire Eoghainn. This necessary change of direction on the descent to the arête complicates the apparently straightforward route. The obvious surface feature near the summit of Ben Nevis in winter is the emergency bivouac shelter a few feet from the summit; built on the ruins of the Observatory and on the spot where the Observatory tower used to stand. This tin shelter is like an ice-box in winter, though it continues to save lives from the crippling effects of the wind.

To find the arête in bad conditions, steer 130 degrees (true) from the shelter for 400 yards, descending meanwhile, then turn east to reach the arête and the head of Coire Leis. From the arête a slightly steeper but uncomplicated slope leads down into the floor of Coire

Leis. Following a fatal accident on Nevis, Dr Duff oversaw the erection of direction posts indicating the safe descent route to the arête. Duff's original pair of three-foot wooden posts were later added to, but only after the terrible accident involving the cadets.

On a more positive note for 1954, Macphee, then President of the SMC, celebrated his completion of all the Munros, his 100th ascent of Ben Nevis, and his 100th night in the CIC Hut. To complete these personal achievements, the new Climbers' Guide to Ben Nevis was published, written by Macphee and containing, as a last-minute addition, descriptions of Sassenach and Fives Wall. The guide book marked a change in format by the SMC in being pocket-sized, in the dimpled cover of red board which was to become a familiar sight on Scottish crags for over twenty years.

Summer climbing in 1956 opened on Nevis on All Fool's Day, with Tom Patey and Jerry Smith climbing the 650-foot Severe Rogue's Rib on the west flank of Tower Ridge. At that early stage in the season, the gully immediately right of the rib, The Italian Climb, was filled with snow and ice. The Aberdonians, climbing in nailed boots, were forced by slabby rock to climb the ice pitch in the gully. They then moved on to the steep and exposed rib which they followed to the upper section. Not long after, Kenneth Bryan and N. Harthill made a complete ascent, climbing the lower rocks in their entirety.

Even better things were to appear during this summer of 1956. Cambridge University M.C. were again up on their post-exam spree. The previous summer Minus One Buttress had been climbed, if somewhat indirectly, by North Eastern Grooves. On June 10 Downes and O'Hara, camping under the stars, were joined by Mike Prestige. O'Hara had been dreaming all winter of a direct route up Minus One Buttress, one which would avoid the left traverse into Minus Two Gully. The next day all three headed for the Minus Face.

Minus One Direct, for the Cambridge students, took a corkscrewing line up the buttress, following the earlier North Eastern Grooves for the first three pitches. On the second pitch they eliminated an aid sling which had been used on the first ascent. The fourth pitch, led by Downes, was the crux. From a large block belay a step right is made on to an exposed rib, jutting out over an overhang. Above is a ledge leading rightward to an undercut groove. The groove requires a committing step up. This leads to another committing move and a third beyond that before difficulties ease off. The rock is perfect, though cracks are blind and handholds scarce.

O'Hara, leading through with Downes, climbed the fine crack above, leading into a regrettable section in the summer looseness of Minus One Gully. A pitch and a half in the gully, climbing up its left corner, then O'Hara traversed left into a cosy if somewhat shattered niche on the buttress. From the niche a fine step left on to the buttress crest is made, where cracked slabs and a small but puzzling overlap lead to the great terrace. This is the reunion with North Eastern Grooves. The giant, 40-foot flake leads on familiar ground to the final, flimsy arête and the North-East Buttress.

8.5   *Alastair Walker on Minus One Direct (June, 1984)*

Since the first ascent of Minus One Direct there have been three variations to the route, two of which have been made inadvertently by parties climbing without guidebooks. The second ascent of the route was probably made by a party from the energetic Cambridge club in 1957, when Mike O'Hara, Ted Maden, David Fagan and Bill Turrall were camped opposite Carn Dearg Buttress. Maden described the three days of perfect weather enjoyed by the party in a Climbers' Club Journal article. (6).

Ten years later, in 1967, the first of the variations was made when Ian Rowe and Peter Macdonald climbed without guidebook. [This was two years before the Marshall guide was published.] At the time they were not fully aware that there were two routes up the buttress, North Eastern Grooves being the original. From the plinth stance at the start of the fourth pitch they moved left as for North Eastern Grooves, realised they were moving off the buttress proper, then made a rising traverse back right above the crux groove, to regain the original line of Minus One Direct below the undercut crack.

In August 1972, five years after the Rowe/Macdonald ascent, Ken Crocket and Ian Fulton made a second variation, again climbing without a guidebook. On this occasion the original line was followed through the crux to the undercut crack. Here it was felt that the

8.6   Alastair Walker on final arete, Minus One Direct, (June, 1984)

crack was leading the climbers off the buttress proper and into the gully, so a rising traverse left was made to regain what was instinctively felt to be the true line of the buttress. Two excellent pitches led to the great terrace and the original finish up the flake and arête.

A later ascent by Crocket in 1976, following the original line with a guidebook, gave a belated realisation of the accidental discovery of the variation climbed in 1972. The variation was named The Serendipity Line, after the Princes of Serendip, characters in a Walpole novel who were always making discoveries of things they were not in search of.

Finally, on August 28, 1983, Noel Williams and Steve Abbot found a variation on the upper part of the route, climbing the first part of The Serendipity Line then breaking out left by a tension move on a peg to climb the Arête Variation, at a grade of VS/HVS. This finishes at the great terrace as for North Eastern Grooves. Whichever variation is taken, or indeed the original line itself, Minus One Direct will give a magnificent day's climbing — through and up an Alpine environment on what many mountaineers would accord to be the best summer route on Ben Nevis.

Three more routes were found on Nevis in the summer of 1956. A Severe on the East Wall of Tower Ridge and two Very Severes on Carn Dearg Buttress. The Severe was Echo

Traverse, by Len Lovat of the SMC and two JMCS members, Ken Bryan (killed in a car accident in Canada in the 1970's) and Norman Harthill. Lovat later went on to write the second Climbers' Guide to Glencoe. Echo Traverse, a neglected route in summer, was later climbed in winter by the Marshall brothers. Its position on an obscure face has contributed to a continued neglect.

The summer of 1956, however, will be remembered for the ascent of a major line on Carn Dearg Buttress. Mike O'Hara recalls how, in August of that year, he was a first-year research student whose work was beginning to fall behind due to too much climbing. He was at that time in the Department of Mineralogy and Petrology in Cambridge, and was in the middle of a big programme of analyses when Bob Downes and Don Whillans called in. They had a motorcycle-sidecar combination with room to spare, but, *"Like a fool I said no . . ."* O'Hara later regretted that decision, because Whillans and Downes went up Nevis to make the first ascent of the major corner line on the buttress on August 30. The line is now known as Centurion. (3).

Centurion had been attempted several times in the past. The first pitch had been climbed by Kellett in June 1944, on which occasion he had come across an old sling 30 to 40 feet up the big corner on pitch two. Jimmy Marshall had made a commendable attempt in 1953. Leading George Ritchie, Marshall attempted to gain the chimney of Sassenach from the left. Failing, as had Kellett, they then turned their eyes on the corner of Centurion. Marshall almost had the crux moves in his hand when demands from his second forced him to retreat.

The first pitch of Centurion takes the small flying buttress, with its deceptive 50-foot wall. A step right then leads into the main feature of the route and one of its hardest pitches, the corner of pitch two. This central corner takes a direct line up Carn Dearg Buttress, midway between Route I and Sassenach. The groove is flanked on its right by smooth overlapping slabs — their appearance brought to mind the battle armour of a Roman centurion.

Whillans, who led seven of the eight pitches (Downes led the masterly seventh pitch), had taken a long time on the second pitch, the groove. This is a fairly open corner, with steep slabs on the right and a vertical left retaining wall. The line follows the crack between the slabs and the wall until one can break left across the wall then up a rib on its outside edge to a ledge vertically above the start.

On the first ascent Whillans had climbed from the belay at the top of the groove up a vicious crack in the left wall, to gain the retaining rib high up. Downes spotted a more subtle horizontal traverse across the vertical wall, gaining the rib lower down. This is the way now followed by parties bent on survival. Above this point the route relents somewhat in angle and difficulty, climbing gradually slabbier rock to cross the traverse line of Route II.

In 1973 Centurion was the scene of a fatal accident. A well-known American climber, Rocky Keeler, was leading the 4th pitch but had strayed on to a direct exit from the diedre, instead of taking the normal way out to the left. He slipped, his single rope cutting on a flake and he fell to his death at the foot of the buttress. His partner, having only a short length of rope, was stranded on the cliff and refused to be lowered, a helicopter dropping a rope to him so as to enable him to abseil to safety. American climbing techniques are based on the use of a single rope, many of their routes having a more straightforward layout than British routes

The final two pitches of Centurion, almost unbelievably, continue the direct line of the route through the huge overhangs above. Downes's contribution to the climb was his masterly route finding on pitch seven, the second crux of the route. This finds its way through the overhangs by a series of jinking traverses on narrow, gangway-like steps, set sideways to the buttress face. One last pitch with (to a tired leader) a strenuous little rib, then the route finishes as abruptly as it begins, at a small ledge.

The ascent of Centurion was a second Sassenach, a national disaster. To make matters worse, the next day Whillans and Downes went out again and climbed The Shield, another Very Severe on the Great Buttress. Above Waterfall Gully, on the north face of the buttress, an enormous flake forms a chimney, the line of the route. On the first ascent on September 1, wet conditions caused the pioneers some difficulty and they gave the route the grade of Very Severe with some misgivings. Both routes however are graded Hard Very Severe in the current guide (7). Less than one year later, in July 1957, Bob Downes was to die from pulmonary oedema during an attempt on Masherbrum.

It was to be three years before outraged Scots could reply with a route of their own on Carn Dearg Buttress, but by 1956 the long-awaited revival of winter climbing on Nevis had begun. In this year we see an inflexion in the curve of Scottish winter ascents. One solitary route and a variation was made during this winter. The route was Neptune Gully, Grade III, on the North Trident Buttress. This was by Arthur Bennet and Jim Clarkson and was the third winter route to be made since Good Friday Climb in 1939 — a period of 17 years. The variation was also on the Trident Buttresses, on March 11, when Ken Bryan and Len Lovat, climbing Central Gully, took the icefall direct. This variation is now graded at III. Hereafter, the curve rose sharply. The revival in winter climbing can be dated precisely to February 1957, as an examination of the record will bear out. In the seventeen winter seasons since 1939 three routes had been recorded. In February 1957 there were five. On the 14th, C.H.C. Brunton and Jim Clarkson recorded a Grade III on Cousins' Buttress, climbing the Ordinary Route. Much of this had been previously climbed by Macphee, Todd and Williams in April 1935 under thaw conditions, probably the reason why Macphee chose not to record the ascent. (8).

Two days later, on February 16, the first route was recorded on the South-East face of the North-East Buttress, overlooking the Carn Mor Dearg arête above Coire Leis. The Cresta Climb, Grade III, was climbed by Tom Patey, Len Lovat and Graham Nicol. It followed a line on this alpine-style face first suggested by Bill Murray, who had reconnoitred this area in the winter of 1947. Like the potentially dangerous slopes above, this face receives any sunlight going and readily builds up ice, particularly on the left section of the face.

The main feature of The Cresta Climb is a shallow couloir about 600 feet long, beginning above and left of a 300-foot rock spur. The couloir leads to the exit cliffs, which include a prominent and steep ice pitch. This pitch was avoided by the first ascent party who traversed right beneath it to break out on to easier ground. The Little Brenva Face, as it is now known, can be climbed virtually anywhere, and though later routes have been recorded, there seems little point in having more than about three recorded routes on this pleasantly sunny area of Ben Nevis.

The mountain was in superb condition that week in February 1957, and those who were staying at the hut made the most of it. On the 18th Slesser and Norman Tennent made the second ascent of The Cresta Climb, finishing by a slightly more direct line through the exit cliffs. Also that day, Lovat and Donald Bennet climbed No.3 Gully Buttress, a highly popular Grade III in later years and a route recommended for its relatively secure but nonetheless exciting positions. As elsewhere on the mountain, good snow-ice made step cutting a delight. But the plum of the day, the week, and the year, was the ascent of the much-sought after Zero Gully.

The news of good conditions had attracted some of the best Scottish climbers from both ends of the country, principally from Glasgow and Aberdeen. The main attraction was Point Five Gully, with Zero a close second. These two gullies were, in effect, the great problem routes of the post-war years. Of the two, Point Five looked to be technically the harder. In addition to their obvious steepness and length, a major stumbling block to an ascent of either gully was spindrift. Even in a day of complete calm, both gullies could be rendered unclimbable by reason of vast icy waves of fine snow pouring down their narrow confines.

That weekend a dozen good climbers had gathered at the hut. From Aberdeen Patey and Nicol had arrived, followed the next day by climbers from the Glasgow area, including Slesser, Bennet, Douglas Scott and Tennent. On the 16th a strong south-west wind was shifting snow down the major gullies, forcing Lovat, Patey and Nicol on to the The Cresta Climb. The other four took to the North-East Buttress. The events that followed were chronicled by the late Tom Patey, in a long and interesting journal article.

When Patey's party returned to the CIC Hut they found visitors,

"two climbers, whose characteristic patois, coupled with a distinct air of authority, stamped them as members of the Creagh Dhu Club."

The two were John Cunningham and Mick Noon, who announced that they intended to climb Zero Gully the next day, much to the discomfiture of Patey and his friends. Shortly afterwards another character entered stage left, as Hamish MacInnes burst into the hut. On

8.7 John Cunningham, (Feb., 1957)

hearing of the competition building up for Zero Gully he had set off from Steall Hut in Glen Nevis to cross the Carn Mor Dearg arête.

"It was impossible", continued Patey,
"to remain indifferent towards such a man: his appearance alone invited controversy. A great rent extending the whole length of one trouser leg had been repaired unsuccessfully with string. In his hand was the famous all-steel hammer-pick, named affectionately by the club 'The Message'".

MacInnes immediately settled the terms with Cunningham; these two, along with Noon, would attempt Zero the next day. Meanwhile, in the small hours of the morning, just as a reluctant search party was beginning to organise itself, the foursome from the North-East Buttress staggered in, *"mumbling excuses about 'Two feet of ice on the Man Trap'"*. The next day MacInnes and the two Creagh Dhu climbers were defeated by avalanches and deteriorating weather. Cunningham and Noon decided to return to Glasgow that night.

8.8   Tom Patey, (Feb., 1957)

8.9   Hamish MacInnes, (Feb., 1957)

Suddenly the die was cast — MacInnes teamed up with Patey and Nicol and an early rise was fixed for the next morning. The gully, to judge from Cunningham's distress, was in excellent condition, apart from spindrift. All that was required now was good weather.

Zero Gully, by 1957, had been attempted several times. On March 15, 1951, two students from Oxford University MC had a narrow escape. Hamish Nicol and Arthur Rawlinson were near the top of the difficult section when the leader fell, ripping out several ice pegs and pulling his second down with him. Through great fortune both survived the 400-foot fall. Hamish Nicol admitted that the traditional rivalry between the two University Clubs, Oxford and Cambridge, was uppermost in his mind. He was utterly determined to beat Cambridge to an ascent of the gully.

Early in the morning Patey, MacInnes and Graham Nicol gathered at the foot of Zero. The steep gully was in perfect condition — surfaced with snow ice, that magic material intermediate in consistency between snow and water ice which can be carved, cut or moulded and which, when present, allows virtually any route to be climbed. A shallow trough ran up and left for 100 feet to below an overhang. A line of steps ended abruptly at a height of 20 feet, the point at which Cunningham had been hit by a warning rattle of ice, recommending a retreat.

Patey set off up the first pitch, climbing in nails.

"I straddled the side walls of the trough, unable to resist a morbid satisfaction in noting that the rope hung absolutely free from my waist to the two at the bottom. They seemed strangely remote and not very interested in my progress, though Hamish would occasionally stir himself to shout 'Straight on up' whenever I stopped for a rest."

Patey gained a small stance at a piece of nylon cord sticking out of the snow. This marked a previous attempt by MacInnes (his sixth!) and Bob Hope, the cord being attached to Hope's frozen-in ice axe which had been used as an abseil point on their retreat the previous month.

The second pitch lay up the overhang, which Patey climbed using tension from inserted ice pegs. Present day climbers use ice screws or drive-ins, but these were unknown in the mid 1950's and quite often the long poker belonging to the hut stove was seen to grace an ice pitch for protection. The technique used by Patey — a rather delicate one in winter — was to rely on rope tension through an ice peg placed as high as possible until the next few holds had been cut. The next peg was placed higher still while hanging on with one hand, and when that was in place tension was taken from that and the lower peg removed to be used again later. The long, flat ice pegs then in use (they were to be seen as late as 1970) had virtually no holding power if pulled in an outward direction.

Above the overhang Patey belayed to a driven-in ice axe, unable to excavate MacInnes's buried ice peg, another souvenir of the MacInnes-Hope retreat during a snow-storm. Thus far, the three climbers had taken less than two hours. The route now led rightward towards the gully proper, taking an exposed traverse between two overhangs. At the end of the traverse Patey stepped round an edge into the gully chute, to gaze up at a gigantic ice pitch rearing up ahead. Patey and Nicol belayed below the steep ice wall and brought up MacInnes for a shot at the lead.

"In went the first ice-piton, and with a violent heave Hamish got a crampon level with where his nose had been. The only indication of his passage was a large bucket hold every 6 feet. The urgency of his climbing indicated that this pitch was to be a vindication of the use of crampons for the benefit of the tricouni-favouring Aberdonians . . . More and more snow came down as the minutes ticked past. Hamish was now out of sight, and we wondered if he was tunnelling the overhang. Every now and then we heard a gasp, 'Thank God for a piton,' but that was all. Two hours elapsed before the signal came to follow on."

The way was now clear to the final cornice. The party, as Patey commented,

". . . moved together, the pace of the party (contrary to the textbook) dictated by the fastest member. Nicol was the most exhausted; he carried the pitons."

Five hours after entering the gully they collapsed on the plateau rim in a triumphant heap. Zero Gully had been climbed. (9).

Outwith the spate of routes made from the CIC Hut that February was one other climb, an ascent by two JMCS members of the Staircase Climb on the rocks flanking Waterfall Gully. Staircase Climb is now graded at IV and though now a neglected route, when in condition would no doubt provide a very technical ascent. The two JMCS members were Dougal Haston and James Stenhouse, both of whom would return again to make their mark on Nevis, in the august company of Jimmy Marshall.

The state of Scottish climbing in 1957 was somewhat bitterly summed up by the streetwise Haston in a later autobiography.

"Scottish climbing was a mess of mediocrity and pettiness. It was full of mountaineers who considered their average talents to be exceptional. The main things in their lives seemed to be club rules, correct committee meetings and good etiquette in huts. These things are fine but climbing should have a place somewhere." (10).

Haston continued to state that arrogant and uncouth as he and his companions were, their climbing ideals were unimpeachable; they wanted only to climb as hard and as well as they could to advance the state of Scottish climbing. In his own brilliant fashion, Haston certainly went on to make history on higher hills, before his death in a lone skiing accident in 1977. To balance his own view, it must be said here that with the exception of one or two individuals, Haston was not popular when a youth. He went out of his way, several contemporaries recall, to offend many decent people. Following an unfortunate motoring accident in Glencoe, which resulted in the death of a hillwalker, Haston left Scotland to live in Switzerland. Here he became Director of the International School of Mountaineering, going on to make several great ascents in the bigger mountain ranges of the world, including Everest, the hard way.

In 1957 Haston met Marshall and, later in the year, Robin Smith. Marshall had joined the SMC in September 1955, his proposer Dick Brown describing him in a covering letter as a *"very competent* mountaineer." (11). In a letter supporting Marshall's application, Len Lovat described him in terms which suggested that the spirit of Raeburn had risen again. Marshall's winter climbing career had begun shortly after his rock climbing with Central Gully on Bidean in December 1949. By December 1952 he was climbing Crowberry Ridge Direct on the Buachaille. At the time he joined he was a 26-year old architect who, according to Haston, recognised the poor state of Scottish climbing, and in Haston, Smith *et al* saw the chance of better days to come. Glencoe and Ben Nevis were to be their proving grounds and, ultimately, the salvation of Scottish climbing.

The increase in the number of new climbs being recorded on Nevis continued in 1958. Of a total of thirteen routes that year, ten were due to one man, a 21-year old native of Bradford called Ian Stewart Clough (1937-1970). National Service with the RAF took him to Scotland, where his love of climbing led to Kinloss and the Mountain Rescue. At this time too he was a pupil on a Mountaineering Association winter course with Hamish MacInnes. Although he was to be heavily criticised for the style of several of his early Scottish ascents, he also came to be accepted by those who knew him as one of the kindest and least selfish characters in the climbing world.

Haston, who in his later years was to enjoy several fine routes with Clough, recollected that in the late 1950's.

"We also didn't have very much time for the routes he [Clough] was doing in winter on Nevis. Later, we found out that they were usually fine and not difficult lines, but at that time we were very intolerant and also suspicious of any Englishman who thought he could climb ice."

At that time, continued Haston, it was genuinely believed that only Scotsmen could climb ice.

The first route of 1958 was a January ascent of The Italian Climb, Grade III, by Jimmy Marshall, A. McCorquodale and George Ritchie. This is the deeply cut gully on the west flank of Tower Ridge, first recorded in summer by Kellett. Starting as a narrow gully, the upper section fans out to the right, where snow slopes lead to the crest of Tower Ridge under the Little Tower. A steep ice pitch which forms low down on the right wall of the gully was first recorded by Steve Belk and Ian Fulton, who rejoined the original line higher up.

The Italian Climb was the scene of a tragic accident in January 1970, when three experienced climbers were swept to their deaths by a slab avalanche from above. By one of those chances of fate the fourth member of the party survived. John Grieve, a teacher from Kinlochleven and an active member of the Glencoe Rescue Team, had set out to do the route with Jim McArtney, Fergus Mitchell, and Mary Ann Hudson. Above the steep lower section Grieve, last on the rope, found his rope badly snagged and released it from his karabiner to shake it free. At that point a huge slab avalanche was triggered, probably by one of the leading climbers and the rope was pulled out of Grieve's hands, leaving him trapped on a ledge.

Twelve years later Grieve described the accident in an SMC Journal article, written about mountain rescue in general.

"When I returned from The Italian Climb the sole survivor of a rope of four, victims of one of Nevis's murderous avalanches, I was summoned to the Police Office in Kinlochleven and suffered an intense grilling lasting for hours by two detectives . . . They asked the same, to me stupid, questions time after time. I now know that Tom Patey, highly distraught with the death of Jim McArtney, contacted the Procurator Fiscal at Fort William and suggested that more than a simple accident had taken place. Tom could not accept that I had survived and Jim had not stomach was witnessing my return to the CIC hut in what . . . might have been construed as good spirits." John Grieve was in fact, in his own worlds, "bloody well glad to be alive." (12).

But, to return to climbs made that year, one was another of Marshall's, the Grade III Number 2 Gully Buttress, with Lovat and Hendry on March 23. In addition there were five easy winter routes by Clough and his friends, while in April Clough found a rising line up the Little Brenva Face of the North-East Buttress with his ascent of Frostbite at Grade III. On this ascent the five climbers found great difficulty in overcoming the dreaded Man-Trap, attempting to climb the seemingly innocuous 12-foot nose of rock by forming a human pyramid.

As if to remind climbers of the narrow safety margins involved in winter climbing, Zero Gully was the scene of a triple fatality on April 9, when three experienced alpinists attempted the gully in poor conditions. They had no ice pitons and were belaying on ice axes. The outcome when the leader fell from the third pitch was inevitable, the two ice axes snapping like matchsticks and all three falling to their death.

Clough returned to Nevis in the summer, making three first summer ascents of gullies. Comb Gully with John Alexander at the end of June, Minus One Gully and Green Gully with Don Pipes on July 5 and 6 respectively. Green Gully had defeated several notable climbers in the past, mainly due to the appalling quality of the rock. Minus One Gully had two short sections requiring the use of aid by Clough, and is still graded at Very Severe.

The last ascent in 1958 was that on September 14, when Haston and Stenhouse made the third ascent of Kellett's Route on Gardyloo Buttress, making a Severe variation in the upper section by following the left rib of the final gully. Haston had just recovered from a motorcycle accident in which he had broken an arm and was shortly to show his promise as a climber. Other climbers too, were ready and waiting for Ben Nevis to come into condition. The next four years were to be remembered by later generations of climbers as perhaps the most inspiring period of climbing that Nevis, and Scotland, has seen.

9.1 Carn Mor Dearg Arête (c.1970)

THE PINNACLE (1959-1960)

Zero Gully had finally received a winter ascent, in February 1957. Remaining still was Point Five Gully as the great winter plum on Nevis, its terrible icy cleft soaring up for a thousand feet between Observatory Buttress and Observatory Ridge. As with Zero Gully, there had been several determined attempts on the gully, some of the suitors being violently repulsed. On January 25, 1956, a Rock and Ice party left the CIC Hut bound for Point Five. The party consisted of Joe Brown, Nat Allen and Nip Underwood. They were confident following a straightforward ascent of Green Gully — a much more benign route under average conditions.

Brown noticed that the rocks were but thinly covered in ice. In addition, the ice was showing different layers. After leading the first pitch he brought up Allen who tied on to two ice pegs, while Underwood remained belayed to a rock spike at the foot of the gully. In retrospect, this probably saved the party from annihilation. The second pitch reared up for 50 feet above Brown's head, culminating in the inevitable bulge. Moving up 30 feet or so to the bulge, Brown banged in two ice pegs for protection and was making another move upwards when the front of the ice bulge fell away, throwing him backwards into space.

Brown hit the ice below Allen and bounced out of the gully, pulling Allen and his two ice pegs out after him. The two fell some 50 feet apart, rebounding out of a hole in the snow at the foot of the gully, Allen badly tearing some leg ligaments. Finally Underwood, with his good spike belay, brought Allen to a halt, Brown then jerking to rest in a tangle of rope. Some strange noises from Brown warned of impending asphyxiation from coils of rope round his neck, but Allen freed him in time. Only Allen was injured, the three shaken climbers making a laborious self-rescue down to the Hut and then to the road.

Certain types of ice — particularly water ice which usually forms from freely running water, as opposed to snow ice which forms from the repeated thawing and re-freezing of snow — show an unsettling and potentially dangerous feature on being struck, known to climbers as 'dinner-plating'. This is a fracturing named after the roughly dinner-plate sized fragments of ice which break off. The old-style ice pegs which were all that was available during the 1950's were particularly liable to cause plating as they were hammered straight into the unyielding and brittle ice. Even modern tubular ice screws can be unusable with some ice, a climber then being in a potentially serious position with little or no protection.

Patey also attempted Point Five, climbing the first pitch in February 1957 before being defeated by spindrift. One month later Noon and Cunningham made the first 180 feet before terrible ice forced a withdrawal. Another contestant for this gully was MacInnes, who went so far as to descend the top 500 feet of the gully on a long length of light-weight nylon, anchored to an ice axe, before climbing back up again. At Easter 1958 Ian Clough met up with MacInnes at the CIC Hut, intent on an ascent of Point Five.

MacInnes had 'The Message', his heavy-weight ice hammer, as he and Clough started up the gully. Clough found the first pitch to be rock slabs coated with water ice, thinning with height. After 25 feet he retreated and allowed MacInnes into the lead. Five hours later a stance was reached, with no belay. The steady beat of MacInnes's hammer then signalled the drilling of a bolt belay. Secured with the bolt, the pair descended, leaving in place a rope.

Clough and MacInnes returned to Point Five the following day, climbing back up the fixed rope. MacInnes was suffering, not too surprisingly, from wrist-ache, and Clough took the lead above the bolt. The ice was poor and the climbers were sorely troubled by spindrift avalanches. Later in the day they were joined by Patey, who had been watching from the CIC Hut. At one point Patey thought they had been avalanched out of the gully, as the two climbers disappeared under clouds of freezing spindrift. The attack on the gully fizzled out shortly after, to be followed by a thaw and the end of winter.

The first month of 1959 saw eight new routes on Nevis, though they took a total of thirteen days climbing. Up at the CIC Hut again, "suffering from a post-Hogmany haze and a slight unsteadiness", were Ian Clough and three friends; John Alexander and Don Pipes, both ex-Kinloss Mountain Rescue Team members, and Robin Shaw of Glasgow University MC.

Three easy routes were climbed during the first week, including Slalom at Grade III, on the Little Brenva Face. On January 7 and 8 an ascent of Waterfall Gully was made, climbing the icy pitch at the start over two days. This use of 'siege tactics', with fixed ropes, was to involve Clough in a certain amount of controversy. To be fair, Clough was to develop into a very competent mountaineer, with successful ascents in the Alps and Himalaya.

The most controversial ascent by Clough was, however, to follow shortly — his sieged ascent of the much sought-after Point Five Gully. The ascent is well-described, both by Clough himself and by Robin Shaw, the climb taking place the week after the ascent of Waterfall Gully. The style in which the two gullies were climbed, depending on aid climbing almost to the exclusion of free climbing, was to lead to Clough's application to join the SMC being rejected that year.

On Monday, January 12, Clough, Alexander, Pipes and Shaw found themselves with heavily laden sacks at the foot of Point Five. For a hundred feet a slab reared up, covered with thin ice with the occasional bulge of snow ice. Shaw described the start of the siege, writing in a University magazine (1).

"We hesitated. 'Aw c'mon', I said hopefully, 'Let's have a bash at it', quickly tying myself on to the middle of the rope with a 'Blow you, Jack' expression. There was a scramble towards the rear but poor Dangle was not quick enough and soon found himself tied firmly on to the 300 feet of doubled three-quarter wt. rope, presented with 'Thor' our modified brickies hammer and a large bundle of ice and rock pegs, and pushed towards the pitch . . . Three hours later Dangle was up two thirds of the pitch and found himself a good peg crack."

Clough then descended, having fixed the rope, to join the rest in tea and sandwiches, Pipes having brought up refreshments from the Hut. Alexander then took a turn and two hours later, as darkness was falling, the bolts placed by MacInnes the previous year were gained at the top of the first pitch. The party then retired to the Hut leaving a rope hanging down the pitch and the remainder of their gear at the foot of the route.

Clough described the second pitch on the Tuesday.

"John climbed the rope and brought me up. While I was having a rest after working on the second pitch for about an hour, John brought up Robin so that he could watch the proceedings. Robin Shaw's appearance was unusual; his climbing outfit seemed to consist of rags held together by no one knew how. This, with his black beard and tousled hair, gave him a Robinson Crusoeish touch." (2).

Clough continued working on the second pitch, spotting a peg high up on the left and another peg under the ice on the right.

"Soon I was standing on an étrier hanging from this peg and knocking in a further rock-peg . . . Next I used an étrier hanging from an ice-peg and, with another ice-peg for a hand-hold, I was over the crux. Another 25 feet up I found a place for a stance . . . Another day's work was at an end."

Pipes, meanwhile, had gone down the mountain and returned with yet more equipment, brought up from the party's base at Cameron's Barn. They now had some 900 feet of rope and about 60 assorted rock and ice pegs. They decided to operate the 'climbing' in a shift system. The next day climbing was impossible due to continuous spindrift and a temporary halt to the climbing was called. Shaw decided that as natural belays and good peg cracks were scarce, a visit to the local blacksmith was in order, to see to the manufacture of some bolts and brackets.

"Two hours later I was in Fort Bill only to discover that the nearest blacksmith was 60 miles away. I was about to return to the hut when I remembered that Dangle knew a mechanic called Sammy in one of the garages. After a bit of a search I found him (a stocky, jovial chap) who devoted the rest of the afternoon to finding out exactly what I wanted and making it, occasionally mumbling. 'Och, it's lucky fur you the boss is no' in.'"

Thursday morning saw Pipes and Shaw trudging up to the gully again on a beautiful clear day. It was to take them three hours of strenuous wrestling with the fixed ropes before they stood at the foot of pitch three. Pipes then spent an icy three and a half hours at his stance while Shaw nibbled away at the next section.

"Robin's crampons were not very good ones and, at first, it was with mixed feelings of amusement and anxiety that Don watched his partner's crampon points curl up as he climbed steps in the ice . . . The climbing was very difficult, although an ice peg or two could be kept above the leader all the while; and at the end of the day only another 30 feet had been forced."

Friday dawned clear and cold, as the next 'shift' of Clough and Alexander left for the gully. After a further seven hours' work they had reached the foot of what was their pitch six, the cave pitch. There they inserted an expansion bolt before sliding back down the ropes in the twilight. They were below the last major pitch in summer conditions — a steep wall of about 80 feet.

At 7 a.m. on Saturday morning, Pipes and Shaw left the CIC Hut. By 1.30 p.m., when Clough and Alexander had gained the top of pitch four, Pipes was already half-way up the steep ice of the cave pitch. This is generally reckoned to be the hardest pitch in Point Five Gully, consisting of a bottle-shaped chimney, narrowing to the inevitable bulge at the top. Pipes took three hours to lead this last difficult pitch, and by the time all four were over it night was falling. The last 600 feet or so involved one small steep pitch and a strenuous ice chimney before the route ended abruptly on the summit rim, gained by Clough's party at 10 p.m.

The first, and controversial ascent of Point Five Gully in winter had taken in 29 hours of actual upward climbing. There had been about 40 hours of work in total in the gully, spread out over a six day period.

"Had we chosen to climb the gully without retreating each day," wrote Shaw, "this would have meant at least three bivouacs. We preferred to have our 'bivouacs' at the CIC Hut, considering it ridiculous to bivouac, for instance, at the top of pitch one."

Shaw concluded this argument with the comment that,

9.2   FWA Point Five Gully (Jan., 1959)

"I have to doubt that Point Five will be climbed in less time, but a party will have to be very lucky to find it in suitable condition to climb in one day."

In September 1959 Ian Clough applied to join the SMC, proposed by Tom Patey and seconded by Jim Bell. Clough was then 22 and had been climbing for over four years. His list of ascents, including two seasons in the Alps, would normally have justified his qualifying and an SMC committee today would have no dissenting voices, yet he was turned down. In 1962 he reapplied and gained admittance. By then Robin Smith had been killed in the Pamirs and as a letter from Clough to his proposer Patey shows, it seems that Clough felt that Smith, who was on the committe in 1959, may have let his nationalistic feelings weigh against the application.

Clough wrote on hearing of Smith's fall,

"The Pamirs accident came as a great shock — I was very upset to hear of Robin's death. I wasn't at all bitter with him personally for trying to black-ball me since that was typically Robin — intensely nationalistic. Although he always seemed to regard me as a rival (why I don't know because I could never climb at anything like his standard) we always seemed to get on very well . . . Terry Sullivan told me . . . that he had spoken with Robin about bombing me out of the club and Robin excused himself by saying he was pissed at the time and having a big hate session against all Englishmen. I think this was probably true — it was a case of nationalism rather than a personal grudge." (3).

One of the reasons put forward in explanation for Clough being refused was his status as a mountaineering instructor. When he successfully joined in 1962 he was a student teacher. There is some validity in this, the SMC do not, on the whole, like professionals in their ranks. The major reason for Clough's initial rejection was the style in which several of Clough's first ascents were done. Point Five Gully and Titan's Wall were viewed by the committee as serious erosions of the contemporary ethic that *'pegs shouldn't replace skill or supplement a blatant lack of same.'* It was felt that as Clough and his companions could not have climbed these routes without recourse to much aid, the whole affair was in bad taste. To end this on a more positive note, Smith was not 'pissed' at the time, nor overly nationalistic. He was, however, obsessive about bringing Scottish rock climbing standards up to the levels of those in England.

A route of a very different nature from Point Five Gully had opened the year's climbing on January 1, 1959, when Robin Smith and Dick Holt did the first winter ascent of the Tower Face of The Comb. This superb buttress dominates the centre of Coire na Ciste, with its wedge-shaped cockscomb challenging the eye. The face looking to Tower Ridge had first been climbed by Ogilvy in 1940, giving a loose Very Difficult. In summer much of the climbable rock here is dangerously shattered. In a ten-hour day, Smith and Holt managed to fight their way up this puzzling face. A good part of their climb must have been done in the dark, as neither climber was renowned for speed.

The Tower Face of The Comb, not surprisingly graded at V, has frightened off several of the leading climbers ever since, and a second ascent has not been confirmed to date. Smith and Holt did not even find it easy going on the buttress crest, as deep powder snow and the elements gave them much trouble.

Another Smith-Holt ascent that January was the first winter ascent of the Orion Face. Smith had been wanting to climb this for some time, following the line of The Long Climb. The two considered the expedition so important that they decided to go north by rail. Somewhat inevitably they missed the train, arriving in Fort William 15 hours behind their planned schedule. At the CIC Hut that Saturday evening they found Clough's party in residence and immediately regarded them as rivals for their route. Holt's article on the ascent described the scene in the hut that night.

"Robin kept up a cheerful but wary demeanour and hatched plots. To allay any fears which the opposition might have they retired early, meaning realistically, and arising just after three secured a strategic advantage. The enemy was so bewildered by these tactics that he supposed a complex double bluff and went back to sleep. Our heroes were able to creep out into the night at half past four — the earliest start that Robin had been known to make in Scotland."

An hour later at half past five, shivering in the pre-dawn gloom, Smith and Holt started climbing, running into difficulties almost immediately on the steep lower rocks below the First Slab Rib. Smith was forced to insert a poor peg on which he made a semi-tension traverse. This allowed a steep smooth rib to be turned and relatively easier ground gained at the full extent of their 150-foot rope.

The second pitch was little easier, with Smith attempting to gain the slabs of the summer route.

". . . Robin had edged along a sloping ledge beneath a steep wall on the right which formed another rib, beyond which were the slabs of the summer route. A 'good' runner was eventually found and following this with a moderate piton he felt sufficiently secure to announce that he would probably fall and to mind the rope. Dick, out of sight, then experienced several intermittent tugs followed by a huge jerk . . ."

Smith had not fallen, though by drawing in the rope tightly Holt almost caused this to happen. The rope ran out when Smith was 30 feet short of the Slab Rib and Holt moved up to the first runner, allowing the leader to reach the corner left of the Rib. The next pitch turned out to be the crux of the day. The obvious way was up the corner for 60 feet, after which the finish was problematic. There was a choice between the crack in the back of the corner or the flanking wall of the Slab Rib. The crack was of knee width, overhanging near the top, while the wall was very steep but with parallel cracks.

The parallel cracks proved to be the only possible way up this section, Smith moving up the wall with wide bridging in crampons and no protection. The hardest climbing was now

9.3   FWA Raeburn's Buttress, (Jan., 1959)

past as Holt led through into the Basin. It was 3.20 p.m. with clouds gathering and the light soon to fade. At this point an escape rightward into Zero Gully was considered but rejected, the climbers deciding instead to make for the North-East Buttress by any feasible route.

On gaining a shelf below the Second Slab Rib they decided that Epsilon Chimney, a possible exit route, had been bypassed. Daylight was now going fast but Smith and Holt continued to climb upwards, finding a series of ledges which led eventually to the crest of the buttress. There remained the Man-Trap.

"Robin, removing a crampon as a gesture, stood on Dick's shoulder, took off, then after a delay, set off back down the face, accelerating under gravity, to land on a large snow padded boulder . . . The Man Trap was avoided.

As the shelf below the last tower was reached the clouds rolled back to coat the tower in gleaming white armour, and, as they moved up this together Orion himself looked down. A fitting finish to a fine climb." (4).

From Holt's description of this ascent it would seem that their route continued above the V-traverse somewhere, perhaps even up Epsilon Chimney by a happy error. On such a vast and confusing face with darkness approaching it is remarkably easy to lose one's bearings. On the rare repeats of the Smith-Holt line difficulties have been found to be high, with the lower section probably containing harder climbing than anything on the Direct Route, which was climbed the following year.

Clough returned to Nevis at the end of January, two weeks after his controversial ascent of Point Five Gully. On January 28 he climbed Central Gully, Grade III, on Creag Coire na Ciste, with John Alexander. This is a route often in condition and though short, at about 450 feet, it can be interesting, particularly if climbed by the right hand of two chimneys. This harder variation was climbed by Ian MacEacheran and Jock Knight a few years later and if followed in icy conditions the climb overall will be a Grade IV.

The following weekend saw the SMC on the hill in strength and four new routes. On Saturday 31, two ropes from Aberdeen climbed Raeburn's Buttress. Ronnie Sellers and Jerry Smith climbed the bottom chimneys of the buttress then finished up Intermediate Gully, the gully to the left of the upper part of the buttress. Following behind this pair, Bill Brooker and Mike Taylor broke out right and finished up the arête of the buttress, plain sailing in nailed boots, taking three and a half hours in all. Raeburn's Buttress is usually reckoned a hard Grade IV by those climbing it today. The deciding factor is probably the short but very steep wall out of the cave belay. If insufficiently iced this can prove impossible.

Elsewhere on Nevis that day the formidable if oddly matched rope of Marshall and Patey was in action. Oddly matched because true to Aberdonian conservatism Patey was climbing in nails, while Marshall was crampon-clad. The route they had chosen was the Girdle of the North Face, following in part Bell's route of 1941. Starting from Observatory Gully below Gardyloo Gully, Patey and Marshall followed the snow ledges running out leftward below Good Friday Climb. These led to Point Five Gully above the steep lower section of that route, the crossing of which proved to be the most awkward part of the day's climbing.

After crossing Point Five, thin bands of ice leading to Observatory Ridge forced a diagonal abseil. The upper part of the Basin was the next objective, gained below the Second Slab Rib and from the Basin the easy shelf leading up to North-East Buttress followed by a spiral finish round Coire Leis completed their short, five-hour crab-crawl. The steps left by Smith and Holt a month previous were still visible.

The snow was just as hard on the Sunday as Sellers and Jerry Smith climbed the Grade IV Pinnacle Arête on the South Trident Buttress. Missing out the initial lower section, snow and ice grooves immediately right of the crest led to the easier arête above the middle section, the arête providing particularly delightful climbing. But the route of the weekend and perhaps the best known to present-day climbers was found on the West Face of Observatory Ridge by Marshall, Patey and Brooker. Hadrian's Wall, as climbed by this strong trio, followed approximately the line of a Kellett summer route, the West Face, Lower Route. The climb was Patey's idea, though the original intention was to climb by what is now the icefall of Hadrian's

9.4   Tom Patey, FWA The Girdle, (Jan., 1959)

Direct. The lack of continuous ice on this enforced a start further left. Also Patey's idea was to have been the route's name — .25!

The Aberdonians were in nailed boots, with Marshall again in crampons. On the fifth pitch, crossing thinly iced slabs, Marshall was obliged to use a peg, making a diagonal abseil to gain easier ground. Brooker, in his habitual position as third man, stood back and enjoyed watching the competition between Patey and Marshall, Aberdeen versus Edinburgh, North versus South, nails versus crampons. When Brooker himself followed the thin traverse he found no need for the peg but then, as he admitted later, *"it's easy if you're third on the rope."* Marshall and Patey were of course leading through on their ascent of Hadrian's Wall. At one point Marshall, who had earlier lost a peg through Patey, banged in to the hilt one of Patey's favourite pegs, a very long ring peg. It's rusty shards are probably there today.

Twelve years later, at Easter 1971, the prominent icefall to the right of the original Hadrian's Wall was climbed by Mike Geddes and Graham Little. Hadrian's Wall Direct, Grade V, is now the line followed by climbers, it being especially suited to front-pointing techniques. The icefall gives two pitches at a fairly high angle before leading up to a small snow-field below the ice chimney, a landmark on the route.

9.5   Tom Patey, FWA The Girdle, (Jan., 1959)

The original Hadrian's Wall is perhaps little easier than the Direct, though of a different nature. It received its second ascent on March 12, 1972 by Ken Crocket and Colin Stead. The ascent was described in a later SMC Journal article, from which the following excerpts paint a little of the atmosphere found on a fairly major step-cutting expedition, as the two Glaswegians had not yet converted to the newly-arrived front-pointing. Crocket led the first pitch and Stead the second, taking the right-hand of two possible grooves. Crocket set off up the third pitch, cutting steps with his single axe.

"The third pitch looked thin, with poorly covered slabs which had to be overcome, but adrenalin was trickling now and we were rarin' to go. Colin wanted me to traverse left, but I put my faith on a narrow tongue of snow-ice which had been caught by surprise and clamped frozen to the slab. On both sides of this tongue decaying molars of dark rock leered through thin snow, while at the top of the slab gaped a hungry chimney . . . Progress up the slab was delicate and with relief I entered the chimney, only to find it full of useless, fluffy snow. Sheathing my old axe I swam and bridged my way up . . . ''

9.6   Tom Patey, FWA Hadrian's Wall, (Feb., 1959)

This little chimney was at the right end of the slabby section. After they had completed the climb, the pair realised that by taking the lower section more directly they had missed out the slab traverse and the diagonal traverse of Marshall completely. The chimney led to a snowfield and the foot of the ice chimney referred to by the original party. The Direct route also leads to this ice chimney. Approaching the chimney, with Stead belayed at its foot, Crocket noticed something ominous.

"Every few seconds he would curl himself up as a silken ribbon of spindrift rushed invisibly down the chimney to explode with an angry hiss at the bottom. The entire upper basin and much of the ridge above was funnelling loose snow down through the narrows of the ice-chimney in a continuous rush."

Crocket set off up the ice-chimney, clinging on miserably to handholds bitterly won in the icy stream.

9.7   Bill Brooker & Tom Patey, FWA Hadrian's Wall, (Feb., 1959)

"At the top I had to move onto the left wall and here the spindrift was worst. I hastily chopped a few handholds, forcing myself to cut them well, and when the next lull came stepped out onto the wall. A sudden rush of snow nearly swept me off but I hung on, cursing feebly and rotating slowly on one good foothold." (5).

Once out of the spindrift in the corner the remainder of the climb went smoothly, though the two climbers were tired as they cut their way on to the summit plateau. With its mixed scenery and grand route finding Hadrian's Wall is a deservedly popular route. The original line is seldom, if ever climbed. It is in condition less often than the icefall of the Direct and, one suspects, is a little bit too complicated-looking for the average modern climber, intent on straight up ice.

At the beginning of February 1959, Marshall, Stenhouse and Haston teamed up for a winter climbing holiday. After a 'training' weekend on Creag Meaghaidh, where they had been joined by Graham Tiso, the trio moved on to Nevis, pushing into an already crowded CIC Hut. Clough and his friends were already in residence. Marshall was intent on climbing Minus Two Gully, the central of the three Minus Gullies. Of the four great gullies on the Ben:

Zero, Point Five, Minus One and Minus Two, only the first two had been climbed in winter; Point Five by the siege tactics of Clough.

Haston later remembered the February 11 ascent of Minus Two Gully in his autobiography.

"For Stenhouse and me it was both a stunner and a mind-awakener. We were supposed to share leads, but after we had followed Jimmy over the bulge it became apparent that his experience and ability were still beyond ours. We were taking as long to second as he was to lead." (6).

Marshall's description of Minus Two Gully in the 1959 SMC Journal read,

"This was a winter ascent *par excellence,* the gully being barred by an impressive ice bulge which proved a bit of an imposter. Difficulties thereafter almost continuous. At the exit pitch below the final forking an *étrier* was used and the left fork followed to the crest of N.E. Buttress, gained at nightfall. By the feeble light of a crescent moon, stars and aurora, the Buttress was climbed. The gully took 8 hours, three pitons being used for protection, and piton belays used at each stance."

Marshall's party regained the CIC Hut at 2 a.m., having begun the route at a traditionally late hour. The next day, February 12, they climbed Hesperides Ledge, Grade III. This is the slanting ledge on the Comb, running up and right above the steepest section of that impressive rock feature. Hesperides Ledge must surely be safer in winter; its loose rocks bound together by ice, but its frighteningly exposed traverses deter most parties from attempting it.

Meanwhile, Clough and his friends had been busy, climbing six routes between February 10 and 12. Perhaps Clough's best discovery was the North Wall of Castle Ridge, where four routes of about Grade III were climbed including Nordwand, a mixed route some 1,400 feet in length which gives interesting route finding while not being technically difficult.

It is worth remarking at this point that in 1959 winter gradings as used now were not yet in use on Ben Nevis. Climbs were described but no grade given. Climbers not in touch with those in the forefront of exploration thus suffered from a slight handicap, though they often had as a rough and ready measure of a route's difficulty the names of the first ascenders and the time taken for the ascent. Cairngorm climbers, on the other hand, had been using a numbered system for several years and the Cairngorm Climbers' Guides by Malcolm Smith were to use this system, numbering grades of difficulty on winter routes from the easiest, I, to the most difficult, V.

Only one winter route remained to be recorded on Nevis that year — Platforms Rib, Grade IV, climbed by MacInnes, Clough, Sullivan and M. White, on March 8. Starting at the foot of Minus Three Gully (then unclimbed in winter), Platforms Rib follows the rib on the left until an overhang is reached. On the first ascent this was climbed using pegs for aid. Above the overhang Minus Three Gully was followed for a short distance before the rib was regained. The 1st summer ascent has been by Bell, Allan & M.B. Stewart, in Sept., 1934.

Throughout April and May of 1959 Clough was active, either in company with MacInnes or other friends. Several routes were recorded on the Secondary Tower Ridge, including a solo ascent of a Hard Severe, Vagabond's Rib, climbing a two-tiered slabby rib left of Vanishing Gully. The next day Clough and MacInnes compounded the Point Five controversy with a peg ascent of the magnificent wall on the right flank of Carn Dearg Buttress. Titan's Wall, as it became, took twelve hours of climbing, 370 feet of the route being new. Lying between Sassenach and The Shield this smooth, cracked wall was responsible for the glint in several climbers' eyes, though probably no one climbing in Scotland at that time had the technique to free climb it.

Attempts to free climb Titan's Wall were made since its first, aided ascent. One notable pair who tried in the late 60's were Rab Carrington and the late John Jackson. Despite their high levels of ability, new standards and skills were required before such difficulties could be overcome. These new abilities arrived in the mid-70's. In June 1977 the route was freed by Mick Fowler and Phil Thomas. It was graded as Extremely Severe (E4). Four days later it received a second free ascent by the Scots team of Dave 'Cubby' Cuthbertson and Murray Hamilton. They climbed it with a slight variation, finishing more directly via an awkward, 30-foot crack.

During the remainder of 1959 three routes were to be pioneered. Two of these were Very Severes on September 19, by two friends of Ian Clough; Terry Sullivan and N. Collingham. The Slant lies on Number Five Gully Buttress, right of Marshall's Fives Wall, while The Shadow is a pleasant and easy Very Severe on Carn Dearg Buttress, parallel to and right of Route II. But the third and final route of 1959, also on Carn Dearg Buttress, was to be remembered not only for its difficulties, which are tangible enough, but also for the essay its ascent inspired one of the party to write, an essay reprinted many times since. The route was The Bat, the party Smith and Haston.

In the summer of 1959 Haston was waiting to enter Edinburgh University as an undergraduate. Meanwhile he collected his weekly unemployment benefit of £2.50 and shuttled back and forth between Edinburgh and Glencoe. As one of the 'Currie Lads', Haston set the molars of the SMC's establishment grinding with rage at several of his escapades. One of these escapades involved Lagangarbh, the SMC Hut in Glencoe.

One of the rooms in Lagangarbh had been painted a dull green, while Glencoe itself was very dark and sombre at the time. Haston was 'into' Kandinsky at the time, and as there just happened to be a stock of paint about; red, yellow, boot polish too, the outcome was colourful. Haston and Ronnie Marshall took out the paints and splashed on the brilliant reds and yellows, setting up candles all around when they had finished.

"The room", remembers Jimmy Marshall, "came alive — we thought it was brilliant — it was an escape from the horrible Glencoe weather — a sunlight corner — but it so happened that a work party had just painted the place!" (7). Haston in 1959 was nineteen.

Robin Clark Smith was already at Edinburgh University, studying Philosophy. Two years older than Haston, Smith was to graduate with an Honours degree. But for his premature death in the Pamirs, Smith would have gone on to study for a doctorate in London. His application form for the SMC, in December 1958, shows a formidable list of hard ascents.

In the early summer of 1959 Smith and Dick Holt made an attempt on the unclimbed central corner on Carn Dearg Buttress — the hanging corner in the middle of the bulging wall left of the Sassenach chimney which was to be called The Bat. Making the traditional late start and beginning via the

9.8 Haston, painter of Lagangarbh, (1959)

Centurion entry, they succeeded in finding a way rightward across the overlapping slabs, attempted in the past by Kellett, Patey and perhaps others unknown. Faced with 40 feet of bulging wall between them and the start of the corner proper, with daylight threatening to fade, they 'retreated' by climbing up Sassenach to meet the night. The next day, wrote Smith,

"We woke . . . to the whine of the Death Wind fleeing down the Allt a'Mhuilinn. Fingery mists were creeping in at five windows. Great grey spirals of rain were boring into the Buttress." (8).

The two abandoned their attempts and left for Edinburgh.

Smith returned to the corner in September with Haston. The two, it seemed, had no great liking for each other, but climbing partners were scarce at that time of year so they teamed up in Glencoe, making an ascent of Carnivore before moving on to Fort William on the Monday. Tuesday at 1 p.m. saw them on the embryonic route, at Smith's previous high point. Smith was intent on climbing the corner and he offered the lead of the next, intermediate pitch to Haston. This was an ugly, overhanging groove.

Haston moved up the groove with care. To quit the groove, he had to place a sling over a small spike, which then allowed poor holds above to be reached. As he moved up the sling rolled off its spike and he barely managed to pull himself on to the ledge above. As Smith followed, more slowly than usual, Haston knew that he too found it difficult. The big corner was now above Haston's belay, rising in two, 35-foot leaps, with a four-foot horizontal roof jutting out between.

Smith, who was wearing a tattered pair of kletterschuh, borrowed Haston's P.A.'s. The impecunious pair had two full-weight ropes, but Haston's had lost five feet of its original 120 feet during an 'experiment' on the Currie Railway Walls near Edinburgh, while Smith's, on loan from a Glaswegian friend, had been 'stretched a little', so that it was now 130 feet long.

". . . and so Dougal at the bottom had quickly tied on to an end of each rope which left me with 15 feet on the one to get rid of round and round my middle to make the two ropes even."

9.9   Robin Smith & Davy Agnew, (1962)

The corner pitch up which Smith now set off looked impressive in its untouched state — a damp crack leading to the overhang, with a crack disappearing out of sight above. The pitch was mossy and vegetated and holds had to be unearthed by pulling off chunks of moss. Smith gained the overhang and as protection to this point had been poor he quickly pounded a metal peg into the crack beneath the overhang, suspended a knotted sling from the peg and stood with his right foot in the sling. Several attempts by Smith to move left and up the corner above produced only a jammed knot for a runner before his initial impetus faded and he retreated to join Haston on the belay ledge.

Changing leads necessitated much time-consuming work by the two; swopping footwear, untying ropes and exchanging ends [in order that the ropes, still running through Smith's runners in the corner, would run smoothly for Haston]. Eventually Haston was back up at the black roof. Their equipment did not include artificial chockstones — these were just about to become available — and at one point in the corner-crack, just above the roof, there was a suitable widening in the crack. Here, according to Smith, Haston succeeded in hammering in a wooden wedge, used both as a runner and as a support for another foot-sling. [In Haston's account of the ascent, written 13 years later, he has it that Smith inserted the wedge, before retreating to the belay for a rest and to exchange leads. (6)].

Haston thought he could see a ledge above the roof and decided to commit himself to gaining it. In climbing as practised at this standard and time, committment implied an all-or-nothing effort; either the climber would safely gain his objective, or he would be in considerable danger of going so far then falling off — and so it proved to be, as Haston set off upwards from the wooden wedge.

"In my overconfidence I'd hopelessly underestimated the angle of the corner. Overhanging it was, and my ledge didn't exist. I found myself with fingers stuck despairingly into a turf that was sliding."

Down below on the belay ledge, Smith was going through the worries and doubts that assail the second man on such hard, exploratory climbs, eyeing his belay points, pulling down the sleeves of his jersey to try and protect his wrists from rope burn, should the leader fall.

"Then came a sort of squawk as Dougal found that his ledge was not . . . Rattling sounds came from his throat or nails or something . . . Then his fingers went to butter. It began under control as the bit of news 'I'm off,' but it must have been caught in the wind, for it grew like a wailing siren to a blood-curdling scream as a black and bat-like shape came hurtling over the roof . . . "

The "bat-like shape" hurtling over the roof was to suggest the name of the route to the pair, in addition to which so much time had been spent climbing in the dark.

Haston fell over the roof head-first and was brought to a shattering halt by the ropes, hanging upside down opposite a not-so-cool Smith who had been pulled off his ledge and was also suspended. The wooden wedge had done its job and was holding under the strain as both climbers scrabbled back on to the rock. By now the inevitable dusk was creeping up the rocks and the climbers were forced to retreat, first by a traverse right to Sassenach, then by an abseil down the ropes in the dark, to land in the mud at the foot of the cliff. The attempts were over for this week, as the pair returned to Edinburgh.

The following Tuesday saw Smith and Haston back under the black roof. This time Smith had a pair of P.A.'s and as it was his turn to lead he climbed up to the roof. Threading his ropes through the peg, jammed knot and wooden edge, he stood in a sling attached to the wedge and at full stretch he was just able to reach two small pebbles jammed in the crack above the roof. Suddenly he felt his stomach lurch as, he thought, the wedge shifted in its crack. Desperately he threaded a tiny nylon sling through the pebbles as the wedge came out and he shot into space, hanging from the jammed knot and peg about 20 feet below the roof.

In a rage now, Smith climbed back up to the roof, moved round it again and sat in slings depending from the two little pebbles. Moving on quickly but feeling his strength ebbing he inserted another peg about 20 feet above the roof, before continuing. Pulling up on this high peg it came out and Smith was once again violently precipitated into space to come to rest below the by now hated roof.

As Smith was hanging from a higher point in the overhanging corner he was suspended away from the lower corner, so Haston lowered him down to the belay. The corner pitch had occupied him for four hours, while night, once again, was flowing up the hill. But Smith's character was very strong in persistence so he made one more attempt, telling the disenchanted Haston that he was going to recover the equipment.

"So I was very sly and said we had to get the gear and climbed past the roof to the sling at the pebbles leaving all the gear in place. There I was so exhausted that I put in a piton, only it was very low, and I thought, so am I, *peccavi, peccabo,* and I put in another and rose indiscriminately until to my surprise I was past Dougal's ledge and still on the rock . . . "

Haston followed in the twilight, leaving all the gear in the corner, then led the next pitch up a groove. At this point, although they had finally cracked the route, some 500 feet of climbing remained before they gained the top of the buttress. Fortunately both climbers enjoyed night climbing and belaying out on the right edge they soaked up the moonlight and the alien views such light provides.

194

9.10   Philip 'Bish' McAra on The Bat corner (1982)

The next weekend Haston returned with Marshall while Smith was exam-bound in Edinburgh. Climbing to the end of the main Sassenach chimney they then moved left to the top of the corner of The Bat and finished by an independent line of grooves. Tied in with a pitch climbed earlier by Smith and Holt, Carn Dearg Buttress had been gifted with a new, hard route. The fact that it had been an all-Scottish ascent probably helped salve the wounds inflicted by Centurion and Sassenach.

Robin Smith had opened 1959 with his winter ascent of The Tower Face of The Comb; he closed the year with The Bat. He was now a 21-year old, fast maturing into one of the most effective mountaineers ever to hit Ben Nevis. The following winter season, Smith and Jimmy Marshall were to climb together on Nevis, where in one week of sustained effort they were to bring to a climax the end of a decade of exciting developments in Scottish mountaineering. In one sense, they were to gain a pinnacle of achievement which can never be bettered. Of the writings that Smith and Marshall left of their week, Jim Perrin made the following observation.

"Robin Smith's literary persona has an attractive, if occasionally coy, ingenuousness, and there is a persuasive quality of enthusiasm & energy about his writing. Marshall's accounts are refreshingly direct . . . " (9).

In fact, 1960 on Nevis opened not with Smith and Marshall but with Clough, who recorded three routes in January. Rogue's Rib, Grade IV, climbed with G. Grandison on January 2, is a technically hard buttress climb immediately left of The Italian Climb. It finds very few takers today. In addition to its low altitude, its steepness ensures that it holds little snow and ice and it is consequently rarely in condition. More often accessible and a good mountaineering route of high quality is Comb Gully Buttress, Grade IV, climbed with Alexander on January 8. The finish taken by Clough, a prominent, rightward curving crack, is probably never in winter condition and most climbers follow the variation finish, taken by Ian Fulton and Davy Gardner in January 1971. This variation moves left to climb ice-covered rocks and a finishing chimney.

On January 29 Clough returned to Nevis, exploring Castle Coire with R. Sefton. In 1940 Rolland and Ogilvy had recorded Compression Crack, a 400-foot Very Difficult right of Raeburn's Buttress. Clough made what he thought was a winter ascent of this route, but later Marshall pointed out that he had climbed a completely new route, so it became Winter Chimneys, Grade IV. Compression Crack itself was not to receive a winter ascent until February 1985, by Martin Hind and Chris Rice.

It may be worth pointing out here that the 'easy slabs and grass ledges', lying above the left wall of South Castle Gully, suggested as an approach route to both these routes, are by no means as straightforward as their appearance would suggest. Their awkward nature and exposed situation are potentially lethal, in addition to which in damp conditions the rock hereabouts is very greasy.

Towards the end of 1959 Jimmy Marshall suffered a series of wet weekends that made him think of giving up.

"I'm going to get married, start a business and to hell with climbing!"

At the time this seemed like a good idea, as he then missed all the wet weekends that followed. Luckily for the history of Nevis and Scottish mountaineering Marshall had second thoughts the following winter, as he described in a retrospective dinner speech.

"Then I thought — I'd better do something, for there's a lot of things that I haven't done yet — that's one of the reasons why we had that great week on the Ben, Robin Smith and I, for I was getting married the month after it and we thought — well, we'd better go out there and do something and we had great weather and a super week of climbing." (7).

Their 'super week of climbing' began on Saturday, February 6, with an ascent of the Great Chimney on Tower Ridge. The grading (IV) given to it would seem too easy, as anyone who looks down the chimney and shudders would agree. At its overhanging chockstone Marshall had to use a sling for aid. Smith, who all through the week seemed to have trouble with a delinquent ice axe, dropped it down the chimney, and after finishing the route abseiled back down to recover it. Sliding down the rope into the gathering darkness,

"I was right at the end of the rope . . . the ends were just sliding over my shoulder when I came upon my axe. The Old Man, who is very bold, went solo down the crest of the ridge and came upon terrible difficulties in the moonlight . . . " (10).

On Sunday, February 7, the traditionally late start was set back even further when Smith had to return to the hut for his forgotten ice axe. The axe worked well on Minus Three Gully however, as Smith battered and bridged his way up an icicle pitch. Marshall led through on the next pitch which turned out to be longer and harder. Eventually they emerged on to the North-East Buttress and so up to the plateau and down by moonlight, Smith pausing only long enough to lose his axe.

Monday saw Smith hunting for the axe again while Marshall waited impatiently below Gardyloo Buttress, the objective of the day. The natural winter line up this buttress lies just right of Kellett's summer line and takes in a slabby corner running up and left to a small overhang. From below the overhang the original line climbs the ice wall to the left. Smith having puffed his way up Observatory Gully, Marshall set off up the first pitch. Conditions, as they were all over the mountain, were perfect, with much snow ice and ice, both easy to cut. Marshall led out a hundred feet and brought up Smith.

Just above Marshall's belay in the corner was an ice-fringed cave, formed by ice drooping over an overhang at the foot of a hanging groove. Smith was all for attempting the overhang but Marshall's judgment was for the line of least resistance and Smith continued

9.11   J.R. Marshall, FWA Smith's Route, (Feb., 1960)

leftward. Marshall, with hindsight, thinks that this decision was possibly a wrong one, as Smith's higher traverses, described below, were at least as hard as the overhang, as well as being further from security.

". . . a nervous traverse left on steep ice, then a happy announcement that it's a doddle. Two hours later, hoarse with singing and groaning. I'm still watching the rope . . . A shout of 'Come on' rakes me back to frigidity; it dawns on me, he's too polite, something is ugly up here besides Wheech; having lived so long for a climber and acquired a cunning commensurate with age, I point out that there is still 50 feet of rope to go; a short exchange of unpleasanteries follows, and the rope continues its neurotic advance." (11).

Smith had given up the search for his axe and was using Marshall's. The senior climber had correctly analysed Smith's politeness and realised that he was shattered and unwilling to continue past a poor belay he had arranged. But continue he did until he dropped the party's only axe.

"It stuck in the ice on top of an overhang five feet below and I crept down to pick it up in a sweating terror of kicking a bit of snow on it."

Smith climbed up and right now, across a great barrel of snow ice. The first six inches of this were uselessly crusted and he used a long ice peg for protection, driving it in as high as he could and cutting steps up past it until it was too low, when the whole procedure was repeated. At least it was repeated until the peg was dropped at the biggest bulge and disappeared into the night. Smith's last chance of retreat was now gone. Continuing to cut steps, he lost his grip of the axe, the sign of a very tired leader,

". . . and it started somersaulting in the air with both my arms windmilling trying to grab it and my feet scarting about in crumbly holds."

Marshall meanwhile was slowly freezing on the belay ledge, as Smith fought to stay on the ice wall.

"Silhouetted against a starry sky the wee bauchle comes into sight, grunts of 'I'm nearly there' go on for another prolonged spell, then a great whoop sears the night."

Smith had reached the foot of the final gully where he belayed on his peg hammer to bring up Marshall. Even seconding this pitch impressed Marshall,

". . . feeling high and deep into the holds, a thrash with the feet for the lower steps, a quick judgment for soundness, then a queer off-balance swing for the next hole - wow! that was a false one - hands slip on the glassy ice, the footholds crunch down, I expect to come off . . ."

Marshall stayed on and completed the pitch, then led through up the final, easy pitch leading to the plateau. Shambling down No.4 Gully Smith found his recalcitrant axe. Smith's Route, Gardyloo Buttress, short at 400 feet though steep, had to wait 11 years for a second ascent in March 1971, by the Cambridge Scot Mike Geddes and Nigel Rayner, who took four and a half hours. Its third ascent came the following month when Kenny Spence from Edinburgh, then leading a party on a mountaineering course, used perfect conditions of snow ice to cut a line of pigeon-hole steps up the buttress. The grading of the route, V, remains inviolate, despite changes in technique. Geddes, on the second ascent, was using the new front-pointing technique.

In February 1975, Ken Crocket and Chris Gilmore made what may have been the fifth ascent, climbing directly up from the ice cave, over the overhang fancied by Smith on the first ascent. Difficulties were experienced on the leftward groove above the icicle due to conditions; a damp skin of snow covering harder ice. (12).

Smith was still exhausted the day after Gardyloo Buttress, but despite this they climbed the Ordinary Route on Observatory Buttress. Originally graded IV, a more realistic grading would be V, taking into account its length and the steep ice characteristic of the hard section of the route. This route was not recorded in the SMCJ along with the other first ascents; Marshall had assumed that Raeburn had climbed the line in winter. This explains it being mistakenly recorded following a later ascent as The Liquidator, 20th February, 1965, Grade V by I.A. MacEacheran and J. Renny. In winter it gives a superb and difficult climb with, in certain conditions, overhanging ice at the crux chimney.

Wednesday dawned wet, but as it cleared around 10 a.m. Smith and Marshall sweated up Observatory Gully towards the fierce, narrow confines of Point Five Gully, still awaiting an ascent since the five-day siege by Clough. Conditions underfoot were still perfect, with snow and ice making the climbing much more secure. Smith charged on up the third pitch,

"I pressed on up a chimney full of evil crusted snow and took an axe belay at the side of the gully. Then the spindrift started drooling down, and just as the Old Man spread himself halfway over the base of ice it grew to a hissing torrent and piled up on his great stomach and pushed him out from the ice while he clawed away for the holds and through the tips of his gloves".

The hissing stream of spindrift eventually ran dry and after one more pitch the gully eased off and Smith and Marshall finished up the gully through swirling clouds and pools of moonlight. The second ascent had taken seven hours in excellent conditions by a team at their peak; subsequent ascents by step-cutting were not always to have such smooth progress, one team being forced to bivouac on the route, finishing the next day. By 1965 Point Five Gully had had five ascents in winter, an average of one ascent a year. Zero Gully had received four ascents up to the end of 1965.

By Thursday morning, Marshall and Smith had climbed five hard winter routes; four first ascents and the second ascent of Point Five Gully. They were plotting the biggest plum of the lot however, the direct ascent of the Orion Face, first attempted by Smith and Holt in January, 1959. Conditions then had forced an escape leftwards from the Basin; this time Smith and Marshall were determined to succeed. But first they had an "off-day", as they woke on Thursday morning to mist and wind.

Crossing the Carn Mor Dearg arête in the teeth of the gale they crossed Aonach Beag and traversed the Grey Coires to Stob Choire Claurigh. Descending to Spean Bridge for refreshment they then took a bus to Fort William — there the fish and chip shop known to climbers as 'Hell's Kitchen' was shut so they had some more refreshment in a pub before being turned out early. Smith and Marshall had agreed to 'borrow' the set of draughts in the pub and the publican, incensed at the loss of yet another set, had called in the police. The climbing pair were hitching a lift back along the road when Smith, reactions slowed by the drink, thumbed the approaching police car. Despite Marshall's suggestion to heave the incriminating evidence over a wall they were consequently given a lift — back to the police station! The two were released in time to catch the last bus passing the Distillery and walked back up to the hut.

Friday, February 12, was cold, and feeling none-too-bright Smith and Marshall had an afternoon's climb on The Comb, making a first winter ascent of Pigott's Route. Avoiding the slabby foot of the buttress, they made use of one of the long, tapering shelves of rock, running from bottom left to the right edge of The Comb overlooking Green Gully. The lead at the "rotten chimney" fell to Marshall, thereafter long ice grooves led to the crest of the buttress. Both the Great Chimney and Pigott's Route were awaiting second winter ascents at the end of 1985; the latter was climbed by a team from Edinburgh at the beginning of 1986. The rotten chimney of Pigott's does not seem to hold snow and ice and the author has retreated on several occasions.

On Friday night the weather improved, the wind fading as quickly as it had sprung up. At last conditions were right for an attempt on the Orion Face, and at one p.m. the pair arrived at the foot of the ice stream depending from the lip of The Basin.

"Even the Old Man recognised he had had his share of cruxes, so he offered me the choice and I chose the first because the third looked terrible . . . " (10).

Smith was mistaken, however, as the third pitch turned out to be easy and the second pitch, led by Marshall, exciting. But Smith had a little adventure at the first pitch, when at 50 feet,

"Wheech's tour had misled him on to a thinly iced slab, where it was obvious he would either waken up or roll back down to the hut . . . " (13).

At the top of the second pitch the climbers were faced with the unknown, as Smith moved out left to the skyline. A series of complaints from Smith signalled arrival on to the easy ground below The Basin, Marshall leading on past to gain the right edge of the depression. A 100-foot ice slope followed by a 50-foot traverse right saw Smith belayed at the foot of the next difficult section on this classically grand mountaineering route — the Second Slab Rib of

The Long Climb. In many winters this rib stands out at some distance, prominently dark against the surrounding snow and ice, as it seldom ices up. It was in this condition on the first ascent, as Marshall began the pitch.

"An exploratory traverse 10 feet round the corner disclosed a well-iced wall, shining green in the evening light and perched over the now impressive drop of the wall beneath: 130 feet higher the hunt for peg cracks failed in the gathering gloom of night and a belay in powder snow brought the sharp edges of frost and fear into the struggle . . . "

The climbing following the Slab Traverse can give incredibly enjoyable situations, as found by later parties.

". . . sustained pitches of IV, no one move standing out as hard, no move easy enough to ignore, no protection, beautiful route finding up parallel grooves, round corners and edges, hard ice all the way and no hanging about." (14).

Reaching the snow slope beneath the terminal towers of the Orion Face, Smith and Marshall found to their dismay knee-deep, floury snow. Their original plan was to spiral up rightward from this point, towards Zero Gully, but doubts as to the safety of a traverse in such conditions made them consider moving left, on to the crest of North-East Buttress. But again the unconsolidated snow would have made this finish dangerous while by now fatigue and darkness were creeping in. They decided to try straight ahead, up the final rocky ramparts of the face.

Smith belayed to rock below the last hard pitch, Marshall stopping long enough to pick up the dry gloves, reserved for the leader of each pitch. A scrabble up a cone of snow led into an icy groove. Here Marshall had to feel the angle by touch, as in the mist and gloom white fog crystals were blurring all outlines. It seemed to him that above lay an enormous cornice; more felt than seen, as he cut steps up the groove.

"About 40 feet up, the groove steepened to a bulge; finding the holds with the cramponed feet was extremely awkward at times, and often moves were made hanging from the handholds whilst the crampons scarted about in search of the 'buckets' cut below."

The bulge now forced him out on the right wall, moving along a short ledge,

9.12   Ronnie Richards, exit pitch Orion Direct (March, 1974)

"then a frightening move, leaning out on an undercut ice hold, to cut holds round a rib on to the slab wall of a parallel groove. The ice here was only about an inch thick and moving into the groove was very difficult; the cat crawl up the thin ice remains imprinted in the memory, for at this 'moment of truth' strains of an awful dirge came up . . . from 90 feet below, 'Ah kin hear the hammer ringin' on somebody's coffin . . .'''

Marshall finally gained a snow-filled groove, where his aching calf muscles could recover. To his side, the top of the first groove was closed over, leaving a steep, icy wall above. He resumed cutting wearily, worrying now about the amount of rope remaining as it seemed to him that he had run out more than 140 feet. Then suddenly there was no more ice to cut, as a gentle snow slope in front of him shone faintly in the cloud-filtered moonlight. The Orion Face Direct had been climbed.

As if stunned by this series of routes nothing more was recorded on Nevis that winter until April 1, when Clough and some friends found a variation to No. 2 Gully Buttress at Grade III, climbing to the left of the original line. Smith, however, had another winter climb to make. On March 23, 1960, Zero Gully received its second winter ascent. Dougal Haston was now a student at Edinburgh University. Dick Holt was President of the EUMC, while Robin Smith was Editor of the Club's Journal, or 'Nocturnal', as it was wittily and aptly called that year.

"I was sleeping off a scoop in the Clubrooms when Wightman came rolling in and said he wanted to go to Nevis so we spent the next night in the C.I.C. Hut".

So began Haston's article in the 1961 E.U.M.C. 'Nocturnal'. (15). This account, written immediately after the event, differs in some small detail from the version in Haston's autobiography, written eleven years later (6); as did Haston's later account of The Bat in the same book differ slightly from Smith's fresh account. In their rush from the *"foulness of the city"*, Haston and Andy Wightman had forgotten to include a rope.

"A solution was on hand, however: the Hut was full of steadfast English muttering earnestly, up Three down Four, up Two down Five, and other Nevis Gully permutations, so we waited until they had departed and went on a scavenge for rope".

They found a spare rope left behind by one of the other residents and set off at the statutory late hour for Zero Gully. The route was in fine condition, with much blue ice, but Haston's weak, out-of-condition arms ran out of strength some 80 feet up the first pitch and the two climbers descended to the Hut with their tails between their legs. But reinforcements were about to arrive.

"The evening was full of hateful mutterings about black rope stealing and bed thieving Scots and the Hut is fully booked. Bed had just been achieved when a grubby Smith arrived."

Smith admitted that he too had no rope, so they slept on the problem and waited to see what the next day would be like.

Another late start, another "borrowed" rope, and the threesome arrived at the foot of Zero. Smith won the toss and set off up Haston's steps of yesterday. Two hours later he was 30 feet higher than Haston's high point and taking a poor belay. When Haston reached the belay, he was so shattered and icicle-like that he let Smith lead the second pitch as well. This contained an evil little bulge which turned out to be an imposter.

". . . and even Wheech using my axe because it was better than his managed to outwit it in less than an hour. In fact he got so chuffed that he battered my axe into the ice with so much enthusiasm that the pick came flying past me . . . "

Wightman, who as third on the rope was apparently on his second ever winter climb was still at the foot of the route, slowly freezing. He tried to untie the rope but his hands were too cold and Haston pulled the rope in and brought him up.

"Now Andy should be called Willie the Weeper for all the moaning he does and sure enough the manky belay sent him off and I left him mumbling and grumbling to himself while I went up the bulge to curse at Wheech for breaking my axe."

Haston led the third pitch, belaying under an ice bulge. Wightman then came up to Smith's belay, while Smith went on to lead the bulge above Haston's head. Smith finished the bulge just as darkness fell completely. On the first ascent Patey, MacInnes, and Nicol had taken only an hour to climb from here to the top, as the major difficulties are concentrated in the first 900 feet. *"We now reckoned on half an hour as the first party were old men"*.

Stopping for a bite of chocolate they found they had one torch between the three of them as for the next few hours they wandered around in the dark, encountering bulges and rock bands. Finally they decided to go rightward and try climbing up Observatory Ridge. While scrambling around on a snow arête, the light from their solitary torch picked out a line of steps below and right, and with a short abseil they landed in the steps and the easiest way up to the plateau.

"It was all hell let loose up there so we quickly beetled off down Four Gully in the dim light of approaching dawn to face court martial for rope thieving by the English dayshift." (15). The CIC log for that week has the entry, *"Zero Gully, quite hard conditions, 'n' hours"*.

In May, Smith recorded his last new route on Nevis with J. Hawkshaw of the Edinburgh University M.C., when he climbed Central Route. Now graded at Hard Very Severe, this climbs the raised rib between Left Hand and Right Hand Routes, on Minus Two Buttress.

In August a fierce route was recorded by a rope from the Creagh Dhu Club. John McLean and Bill Smith climbed the ferocious chimney of Subtraction. This route starts on Minus Two Buttress, crosses Minus Two Gully and finishes up the obvious overhanging groove on the left flank of Minus One Buttress. This very difficult and very underrated climb is certainly in the Extremely Severe category, with several subsequent attempts being defeated by the overhanging groove, a typical Nevis groove, slanting up and left, undercut, smooth.

Of Subtraction McLean has expressed puzzlement at its seeming difficulty, having found no great problems on the first ascent. The second ascent, in 1963, was by the Marshall brothers, Jimmy and Ronnie. Jimmy Marshall remembers it being very hard, while on a later ascent, by 'Big' Ian Nicolson and Dougie McArthur in 1971, the latter took a swing while seconding, which lends more weight to the extreme nature of this futuristic route.

During that same period, in August 1960, Marshall and Stenhouse were running up and down many of the older routes, busy checking descriptions for the new guide. They made a variation start to Bayonet Route while repeating routes on the First Platform.

9.13   J.R. Marshall, J. McLean, W. Smith & J. Stenhouse at CIC Hut, (August, 1960)

The first winter ascent of the Orion Face was the climax of an incredible week of mountaineering on Ben Nevis. The partnership of Smith and Marshall had joined with ideal conditions. But it was more than that. In the ten years that followed other fine and equally hard routes would be won by step cutting. But no other climber would come near to repeating such a sustained effort, nor to writing about that week with such lasting feeling. Just as Murray had been a source of inspiration to them, so they would be for those who followed. Smith would die in the summer of 1962; with Wilfred Noyce on Peak Garmo in the Russian Pamirs. Marshall would go on to record other great routes. And after an intervening decade had passed new techniques would make step cutting virtually obsolete, fixing more firmly that week of climbing by Smith and Marshall as the very pinnacle of Scottish winter mountaineering.

10.1   Alexander Macdonald of Keppoch (c. 1745)

OF WHISKY, FOOT-RACES & CARS, & ALUMINIUM

WHISKY

Up until the mid-1970's, most climbers began their approach to the north face of Ben Nevis by walking up from the Ben Nevis Distillery. Leaving the main road, the heavily-laden climber would walk through the distillery gate which never seemed to be closed, and which bore the crest of the Clan Macdonald, tiptoe across the courtyard, and turn a corner to gain the far side of the distillery. Here there was a large open shed containing wooden casks. These were, of course, empty, but some must have been used, as the sweet smell of whisky was always in the air. So a dark night's walk up Nevis often began with an appreciative lungfull of whisky-scented air, courtesy of a long-dead Highlander named Long John Macdonald.

Long John Macdonald, who gave his name to the Long John blended whisky produced by the present distillers, Long John International, is believed to have been born about 1798, in a house at Torgulbin in the Spean Valley. His birth date cannot be precisely known, as the

Catholic records of Fort William start in 1820. He was known as Long John to distinguish him from other members of his clan — though visually his great height would have been sufficient.

The family tree shows that Long John could prove a pedigree going back to John Macdonald, Lord of the Isles in the fourteenth century. John Macdonald, Lord of the Isles, lived and married royally, to Princess Margaret, daughter of Robert II, King of Scots. Margaret was also a great-grandaughter of Robert the Bruce, the Scottish monarch who so resoundingly defeated the English army at the Battle of Bannockburn in 1314, and so gained independence for Scotland.

Long John's branch of the Clan Macdonald was started by Alexander Macdonald, a son of the Lord of the Isles. He was also known as Alisdair Carrach and was the first chief of the Macdonalds of Keppoch, a branch long known for their fighting spirit. The seventh chief, Ranald Mor Macdonald of Keppoch, rebelled against the Scottish crown, paying dearly for it by being beheaded in 1547.

The great-grandfather of Long John, Alexander Macdonald, had been studying at Glasgow University when the first Jacobite Rising broke out in 1715. He joined the Earl of Mar immediately, took part in the disastrous rout of Sheriffmuir and fled to France, finishing his education there and afterwards joining the French army, serving as an officer for several years before deeming it safe to return to Scotland.

By 1743 Alexander Macdonald was at work for the Jacobite cause, returning to France that year to meet with Prince Charles at the French court. The story of Prince Charles Edward's landing in Scotland to raise the clans, and the march of events leading to the invasion of England and the long retreat to Culloden is only too well known. That last battle to be fought on British soil took place in April 1746 on the wind-swept moor overlooking the cold waters of the Moray Firth. At the war council preceding the battle, Alexander Macdonald advised against a face to face confrontation with a better armed and numerically superior force. Along with other dissenting chiefs he was overruled. He died with his brother Donald, leading a charge against the guns of Cumberland's army.

Fifty years or so after Culloden, probably in the year 1798, Long John Macdonald was born. His father, Donald Macdonald of Torgulbin, was a farmer, as were his seven sons, with the exception of Angus who fought at Waterloo. For as long as the Highlanders could remember, the making of whisky on a small scale had gone on, the clansmen distilling their own from the raw materials readily available; barley (or some other grain), peat, and the good and plentiful Highland water. Indeed, in Gaelic the name of whisky is 'uisge beatha', which translates as the 'water of life'. There is no evidence that Long John or his family was in any way involved in illicit making of whisky, but it is certain that when the Government in London passed an Act of Parliament outlawing private stills, Long John applied for and was granted a Licence, building a distillery at Fort William in 1825.

His original whisky was called *'Long John's Dew of Ben Nevis'*, an appropriate-enough name for a drink made at the foot of Britain's highest mountain. A description of Long John — the man, not the drink, can be found in a book by Alexander Smith, published in 1864, and titled 'A Summer in Skye'. Smith went to Fort William, meeting Long John and writing the following short portrait.

"When a man goes to Caprera, he, as a matter of course, brings a letter of introduction to Garibaldi — when I went to Fort William, I, equally as a matter of course, brought a letter of introduction to Long John. This gentleman, the distiller of the place, was the tallest man I ever beheld, and must in his youth been of incomparable physique. I presented my letter and was received with the hospitality and courteous grace so characteristic of the old Gael. He is gone now, the happy-hearted Hercules — gone like one of his own drams!"

The Ben Nevis Distillery had been going for some 23 years when Her Majesty, Queen Victoria, paid it a visit. She was partial to 'a drop of the cratur', perhaps due to the influence of her Highland servant John Brown, and on visiting Fort William in 1848 honoured the distillery with a visit. The Illustrated London News for April, 1848, records that,

"Mr. Macdonald has presented a cask of whisky to Her Majesty, and an order has been sent to the Treasury to permit the spirits to be removed to the cellars of Buckingham Palace free of duty. The cask is not to be opened until His Royal Highness the Prince of Wales attains his majority."

The whisky would no doubt have been finely matured some fifteen years later, when the Prince of Wales, later to become King Edward VII, reached his majority. A renowned gourmet, no doubt he enjoyed the tipple from the Royal cellars.

Long John married in 1835, having built up the family fortunes lost after Culloden. When he died in 1856, at the age of 58, his son Donald Peter Macdonald took over the distillery at the age of 20. The son was so successful that he opened a second distillery, the Glen Nevis. This stood near the mouth of Glen Nevis, but no longer exists. Long John was buried in the Braes of Lochaber, at the small Catholic Chapel of Killichyril, built on top of a steep hill and commanding the peaks of Roybridge and Glen Spean.

As for Long John's distillery, it has gone from strength to strength. There are now four distilleries belonging to Long John International, including the Ben Nevis Distillery. The New Strathclyde Distillery, built across the River Clyde from Glasgow Green, is the Long John grain whisky distillery. The original building was a mill, but it was converted into a distillery, using the pure water of Loch Katrine in the Trossachs.

The third Long John distillery lies far to the north, with the Tormore Distillery on Speyside. With Tormore, Long John International built the first completely new malt whisky distillery to be opened in the Highlands this century. The water here is from the Achvochkie Burn, which runs out of the Loch-an-Oir (the Loch of Gold). The Tormore Distillery began producing in 1959. To reach the fourth Long John Distillery we have to leave the mainland and sail west, for this distillery is none other than Laphroaig on the Hebridean island of Islay. The Laphroaig Distillery was started in 1815, and has been producing a highly favoured malt whisky of the same name ever since.

10.2   Ben Nevis Distillery (c. 1980)

Long John whisky is a blend, using a mix of malt whiskies from various distilleries and grain whisky from the New Strathclyde Distillery. It owes at least some of its distinctive colour and taste to the peaty Laphroaig, and much to the mysterious and, some say, magical happenings that begin when the components are married and allowed to mature in the cask. As mentioned at the beginning of this section, the way up Nevis is now rarely begun by the Ben Nevis Distillery start, so climbers miss out on the aroma of whisky at the start of an ascent. For some, however, a good day or weekend up Ben Nevis may be toasted with a dram of this country's distinctive spirit, and for many of them the chosen brand will most appropriately be — Long John.

THE BEN NEVIS FOOT RACE

On the first Saturday in September each year the Ben Nevis Race is held, upwards of over 400 men and women vying with each other to be the fastest to run to the summit and back to Fort William. This arduous race — the course is about 14 miles long following the tourist path, though a runner can shorten this somewhat by taking a more direct route — began to enter the record books in 1895. That year, a local hairdresser, William Swann, ran from the old Post Office at the far north end of the High Street to the summit and back again in 2 hours 41 minutes. This was the first and last race to leave from this point, as three years later the Post Office location had been moved before William McDonald from Leith made the return journey in 2 hours 27 minutes on August 2, 1898.

Two months later Willie Swann regained his leadership, with a time of 2 hours 20 minutes, on October 29. These early attempts at the record were in the nature of solo runs, but on June 3, 1898 the race gained a more competitive look when Mr Menzies, a local hotel proprietor, offered a gold medal to the first man to finish. The race started from the Locheil Arms Hotel, Banavie, to the sound of a shotgun and the winner was a local gamekeeper, Hugh Kennedy, in a time of 2 hours 41 minutes. The distance was about one mile longer than the course from the new Post Office. This was the first race to be run under Scottish Amateur Athletic Association rules, the starter being William Lapsley, their official timekeeper.

The summit Observatory was still running in 1899, of course, and Hugh Kennedy's arrival at the summit was relayed to the waiting public at the start by a telegram from the summit. There were nine other runners besides Kennedy, including McDonald of Leith, who came in a long way behind as second man with a time of 3 hours 13 minutes. Perhaps to salve his price, McDonald made a solo run on August 29, making his run from the new Post Office in 2 hours 18 minutes.

Women were for a long time barred from entering the race, though unofficial entries were common. Their history is almost as long as that of the men and begins in 1902 with Miss Lucy Cameron of Ardechive running to the summit in 2 hours 3 minutes. The previous day, it must be recorded, she had walked up Nevis to look at the route, while the day before that she had walked from Ardechive to Fort William. Later that same year, on July 19, Elizabeth Tait, the post-woman at Corrour, made the ascent in 1.59.30, a record that was to stand for seven years. Both of these ascents were made from the new Post Office.

There were two races in 1903, the first of which, for the ascent only, began at Achintee and was started with a shotgun by Major Cameron, factor to the Cameron Lucy Estate. Among the seven starters was Ewan McKenzie, the Observatory roadman. The Observatory had only one more year to run at this time. Unfortunately there is no record of the race times, but at the second race, taking in the full return course starting at the Post Office, Ewan McKenzie returned a winning time of 2.10.6, on September 28.

McKenzie, as the roadman, would not only have a unique knowledge of the route and

10.3   Start of Ben Nevis Race (1903)

all its variations, his daily work on the mountain, weather permitting, would keep him at a good general level of fitness. He once participated in an experiment designed to examine his work output, running from the start of the slopes to the summit in 1.08.00. This experiment, conducted by the Edinburgh physicist J.Y. Buchanan, determined that McKenzie had developed one-third horsepower over his ascent.

McKenzie was one of three running in the September race of 1903. One of the other runners, R. Dobson from Glasgow, collapsed during the race and had to be carried down. He remained unconscious for ten hours before being brought back to life by a local doctor. The second man behind McKenzie was Hugh Kennedy of Banavie, in 2.21.00.

In October 1904 the Observatory was finally closed, the prediction on that wet and cold day being that there would be no more racing on the hill. There were certainly no more races recorded until 1937, with one exception. On September 14, 1909, on a beautiful autumn morning (there was a touch of frost), a Miss Wilson-Smith of Duns, Berwickshire made a new record for the ascent. Starting alone from the Post Office, she gained the summit in 1.51.00. Four days earlier, she had run from Achintee to the summit in three hours, but as a woman this was not recognised as a record.

In 1937, some 34 years after the last organised race, the Depute Town Clerk of Fort William revived the event. The race was held for the next ten occasions during the summer

10.4   Ben Nevis Race (1985)

months, suitable for the spectators, but often too warm for participants, the ideal conditions being an overcast day with a cool breeze and damp underfoot, which helps bind the otherwise loose scree of the slopes. The record set by McKenzie in 1903 was finally broken in 1939, D. Mulholland of Ardeer finishing with a time of 2.3.43.

There were no races in 1940 or 1941, and in 1943 a new starting place was chosen, being the King George V Park. This resulted in a new record by Duncan McIntyre of Fort William, at 2.4.30. McIntyre, a local butcher, was later to serve as the Honorary President of the Race Association. The following year C.P. Wilson of Kilwinning returned his fourth win since 1937, at the ripe age of 47.

Races stopped again until 1951, since when they have been a regular event. In that year the Ben Nevis Race Association was formed, taking on the organisation necessary for an event becoming more and more popular. The starting point in 1951, as in 1943 and 1944, was the King George V Park, the change being necessitated by the growth in traffic in the High Street. The new course was about one and a quarter miles shorter, and taking advantage of this Brian Kearney, a Fort William joiner, set a new time and was the first to break the tantalising two hour barrier, of 1.51.18.

10.5   Ros Coates, Ben Nevis Race (1985)

A solo ascent was made in September 1955, by the 16-year old daughter of a local doctor. Kathleen Connochie was accompanied by her trainer, Duncan McIntyre, who himself had set a record in 1943. She finished in 3.02.00, having reached the summit one hour and 55 minutes after leaving the King George V Park.

The knowledge of local runners obviously played a large part in the winning lists for some years, as Fort William runners won the race for the next four years, until Pat Moy, Vale of Leven, took the title away from them in 1956 by crossing the winning line in 1.45.55.

Over the decades the number of participants has continued to increase, growing from about 100 in the early 1960's, to 200 by the late 1970, until by the start of the 1980's it was a vast event drawing some 400 runners from all over the country. The Lochaber Mountain Rescue Team, who supervise mountain safety during the race, expressed concern in 1981 about the perils that such large numbers of people on the hill could bring, especially in poor conditions. This concern has been shown to be necessary, as a tragedy which occurred in 1957 indicates. One of the runners lost a shoe near the summit and took shelter below a rock. Despite being found by a rescue party he died of exposure on the way to hospital, his sparse clothing being inadequate for a prolonged halt on the mountain. In 1980 the weather was deemed so severe that the race was cancelled for that year.

Women were 'official' participants from 1982 onwards, starting at the same time as the men. The women's record, held by Kathleen Connochie since 1955 still stands, as her time of

3.02.00 is for the King George V Park start. Since 1971 the race has begun from the New Town Park and the women's record at present is the 1.43.25 held by Pauline Haworth of Keswick A.C., made in 1984. The present men's record was also made in 1984 by Kenneth Stuart of Keswick A.C., at 1.25.34.

In 1985 the Ben Nevis Race broke another record with over 500 entries before the race started, at 2.00 p.m. on Saturday, September 7. The winner was H. Symonds of the Kendal A.C., in a time of 1.28.00. The fastest woman was Angela Carson of the Eryri Harriers, with a time of 1.52.45. The poor weather and soggy ground, following an abysmal summer of near-continuous rain, ensured that the records of 1984 would be very hard to beat. Out of the field of 438 who completed the race was No.321, the legendary Eddie Campbell of the Lochaber A.C., who has won the race three times. The 1980 cancellation prevented Campbell from completing his 30th run in a row.

The 1985 list of runners also includes several enigmatic runners who prefer to remain unknown, including No.541, who finished in the respectable time of 1.47.04. But whether it is a runner's wish to run anonymously or carrying a club's name, the Ben Nevis Race remains an annual challenge to those who enter, the most demanding mountain run in this country.

CAR ASCENTS

Another ascent of Ben Nevis was one first made in 1911 and repeated by the same man in 1928. Henry Alexander Jnr did not make his two ascents under muscle power however, but while driving a standard production car from his family's Ford agency in Edinburgh. In 1911 Alexander was driving a 20-horsepower Ford Model T; the car with which Henry Ford revolutionised both the motor industry and factory production. The Model T was light, simple and rugged, and could be bought *"in any colour you wish — as long as it's black."*

The 1911 ascent of Ben Nevis was a publicity stunt set up by Ford. It was a period in which the car was still proving itself superior to the horse and long-distance car runs were in vogue: the Pekin-Paris Run; Paris-New York-Paris Run; trans-Australia, north to south; and other punishing runs in the Alps of Europe. Ford heard that a track existed leading to the summit of Ben Nevis and a feasibility study began.

The first section of the Observatory bridle path, leading to the old Halfway House near Lochan Meall an t-Suidhe, was quickly recognised as being impossible. Many parts on this section were too narrow for the Ford's wheelbase. The next start looked at involved leaving the road at the Ben Nevis Distillery but again it was found to be too difficult. Finally it was decided to drive the car over boggy terrain near Inverlochy, to join the present day track near where the Halfway House then stood.

As the Model T was a fairly light car parts of the boggy route would support it for long enough to allow its progress. Even so, ten days were taken in order to reconnoitre the route to the lochan, wooden planks being placed at strategic points as temporary bridges. It took three days careful driving to reach the Halfway House, the car having to be rescued three times by rope from boggy ground.

Once at the Halfway House further progress was by no means easy. There were three miles of rocky trail left to negotiate, the top section of which was snow-covered. Only in the latter section could the driver relax slightly, as the trail became slightly wider than the car's breadth near the summit. On the summit plateau a path had to be cut through snow in parts, before its triumphant arrival at the now deserted Observatory and closed summit hotel, the season still some time away.

The descent was very different, taking only two and a half hours. Its arrival in Fort William, preceded by pipers, was the signal for much excitement, with a local holiday being declared and a banquet at the Caledonian Hotel. As for the real hero of the ascent, no repairs or replacements were found to be necessary, and after a slight adjustment to the brakes the Model T was driven back to Edinburgh by Alexander.

Seventeen years later, on September 13, 1928, Alexander repeated the feat, this time driving a Standard New Ford touring car — the Model A. The ascent on this second occasion took only one day, putting to good use the experience gained on the first occasion. Starting at 10.30 a.m. the Halfway Hut was reached at 1 p.m., where an oil change was made. By the

10.6   First Car ascent (1911)

time the summit was gained, with four passengers on board for the last quarter of a mile, darkness had fallen, and the car was left there overnight before being taken down the following day.

Three weeks later on Saturday, October 6, George Simpson from Edinburgh made an ascent driving what was then Britain's smallest car, the Austin 'Baby' 7. The car on this third occasion was a standard Austin Seven tourer, with 12,000 miles to its credit. One passenger was carried, in addition to spares and equipment. The first-speed gear ratio was slightly lower than standard but otherwise both gearbox and back axle were standard. The car used chains on its rear wheels and assistance was given only at places where it was necessary to prevent excess wheel spin.

The Austin took seven hours and 23 minutes to reach the summit and the speedometer showed that while the distance travelled on the map was five miles, the car's wheels had revolved the equivalent of eight miles, the difference being due to wheelspin. Despite this there was no noticeable wear on the treads. About one and a quarter hours was lost in repairing the chains at intervals, but this time was included in the total ascent time given above, as was a half hour rest at the Halfway Hut. No water was required to be added to the radiator.

After a rest at the top the descent commenced, the latter half being made in darkness. Despite this the car made it safely down in two hours and two minutes, thus having the distinction of being the first car to make the return journey in one day.

The Austin's climb was monitored by George Douglas, Trials Secretary and Official Timekeeper of the Scottish Western Motor Club, who also wrote the official report of the ascent. Commenting on the condition of the Austin following the ascent, the report noted that —

"The rear mudguards were both bent owing to the chains coming adrift so often, and one spoke was broken. This was the only damage done to the whole car, and that only because when the chains went to pieces they had to be lashed to the spokes. The car was driven from Edinburgh to Fort William and also back again after the Climb without any adjustment being necessary.

This speaks well for the reliability of this make of car. Only those who have seen the track to the summit can realise the gruelling that any machine with more than a single track is subjected to in making the ascent and descent, and no praise is too great for the way this small car behaved."

Other objects have of course been taken up Britain's highest mountain — motorbikes, bedsteads, a piano, wheelbarrows (the Observatory staff were once amused by a man pushing a wheelbarrow from Land's End to John O'Groats, ostensibly to 'raise the wind'). The list is probably endless. The summit has been left in unusual ways as well — balloons and hang-gliders being only two methods. Some of these deeds have merit, some indeed have been done for the purpose of raising funds for charity, but all of them have taken place on the open mountainside. For the next section we have to go underground, to learn of a remarkable tunnel through the mountain.

ALUMINIUM

A few great works are destined to remain largely hidden. One such work is the Lochaber Water Power Scheme, the first phase of which is described here. Leave Fort William going north and a factory complex will be visible on the right, lying on what was originally a boggy moor under the slopes of Meall an t-Suidhe. The factory belongs to British Alcan Highland Smelters Ltd., a subsidiary of British Alcan Aluminium Ltd., manufacturing the metal aluminium, renowned for its light weight and great strength, when alloyed with other metals. To the climber or walker going up Ben Nevis the factory may seem just another factory, jarring perhaps against the backdrop of mountains, with its line of five massive pipes running up the north flank of Meall an t-Suidhe. What is most interesting about it however is because so much of the impressive engineering work carried out over 50 years ago is buried underground. The story of this massive Lochaber Hydro Scheme ties together the unlikely companions of rainfall and aluminium.

The British Aluminium Company was founded in 1894. Lord Kelvin joined the board four years later, taking a keen interest in the new company. It was at Foyers in Inverness-shire that aluminium was first produced in commercial quantities by the electrolytic method. This was in 1896, with an annual output of 200 tons. British Aluminium (B.A.) acquired the U.K. rights to two important processes. The first was the Bayer process, used for the production of alumina, or aluminium oxide, from the earthy mineral bauxite. The second was known as the Hall-Héroult process, from its two inventors, the American Hall and the Frenchman Héroult. This process reduces alumina to aluminium. With the later siting of smelters at Kinlochleven and Fort William, opened in 1909 and 1929 respectively, and a third smelter at Invergordon producing in 1971, B.A. is the country's largest producer of primary aluminium, with a total capacity of about 138,000 tons per annum.

A large supply of low-voltage electric current is necessary for the Hall-Héroult process. During the First World War increasing demand for the metal induced a search for more power. Water power being cheaper than steam power, the original intention was to utilise the catchment areas of Loch Laggan and Loch Treig, driving a 7-mile tunnel from Loch Treig to Kinlochleven. Here, a second powerhouse would be built. However, strong local opposition vetoed the plan.

As an alternative, a new Order was promoted, leading to an Act in 1921, allowing for the construction of a 15-mile tunnel from Loch Treig to the head of Loch Linnhe. Owing to poor economic conditions construction did not begin until 1924. One advantage of the second plan, offsetting the extra length of tunnel required, was the considerable amount of water available from the slopes of the Ben Nevis range of mountains. The scheme planned for a catchment area of 303 square miles, extending from Loch Linnhe to the upper reaches of the River Spey. Rainfall variation is considerable in this area, with the lowest at Laggan Bridge showing an annual average of 41 inches, to Ben Nevis itself, with 161 inches.

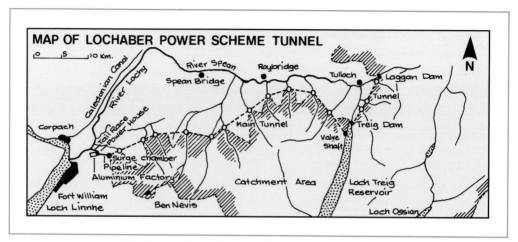

10.7   Fig. 1 – Map of Lochaber Power Scheme Tunnel (1929)

Lochs Laggan and Treig form the principal reservoirs, connected by a tunnel two and three-quarters of a mile long and 15 feet in diameter. Loch Laggan was extended by dredging the outlet and building a dam across the Spean four and a half miles below the loch, 700 feet long and 130 feet high. The height of the surface of Loch Laggan was to remain unchanged at 820 feet above sea level, while the height of Loch Treig was raised by a dam from 784 feet to 819 feet above sea level. The amount of available water from Loch Laggan, calculating on a 16-foot fall, was 1,480 million cubic feet, while Loch Treig, the larger of the two, had an available capacity of 7,838 million cubic feet, calculated on a drop of surface level of 124 feet maximum.

In addition to the natural catchment areas, the flood waters of the Spey in excess of 40 million gallons per day are diverted across the watershed to the River Pattack by means of a dam, while a subsidiary conduit taps the River Mashie, a tributary of the Spey. From Loch Treig water runs down the very gentle gradient of 1:1100 through the 15-mile long horseshoe section pressure tunnel, having an equivalent mean diameter of 15 feet, 2 inches. Along the line of the tunnel eleven major streams are tapped by dams, their excess water entering the tunnel by vertical shafts. As the average area rainfall is high, the water collected by these intakes contributes 16% of the total power available.

Intake Number 11 is well-known to climbers going up Ben Nevis, as it taps the Allt a'Mhuilinn. From this intake, known simply to climbers as 'The Dam', the tunnel runs west to a surge chamber, situated near the top of the pipe-lines visible on the north flank of Meall an t-Suidhe. From the outlet of the tunnel through Ben Nevis, five pipes, each about six feet in diameter and 1,000 yards long lead to the power station. As the turbines have their nozzles at a height of 19 feet above sea level, when Loch Treig is full the maximum head of water available is exactly 800 feet.

The Lochaber Scheme was carried out in three phases. The first phase began in 1924, and comprised all the works to the west of Loch Treig. This was the largest stage and included the 15-mile tunnel. Completed in 1929, the first phase cost about £3 million. The Engineers were Messrs C.S. Meik and W.T., later Sir William, Halcrow of Westminister, London. Meik died in 1923, two years before main construction work had begun. Principal contractors were Messrs Balfour, Beatty & Company Ltd., while the main turbines and generators were by English Electric.

The second phase began in 1933, when Loch Laggan was extended by a dam to provide extra storage capacity. At the same time the capacity of Loch Treig was increased by the building of a 40-foot dam. Raising the level of the larger loch meant diverting one and a half miles of the West Highland Railway Line. The third and final phase was the damming of the River Spey, the water then being fed back to Loch Laggan by a tunnel just under two miles long. This final stage was finished in 1943.

As preliminary work to the main engineering task of driving the 15-mile tunnel, a railway was built connecting Loch Treig to the power-house site. A temporary power plant was also necessary and was built on the River Spean to take advantage of the falls in the Monessie gorge. The power generated by this hydro-electric plant was 6 Kv, raised to 11 Kv for transmission by aluminium cables throughout the works. The total length of transmission line was eventually 25 miles, with 460 volts available for general use. Apart from lighting and various electrical motors, such as pumps, concrete-mixers and so on, most of the power was used for driving air-compressors for rock drilling.

The contract drawn up specified that a railway be built from the power-house site to Loch Treig. A clause stated that if the railway and temporary power plant be completed within nine months from the date of commencement then a large bonus would be paid, reducing week by week after nine months was up until it became zero after 12 months. The contractors earned the bonus.

The main railway was of three foot gauge and was built mainly of 30-pound rails. Its maximum gradient was 1 in 30, the longest haul being at the west end where the line rose from 20 to 650 feet above sea level in under three miles. Numerous streams were crossed on viaducts, built mainly of timber and sometimes of steel girders. Two steam trains ran according to a time-table in each direction daily, carrying mail and stores for the camps. There were in total 26 miles of three-foot gauge, and 20 miles of 2-foot gauge.

A reinforced concrete pier was built at the head of Loch Linnhe, to be available for the handling of construction materials early in 1925. The pier was designed to carry five-ton electric portal cranes and was laid out so as to accommodate ocean-going vessels. The main road out of Fort William was diverted and regraded for a length of 1100 feet to allow for a uniform gradient on the railway connecting the factory to the pier.

At each adit and shaft along the tunnel construction camps were set up for workmen.

Sleeping huts had separate bedsteads, mess and recreation rooms, drying sheds for wet clothing, stores and canteens. A camp hospital was built near adit No.5, with a doctor in constant attendance on the scheme. At the height of construction, 3,000 men were in employment, and £75,000 was spent on camps.

The main tunnel had four working shafts and seven adits. The route of the tunnel did not take a straight line, but was chosen to afford convenient access by the vertical shafts and horizontal adits. In addition to the construction shafts, intake shafts were sunk at eight points, the depth of these ranging from 163 to 271 feet. The cross-sectional area of the main tunnel increases from 169.3 square feet at the beginning, to 181.2 square feet in the middle, reaching a maximum of 193.5 square feet in the last third before the surge chamber. These increases in cross-sectional area allow for the additional water taken from the 11 side streams. There is a 72-foot drop in the 15-mile tunnel, a gradient of 1 in 1100. The tunnel is designed to carry 1,600 cubic feet of water per second, giving a velocity in the largest section, from adit No.7 to the surge chamber, of 8.27 feet per second.

The velocity is lower in the initial section, from the intake at Loch Treig to adit No.3, being 8.1 feet per second, and intermediate in the middle section. Theoretically, an object being carried through the tunnel at a maximum velocity in all sections would travel the 79,723 feet from Loch Treig to the surge chamber at the top of the pipe-lines in a time of about two hours and 40 minutes, a speed of just under 6 m.p.h. There are frictional losses of course, which were minimised by lining the tunnel with concrete.

The main tunnel, one of the largest of its kind in the world on its completion, passes through a wide variety of rock types. For the most part metamorphic schists had to be driven through, with Lairig schist at Loch Treig leading to Eilde flags and Leven schists and finally Ballachulish limestone near adit No.9. The schists were to cause the tunnellers great trouble. The flags were exceedingly hard, virtually quartzitic. The limestone traversed by the tunnel was impure, and where it came near the Ben Nevis granite it had been altered by heat to a hard calc-silicate hornfels. Two granite masses were tunnelled through, one near No.7 shaft and the other from a point east of No.10 adit to the portal. The rocks around Ben Nevis and its companion hills have also been intruded by numerous parallel igneous dykes, running NNE and SSW. Some of these dykes are up to 100 feet thick, though most are only a few feet thick.

The tunnel was bored out from 22 faces. The usual method of drilling involved a short top heading and a bench, the heading being 10 to 15 feet ahead of the bench. There were usually 22 to 30 holes drilled in the heading, 8 to 10 feet deep, with five to nine holes in the bench. In a blasting round of 26 holes in the heading there would be six cut holes, eight easers, and 12 trimming holes. The average advance gained by a blast was about eight feet, ranging from four feet in the very hard hornfels, to about 10 feet in softer rock. The amount of gelignite used per round averaged about 180 pounds for a 'pull' of eight feet (about 64 cubic yards of rock).

10.8   Drilling work on tunnel (1925)

Four percussive pneumatic drills were normally used in attacking the heading, bolted to vertical steel columns. At the same time one or two drills were used on a horizontal bar for drilling the bench. The drills ran off compressed air at a pressure of 80 p.s.i. After trying various work patterns, the tunnel driving settled into a routine whereby the day was divided into two shifts of ten and a half hours working time each. Work was arranged so as to complete a cycle of operations in 24 hours; drilling, firing, removal of spoil. The latter was, as in most tunnel work, the factor governing the rate of progress. Different mechanical methods of spoil removal were tried, but eventually most of the spoil was removed by manual labour.

The progress of the tunnel varied considerably, with a maximum advance of 91 feet in one week, or 350 feet in four weeks. With all 22 faces fully operational, 900 to 960 feet per week was achieved. It had been the original plan to begin lining the tunnel in the various sections after the excavation had been completed, but in several of the longer drives concreting began before the section was finished. Steel forms were used for the concreting, made in panels to fit the radii of the tunnel-section. The usual lengths of forms were 32 and 64 feet. As mentioned before, the function of the concrete lining was to reduce friction in the tunnel; the solid rock walls being sufficient support for the tunnel as a whole. Lining was done at a rate of about 100 feet per week when all went smoothly.

The eight intake shafts were of two sizes. The larger had a water-inlet pipe five feet in diameter, while the smaller had a diameter of three feet six inches. In December 1929 the first tapping of aluminium was made, the water for power being obtained from the side streams until the intake was opened at Loch Treig. The surge chamber, a kind of open safety valve designed to reduce the effect of variations in water pressure, was built in solid granite to a diameter of 32 feet, 30 feet when lined in concrete. Its height is 240 feet. From the surge chamber two 12-foot branch tunnels connect to the pipeline, enlarging to a chamber 32 feet wide and eight feet high, which forms the entry to the bellmouths of the pipes.

As a precursor to all this tunnelling, drilling, blasting and burrowing a complicated triangulated survey was carried out over an area of 75 square miles, using as a base-line a straight section of the railway of about 5,000 feet in length. As a verification of the accuracy of the survey another base-line, about 3,000 feet long and 11 miles from the first was measured. The difference between its measured and calculated lengths was one inch.

One of the most interesting features of the Lochaber scheme, and one which had not before then been carried out in Britain, was the making of an underwater intake at Loch Treig. The underwater slope of the loch at that point was found to be virtually free of debris and quite smooth, probably glacially polished, with a slope of about 1/3 to 1. Tunnelling was started from the valve shafts and moved towards the loch until within 85 feet of the water, at which point pilot holes 35 feet long were drilled to test for fissures. At a point 30 feet from the loch a vertical fissure was met which connected directly to Loch Treig. The crack was grouted and tunnelling continued until the wall of rock separating the tunnel from the loch was only 16 feet thick in the centre and 20 feet thick at the sides. The end face of the tunnel stayed remarkably dry despite being drilled with 134 holes, from 10 to 35 feet deep. Some sprang a leak and gave a considerable flow of water until they were plugged.

Behind the end face a sump was excavated to contain any rock shot inwards by the blast. The holes were drilled to within two feet of the loch. The next step was to construct a bulkhead of solid concrete 100 feet downstream of the valve shafts. The minimum thickness of the bulkhead was four feet. When everything was ready, the drill holes were filled with 3,435 pounds of blasting gelatine and four separate initiators were cross-connected so that even if only one detonator functioned the whole charge would still be set off. The concrete bulkhead, which had a four foot by two foot safety aperture through it, had this covered with a one inch thick steel plate. The tunnel was then filled with water between the bulkhead and the end face until the level in the vertical valve shafts was higher than loch level. The level of the end face was 105 feet below the surface of the loch.

On January 3, 1930, the charge was fired. Gases bubbled to the surface of the loch over an area of about 240 square feet and waves of up to four feet high were induced. The explosion was later shown to have removed about 3,000 cubic yards of rock. The shot-back rock filled the sump as planned and was heaped up for more than half the tunnel's height. The steel plate over the safety opening in the bulkhead was split cleanly along both diagonals, the pieces being found later down the tunnel.

While the tunnel was being driven the pipelines and power house were also being constructed. Two pipes were built for the first phase of the scheme, the entire project requiring a final six (there are now five pipes). The total length of the pipeline is 3,240 feet. The diameter of the pipes is five feet nine and a half inches for the top 1,228 feet, five feet six inches

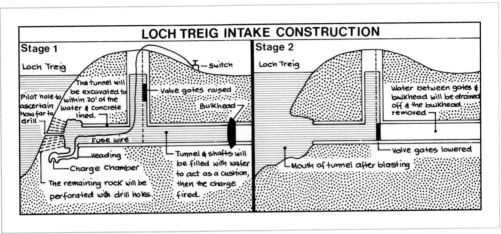

LOCH TREIG INTAKE CONSTRUCTION

Stage 1

Loch Treig

Pilot hole to ascertain how far to drill

The tunnel will be excavated to within 20' of the water & concrete lined.

Fuse wire

Heading

Charge chamber

The remaining rock will be perforated with drill holes.

— switch

Valve gates raised

Bulkhead

Tunnel & shafts will be filled with water to act as a cushion, then the charge fired.

Stage 2

Loch Treig

Water between gates & bulkhead will be drained off & the bulkhead removed

Valve gates lowered

Mouth of tunnel after blasting

10.9   *Fig. 2 – Loch Treig Intake (1930)*

for the middle 1,159 feet, and five feet three inches for the final 638 feet. The thickness of the metal varies from half an inch to one and one eighth inches. Made of welded mild steel, the pipes were manufactured in 30-foot lengths by the South Durham Steel & Iron Company Ltd., each length being of two or three plates lap-welded. The weight of each pipe ranged from five and a half to eleven and a quarter tons. Circumferential joints were electrically welded inside and outside *in situ*.

Valves at the top of the pipeline control the flow of water. Perhaps surprisingly to the non-engineer, the greatest danger to the pipe system lies not in flooding, but in a pipe collapse due to a vacuum. Anti-vacuum valves were built to circumvent this possibility. Should a full-area pipe-burst occur at the bottom end of the pipeline, the upper end would collapse with an excess pressure of about 18 p.s.i. The anti-vacuum valves were designed to pass the maximum amount of air, about 1600 cubic feet per second, with an internal drop in pressure of about three and a half pounds per square inch below atmospheric pressure, therefore providing a safety factor of five.

The power house was excavated out of rock, and is 270 feet long by 63 feet wide. For the first stage of the scheme five turbines were installed, Pelton wheels with their nozzles 19 feet above sea level, and 800 feet below the full height of Loch Treig's surface level. Each of the five units consisted of a single runner wheel with two jets developing up to 10,000 h.p. and driving two DC generators. The current was then passed along aluminium conductors to electric furnaces in the adjoining factory. Below the power station a tailrace runs into the River Lochy.

The power station now has a total installed capacity of 125,550 h.p. There are twelve main sets of 10,000 h.p. each, the turbines working at a normal speed of 250 r.p.m. The total capacity is 82,250 KW, of which about 95% is used to operate two lines for aluminium extraction, each line consisting of 60 to 70 reduction cells of the Soderberg anode type, operating at about 100,000 amperes.

The actual production of aluminium is done by a reduction process at a temperature of about 1,000 degrees Centigrade. When climbers speak of a 'white hell' after a trying day in winter they little realise how close they were. Aluminium oxide (alumina) is dissolved in molten cryolite (sodium aluminium fluoride) in an electrolytic cell. Direct current of high amperage is passed through the cell from the carbon anode, through the molten cryolite, to the carbon cathode. The alumina in solution decomposes, with the aluminium passing to and collecting on the cathode to form a molten pool lying under the cryolite. Oxygen released from the alumina passes to the anode, forming carbon dioxide. The anode is progressively consumed and the carbon is regularly replaced by feeding carbon paste to the top of the self-baking anodes.

The molten aluminium collects in a pool on the cathode. In simple terms this consists of a carbon-lined, thermally insulated steel box with steel bars joined to the carbon to carry the current. Metal is periodically removed by suction tapping for transfer in liquid form by a crucible. In the casting complex aluminium can be found formed into ingots, rolling blocks, wire bars or extrusion billets. Two tons of alumina are used to produce one ton of aluminium by the above process, known as the Hall-Héroult process. In doing so, half a ton of anode carbon is consumed and 16,000 to 18,000 units of electricity used.

The bauxite used by the industry originates mainly from Ghana, while alumina is produced at Britain's only alumina plant in Burntisland, Fife. Burntisland's production goes to the bauxite chemicals industries. The alumina for Invergordon comes mainly from the Caribbean area, rail and road tankers supplying the smelters at Fort William and Kinlochleven with alumina delivered at Invergordon. In addition to employing about 500 at Fort William, B.A. Highland Smelters Ltd., operates one large sheep farm and has several other properties under tenant farmers. Re-afforestation was begun in the late 1940's. Inverlochy Village was built as a direct consequence of the need for extra housing for the workers at the smelter, with almost 300 new houses.

The average climber is aware that much of his climbing hardware uses aluminium; its properties have made possible huge improvements in safety and weight-saving. It is perhaps ironic that the high rainfall in this area, so often complained about, has made it ideal for the Lochaber hydro-electric power scheme. The magnificent feat of the tunnel blasted through 15 miles of solid rock has permitted the Fort William smelter to produce much of that very same aluminium.

11.1   Ken Crocket, Vanishing Gully, (March, 1974)

CONSOLIDATION (1961 – 1969)

In a great leap forward, Scottish winter climbing had come of age. Looking back to early days, the hills in winter had been regarded as good training for the Alps, then interesting for themselves in a narrow sense, before the realisation dawned that here at home could be found adventure enough, satisfying in itself — the Alps were great, but so was Nevis and other notable Scottish hills in true winter conditions.

Future years would see a small but significant counter-current grow, as mountaineers from other countries began to hear of and read about Scottish winter climbing. The gullies and buttresses of Nevis would soon hear accents European and Transatlantic. But a few years of relative peace remained, as the slow and hard work of step-cutting, particularly on the more difficult routes, limited the number of aspirants.

The winter season of 1961, as in the previous year, was opened by Clough and Grandison. The route on this occasion was Tower Scoop, Grade III. This lies below Gardyloo Buttress and gives a two-pitch climb, variable in difficulty. The prize find came later that month however on January 15, with the ascent of Vanishing Gully by Ronnie Marshall and

11.2   J.R. Marshall, FA The Bullroar (June, 1961)

Graham Tiso. The route description by the climbers was a classic in understatement. *"The climb had four ice pitches, three of which were steep"*. In fact the crux pitch, led by Tiso, is often overhanging for a stretch and this superb climb is generally agreed on as being a Grade V.

Vanishing Gully lies on Secondary Tower Ridge, between West Gully and The Italian Climb. Its first summer ascent was probably by Archie Hendry, in the summer of 1943, though it was first recorded by Kellett in September 1944. At its foot the ice may be barely a foot wide: it slowly widens to a shallow chimney leading to the crux section. There will often be a cave belay here, though in exceptional conditions this can be covered, providing a huge bulging wall of ice of over 100 feet. Following the crux pitch a shorter easier ice pitch leads to the shelf of 1934 Route. If the shelf is followed rightward more enjoyable if easy climbing can be had, otherwise a more direct line on the buttress to the left leads to Tower Ridge proper. It is probably safe to comment that Vanishing Gully was one of the best winter routes to be recorded in the 1960's. Interestingly, Tiso does not recollect there being any great difficulties.

The third and last new winter route of 1961 was also in January. George Wallace and Robin Shaw made an ascent of the 1931 Route, Grade III, on January 21. This was originally recorded as a completely new route. Marshall later reconciled it with the older climb.

The snow finally went and the summer of 1961 arrived. With it came Marshall and Stenhouse, up for a weekend at the end of May. The weather had been poor, with heavy rain for several days. Finally, on May 30, the rain stayed away, though low mist clung to the rocks and Marshall and Stenhouse began their long weekend with a route on Number Five Gully Buttress. The Chickenrun, Very Severe, lies right of Five's Wall, the Severe with which Marshall had first entered the lists on Nevis, in 1953.

The weather continued fair for Marshall and Stenhouse and the following day another line was climbed with The Brass Monkey, Hard Very Severe. This route lies on the eastern flank of Tower Ridge and climbs the deep crack in the corner formed where Echo Wall turns out towards Observatory Gully. Across the void to the right is the deeply-cut Great Chimney, the Severe first climbed by Macphee and A.G. Murray in 1935. Marshall had to use two pegs to gain the crack proper and near the top of the penultimate pitch was forced to make a move on to the right wall. The following summer McLean and W. Smith succeeded in climbing the crack in its entirety.

On June 1, with the sun breaking through at last they climbed Carn Dearg Buttress by one of the finest lines in Scotland — The Bullroar. This 800-foot Hard Very Severe route is a masterpiece of route-finding, making a rising traverse rightward across the great undercut slabs of the buttress to finish up corners and grooves parallel to The Bat finish. The crux of the route, most unusually for the buttress and indeed Nevis, is a friction move on the fourth pitch, stepping down and right in the middle of the vast slab. A fall here by the second, and it has been known, will result in a pendulum under the overlap below.

A small but constant weep of water hits the top of the Bullroar slab. On a summer's morning the sun will keep the slab dry, but beware the climbers who start late, for as the sun moves off the slab in the early afternoon the weep gains a hold and a wet patch moves slowly down the slab to reach the traverse line.

The Bullroar traverse continues across the buttress, crossing the line of Centurion. The section immediately after the junction with Centurion gives delightful climbing with perfect rock and good situations. Of all the summer routes recorded on Ben Nevis by Jimmy Marshall it is fair to consider The Bullroar as his greatest legacy. Its name derives from the aboriginal device, whirled in the air to produce a roaring sound during young men's initiation rites.

Ian Clough and Keith Sutcliffe were on Nevis that same weekend and recorded three routes. On May 31 they made an impressive girdle traverse of Carn Dearg Buttress. The Orgy, Very Severe, all 2,000 feet of it, starts up Route I and finishes near Evening Wall. In between it descends parts of Centurion and Sassenach, crosses The Bat and Titans Wall, and follows The Shield for 300 feet.

The next day Clough and his companion recorded two other climbs on the Great Buttress. Mourning Slab, Very Severe, climbs the slab corner on the right of No. 5 Gully. Taking advantage of the dry conditions, they climbed this now rarely followed summer line. Four years later it would be climbed in winter to give one of the busiest routes on Nevis — The Curtain. This pair's other route that day was a Severe, also on Carn Dearg Buttress. The High Girdle starts left of Mourning Slab and crosses Route I to follow Route II to the outer edge of the buttress. Continuing to Evening Wall and past, like its lower companion girdle, this route is rarely if ever repeated.

Surprisingly, that weekend with its six routes by the above four marked the end of the first ascents for 1961. Perhaps even more surprisingly, no routes were made the following winter, with the sole exception of an ascent of Harrison's Climb, on the North Wall of Carn Dearg Buttress. The parentage of Harrison's Climb has been a varied one, with at least five parties having a hand in it. The route, which lies left of Cousins' Buttress, was first climbed in 1929 by Alexander 'Sandy' Harrison. Joining the SMC in 1918, Sandy Harrison was President from 1945-1948, and at the time of writing is the Honorary President. Next came Macphee in 1935, traversing leftward above the chimney of Harrison's Climb in thawing conditions. He was followed in 1957 by Brunton and Clarkson, who are credited with the first winter ascent.

Early in 1962, the first complete winter ascent of Harrison's Climb by the original line was made by Norman Tennent and Malcolm Slesser. Two pitches on the face led to the foot of the chimney pitch, separating Cousins' Buttress from the main wall on the left. In good icy conditions a fantastic fringe of icicles builds up at the top of this impressive face, stabbing downwards at a climber approaching from below. Climbing in tricouni-nailed boots, Tennent stepped on to the foot of the fifty foot ice wall, and in a later essay revealed the leader's thoughts on an ice pitch.

"The start often seems the worst, and this bulge is no exception. Think. Start at the bottom left, and work right, then perhaps left again. Cut as many steps as you can before you start. Move up slowly, you've all the time in the world. You can't stay on at this angle. You can; must. Keep cutting well ahead; out on to the right wall. You can't hold on to ice without a handhold. Blast! I need a step at the height of my left knee. It's no good thinking the angle eases. Keep cutting. The steps are there, even though full of snow. How can my fingers be so cold? Are burnt fingers more painful than frozen ones? That wall looks the steepest yet. Keep your distance brother, and cut with both hands. Out on to the nose. The holds are all there, because you made them. Keep on cutting. You died a long time ago; now you are really living. Over the top, finish the job, give us the tools. Why keep the head; keep the feet first. Could probably finish with fewer holds, but that would be a piece of impertinence. Taking a liberty. Technique or *The Art of Love: Les Liaisons Dangereux*" (1).

Above the chimney Tennent and Slesser made the exposed traverse leftward above the big wall, with a curtain of vertical ice above barring access to easier ground. After they had made the left traverse and were climbing upwards again an avalanche came sweeping down, obliterating the ice wall but luckily missing the two climbers who went on to finish the route.

Summer 1962 saw several easy Very Severes climbed by Clough and Grandison, including the 955-foot Astronomy on the left side of the Orion Face. This follows a line of cracks and grooves parallel to Minus One Gully and tends to be a somewhat grassy line in summer. The excellent Left Edge Route on Gardyloo Buttress was finally climbed, also in June, by the brothers Marshall and George Ritchie. Many old pegs and carabiners were found on the route, marking the sites of previous attempts; by Ogilvy in 1940 for example. Their route finished up the Direct Finish made by Haston and Stenhouse in 1958. The summer of 1962 also saw the death of Robin Smith in the Pamirs. Smith had been roped to Wilfred Noyce, when both climbers had fallen to their deaths on Peak Garmo, walking over an edge on relatively easy ground in poor conditions.

In June the Marshall brothers and George Ritchie recorded an important variation start to The Shield, adding several, hard pitches to the bottom section. Their direct start climbs the lower chimneys, these having being bypassed by Downes and Whillans in 1956. The ascent included a fall by Ritchie. Marshall considers the route to be as good as Centurion, though its position on the flank of the buttress seems to have led to a state of neglect.

Another major ascent of 1962 was a hard and direct line on Carn Dearg Buttress — Torro. John McLean, Willie Smith and Willie Gordon of the Creagh Dhu arrived on July 25. The route starts up the left side of the small subsidiary buttress taken by the first pitch of Centurion. Difficulties begin immediately upon leaving the ground, with a strenuous and gently overhanging groove to be tackled. A peg was placed here on the first ascent for protection while a sling was used for aid on pitch four, moving over an overhang. On the penultimate pitch McLean traversed hard left; most climbers at this point continue straight up.

11.3   *J.R. Marshall, FA The Shield Direct (June, 1962)*

A peg, contrary to the route description published later, was not required for aid on the last pitch but was another protection placement.

Subsequent parties thought that aid pegs had been used on pitches 1, 4 and on the last pitch. In fact, according to McLean, no aid pegs were used, a sling for a hold on pitch 4 being the only point of aid on the entire route.

John Cunningham and Jimmy Gardiner were on the route next but did not finish the climb, missing out the last pitch. The second complete ascent, climbed completely free, was accomplished by two of the 'Dumbarton Boys', 'Big' Ian Nicolson and 'Wee' Ian Fulton, in June, 1970. The two Ians were members of a small group of technically accomplished climbers who lived in and around Dumbarton, climbing skills honed to a fine edge on the exacting boulder problems of Dumbarton Rock. Other climbers from this informal group included Rab Carrington and John Jackson. Several went on to join the Creagh Dhu Club; at least two were to enter the SMC. Ian Fulton described their ascent, made that beautifully sunny day.

"Ian started climbing and was soon performing ridiculous bridges across the bulge. My mind began working overtime as I compared my leg span with his; there would have to be another way. A few funny moves and he was up to a good resting place on the right. A couple of unusual layback moves round a jutting flake led to the foot of a smooth sweeping groove which was quickly climbed to the big comfortable belay. The rope came tight and it was time to go . . . I nervously fumbled my way up to the bulge and removed the protection. Think what you are going to do, don't hang on your arms, work out the moves."

Fulton worked out the alternative way round the bulge and 20 minutes after Nicolson had begun the route the two were reunited on the belay. Fulton found the slab on the second pitch troublesome due to the very dry conditions.

"My feet kept slipping on the dry moss so a well timed grab was made for a big jug and I quickly hoisted myself up the short overhanging groove to the belay. An interesting pitch"

The fourth pitch was soon reached, with the aid sling waiting to be eliminated. Nicolson was determined to free this,

"So up and down he went trying all the different permutations of holds until a high step up with undercut hand holds allowed him to layback round the upper overlap".

The point of aid had been eliminated. Torro then takes a long run-out up smooth water-worn slabs, topped by an overlap below the broken ground near Route II. It breaks through these overhangs using the seventh pitch of Centurion. Nicolson set off up the last pitch.

". . . ridiculous bridging moves brought him up level with the decaying stumps of two old pegs, only to find progress stopped by two loose blocks. Pulling the rope out of the way he trundled them off and we watched, fascinated, as they bounded down the slabs and over the edge. Ian disappeared into the groove. Judging by the sound effects, it seemed to be strenuous but in due course he emerged on the ledge above. He smiled slyly and casually tossed down the fact that he had just done the crux". (2).

The crux is a shallow, vertical V-groove, undercut and with no crack in the back, the sort of problem usually found on outcrops, but the long reach and athletic physique of Nicolson

11.4   Torro

had won the day. Torro is presently graded as an Extremely Severe, E1. It should perhaps be remembered that the first ascent party did not possess much in the way of today's protection equipment, such as manufactured chockstones. Their carrying and occasionally using pegs for protection was standard practice right through to the end of the 1970's. Only then with improved equipment could leaders have the confidence to leave pegs behind in summer. What McLean's party did carry though were the first prototype chockstones — engineering nuts with drilled out threads.

The poor winters which had opened the 1960's retreated slightly in 1963 and several winter ascents were made. The first of these was Wendigo, Grade IV, by Tom Patey and Joe Brown on February 24. Wendigo is to be found on Creag Coire na Ciste, just left of North Gully, and provides difficult technical climbing on mixed ground, Patey's favourite climbing. This was to be Patey's last new route on Nevis; in June 1970 he was killed abseiling off a sea stack. The climbing world was to be all the poorer for the leaving of this colourful man. G. Graham Macphee was killed in February 1963, on a mountain in the Canary Islands. He was descending the summit cone of El Tide, normally a walk but on this occasion plastered with an unusual amount of snow and ice. He had just recently entered his retirement.

In March 1963 another well-known pair of mountaineers recorded a short but hard winter route, when Dougal Haston and Dennis Gray climbed Winter Chimney. This takes the chimney, really more of a corner, lying in the back of the bay which defines the right edge of Gargoyle Wall, on No. 3 Gully Buttress. It's feasibility depends on the amount of ice to be found at the top of the chimney. Here an overhang forces one rightward on to a steep slab and so to the top.

Summer routes in 1963 were limited to an alternative start to Left Hand Route by Clough and friends, and a prominent line on the Douglas Boulder, Cutlass, Very Severe, by E. Cairns and F. Harper on July 6. This 400-foot line takes the clean-cut corner left of the south-west arête of the Douglas Boulder, and was the first Very Severe route on the Boulder.

The brothers Marshall, along with Stenhouse, saw in the last routes of 1963 with two winter ascents in December. Thompson's Route received its first winter ascent and at Grade III/IV gives delightful and steep climbing, particularly in the lower section, where a narrow groove line cuts up through the buttress wall. The other winter ascent in December was the Grade III/IV Jubilation, weaving up through the Central Trident Buttress to give Alpine-like climbing up the open slopes above. Snow conditions must be safe before considering an ascent.

As the 1960's progressed, so the number of outstanding first ascents decreased. There were obvious exceptions of course, but in the main exploratory climbing on Nevis had passed a peak and climbers were content either to slowly complete obvious gaps in the cliffs or repeat earlier lines. Jimmy Marshall was busy researching for the new edition of the Climbers' Guide to Nevis; he would go on to record more than a dozen first ascents. As Marshall's ginger group slowly declined in numbers; some moving elsewhere, some dying, some inevitably losing the momentum of their early hard days, other groups sprang up, including The Squirrels Mountaineering Club.

The Squirrels, taking their name from an Italian Alpine group, were based in and around Edinburgh. In 1964 they moved their activities from Glencoe, where they used a renovated war-time defense bunker appropriately called 'The Drey', to Ben Nevis. Ian MacEacheran and Dave Bathgate made the third winter ascent of Point Five Gully, suffering a cold bivouac half-way up the route in the process. The winter of 1964, however, produced no more than a one-pitch variation finish to North Gully, Creag Coire na Ciste, by Bathgate, Jock Knight and Alisdair 'Bugs' McKeith.

In June 1964, Marshall climbed two routes on the South Trident Buttress, The Clanger, Severe and the Very Severe Sidewinder. Also that June Dougal Haston made his last route on Nevis with Robin Campbell, climbing the pleasant rocks left of Minus Three Gully to record the Very Severe Wagroochimsla. The minimal route description left by this pair is easily augmented, once it is realised that the route name is a derivation of WAll, GROOve, CHIMney, SLAb.

In July, Marshall and George Ritchie left the CIC Hut in a downpour and made for the Minus Face and the unclimbed (in summer) Minus Three Gully. The pair splashed up the gully for some way then came to a slabby groove with a bulge. Ritchie tried this but was beaten back. Marshall took over and soon gained the high point and a stance on slings. From here two possibilities suggested themselves; a clean slab corner on the left with about an inch of surface water, or a right forking, bulging crack. Marshall decided that the crack on the right was to be the way.

". . . with gasping warnings to the grey old man below, the crack is entered, what a thrutch! socks are thrashing, knees rammed survivally into the crack, and gains upward secured by fingery sprags inside . . . Suddenly one of these wee sprags breaks, and I am leaning out backwards on knees, hands slipping green from the bowels of the crack, a backward snatch finds the cowardly provident right-wall sling, enabling the thrust back into the crack and a grunting progression to stand established in what is now a chimney". (3).

All three of the Minus Gullies had now been climbed in summer; indeed, with the ascent of Minus Three, all of the Nevis gullies on the north face had received a summer ascent. The one outstanding winter problem remaining, at least in the classical sense, was Minus One Gully. Lack of suitable conditions in this case delayed an ascent for a further ten years; it was certainly not due to a lack of suitably qualified applicants or determined attempts.

The summer of 1964 moved wetly towards the autumn and at the beginning of September wee Brian Robertson and Fred Harper sweated their way up to the Hut in uncharacteristic sunshine. Robertson had been studying the possibility of a new line on Carn Dearg Buttress between Centurion and The Bat, skirting just right of the former line. The overhanging cracks right of the first pitch of Centurion were wet however and instead Robertson scurried his size four PA's up the first pitch of Centurion to belay at the large block.

From here, most climbers would have followed the traverse of The Bat before breaking away and up over the slabs and overlaps above. But Robertson was possessed with a peculiar stubbornness of purpose and instead made several difficult and devious moves. Traversing rightward from the foot of the Centurion corner, parallel to and lower than the Bat traverse, Robertson used a channel peg to gain a lower slab, before continuing to a peg belay near the end of the slab. It was now 8 p.m. and fixing the ropes the two climbers abseiled down from the belay.

The following day, Tuesday, Robertson and Harper repeated the previous day's climbing, ending back at the peg belay. From here Robertson followed an open corner with one peg for aid leading to the block belay on The Bat. A move down left led to a ledge near the loose block on The Bat traverse, and here Robertson belayed. All this tortuous, though no doubt difficult climbing at the start of Robertson's route is now avoided, climbers preferring the more logical course of following the second pitch of The Bat to gain the same point. Robertson now started up the futuristic fourth pitch, one which has rejected several later attempts. After a few moves he spotted a chockstone high up on the right.

"Being a bit on the small side, I was too wee to reach it . . . With my eyes firmly fixed on the sky, my teeth firmly pressed together, I prepared my body for a peel as I moved up. My forefinger managed to hook itself round the stone, then, after many miserable attempts, I threaded a baby-nylon for a runner. Groping about with my right hand, I found a crack somewhere up on the right, then I managed to get my right P.A. foot flat on the upper slab . . . It looked all right, so I pulled myself up on to the slab".

Robertson was now committed to climbing up the vast slab above the overhang and made for two small holds at head-height.

"As soon as I did stand on these holds . . . I had the sneaky feeling that I was going to make a rapid departure from the rock. One finger, jammed in a bit of muck level with my waist, kept all my ten stone in contact with the rock, and it was failing fast. Somehow, I wangled an ace into a crack. Just as the rope was clipped in, my trusty forefinger gave up the ghost . . . Hanging from the peg, I suddenly felt very tired".

Robertson and Harper retired once more to the CIC Hut, where the next day they were joined by two of their friends, "hoods from the Glasgow Etive Club — 'immy (Weed) Graham, and Drew Campbell". Harper decided to withdraw from the siege at this point, so Wednesday morning saw Robertson and Graham back on the route. This time they took the more sensible course of following The Bat to gain their belay and equipment. Robertson was soon at Tuesday's high point and with further climbing gained a belay up and right. On the next pitch an overlap led to a vertical crack, near the top of which a rightward traverse led to easier ground, half-way up the buttress. More climbing lay ahead of Robertson and Graham, including a small roof overcome by using a jammed-nut and an étrier, but the major difficulties were over on this route — King Kong.

The account by Robertson of the first ascent of King Kong (4), leaves out mention of most of the aid points given in the route description — about a dozen in total. Attempting the second ascent in 1966, John Cunningham, Con Higgins and Ian Dingwall were forced off line on the fourth pitch finding instead, using several points of aid, a new way up the slabs right of Centurion. The second ascent, in June 1970, was by Ian Nicolson and Norrie Muir, taking the entry as for The Bat and eliminating the aid completely. Graded at E1 in the current guide, King Kong is a route in the modern idiom; subtle of line, uncompromising in severity.

The decline in exploratory climbing on Nevis continued through the 1960's. During the last five years of that decade there were 17 routes and a variation made, seven by J.R. Marshall whose guide was to be published in 1969. A further four routes were by Clough who had now left the R.A.F. Mountain Rescue Team and with Hamish MacInnes was running the Glencoe Mountaineering School.

Three winter routes in February 1965 was the sum total that winter. Jimmy Marshall and J. Moriarty ('Eli', the gentle giant, and a regular partner of Dougal Haston), made the first winter ascent of Green Hollow Route on the First Platform at Grade IV. This gave sustained and delicate climbing up thinly iced grooves. Also that month, Marshall teamed up with Dick Holt and a relative newcomer to Nevis, Robin Campbell. By his own confession, Campbell had chosen Edinburgh University for his undergraduate studies on the sole criterion that Smith and Marshall were climbing out of that city. Campbell later went on to edit the SMC Journal (1965-1975); at the time of writing he is President of the Mountaineering Council of Scotland.

Marshall, Holt and Campbell found a tenuous winter line right of the Italian Climb, starting up the steep wall about a hundred feet right of that route. A rising left traverse, a horizontal ledge leading right and a system of snow and ice-filled grooves above completed this hard Grade IV. A second ascent is not known, and certainly unusually heavy conditions would seem to be necessary. Their route approximates to a disappointing summer line first climbed on June 21, 1957 by the Cambridge University M.C. team of Ted Maden and Mike O'Hara, and named by them The Ruritarian Climb; now known as The Chute.

The third winter ascent of February 1965 climbed what is easily one of the most frequented lumps of ice on Nevis. Every winter without fail, though it does fall down during a prolonged thaw, a continuous cataract of ice forms over the wet rocks of Mourning Slab, first climbed in summer by Ian Clough and Keith Sutcliffe in 1961. Named 'The Curtain' long before it was climbed, this is a good winter route which leads nowhere in three pitches, but gives excellent and surprisingly varied ice climbing while doing so. The first ascent in February 1965 was by two of the Squirrels, Dave Bathgate and Jock Knight. The previous weekend Bathgate and Ronnie Marshall had climbed 70 feet of the first pitch before high winds and blowing snow forced a retreat.

The first pitch of The Curtain, a great slab at a reasonable angle, gave Knight a full run-out of 150 feet to a small ice-cave belay at the top of the slab. Many leaders miss the peg runner some 50 feet up on the right wall, though if the ice on the slab is of sufficient thickness ice screws provide adequate protection. Bathgate started up the second and crux pitch, traversing left below a bulge, up a short wall, then back right above the belay to the steepest and hardest section of the route. He tells the story in his own words.

"Twenty feet above me rose a great barrier of vertical ice, tapering and decreasing slightly in angle towards the left, where it met the rock. The intervening twenty feet of 80° ice

11.5   The Curtain (March, 1979)

had to be climbed before I could see if a leftward traverse to the rock was possible. Moving up into new footholds, I noticed something wrong with my right crampon. I looked down and, with the adze of my axe, just caught the front half as it slipped off. I took off the other half and clipped both pieces into a karabiner . . .''

Bathgate managed to reverse back down to the belay, using his well-made holds. There he tied the crampon together and set off up the pitch again.

''Back on the ice and cutting up the steep section, I had to form holds that I could hang on to for as long as possible with one hand; there could be no tension assistance, for I had taken a zig-zag line. After making the normal incut hold, I chipped the sides away, leaving a mound of ice, like half a tennis ball, sticking up in the middle of the hold. Fingers could then spread and the thumb grip. Such a hold is possibly only on the hardest ice. I fixed a third screw at the beginning of the leftward traverse. I cut a handhold, then a foothold big enough for both feet; step across with the left foot, then cut another hand and foothold; bring the right foot across beside the left, then put the left foot in the last hold. Begin again. My left arm was as strong as a wet newspaper by the time I reached the rock ledge 25 feet away, with its sound rock peg.'' (5).

Knight led through and finished the route, climbing the very steep start of the last pitch with tension from an ice screw. Equipment advances since the start of the decade had included the introduction of tubular ice screws, manufactured by the West German firm Salewa. The same company was also responsible for the introduction of the two-part, hinged crampon, adjustable in length. These were very quickly recognised as being superb for mixed climbing. Until then, the favoured crampons were made by Grivel, the French manufacturers.

Originally graded at V, The Curtain is a IV in the current guide, due to its short length and lack of sustained high-angle ice. Protection on the climb being generally good, the ease of access and regularity of being in condition have led it to being a route which suffers a constant stream of ascents. In a busy settled spell so many teams can have kicked their front points up the route that a deep groove may be seen on the first pitch. Despite this indignity, and an air of being an 'ice problem', the climbing on The Curtain is to be recommended.

Another hard route was climbed that winter of 1965, and also by a pair from the Squirrels. Ian MacEacheran and Jim Renny made an inadvertent second ascent of the Ordinary Route on Observatory Buttress, first climbed, but not recorded, by Smith and Marshall in 1960. They named their route The Liquidator, thinking it was a first ascent. Many climbers would regard the route as a Grade V, with a very hard icy chimney high on the climb, and slabby rocks at the foot of the buttress.

Exploration on Nevis in 1965 was completed with an August Creagh Dhu ascent of Rolling Stones, Very Severe. Climbed by John Cunningham and Con Higgins, this forgotten route climbs the vast wall below the Great Tower, on the East Flank of Tower Ridge. Appropriately enough, the Marshall brothers returned to this wall in February 1966, making two winter ascents. East Wall Route, Grade II, was probably a reconnaissance for the harder Echo Traverse, Grade IV. The former route followed an old Difficult climb, traversing right to gain Tower Ridge crest, while Echo Traverse shoots upwards from the easier line, climbing exposed and sustained rocks. Great difficulty was experienced crossing a heavily iced slab, Marshall having to use rope tension from a rock spike. Like so many of Marshall's technically difficult mixed routes on Nevis a second ascent has not been verified.

Marshall continued to dominate Nevis climbing in the mid 60's, returning in September with his younger brother Ronnie to climb two hard and excellent lines. The Knuckleduster, graded Hard Very Severe at least, climbs a superb line on Number Three Gully Buttress. The main bulk of this buttress forms a steep face looking down to Lochan Coire na Ciste. Gargoyle Wall lies on the right edge of this face. The Knuckleduster takes the very prominent groove towards the left side of the smooth buttress face. Fated by its altitude to be climbed infrequently, this classic Marshall line received its second ascent by Big Ian Nicolson.

The second route by the Marshall brothers that September took a central line up the great slabby face left of Point Five Gully. This face had first been attempted by Jim Bell in 1936, in wet weather, and later by Bell and Hamish Hamilton in July 1937. They found the rocks impossible, given their footwear, and moved left to climb the West Face, Upper Route, on the left edge of the great slabs. The ascent by the Marshalls found the rocks to be Very Severe. Both The Knuckleduster and Pointless were climbed on the same day, September 4.

Later that month Ian Clough returned with a partner from Fife, George Farquhar. They climbed an easy Very Severe on the left flank of Carn Dearg Buttress, P.M., lying to the right of Clough's earlier Mourning Slab. On the following day, September 22, Clough and Farquhar recorded a girdle traverse of the Minus and Orion Faces, giving a 2,000 foot Very Severe. This monster girdle, named Marathon, included the cruxes of Right Hand Route and Minus One Direct. It continued by the Great Slab Rib of the Long Climb, finally finishing at the top of Slav Route.

New routes in 1967 opened with a near-tragedy, perhaps the closest call that Jimmy Marshall has had on Nevis. Climbing with Robin Campbell on February 25, the two had finished the first winter ascent of Newbigging's 80 Minute Route. The grading at III is probably conservative, as the crux pitch is a 100-foot groove climbed delicately on thin ice with few positive holds. Descending from the First Platform by the traverse leftward into Coire Leis, Marshall came off due to soft snow, but brought himself to a halt just above the cliff edge below. This same spot was the scene of a fatal accident in January 1983, and great care must be observed here, as in other spots where steep snow lies above a drop.

The only other winter ascent of 1967 was one which led to some grim amusement. Back in June 1964 Marshall and Stenhouse had been climbing on the South Trident Buttress, checking out Kellett routes for the forthcoming Nevis Guide. Looking for a groove in the middle tier they found and climbed a prominent specimen which fitted the description except for the finish. Here Kellett had mentioned a choice of routes; Marshall and Stenhouse had had to climb a vertical wall of unbelievable looseness. At the time Marshall filed the route away in his mind as a possible winter line.

Next February, Marshall and Moriarty returned to the groove, where Marshall pointed Big Eli up the big pitch. Eli climbed the 40-foot entrance wall, glazed and awkward, to a string runner, then moved leftward a little into the groove. Marshall tells the story of what happened next:

"Winter's worries assailed me, the axe belay was useless, the peg doubtful . . . Muffled mumblings and excuses filtered down the rope; brittle ice, glazed bulges, etc; the gut began to tighten . . . Och, he'll be alright, he's so tall he's over most problems before they start, the happy thoughts prevail and I peer into the grim corrie below. The rope moves up, good, that's the bulge over, and then — a great rasping, rumbling, thrashing, tumbling offends my ear. I race the rope back through the string runner. Jesus Christ! there isn't a higher runner. Eli streaks out off the groove head down like a 225 lb. torpedo, my eyes are on stalks as he smashes a crater from the ledge and bounces out into orbit . . . " (6).

11.6   Ed Jackson & Stuart Smith, finish of Central Gully (February, 1978)

Thinking of the 500-foot drop below, Marshall was pulled up against the belay peg which creaked alarmingly as the rope bit through the winter layers of his clothing. Amazingly, Eli's bloodstained face appeared below, as both climbers regained their footing. Other than a deep cut on the bridge of his nose Eli was unhurt, as the two shattered climbers made their way down.

Two winters later, in March, 1967, the determined Marshall returned to the groove again, this time with his brother Ronnie and Robin Campbell. The latter had now been with Jimmy Marshall on various escapades on Nevis, including the occasion when Marshall had come close to grief on the descent from the First Platform.

"I thought . . . of one day when he slipped briefly, stopping himself on the brink, and meeting my specious concern with silent seethings and a steely glare. But most of all I thought of his ungovernable rage when thwarted . . . " (7).

Jimmy led the difficult pitch then brought up the other two. Campbell was then pushed into leading the next pitch, an open bay from which the exit was an overhanging chimney.

"He leered at me, thrusting his red beak through the porridge 'On ye go, son! Up thae cracks. It's nae bother noo I've done aa the hard bits'. High above, I fumbled at a bitter overhang, bare of snow or holds. I thought he'd better hear about it. 'It won't go, Father. It's too steep'. 'Whaur's your spunk, laddie?' he bellowed. 'Do your share, ye wee bastard! Does your puir auld Faither have to dae it aa fur ye?'"

Campbell tried the overhang again but to no avail. He was about to come down when a great cloud of swirling snow descended, blotting out visibility. Taking this chance, Campbell shuffled rightward into an easy groove which led to a chimney.

"I slotted myself in and, thus hidden, made progress to the roof, deaf to his rantings. I'll get him yet, I thought, I see a hole. So I did; deep in the chimney's frosty innards there was light."

Campbell squeezed through the narrow slot and emerged above the difficulties. When Ronnie came up he had to remove some clothing to pass through the squeeze, so they guessed that Jimmy might have difficulty with the chimney, might even stick in fact,

". . . and maybe for a long time at that, and it could just be that a big hoodie craw might come along and take a fancy to his wee beady eyes."

But Jimmy was very cautious,

". . . he stuck his head through to glare and curse, then backed off, roaring for a coil to be thrown to him. 'Throw me a rope, ye wee scut! Ye'll no lead the way again. I'll see to that, mind ye!' Uncle and I hauled him up howling with rage and beating the cold rocks in his shame. Well, that set him back a bit. He led the rest of the way, which was easy, but you could see he was livid. He took us off the buttress by a maze of floury terraces and snowy chimneys, showing off his local knowledge. Back in the stinking hut we thawed out, but he was still giving me the cold eye. 'Ah'll get ye fur that, runt. 'Ah'll get ma chance, ye'll see'. We left it at that. He had to wait a while; till what passes for the summer came, in fact . . . " (7).

As for the route, the last paragraph of this account belong to Marshall.

"Months later during a balmy spring walk around the corrie the whole scene clicked into place. Our route was not Kellett's Groove Climb after all. That climb lay tucked in a corner well to the left, a tiny little chimney, ours loomed and leered in splendid scale above, a classic Nevis joke". (6).

Named, appropriately enough, The Clanger, Marshall's route is Severe in summer and a Grade IV in winter, when the description mentions a through route for thin men.

The 1960's were winding down fast. A variation to Minus One Direct was made by Peter Macdonald and Ian Rowe, climbing round and above the original crux to rejoin the route above. Perhaps the best find of 1967 was the September ascent of Psychedelic Wall, Very Severe, by John Jackson and Ronnie Marshall. This is a good climb, if somewhat loose and messy. With the soon to come revolution in winter climbing it would become known as an excellent winter route.

1968 had one solitary route recorded, Turret Cracks, Very Severe, by Ian Clough and D.G. Roberts. Following a thin crack line left of the prominent line of chimneys on the vertical final tower of The Castle, this short route came too late to be included in J.R. Marshall's definitive guide, then at the mercy of the publisher. The last two routes recorded in the 1960's came in 1969 with, in February, the Grade III Route Major by Clough and MacInnes, and in September the Very Severe Teufel Grooves, by Dave Bathgate and John Porteous.

Route Major is a very fine winter route, closely following in its lower part Macphee and Williams' Eastern Climb on the Brenva Face. It is not a route for the inexperienced, despite its relatively easy grading, as it has some complicated route finding. In the more lean winters of recent years, it has rarely been in obvious good condition. In March, 1969, Ian Clough had published his guide to winter climbs on Ben Nevis and Glencoe. This useful, compact guide filled a gap until Marshall's Ben guide came out, and continued to be of use in Glencoe particularly, despite some historical inaccuracies. (8). Clough was killed in an avalanche on Annapurna, in 1970.

Teufel Grooves takes a good looking line of grooves on Raeburn's Buttress; right of The Crack. Like many of the later routes, knowledge of this route is scanty, and it does not appear in the latest edition of the guide. In 1969 Torro had its second ascent by Nicolson and Fulton, described earlier in this chapter, while on Sassenach John Porteous had an exciting time when an infamous rotating block in the big chimney pitch decided to stop rotating and start flying. Porteous was hanging on to the block at the time, but a runner held him safely. Later he was to be seen ruefully exhibiting the mangled karabiner.

Another seeming lull had fallen on Ben Nevis. Talented climbers were about though the publication of Marshall's guide, in its soon to be familiar blue cover, seemed to say it all. But strange hammering sounds were heard in various workshops around the world, as the conventional shape of the ice-axe was changed and bent into something new. Front-pointing was about to be sprung on an unsuspecting public.

12.1   *Ken Crocket, Harrison's Route (1980)*

REVOLUTION (1970 – 1985)

Until 1970, winter routes were climbed in virtually the same style as they had been climbed at the turn of the century, a single cumbersome ice axe laboriously wielded by the leader who hewed a line of hand and footholds. The early climbers had used larger axes and cut when feasible with both hands. This made it very difficult to cut steps on near-vertical ice, but the gradual shortening of the ice axe shaft made steep angles less of a strain.

Steep pitches of snow and ice were cut one-handed from about the 1930's onwards. Douglas Scott had his short axe custom-made by a blacksmith in 1936, but no British manufacturer seemed willing to take on such a tiny market, and long shafted European makes continued to be the only axes available — Stubai, Aschenbrenner, Grivel, etc. A climber bought the axe available in his local sports shop then had it shortened. Crampons came into more general use in the 1950's and helped lessen the leg-strain of standing in holds and kicking steps up easier angled slopes.

Ice daggers were used by a few climbers for balance — notably by John Cunningham who, with Bill March, climbed Zero Gully in under six hours. This was in 1970, effectively the year in which front-pointing experiments first came to the notice of British climbers. Before then, direct aid from long ice pitons was the only real assistance a leader could expect to find on an ice pitch. Hamish MacInnes, the 'Old Fox' of Glencoe, had been experimenting with ice axe design since about 1965, working with metal shafts. His early designs for inclined picks did not go far enough with the angle of inclination however, his contributions to front-pointing coming a few years later.

In 1970 the Americans Yvon Chouinard and Doug Tompkins visited Scotland. Chouinard, long an innovator when it came to producing climbing gear had brought out his design of rigid crampons, for use on ice. In some ways these were a refinement of the Austrian modification to Grivel's twelve point crampons, the latter first appearing in 1932. The Grivel crampons were excellent for Scottish conditions, though did tend to be brittle. Salewa crampons, lighter and with straight inclined front-points, took over from Grivel in the 1960's. The Salewas were hinged and of particular use on buttresses and mixed climbing. As their length could be adjusted, they also fitted the boot more snugly, increasing confidence.

To go with Chouinard's crampons he brought his curved ice hammers, again designed for pure ice. The two Americans climbed Raven's Gully in Glencoe, in February 1970, making the first winter ascent of the Direct Finish (1). The sight of their ice hammers spurred a few observant Scottish climbers to experiment on their own. The crampon technique used by the Americans was one never taken up by British climbers, being the French style known as 'pied a plat', in which the feet are often placed flat on to the slope. British climbers used the German/Austrian front point technique, more suited to the 'normal' terrain found on local mountains. The amusing fact about Raven's Gully is the limited amount of pure front-pointing normally possible in its rocky confines.

Like most innovations front-pointing took a few years to become accepted. Some adventurous climbers began in 1971, with blacksmith-made axes. One of the earliest and most influential climbers to take up the new technique was Mike Geddes, a Scot from Edinburgh who went south to study chemical engineering at Cambridge University. Interested by an article in 'Mountain' at the end of 1970 Geddes bought a Chouinard hammer and also persuaded a blacksmith to make a copy of a Climax. Other climbers front-pointed using alternative equipment, such as the Salewa half-round ice screws wielded by Norrie Muir in 1970. These were never satisfactory, however, and Muir failed on The Curtain with such gear.

Even more climbers adapted to the new technique half-heartedly, testing the water if not the ice with cold feet, loath to buy two expensive tools when one old axe would suffice. This led to hilarious episodes with climbers trying to lead pitches in mixed style, which inevitably meant cutting steps. Within three years however the conversion would be complete for all but a few.

12.2   Allen Fyffe, FWA Astronomy (March, 1970)

The 1970's opened with a conventional Grade III in February by Norrie Muir and G. Whitten, Garadh Buttress. Possibly climbed before, this leads up the rocks right of Garadh Gully. The following month saw a new Grade V on the Orion Face, when Kenny Spence, Allen Fyffe and Hamish MacInnes followed a line approximating to the Clough V.S. Astronomy. The route was sustained at a reasonable level, linking a series of snow patches by iced grooves and corners. True to MacInnes's character the ascent was unconventional, the second and third men using jumars. Despite that time-saving technique, a late start enforced a bivouac on the North-East Buttress in bad weather, following a ten-hour ascent of the route. Soon after their March ascent, the winter fizzled out in a series of thaws.

By April 1970, the lines on Carn Dearg Buttress had been for the most part either climbed or tidied up. There remained one obvious feature between Torro and The Bullroar, known as the Weep. This was a dark, wet patch which originated from the green garden on Route II, oozing water and slime down over the slabs and overlaps below, finally drying up on The Bullroar slab traverse.

Con Higgins and Robert 'Rab' Carrington attempted it in 1967, but were beaten by a wet slab on the second pitch. In April 1970 the Weep was dry from the winter frosts, waiting for the summer rain to begin its dribblings on the slabs below. Carrington had returned with Ian

Nicolson that year to try the line again.

Cowslip — for the proposed new route had already been named — began just left of Torro, following a faint groove running up leftward to a stance below overhangs. Carrington led up the second pitch, making a hard move to gain the slab above. He found himself committed, in a poorly-protected situation.

"With an ingenuity born through fear, I managed to wangle in a couple of tatty 5mm runners. In front of me lay the black, overhanging corner I was hoping to climb. Padding up the slab a bit, I got a mucky finger-hold in the depths of the corner. This allowed me to get my feet right up to the roof. The position was precarious: the fingers of my left hand, jammed in the corner, were holding my arching body to the rock, while my right hand was groping for a hold on the lip. One last push and my fingers curled round an edge; luckily it was good, because my feet came off almost at once, leaving me flailing in space, hanging on by my fingers. A quick heave and I landed on the ledge like some floundering porpoise." (2).

The key to the route had been found and Carrington and Nicolson soon found themselves under the final overhangs of the great buttress. Here, seemingly impossible rock forced them to traverse first right, overlooking the final pitches of Torro. Unhappy, they eventually traversed hard left under the rock to finish up the Clough/Farquhar route P.M. Cowslip is given a grade of E2 in the current guide, making it the hardest route on the buttress through the 1970's.

June 1970 introduced the Glasgow based 'Steam Team' to Nevis. This healthily unconventional association had begun routinely enough, for some of them were members of the JMCS. Soon tiring of what was to them that Club's polite restraints, independence was chosen by Stevie Docherty, Bobby Gorman, Norrie Muir and others. Excess energies were on occasions diverted to new and exciting ways of entering the CIC hut without the usual paperwork — events which were to lead to confrontations with the Custodian. More useful energies led to one of the best finds of the decade on Nevis, with the first routes to be recorded on the steep central buttress of the Central Trident Buttress.

That June of 1970 Norrie Muir and Ian Nicolson began a burst of hard climbing on Nevis. On the Saturday of their long weekend they made the second ascent of King Kong. Sunday was reserved for Central Route and Sassenach, while on the Monday the new buttress was officially breached with an ascent of Heidbanger. Probably about E1, this excellent route climbs the centre of the crag, starting just left of a prominent crack. Muir returned seven years later with Arthur Paul to climb the true start by the prominent crack.

The 300 or more feet of the new crag on the Central Trident Buttress highlighted the amazing neglect suffered by Ben Nevis. The buttress is steep — very steep, drops of water on a wet day falling 200 feet free from the top overhang — while the rock is sound. In August

12.3   Comb Gully Buttress (March, 1976)

1971 Stevie Docherty returned here with Davy Gardner, to record Metamorphosis, reputedly the best line on the crag. To complete summer ascents in 1970, Robin Campbell and Fred Harper recorded Gutless, Severe, on the Douglas Boulder, climbing the dirty chimney left of Cutlass.

The Nevis winter season of 1971 opened on January 3 with Davy Gardner and Ian Fulton making a logical variation finish to Ian Clough's Comb Gully Buttress. The two climbers were cutting steps, not yet being converted to front-pointing, so the crux pitch consumed several hours of hard climbing on ice. The original finish, as climbed by Clough, takes in a rightward-curving chimney on the steep, final rocks. This is not a line which holds snow or ice, however, and is now not followed, climbers taking the Fulton-Gardner variation. The buttress is an enjoyable Grade IV.

Marshall and Campbell were back on Nevis again in February 1971, climbing a line of discontinuous chimneys on the right flank of the South Trident Buttress to record Joyful Chimneys, Grade III. In March Docherty and Muir, attempting the second ascent of Orion Direct, made a variation start to that route, entering the Basin via steep grooves just left of Slav Route. They made two attempts on the great face that winter, one of them being abandoned half a pitch short of the Basin due to a sudden thaw. The two Glaswegians were using bent-down axes at this time.

Another climber using home-made or 'converted' equipment during the 1971 winter was Mike Geddes. Then a student at Cambridge he would make the long trip to Nevis, hitching up to Edinburgh on Friday to connect with a pre-arranged lift to Fort William. On the Sunday afternoon, using the extra time provided by the new technique, Geddes and his companion would wearily begin the tedious return to Cambridge.

On March 15 Geddes and John Higham climbed Aphrodite, Grade III/IV. This 600-foot line climbed the steep mixed face between Green Gully and No. 3 Gully Buttress, beginning about the centre of the buttress and moving up and left to finish up grooves overlooking Green Gully. Three days later Geddes and Harold Gillespie, the latter in the JMCS, recorded a route right of Glover's Chimney. The White Line, a 900-foot Grade III, was almost certainly a repeat ascent of the line taken by Goodeve's party, during their epic 29-hour ascent of Tower Ridge, in 1907, (see Chapter 4 for a full account of this story).

Geddes' major contribution in 1971 came in March with his second ascent of Smith's Route on Gardyloo Buttress and a third ascent of Observatory Buttress, both with the Edinburgh climber, Nigel Rayner. Their ascent of Gardyloo Buttress in four and half hours came 11 years after the Smith-Marshall first ascent, and sounded the beginning of the end for step cutting.

Also climbed by Geddes was Point Five Gully. Geddes led three others up the initial, difficult pitches, the three prusiking behind Geddes, before the climbers continued as two ropes; Geddes and Higham first, followed by Gillespie and Alan Rouse, the latter a young novice. Point Five Gully had its next front-pointed ascent in April by John Cunningham and Bill March, whose impressive two and three quarter hour ascent apparently made note of climbing time only. Also in April came the third ascent of Smith's Route, on this occasion Kenny Spence leading a climbing course party up in superb snow conditions.

The first major new route to be climbed on Ben Nevis using front-pointing was the April ascent of Hadrian's Wall Direct by Geddes and Graham Little. This was their third or fourth attempt on the line, each day the two climbers starting to climb a little earlier as the daily temperature slowly rose. Little, who had just begun climbing, followed Geddes up the hard pitches by prusiking. Hadrian's Direct, originally graded at IV, begins up two very steep ice walls to enter the chimney taken by the original line. Its present grading at V is probably more appropriate, given the length and nature of the climbing. It remains a firm favourite, often in condition and always exciting. The second ascent of Hadrian's Direct was that of Quinn and Lang, by cutting, in February, 1973. (See later this Chapter).

The second front-pointed ascent of Hadrian's Direct was probably that of Ian Sutherland and Ian Skyes, on March 10, 1973. As an interesting point, the original recording of Hadrian's Wall Direct, in the CIC Log Book, had Grade V. This has been altered to IV in a different ink, suggesting that the first ascent team were themselves unsure of the grade. (Or, just as likely, that someone else disagreed with the grade, without having actually climbed the route.)

The winter of 1971 gave way to summer and the finding of another new crag on the north face of Nevis. The North Wall of Castle Ridge is the first piece of rock seen by a climber walking round by the Lochan Meall an t-Suidhe approach. The foot of the very steep upper wall is best gained by traversing round Castle Ridge from the bay below the Castle. The first route here was found by Dave Bathgate and G. Anderson, on July 10. Plastic Max, a 500-foot Very Severe route, was followed in September 12 by another route, climbed by Norrie Muir and R. Schipper. Night Tripper, a 600-foot Hard Very Severe, lies fairly close to Plastic Max, but as neither route have in all probability received second ascents their grades and precise locations remain in some doubt.

With ascents of a Severe on the Douglas Boulder by Klaus Schwartz, an instructor at the nearby Loch Eil Outdoor Centre, Metamorphosis by Docherty and Gardner on the Central Trident Buttress, and a Hard Very Severe, Arthur, by Schwartz and G. Webster on No. 3 Gully Buttress, the summer ascents of 1971 were over — with one notable exception. In September Norrie Muir made the first solo ascent of Centurion. Muir had arrived at the foot of the buttress, intending to solo the route, when he met a pair of local climbers.

Now Muir, like many other climbers, does not like the first pitch of Centurion, the 50-foot deceptive wall leading to the start of the corner. He led this pitch roped then handing over his equipment to the two climbers soloed the remaining seven pitches of the Hard Very Severe. On arriving safely back at the foot of the buttress Muir, to satisfy his mind and complete the route, soloed the first pitch. He then abseiled back down, the route complete. Earlier that year, in July, he had soloed Astronomy. Muir was to be one of the most active of climbers on Nevis though after marriage in 1973 he stopped climbing until 1976.

January 1972 saw the Steam Team in operation again, with first winter ascents of Wagroochimsla, Grade IV, by Docherty and Adam, and Left Hand Route, Grade V, by Docherty and Muir. The latter route included a tension traverse and considerable excitement on the slab pitch. Muir was leading this with a bent-down Stubai hammer and an axe. When one of his crampons fell off he was forced to cut steps to finish the pitch. The fun didn't end there, Docherty dropping Muir's axe. Somehow the two Glaswegians finished the 900-foot route, but due to powder snow a late finish made the logical continuation up or down North East Buttress impossible. The two climbers then abseiled down Right Hand Route, Muir going first with the only head torch. This led to a surprise for Docherty on one abseil, when Muir came to the end of the rope and continued going down for a further 30 feet solo.

In February, the triumvirate of Campbell, Carrington and Marshall made the first winter ascent of Newbigging's Route, Far Right Variation, a 600-foot Grade IV. This is the natural winter line up this part of the buttress, taking in thinly iced corners and slabby grooves. (Carrington is said to have been so impressed by Marshall's single axe technique on this route that he seriously considered reverting to that method). Carrington and Marshall also teamed up that February for an ascent of Left Hand Chimney, Grade IV, on the Douglas Boulder.

12.4   Alastair Walker on Serendipity Variation, Minus One Direct (June, 1984)

The major winter ascent during February 1972 however was the long-awaited second ascent of the Orion Face Direct, first climbed by Smith and Marshall 12 years earlier. This was made by front-pointing techniques, the climbers being Mike Geddes and Alan Rouse. Both were continuing to travel from Cambridge, making their long-distance and highly profitable trips three or four times a winter. Both climbers were also continuing to use home-made ice tools, though Rouse by now had bought a Terrordactyl. This latter was the ice tool designed by the practical MacInnes, and originally named after its silhouetted resemblance to the prehistoric flying reptile the Pterodactyl. (Inevitably the name was changed for commercial purposes.)

Unfortunately for Rouse his Terrordactyl was one of a number manufactured in the early years which bent during use. Rouse, wearing glasses, had a hard time seconding the slab traverse, his vision obscured by snowed-up spectacles and his efficiency, unknown to him at the time, impaired by a next-to-useless Terrordactyl pick.

Geddes and Rouse made the second ascent of Orion Direct harder for themselves by carrying sacks with all their weekend equipment. Finishing the route at about 9 p.m., they then had to head back down to Cambridge trusting to rule of thumb — hitching lifts on the road. Cambridge was not reached until late the next day. Climbers don't come much keener than that!

Kellett's Right Hand Route received its winter ascent in March, by Carrington and Rouse, at Grade V. This sustained route added to the growing concentration of long, hard winter lines on the Minus and Orion Faces. A Grade II on the North Wall of Castle Ridge and a Grade IV immediately right of Slingsby's Chimney completed winter ascents for 1972, the last season in which winter routes of any note climbed by cutting would be recorded.

August 1972 marked the beginning of summer climbing on Ben Nevis, at least as regards new rock, with a variation to Minus One Direct by Crocket and Fulton (see Chapter 8). The first complete route to be climbed however was a line on the South Trident Buttress, by the now ubiquitous Norrie Muir and D. Regan. Submitted with the suggested name of Pink Dream Maker, the line was climbed later the same summer by Jimmy Marshall and Robin Campbell, who encountered some loose rock. Campbell now thinks that Muir's ascent went where stated, and that Muir was not, in fact, "suffering from hallucinations" (3). The route was named Strident Edge by Marshall and Campbell.

Other good routes from the summer of 1972 included Big Ian Nicolson's Sioux Wall on No.3 Gully Buttress. As with other excellent climbs on high crags, this route suffers an unjustified neglect. By visual inspection it would seem to provide a superb face climb, taking a rising line up the buttress right of Marshall's Knuckleduster — itself a neglected route of great appeal. Nicolson's naming of the route was a witty attempt to circumvent the New Routes policy of the SMC, eponymous route names being frowned upon. (His wife's name is Sue.)

The autumn of 1972 was the best for many years, with the Scottish Highlands a blaze of golden colours. The September 4 ascent of Nicolson's Sioux Wall was the first of several routes climbed in September and October. Campbell recorded two routes on the Central Trident Buttress with the delightful names of Gutbuster, Very Severe, and Nosepicker, Severe. These two routes climbed the diamond-shaped buttress between Central Gully and Jubilee Climb.

Finally came four routes from Paul Nunn. On September 30, Nunn and M. Curdy climbed Dissection, Very Severe, taking a direct but admittedly contrived line starting between The Shadow and Route II, Direct Start. On a return visit in October, Nunn and Paul 'Tut' Braithwaite recorded three short Very Severe routes on the steep upper wall of Number Five Gully Buttress. Their technical grade is very probably more than Very Severe, but until 1977 the SMC Journal, wherein are published new climbs done in Scotland, did not sub-divide the climbs of Very Severe standard and above.

The superb autumn of 1972 was offset by the disappointing winter and summer of 1973. One route only was recorded for that entire year. Boomer's Requiem, Grade IV, by Con Higgins and Dougie McArthur. This followed a prominent icefall left of Raeburn's Buttress. In March Geddes and Rouse climbed Minus Two Gully, on what was probably the second ascent, 14 years after Marshall had led the youthful Haston and Stenhouse up the gully.

The advantages of the new winter techniques were again highlighted during that otherwise poor season of 1973, when Ian Nicolson soloed Point Five and Zero Gullies in one morning. Nicolson was climbing six days a week at this time on the Glencoe winter courses set up by Clough and was at the peak of fitness. His partner for the day was Dave Knowles, an English émigré also living in Glencoe. Knowles, an excitable, energetic climber, was killed several years later on the Eiger, assisting in the production of the film 'The Eiger Sanction'.

Nicolson disclosed nothing of his plans that day to Knowles, as they quickly trotted up the Allt a'Mhuilinn path. On arriving at the foot of Zero Gully Knowles was quietly informed that he could come along on the route, but that Nicolson intended to solo it. Both climbers set up into the thick swirling mist, Nicolson in front using his Terrordactyls. Every so often he would stop and wait for his friend, giving confidence on the steep parts. This held him up slightly, but even so Nicolson emerged at the top of Zero one hour after entering the gully, with Knowles ten minutes behind.

Descending Tower Gully, Nicolson traversed over to the foot of Point Five. Knowles declined to solo this time however, teaming up instead with a third climber. Nicolson finished Point Five Gully in 50 minutes, arriving back in a Fort William pub just after 1 p.m. in time to polish off a well-earned pint of beer.

Most winter climbers actively engaged on Nevis had now converted to front pointing. As there was at this time very little choice in the way of ice tools, climbers decided on either the curved Chouinard gear or the straight inclined Terrordactyls, though a few, as described earlier, adapted or had made for them their own weapons. All systems worked to a degree, assuming a climber had confidence in his particular choice. The MacInnes designed Terrordactyls probably had a slight advantage in mixed conditions, though many agreed that they were not as good on ice.

Those climbers who started winter climbing after the equipment revolution knew no other way of course, for no one was going to revert deliberately to step cutting. To paraphrase an earlier writer, those lucky climbers who had begun in the step cutting age and then changed would always feel that they had been members of a privileged class, that they had tasted of a fabulous, yet dangerous liqueur, the recipe for which was long forgotten. Most converted climbers also felt a sense of relief at the passing of step cutting, but it was relief coloured with a little sadness.

"Strength and endurance were major factors in the years before the early seventies, when climbing ice meant hanging on with one Dachsteined hand while chopping holds in stubborn ice with the other, all with a usually ill-balanced, cut-down axe, twice as heavy as some modern tools. A good step-cutter had to be ambidextrous, to permit cutting on either side and to allow the alternate arm to recover its strength. But if the effort was high, the rewards were higher still. Each pitch was a route in itself; to be worked out and worked on.

The climber on a hard route was constantly aware of the fine line between satisfied fatigue and dangerous exhaustion". (4).

February 23, 1974 marked the end of an era, when the last gully on Nevis received its winter ascent. Minus One Gully was climbed that day by Ken Crocket and Colin Stead to give an enjoyable Grade V outing. The difficulties lay, not so much in the actual climbing, though it is not the easiest Grade V on the mountain, but in finding the key section in climbable conditions. This was the overhanging cave pitch low down the gully which had stopped all parties attempting the route to date, including an attempt by Rouse and Carrington in April, 1972. Indeed, according to a local climber, there had been over twenty attempts on the route.

Crocket and Stead soloed the first easy pitch of Minus One Gully then roped up for the cave pitch, Stead tackling the icy corner. Both climbers describe the ascent, Crocket beginning with Stead's attempts on the overhang.

"He was making no progress with the overhang and to my impatient eye seemed to be tiring. A loose suggestion to use a screw ended in technical failure as he made a soft landing on the snow-cone. Finally, caught between my impatience and the improbable left wall, he announced a tension traverse. I was impressed when he admitted it was his first . . . Fascinated, I watched an apparent revolt against gravity as he teetered across from snow lump to snow lump, outlined starkly against a lowering grey sky. The climbing was obviously impossible — yet he was succeeding." (5).

Crocket managed to second this section by climbing the ice boss directly, then led through on the second pitch, a steep ice wall above an overhang.

"I traversed left under a bulge in the open gully — it was now more of a scoop — and found a steep wall of hard snow. I still had an adrenalin high from following the overhang and clumsily smashed a fingernail on a protruding lump of ice".

[A hazard commonly experienced by terrordactyl users, these axes having a limited clearance between shaft and slope due to steeply inclined picks.]

"When I came to follow", wrote Stead — "I found an impressively steep ice wall, which was pointed up from one resting place to another, with blood-drained arms and bruised knuckles, removing his one protection screw on the way. It was a good pitch". (6).

Both these climbers were SMC members, climbing during a period which marked the beginning of a rise in that club's activities. Minus One Gully had been one of the few major

12.5 *Colin Stead, FWA Minus One Gully (Feb., 1974)*

lines unclimbed by Marshall and his contemporaries, due to its rarely being in amenable condition. With its companion routes Minus Two Gully and the Orion Direct, it completed a great trilogy of major classic winter routes, Alpine in magnitude, Scottish in nature.

March 1974 brought better settled weather to Nevis and five more lines were climbed by various parties. The Creagh Dhu were responsible for two lines, Brian Dunn and Con Higgins finding a Grade IV on March 3, with East Face, a prominent groove line starting below and right of Zero Gully and leading up the entire length of the East Face of Observatory Ridge.

Two days later, Dunn and Higgins were joined by Dougie McArthur for an ascent of Minus Two Buttress, Grade V. This 900-foot route starts 40 feet left of Minus Two Gully and climbs the sustained rocks of the buttress to gain the crest of North-East Buttress.

On March 9 it was the turn of the SMC again, with Doug Lang and Neil Quinn making an ascent of Left Edge Route on Observatory Buttress. This Grade V climb followed a Bell Severe, 400 feet to the Terrace running across the Buttress with another 350 feet leading to the plateau. The three long pitches leading to the Terrace took some five and a half hours of sustained climbing by the Dundonians, a measure perhaps of its difficulty.

Quinn and Lang were one of the most consistent ropes climbing during the 60's and 70's. Quinn was unusual in that he did virtually no summer climbing, other than the occasional easy route — and that was sometimes done in order to make a reconnaissance for a possible attempt in winter. With several other local climbers, they were active in areas across the breadth of Scotland: Creag Meaghaidh, the Cairngorms, Ben Nevis. Quinn and Lang were one of the last of the active ropes to convert to front-pointing but their abilities on snow and ice continued strongly after the technical revolution.

As a pair, the two Dundonians are physically disparate — the ectomorph and the endomorph, Laurel and Hardy, with the broad-beaming Quinn offset by the greyhound figure of Lang. Their inevitably late arrival at the CIC Hut on a Friday evening would be the signal for

12.6   Neil Quinn at CIC Hut (March, 1974)

general hilarity, as Lang produced a great cabbage head and half a turnip for the next evening's dinner. (According to Lang, the food arrangements were usually engineered so that the actual carrying of the food fell to him.)

Quinn virtually stopped climbing in the early 1980's, taking to marathon running instead, but before then the two made some exciting ascents, including the second ascent in February 1973 of Hadrian's Wall Direct. Quinn described their epic 17 and a half hour ascent in a later Journal article. It was almost certainly the only one to have been made by cutting. (Though Crocket and Stead climbed the original line by cutting.) Lang led the first pitch, cutting its 150 feet in three hours. Quinn took over and set off up the next pitch, normally the crux in winter, with a section of near vertical ice.

"I cut holds up this final section in several sorties and at last make a move up the wall but reaching the top holds I can't let go to cut any more, not even to plant a screw or a Chouinard hammer. So down again and I put a screw just below on the right for tension. This results in dinner-plating of the right hand holds. Oh well, try the left and once again the hand holds are very effectively removed. I go back down the wall to the halfway stance to think . . . "

Quinn eventually succeeded in overcoming the ice bulge but by the time both climbers were at the foot of the chimney darkness had descended, an ever-present threat hanging over a lengthy step-cutting expedition. They continued up the chimney and ran out several rope lengths above, slowly being forced rightward. Lang belayed below a bare wall, not far from the plateau.

"There's a bare holdless ten-foot corner on the right and an open groove leading to an overhang on the left with a practically bare wall between. Very interesting, but at midnight shattering. Lang smugly gives advice from the security of his phoney belay above. He suggests hauling the sack *[the Dundonians habitually climbed with one rucksack]* but we've wasted enough time so I try it with it on". (7).

Quinn managed to struggle up the wall Lang had just led and continued past the belay after leaving the rucksack again. Thirty feet further on he reached an impasse with bare holdless rock. Frustratingly he could see the summit slope twenty feet to the right. Lang had a go at the pitch but could make no further progress, so the two climbers decided to try and sleep on the miserable belay ledge. After a short period of this, during which Quinn was frequently awakened by snow kicked down by a restless Lang, they made a move at retreat, almost immediately finding a good belay for the abseil rope.

One abseil, a down-climbed pitch and a traverse left and a snow gully was gained allowing the tired climbers to struggle up to the summit. The entry in the log book for their ascent was headed "A Comedy of Errors . . . ".

More straightforward was the Quinn and Lang ascent of Slav Route on March 23. Theirs was the first complete ascent of this sustained route, but only just, as on a prior occasion Con Higgins and Brian Dunn had climbed all but the last 80 feet of the route before circumstances forced them to traverse right into the easy finish of Zero Gully. For that reason Higgins decided not to record the ascent.

From this point on the pace of winter climbing in particular increased, with areas of Nevis opened up by front pointing unlikely to have been possible by step cutting. (Many of the routes climbed in the last ten years covered by this history of Ben Nevis have not yet received sufficient ascents, or even a second ascent, for a true assessment of their grades. As a consequence, a selection of what appear to be the most interesting routes has been described. Few have been left out.) One such area was Indicator Wall, whose development well illustrates the jerky, irregular pace at which trends in winter mountaineering tend to advance — a result, perhaps of the climbing conditions, equipment and individual endeavour.

Winter routes on Indicator Wall began in February 1975 with a fine ascent of the Indicator Wall ice fall by Gordon Smith and Terry King. The route was graded, perhaps modestly, at IV/V. An interval of three years then occurred, until a good spell of hard ice in

January and February of 1978 saw no less than four routes. Mike Geddes and Con Higgins opened the salvo with Albatross, Grade V, on January 21, a line which starts up the left corner of the central slab before breaking out left to finish up the steep grooves and chimneys on the upper wall.

The following day, Norrie Muir and Arthur Paul started at the toe of the buttress opposite the left edge of Gardyloo Buttress, climbing up directly to give a winter ascent of Psychedelic Wall at Grade V. Mike Geddes returned on February 11 with Alan Rouse, and after following Gardyloo Gully for 100 feet or so broke out left to produce a Shot in the Dark at Grade IV. Finally, to

12.7   Doug Lang, FWA Slav Route (March, 1974)

complete the 1978 quartet of routes, a week later on February 18 Davy Gardner and Arthur Paul climbed a line just right of Psychedelic Wall to give Caledonia, Grade V. This goes up to share the same first stance with Shot in the Dark before crossing that route and heading up and right.

Then followed a period of uncertainty, as few climbers were completely aware of either the quality of climbing or indeed of what went where, a situation not completely unheard of before. Another four years passed, until in 1982 Dave Cuthbertson and Rudy Kane broke on to the central slab, moved right under a series of undercut grooves before finally breaking out higher up on the face to record Stormy Petrel, Grade V. That confusion still existed was shown by the recording in March 1983 of a line left of Stormy Petrel. In fact this gave a fine Direct Start to Albatross, taking in a natural gully line perhaps more often in condition than the original start. Another winter ascent, made in March of 1975, was that of the short North West Face on the right of Observatory Buttress, by Fred Craddock and Colin Stead.

Perhaps the most interesting ascents of the 1976 winter season (there were no summer routes made until 1978) were the February 7 ascent of Harrisons Climb Direct at Grade IV by Ken Crocket and Chris Gilmore, and Astral Highway at Grade V by Con Higgins and Alan Kimber on December 28. Harrison's Direct was virtually a new route, the only pitch which had been climbed before being the ice pitch up the left flanking chimney of Cousins' Buttress. This had been climbed in 1962 by Slesser and Tennent (see Chapter 11 for Tennent's description of their ascent).

12.8   Chris Gilmore on FWA Harrison's Direct (Feb., 1976)

Harrison's Direct took in the summer variation start which gave a superb steep ice pitch in the excellent conditions found. After climbing the chimney pitch, again heavily iced, the route took to the rocks of the Ordinary Route on Cousins' Buttress. This section of mixed climbing maintained the interest of the route, one of the most enjoyable ascents the author has made on Nevis.

Astral Highway is a route of a very different nature, climbing the huge Orion Face. Following the Orion Face Direct as far as the top of the Basin, it then takes to a groove system between Epsilon Chimney on the left and the second Slab Rib on the right. This was an early ascent of the face for the season, made on December 28 by Higgins and Kimber.

Norrie Muir resumed his suspended climbing career in the summer of 1976. His contributions to climbing on Nevis was soon to show with four winter routes in 1977. Con Higgins was now living in Fort William, working at the Outdoor Centre based at Corpach. In moving to the 'Fort' he was joining an increasing number of climbers stationed there, all apparently immune to the high rainfall. With Kimber, an instructor at the Centre, Higgins climbed The Lobby Dancer, Grade V, approximating to the summer line of Night Tripper on the North Wall of Castle Ridge. The Lobby Dancer takes to the grooves right of the overhanging wall on that route. Dunn and Gardner that same month made an ascent of Continuation Wall next to Boomer's Requiem, at Grade IV.

Late in March 1977, Muir and Paul were defeated on an attempt at climbing Minus One Buttress, gaining a height of only 20 feet. They were back the following weekend and, like Crocket and Stead on Minus One Gully three years earlier, they experienced conditions of excellent snow ice allowing an exciting if secure ascent of the buttress. The same pair were back on April 14, making an ascent of Rubicon Wall, Grade IV. Somewhat surprisingly, this seems to have been the first winter ascent of the 1933 Hargreaves route.

Though no summer lines were recorded in 1977, the first waves of the revolution taking place in rock climbing lapped at the rocks of Ben Nevis when in June Mick Fowler and Phil Thomas made the first free ascent of Titan's Wall on Carn Dearg Buttress. This had been an old aid route of Clough and MacInnes, first pegged in 1959. There had been attempts at free-climbing the great cracked wall, including an attempt by Carrington, but these had petered out in the face of its great challenge. Graded at E4, its ascent brought to Nevis the new age of rock, the message carried by a new breed of climbers who treated this sport as any other serious sportsmen and trained hard for self-improvement.

Four days later, Dave Cuthbertson and Murray Hamilton made the second free ascent, finishing by a slightly different, awkward 30-foot crack. Titan's Wall climbed free rates as one of the most difficult on Ben Nevis, nothing surprising to any innocent who has wandered under the magnificent expanse of Carn Dearg Buttress and looked up in awe.

1977 came to an end with three winter routes, two by Muir and Paul on the face left of Hadrian's Wall. Abacus and Antonine Wall were both graded at IV, climbing icy grooves to gain the crest of Observatory Ridge. Finally, an interesting Grade V was recorded on December 29 by Mike Geddes and Brian Hall. Geddes was now living in Fort William, having moved there in 1977. Sickle, the line climbed by Geddes and Hall, lay up the slabby wall right of Hadrian's Wall Direct, climbing a steep, iced corner to join up with Hadrian's Wall above that route's chimney.

The winter season of 1978, as mentioned earlier, saw the development of Indicator Wall as a new winter face. That February a harbinger of the technically difficult and very serious routes that would appear with increasing frequency arrived with the ascent of The Great Glen by Paul Braithwaite and Paul Moores. This short but desperate route at Grade V followed the shallow groove right of Smith's Route, Gardyloo Buttress. On the same day, February 12, one of the best contributions by Geddes (from a long list of superlative ascents) was made with the ascent of Route II on Carn Dearg Buttress, climbed with Rouse.

The hard winter men had been eyeing Carn Dearg Buttress for years, waiting for conditions which never seemed to come. The great summer classics like Centurion and Sassenach could never hold sufficient snow and ice to be more than uncomfortable rock climbs, and the best opportunity for a winter climb, it was felt, would have to wait for the vast central slabs to ice up.

Route II had received its first ascent in June 1943, by Kellett and Arnott Russell, the latter a student plucked out of the CIC Hut for a second man. A little known winter attempt was that made in the early 1960's by Haston and Wightman. This ended when Wightman took a leader fall of over 100 feet on to a poor belay.

When Geddes and Rouse left the CIC Hut that February morning in 1978 the sky was clear and the waiting line across the slabs of the buttress unusually white. From the bottom of the large smear of ice known as The Curtain the two climbers traversed easily right to reach the chimney of Route I. Rouse led the first pitch up the chimney then Geddes climbed through to launch himself on what proved to be the crucial traverse. Rouse described this section.

"It was obviously going to be a hard pitch. The snow would not support our weight unless, by chance, crampons bit on a rugosity beneath while sloping handholds allowed only leaning moves to clear the next few feet. It was time-consuming and strenuous on the calves. Standing on sloping footholds in crampons needs precision . . . " (8).

Route II is a serious climb, as every move takes a climber further out across the buttress face and further away from an easy retreat in the face of difficulties. In one of these twists of fate the route received a second ascent a few days later, by Gordon Smith and Ian Sykes. This ascent began by the Direct Start, giving several hard pitches low down before joining with the normal route. Both parties, naturally enough, have strong feelings of pride in their respective lines, though Geddes felt that the ascent by the original line is the more natural winter route.

12.9   Tom Prentice, crux pitch Caligula (1984)

The following weekend, February 18, the partnership of Lang and Quinn made their last new route on Nevis with American Pie, Grade IV, on the North Wall of Castle Ridge. At a length of 2,500 feet, this is one of the longest routes on Nevis, and consequently Britain.

Geddes and Higgins took advantage of a later winter season with two April ascents. Burrito's Groove, Grade IV, on April 8 was one of three recent routes on Number Two Gully Buttress, climbing a groove line left of the original line. It is often in condition and well recommended by its originator. The following week, on April 14, Geddes and Higgins climbed the steep slabs and grooves between Hadrian's Wall and Point Five Gully. Geddes had already attempted a climb here in February, finding that the slabs, as usual, had insufficient ice. Competition was raising its ugly head at this time, with so many good and active climbers living in and around Fort William. One of the climbers chasing lines was Gordon Smith, and when Geddes attempted a line next to Sickle in February 1978, Smith appeared a few days later and made the first winter ascent of Pointless, thinking that Geddes had failed on that line.

The climbing on both Galactic Hitch-hiker, Grade V, as Geddes and Higgins named their route, and Pointless, Grade V, is of a serious mixed nature. On Galactic, the original start as taken by the pioneers is hard, and has often been missed out by subsequent parties who have started up easier ground further left. Subsequent ascents have also suggested that Galactic Hitch-hiker should be given a Grade VI, which, if the case, would make it the first route on Ben Nevis of that grade.

Two months later, in June 1978, rock climbs were again being recorded on Nevis, with two hard routes on Carn Dearg Buttress. The startling rise in rock climbing standards, first seen in England in the early 1970's, had reached Scotland by about 1976, and Nevis in 1977, with the first free ascent of Titan's Wall. The young Scottish climbers setting the pace in the north moved up from Glencoe, where they had been busy in 1976 and 1977, to explore the cliffs of Nevis in the summer of 1978. This second climbing revolution manifested itself in two routes on the great buttress of Carn Dearg.

On June 2, a very steep line was found up the most imposing part of Carn Dearg Buttress. A tenuous, hanging groove to the right of Sassenach, taken in part by this line, had been known to local climbers for years as 'the big banana groove' (see below). As with most lines that were well-known, it was also too difficult for prevailing standards. The route, christened Caligula and graded at E3, received an all-Scottish ascent, with three young climbers from the new wave, Dave 'Cubby' Cuthbertson from Edinburgh, and Dougie Mullin and Willie Todd, the latter pair from Glasgow. Caligula moves across right midway up the banana groove. Cuthbertson, who lives for and by mountaineering, later joined the SMC, and continues to climb at a high standard.

The other line on the Great Buttress was climbed over two days by Ken Johnstone and Willie Todd. Adrenalin Rush, at E3, is a fairly direct line taking in the slabs and roof just right of The Bullroar. Crossing the crux traverse of The Bullroar it breaks through the roof above then makes a right, rising traverse to a junction with Centurion.

Elsewhere on Nevis that summer of 1978, Con Higgins and H. Woods made a June ascent at Very Severe of the winter line East Face, on the Zero Gully face of Observatory Ridge, while on the First Platform John Mackenzie and two friends found a Severe right of Ruddy Rocks with Rain Trip. Interestingly, there would be no rock climbs recorded for the next two years, as a succession of wet weekends swept over the north face of Nevis, though winter routes of a high standard would continue.

From about the mid 1970's onwards the Scottish winters have been generally unspectacular. There have been some good spells, naturally, but these seem to have been further and futher apart and of shorter duration as the decade advanced. Whereas 1978 was a peak year for the decade on Ben Nevis, with 11 first winter ascents, all of which were Grade IV or above, the next six years, from 1979 to 1984, saw an average of only three winter lines per annum, despite the increased number of winter climbers. This decrease in winter ascents can be only partially blamed on the weather, however. Several of the active local climbers moved on, thereby lowering the competitive flame that had burned in the Fort William area for some years. Geddes was to move back to Edinburgh, recording one more route in 1979.

Higgins was to emigrate to the United States. Norrie Muir, a complex Glaswegian, (a qualified fitter with a Diploma in Business Studies), was to stop winter climbing a few years later.

March 15, 1979 gave the first good conditions of the year, and also the first recorded Grade VI on Ben Nevis (and Scotland). The New Routes Editor of the SMC Journal had no reservations about publishing that grade for the first winter ascent of The Shield Direct, climbed by Mick Fowler and A. Saunders. Even a stroll up to the foot of that route would convince the sceptical that winter climbing had taken a quantum leap upwards in difficulty.

Five other hard routes were climbed in March 1979. Arthur Paul would team up with Davy 'Paraffin' Sanderson to make two Grade V ascents. The first of these was Gemini on March 23. This climbed a line in the vicinity of Evening Wall, which several teams had been looking at for some years, waiting for the right conditions. (The 'right conditions' for some routes are often very difficult to predict, on some occasions being for a few days only, and that at midweek.) Three days later they climbed the 900-foot line of Alchemist, on the North Wall of Castle Ridge.

On the same day as Alchemist received its ascent, Tut Braithwaite and D. Pearce climbed The Shadow at Grade V. This followed the summer line first climbed by Terry Sullivan in 1959, starting just right of Route I and crossing the exposed slabs of Carn Dearg Buttress by a line parallel to and lower than Route II. As with other Braithwaite lines, its low-key reporting has led to it being overlooked, even though it can be no easier than Route II and almost certainly more sustained. It probably, as with The Great Glen on Gardyloo Buttress, awaits a second ascent at this time.

On April 8, Higgins and Geddes climbed Purgatory Wall, Grade V. This was to be the last Nevis route recorded by this fruitful pair, and followed a line on the steep wall right of The Lobby Dancer, on the vast, sprawling North Wall of Castle Ridge. (The route name was first submitted as Last Day in Purgatory, a title which sounded too pretentious to the SMCJ New Routes Editor, who at that time did not realise that Higgins was preparing to leave the country and was, in effect, saying farewell to the joys and miseries of winter climbing in particular. Higgins, like any canny Scot, bided his time and with a change of Editor corrected this oversight several years later.)

Mike Geddes, one of the most prominent winter climbers in Scotland in the 1970's, died in September 1985, after an illness. His repeat ascents of the hard Smith-Marshall routes and his early recognition of the promise of front-pointing were significant contributions to Scottish winter mountaineering.

The 1980's have so far seen mountaineering on Nevis played out in a low key. Most new routes recorded have been winter ascents — despite the blazing summers of 1983 and 1984. Many of the young and active rock climbers who are climbing at high standards are not recording routes above the tree-line, and this despite the fact that there exists much untouched good rock. This does not imply laziness on their part. The nature of rock climbing near the present ceiling of ability is such that potential lines often have to be inspected by abseil, offending moss or other vegetation removed and crucial sections inspected visually for holds and protection. This time-consuming procedure is often necessary before attempts at a first ascent, some of which have required several days or even weeks effort. All of this makes an attempt on a hard mountain line very difficult.

Many climbers are loth to make the walk to the north face of Nevis two days in a row. They are even less enthusiastic about carrying camping equipment. Access to the CIC Hut remains difficult for the ordinary user, who due to the usual vagaries of weather may decide to climb on Nevis at short notice. It would be naive to maintain that some recently joined members of the SMC had not joined with the use of that hut in mind.

Despite these drawbacks, routes have continued to be found on the cliffs of Nevis, if at a reduced flow compared to the 1970's. The winter of 1980 was poor with three routes, two of which, however, were at Grade V. Journey Into Space marked Con Higgins' farewell to Nevis, climbed on March 8 with Alan Kimber. This was a truly Orion Face Direct route, climbing directly out of The Basin between Astral Highway and the Second Slab Rib.

Interstellar Overdrive, climbed on April 12 by R. Anderson and I. Kennedy, takes to the ribs and grooves between Pointless and Point Five Gully. A hard solo winter ascent was that of Slav Route by Mal Duff. Of a very different nature from these two routes was Norrie Muir's and Tam McAuley's recording of the Grade II Fawlty Towers, climbing the first icefall right of West Gully, Douglas Boulder. Two winter routes in 1981, the first being the February 21 ascent by Graham Little and Bob Richardson of the Grade IV Left Flank, following a ramp and icefall out right from above the first main ice pitch of Comb Gully. In March, K.Leinster, A. Paul and G. Reilly climbed the Grade V Augean Alley on Gardyloo Buttress. Some 400 feet long, this climbs Kellett's Route, starting midway between Left Edge Route and Smith's Route, finishing up the upper section of the buttress by following the Haston/Stenhouse summer variation to Kellett's Route. Two Very Severes by Muir and McAuley completed first ascents for 1981.

Bayonet Route received a winter ascent at Grade III, on March 7, 1982, by Ian Griffiths, Ed Jackson and Colin Stead. The latter also climbed the 300-foot Right Hand Wall Route variation at Grade IV on March 22 in company with Colin Grant. Stormy Petrel, Grade V was climbed this season, as mentioned earlier in the description of the Indicator Wall routes, its ascent by Cuthbertson and Kane bringing that face further into the modern light.

Earlier in 1982, on January 28, the Edinburgh climber Mal Duff and the Aberdonian Andy Nisbet teamed up to record Venus, Grade IV/V. This follows the right-bounding arête of Green Gully for two pitches then takes to the grooves of Aphrodite on the left to finish. At the end of 1982, on December 18, the icefall on Central Trident Buttress was climbed by John Murphy and A. Cain. Mega Route X, as it was named, approximated to the summer line of Steam, and had been eyed by many climbers for some years, as its ice approached the ground only to crash to the ground with each thaw. At Grade V and 200 feet it is a short hard ice exercise. Murphy and his partner climbed one pitch then abseiled off, returning the next day to climb up by an adjoining line before moving right and finishing up the final pitch. An ascent was made the next week, climbing the entire line in one go, by Martin Lawrence and Roger Webb. Precedence for this route is best left to the next guidebook author.

The winter season of 1982/83 saw three winter routes. The first was a 550-foot Grade IV just right of the above-mentioned Aphrodite, on Number 3 Gully Buttress. This was Quickstep, climbed on March 26 by R. Townsend and T. Bray and climbing the obvious corner to the left of Two Step Corner. Another line climbed some time that winter of 1983 was Shot in The Light, Grade IV/V, climbed by P. Thornhill and A. Saunders and at 330 feet in length taking the right wall of Gardyloo Gully, left of Left Edge Route. Finally, from the winter of 1983, Arthur Paul and Dougie Hawthorn succeeded after several attempts in climbing a hard line on the Orion Face on April 12. Urban Spaceman, a 1,000 foot Grade V, takes a line on the face between Astronomy and the Orion Direct in its lower section, and between Astronomy and Epsilon Chimney in its upper part. Its originator recommends it, rating it highly for length, quality and variety.

Moving to the summer, on August 28 Minus One Direct received a variation by Steve Abbot and Noel Williams. The Arête Variation, at VS/HVS grade, climbed the earlier Serendipity Variation in part, then broke away to gain the arête, using a peg for tension. (More details of the Minus One Buttress variations are given in Chapter 8).

Just right of Sassenach lies a narrow stretch of wall, the right arête of which is the left-bounding arête of Titan's Wall. On the wall is an obvious groove line, known for years as 'the big banana groove'. This had been climbed in part by the line of Caligula, but on August 21, 1983, two Edinburgh climbers, Murray Hamilton and Rab Anderson, made the first complete ascent of The Banana Groove.

Perhaps the main summer event of 1983, however, was the ascent of Agrippa by Pete Whillance and Rab Anderson, on August 29. Agrippa climbs the improbable left arête of Titan's Wall, on Carn Dearg Buttress. Whillance, an immensely strong climber from Carlisle, had been over in the Cairngorms with Anderson and two others, but deciding the weather in the west looked better moved to Nevis. On Sunday, August 28, they went up to Carn Dearg Buttress, Whillance having designs on the arête. He decided that the easiest way to clean the route was to climb Centurion then traverse right to drop the 300-foot cleaning rope down the line. Whillance decided to lead Centurion using the cleaning rope, which was non-stretch and not designed for climbing. His apparently endless lead perplexed a few onlookers.

After a day spent scrubbing clean the arête and climbing the ropes all three were tired. The wind had risen by now, but Whillance decided to leave the rope in case the weather improved the next day. The Monday was dull and windy, and not at all promising as they trudged back up the Allt a'Mhuilinn. It was cold weather for such climbing, and the climbers went for a stroll round the crags, hoping for an improvement. After a few hours Whillance decided to abandon the route and prusiked up the rope to abseil back down the line of Titan's Wall. The ropes were coiled and the party ready to descend when Whillance suddenly changed his mind.

The second pitch of Agrippa was the crux pitch, with poor protection and the wind blowing the ropes out in a scaring fashion. Luckily there was a loose block on the arête which the climbers could rest on, wrapping both arms round it in a spectacular position. Rab Anderson described the action.

"Moves up and left gain the crux on the left side of the arête. With the wind blowing, fingers going numb and runners below his feet Pete decided to go for it. Just as he was reaching the belay ledge a gust of wind caught the rope as I was dragging it through the sticht plate and I nearly pulled Pete off!". (9).

Agrippa, at 250 feet, is graded E5, with technical pitch gradings of 5c, 6b, 5c. In a technical sense, it is the most difficult rock climb on the north face of Ben Nevis. The second ascent was that by John 'Spider' McKenzie in the summer of 1984.

The winter season of 1983/84 began on December 17, when Arthur Paul, Colin McLean and Dougie Hawthorn made an ascent of Right Hand Chimney on Moonlight Gully Buttress at Grade III; Haston and Smith had almost certainly climbed the chimney about 1960, while the top two tiers of the buttress were climbed by Crocket and Gilmore in 1974.

There were few first winter ascents in 1984. On March 3 Cuthbertson and C. Fraser made a True Finish to Waterfall Gully, while the following day Mal Duff and John Tinker made an ascent of Point Blank, Grade VI. This followed the tenuous sliver of buttress between Point Five Gully and Left Edge Route. Duff noted that after the third pitch of Point Blank it was possible to keep to the edge overlooking Point Five Gully, a variation which had been done earlier by D. Wilkinson and friends. Wilkinson had started up Left Edge Route however, a continuous ascent of the edge still being awaited.

It seems that only six climbers took advantage of the glorious summer of 1984 on Nevis. In May Doug Hawthorn and John Grant recorded a route on the First Platform, left of Newbigging's 80-Minute Route, a 400-foot E2 on excellent, rough rock, while in June, Williams and Hawthorn had teamed up to make a Hard Very Severe ascent up the big corner between the above route and Newbigging's 80-Minute Route. But most of that summer's routes were done by two ropes. One of them was Norrie Muir, who in company with George Adam recorded no less than six routes, three each in July and August. Most were at an easy grade, four being Very Difficult, with two on the Douglas Boulder. A third Very Difficult, Gaslight, follows for the most part the right edge of Moonlight Gully Buttress, just right of the

Right Hand Chimney, while Vanishing Glories is 400-foot Very Difficult on the Coire na Ciste face of the Garadh Buttress.

The Banshee, Very Severe, was climbed on August 11 by Muir and Adam, following corners and grooves between Sioux Wall and Thompson's Route on No. 3 Gully Buttress. On the same day Muir and Adam climbed The Rattler, Severe, starting left of The Groove Climb on the South Trident Buttress. The other pair recording routes in the blazing heat of '84 were Arthur Paul and Dougie Hawthorn, who between them found five routes of Severe and above, climbed over four busy days.

12.10   Dave 'Cubby' Cuthbertson (April, 1979)

Opening their salvo on Monday, July 2 they climbed Last Stand, a 360-foot Hard Very Severe, on No.3 Gully Buttress, climbing the arête between Knuckleduster and Sioux Wall. On July 3 the 300-foot Hard Very Severe Clefthanger followed a corner system to the right of Tower Cleft, while on the same day they found The Urchin, a 200-foot E1 left of The Great Chimney on Tower Ridge, following the first leftward-facing corner crack. On the Wednesday Paul and Hawthorn were back on No.3 Gully Buttress, recording Chinook, 210 feet, at Hard Very Severe. This climbs the arête to the right of the final corner of Two Step, and when preceded by an ascent of Nicolson's Sioux Wall would make for a superb combination. The final route from Paul and Hawthorn was with a Thursday ascent of Saxifrage, a Severe on Raeburn's Buttress, following a thin groove some 30 feet left of The Crack. Also climbing on Nevis that summer of 1984 was Noel Williams. In the previous year he had found a variation on the upper part of Minus One Direct. Embarrassed by the use of a peg for tension he returned with Willie Jeffrey on July 6 and succeeded in climbing his Arête Variation free.

The winter season of 1984/85 began early on with a solo ascent of Centurion by Dave Cuthbertson in powder snow conditions. This was the second solo 'winter' ascent, the first being in 1975 with a two-day ascent by R. Millward. On New Year's Day, 1985, Hawthorn and Paul made a winter ascent at Grade V of Clefthanger, first climbed by them the previous July.

On the 19th of January Mal Duff and John Tinker recorded Sod's Law, Grade V, beginning below Route I on Carn Dearg Buttress and taking the chimney on the left. Also apparently climbed in that January of 1985 was a so far mystery route, going under the obscure name of Jazz Discharge Party Hats, by M. Millar and S. Smith. This Grade VI route on the Orion Face climbed the crest of the buttress left of Journey Into Space. Trending rightward under roofs there was a lack of belays and runners, and one pendule was used. At the moment its relationship to Journey Into Space and other routes on the face is not clear, and there are some indications that it may not have taken a completely original line.

On January 26 Martin Hind and J. Christie climbed Mercury, a line between Pigott's Route and Green Gully, and graded at IV. Their route took the first pitch of Green Gully, traversing left below the first peg belay of the gully to below an obvious chimney-crack with a chockstone. The next pitch was the crux, and according to Christie's description,

"consisted of climbing handsize lumps of ice some how stuck to the wall, axes occasionally jammed in cracks, tufts of moss & anything else that aided upward progress. Pitch 2 took 2 hrs to lead & was hard." (10).

Mal Duff and John Tinker were responsible for one other winter ascent in 1985. On February 16 they climbed Diana, Grade V/VI, on Number Three Gully Buttress. This route, the hardest winter line on the crag, starts up an icefall some 40 feet left of No. 3 Gully Buttress Original Route and trends left to grooves and corners before taking a steep icefall on the right wall of a huge corner. Its makers highly recommend the route.

Martin Hind was busy in February on Nevis, making the first winter ascent of the summer route Compression Crack, first climbed by Rolland and Ogilvy in 1940. This was the route which Clough thought he was climbing in January 1960, making instead a first ascent called Winter Chimneys. Hind found the second chimney pitch particularly difficult, the route being Grade V. On that day the Carn Dearg plateau lived up to the name given to it by Clement Wragge, 'The Plateau of Storms', as Hind was blown some 30 feet through the air while walking towards No. 4 Gully. (On the same day the author had a Dead Man blown off his harness by a sudden gust of wind while climbing on the Central Trident Buttress.)

The summer of 1985 has gone on record as the worst for weather for over a century. Certainly in Scotland after the end of June there was no let up in the steady rain that fell, excepting one weekend in September. The amount of rain and lack of sun enforced a virtual ban on climbing on the north face of Ben Nevis, with no new routes being recorded that summer.

The start of the winter season of 1985/86 took place in November, with a winter ascent on Observatory Ridge left of Abacus. At Grade IV and about 350 feet in length, this route was climbed by Paul and Hawthorn and followed a Very Difficult route first climbed by Norrie Muir and Hawthorn in May 1984.

The final note in this 400-year history of Ben Nevis took place with a winter ascent on Moonlight Gully Buttress, on Sunday, December 22, when Ken Crocket, Alastair Walker and Bob Richardson climbed the 550-foot Grade III/IV Phosphorescent Grooves. This climb followed an interesting rising traverse line on the No.5 Gully wall of the buttress. Pitches three and four presented difficulties, with the line as a whole being fairly sustained.

We have come to the end of this history, with an artificial line drawn across the end of 1985. We have to stop at some point, and 400 years from the start seems as good as any. If this story of Ben Nevis as regards its climbing history seems to end in the air, then that is because with such a magnificent mountain there can be no end. Those who climb on its northern cliffs may eventually cease making the walk up the Allt a'Mhuilinn and go elsewhere in search of adventure. Some switch to other, less demanding mountains or sports. Some stop climbing for a few years, raising a family and building a career. It takes time and determination to continue mountaineering through all these activities. But all who have enjoyed a good day on Nevis will have a memory rich in the experience of a unique British mountain, one they are unlikely to forget.

If the feeble scratchings of man leave any mark on this great mountain then it will not be seen on the rocks — time and weather will soon take care of that. Go to the written page, and there find the thoughts and actions of those who have pioneered new ways on Nevis. If this history encourages a few to go to the original sources, then it has succeeded in the main. If some go on to repeat the classic routes, pioneer new and harder ways up the old rocks and icy slopes of Nevis and set their thoughts down on paper — the heritage will continue.

Note: Each derivation or translation is followed by the suggested phonetic spelling (Ph.) In this, pronounce 'A' as in Apt. The sound of these place-names as rendered by a native Gaelic speaker is usually completely different from most attempts commonly heard, and the reader is urged to try and hear the music of this language as spoken by a native. For references see Bibliography for Chapter 1.

Achintee. Probably from the (Ga.) achadh an t-sithidh, or 'field of the shaped hill', the hill in this case being Meall an t-Suidhe. Sithe, or sithean in (Ga.) means 'mound shaped hill', and is often associated with fairies, or sithichean. Alternatively, according to MacMillan neither the topography nor the local pronunciation favour this derivation. Sitheadh in (Ga.) means 'quick onrush', which could refer to the wind, so 'field of the stormy blast' as suggested by MacMillan is not impossible. (Ph.) *Achu an cheehee.* Using 'ch' as in loch, 'u' as in up, achu an. Using 'ch' as in 'cheat', cheehee.

Allt a'Mhuilinn. (Ga.) for 'the mill burn'. It is also known to an older generation as Allt Domhnall an t-Siucair, (Ga.) for 'Donald of the sugar burn'. Mothers used to admonish their naughty children by telling them that 'Donald of the sugar' would come and get them. Another old name is the Allt a'phriosain, (Ga.) for 'the prison burn', after an old prison. (Ph.) *Owltt a vooleen.* Owltt, 'Owl' + 'tt'.

Allt na h-Urchaire. (Ga.) for 'burn of the shot'. Modern name is the Red Burn. As (Ga.) for red is dearg we might guess that at some time a story was connected with the burn, perhaps of hunting. (Ph.) *Owltt na Hoorichiru.* 'Ch' as in loch, 'u' as in up.

Ben Nevis. (Ga.) Nibheis or Nimheis. The late Professor Watson suggests an old Irish word 'neamheis', meaning 'terrible', and also a (Ga.) word 'ni-mhaise', meaning 'no beauty'. W.C. MacKenzie has made an attempt to associate the Irish 'neamhaise' with the Scottish 'uamhais', or 'dread', thus drawing in the two Scottish mountains Nevis and Wyvis (both, interestingly, large shapeless masses from certain angles). The word 'neamh' in (Ga.) means 'a raw and bitingly keen atmosphere', and is sometimes confused with the (Ga.) word 'neimh', meaning 'poison, bitterness, and malice'. (Ph.) *Ben Neevish.*

Càrn Beag Dearg. The little red rock or mountain. (Ph.) *Carn Bayg Jerrag.* 'Carn as in Carnivorous, 'Bay + G', 'G' as in good, 'Jerrag', 'G' as in good.

Càrn Dearg. The red rock or mountain. The mass of rock seen from the climber's point of view in the Allt a'Mhuilinn is andesite, and therefore dark grey, but from the Fort William side the flanks of Càrn Dearg are of the surrounding red granite. (Ph.) *Carn Jerrag.*

Càrn Dearg Meadhonach. The middle red rock or mountain. The intermediate point on the ridge between Càrn Mór Dearg and Càrn Beag Dearg. (Ph.) *Carn Jerrag Me-an-och.* 'Och' as in 'Och Aye!'.

Càrn Mór Dearg. The big red rock or mountain. The ochre-coloured granite screes of this mountain above the Allt a'Mhuilinn are an obvious contrast to the darker andesite of Ben Nevis. (Ph.) *Carn More Jerrag.*

Coire Eóghainn. There is some doubt as to whether this should be translated as John's coire or Ewen's coire. The (Ga.) for John is Iain or Eoin. (Ph.) *Corry Ee-o-in.* Said quickly with emphasis on the 'o'.

Coire Gaimhnean. Coire of the yearling deer or cows. One yearling is gamhainn, with the plural gaimhne. Grammatically it should be written Coire nan gaimhne. (Ph.) *Corry Guynone.* 'Guy' + 'none'.

Coire Giùbhsachain. Coire of the little pine forest. (Ph.) *Corry Geeoosachan.* 'G' as in good, 'Ch' as in loch.

Coire Leis. The leeward or sheltered coire. (ph.) *Corry Laysh.*

Coire na Ciste. The coire of the chest or casket. (Ph.) *Corry na Quichechu.* 'Quiche' as in 'Quiche Lorraine', 'Chu' as in 'Chugg'.

Corpach. (Ga.) A'Chorpaich. 'Ground under which there is decayed wood'. MacMillan states that this is descriptive of the peaty soil of Corpach Moss and is more feasible than the more popular derivation of 'body-place', where the illustrious dead are said to have rested before being shipped to Iona for burial. (Ph.) *A Chorpeech.* Both 'Ch' as in loch.

Lochaber. (Ga.) Lochabair, 'the confluence loch', named as the main rivers and burns flow into it, and giving the district its name. Now known as Loch Linnhe (see below). (Ph.) *Llochappir.*

Loch Laggan. (Ga.) for 'loch of the small hollow'.

Loch Linnhe, In (Ga.) known as An Linnhe Dhubh, 'the dark channel'. (Ph.) *An Leena Ghoo.* (The 'h' is aspirated to soften the 'g' sound.)

Loch Tréig. Derivation uncertain. May be from *Treig,* (Ga.) for 'forsake', thus giving 'the foresaken loch'. (Ph.) *'trake',* as in drake.

Meall an t-Suidhe. (Ga.) for 'hill of the seat', with its associated lochan. This is the popular derivation, though MacMillan thinks that 'hill of the stormy blast' may be a contender. (See entry for Achintee). (Ph.) *Meowll an tooyee.* 'Meow' as in cats.

Meall Cumhann. 'Narrow-shaped hill'. (Ph.) *Meowll Cooven.*

Polldubh. (Ga.) Poll Dubh, 'the dark pool'.

Steall, An. 'The waterfall'. (Ph.) *Steowll.*

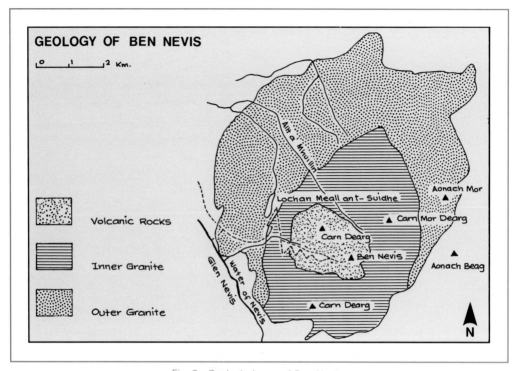

Fig. 3   Geological map of Ben Nevis

THE GEOLOGY OF BEN NEVIS

An aerial view of Ben Nevis, or one looking over from Carn Mor Dearg, gives one the impression of an incomplete and long dormant volcano, jagged rocks rising out of the surrounding foothills. The black lava forming the cliffs and providing the climbing is andesite, named from the type rock first described from the lavas of the Andes Mountains in South America. The gentle foothills are formed of granites and the older, underlying schists, such as these found forming the Polldubh crags in Glen Nevis. The fact that any andesite has been preserved at all is due to an accident of geology.

The andesite erupted in a series of flows and explosions. The flows varied from less than 15 feet to more than 100 feet in thickness, and give to the rocks the basis of their finished architecture. The flows were poured out during quieter periods in the activity of the volcano, but intervening beds of agglomerate indicate explosive phases, when a molten jumble of rocks was spewed out. An example of the agglomerate is well seen just in front of the CIC Hut, where slabby outcrops exhibit the rough mosaic-like finish of agglomerate, stones and blocks of rock cemented into a rough-weathering mix. The agglomerate contains large fragments of andesite, red felsite, and lighter-coloured quartzite.

The dip of these rock beds, the andesite flows and agglomerates, is toward the centre, being steeper near the margin. Standing near the CIC Hut and looking up at the cliffs, on the left the beds which form the Orion Face will be seen to dip down to the right, while in Coire na Ciste, the rocks forming the Comb dip down to the left. In fact, to the right of Tower Ridge any major ledge will be seen to slope down to the left e.g. Ledge Route on Carn Dearg Buttress. The dip of the flows should not be confused with the often more obvious gully and chimney lines, formed by lines of weakness such as dykes. The dip of the rock is obviously of some importance in determining the slope of holds and incuts.

The next stage in the formation of Ben Nevis involved the formation of a ring-shaped fault, allowing a subterranean block to sink into the underlying molten rock, or magma. The space left by this subsidence was filled by the Outer Granite. Over a long period of time this uprisen granite became exposed at the surface by erosion, where it consolidated and cooled. A period of dyke formation then occurred, igneous dykes being injected in a general NNE-SSW direction. Some of these dykes, as observed by the Lochaber Power Scheme tunnellers, were upward of 100 feet thick, though most were of the order of a few feet in thickness.

Following the dyke phase, a further subsidence occurred, confined to the central area. This admitted more molten rock to swell up, giving the Inner Granite. Then there took place a geological event which is probably unique to Ben Nevis, an event which preserved for future climbers the cliffs of the north face. The roof of the subterranean furnace collapsed, and a huge block of schist, with its cap of andesite, plunged into the still molten Inner Granite. The Inner Granite was chilled by the cooler descending mass. As this latter plug descended, friction on the walls of the cauldron slowed its descent, so that the falling plug became basin-shaped, explaining the tendency for the rocks of the central mass to be steeper near the margins. The edges of the central mass also became cracked and were penetrated at many points by veins of molten granite. The final phase of igneous activity seems to have been the injection of some more dykes, penetrating the margin of the Inner Granite.

After the violent excesses of vulcanism, subsidence and forced injections of molten rocks, there came the more gentle but just as effective forces of erosion. Millions of years of frost and sun, rain and wind, did much to shape and change the landscape. As the lavas had been protected by their collapse into the subterranean cauldron, they emerged into the daylight at a late stage. The fact that they had originally been underground and are now the highest rocks of this country goes to show how much the landscape owes to the forces of erosion. Some 18,000 years ago, most of Britain was covered by the last great glaciation. Huge glaciers and ice sheets moved slowly over the country, grinding down the rocks and shaping the scenery into a form we would recognise as today's. The ice scooped out rocky basins, Coire na Ciste and Coire Leis being fairly typical examples, with tiny lochans at their

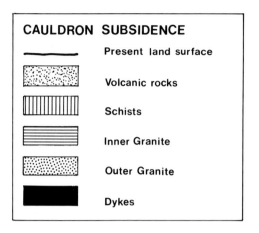

CAULDRON SUBSIDENCE

——	Present land surface
	Volcanic rocks
	Schists
	Inner Granite
	Outer Granite
▮	Dykes

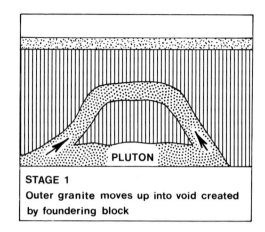

STAGE 1
Outer granite moves up into void created by foundering block

PLUTON

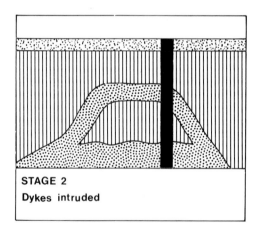

STAGE 2
Dykes intruded

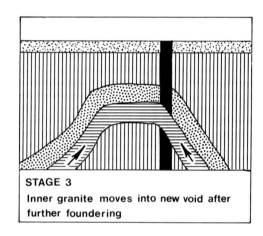

STAGE 3
Inner granite moves into new void after further foundering

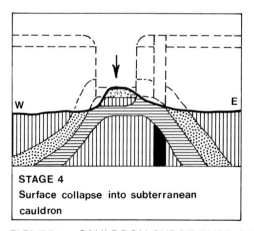

W   E

STAGE 4
Surface collapse into subterranean cauldron

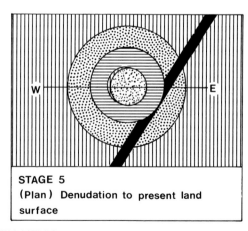

W   E

STAGE 5
(Plan) Denudation to present land surface

FIGURE 4   CAULDRON SUBSIDENCE OF BEN NEVIS

deepest points. The back walls of the coires were worn down, forming narrow arêtes such as the Carn Mor Dearg arête. Rocky outcrops were polished and smoothed down to finish up like the slabs opposite the CIC Hut.

The relatively slight metamorphism of the lavas indicate to a trained geologist that the present level of exposure is near the top of the intrusion. The andesite at this level was not heated to a great degree, having sunk through a small depth of molten granite. An analysis of the andesite of Ben Nevis shows some differences from the other two lava suites of Devonian age, at Lorne and at Glencoe. On Ben Nevis the flows show a much more restricted range of composition, being (to be strictly technical) hornblende- and hornblende biotite rhyodacites. They contain crystals of plagioclase, brown and green hornblendes, biotite (brown mica), and iron ore. Indeed, there are abundant if minute grains of iron ore, which may help explain an old report of a magnetic rock near the summit, which contained sufficient iron to force a compass needle out of alignment. Perhaps a new survey of the summit rocks might uncover an iron meteorite, an alternative explanation for the magnetic rock.

All of the above rocks will be seen on a careful walk up the Allt a'Mhuilinn, schists leading to the Outer Granite. The Dam over the Allt a'Mhuilinn is built on the Porphyritic Outer Granite; follow the burn upstream and it leads in just over one mile to the Inner Granite. The CIC Hut is on andesite, but only just, as a glance over the burn towards the slopes of Carn Mor Dearg will indicate the red rocks of the Inner Granite. A walk along the Carn Mor Dearg arête will show andesite abutting against the Inner Granite, with dykes running across the arête. This igneous complex may have been an accident of geology, but it was a fortunate accident, which has preserved for climbers the rocks of Ben Nevis.

A P P E N D I X   C
THE MAPPING OF BEN NEVIS

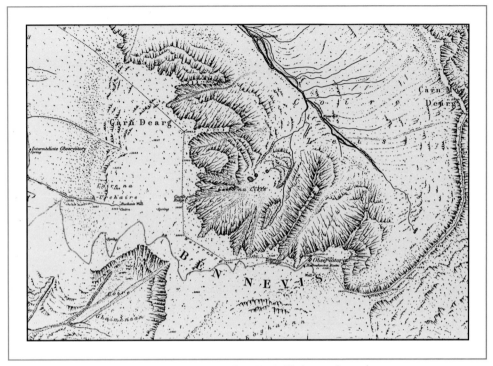

Fig. 5   1902 6'' map of Ben Nevis (Ordnance Survey)

By Graham E. Little

Of the thousands of hillwalkers and climbers ascending Ben Nevis every year the vast majority will be carrying a map, although few will be aware that man's earliest cartographic interest in the mountain dates back to the sixteenth century.

The earliest maps of the Scottish mainland were concerned primarily with communication, whether by path, track or water. Mountains, merely serving to hinder this process, were of relatively little interest and were therefore depicted in a very stylised fashion with no individual identity.

One of the most prolific of the early map makers was the redoubtable Timothy Pont, who travelled throughout Scotland between 1583 and 1611 often suffering great privitations in pursuit of his chosen task. He was probably the first cartographer to depict the name Ben Nevis on a map. Robert Gordon, a graduate of the University of Aberdeen and described at the time as 'doyen of geographers', revised Pont's maps between 1636 and 1648. Thirty six of Pont's updated Regional maps were published in Johan Blaeu's Novus Atlas in 1654.

By the middle of the eighteenth century a Military survey of Scotland was in progress under the guidance of William Roy who by 1781 reached the rank of Major General. Roy is often considered the founder of the Ordnance Survey although he died before it formally came into being. Using basic theodolites, without telescopes and fifty foot chains Roy and his colleagues produced the 'Great Map' in under ten years at a scale of 1":1000 yards. Ben Nevis is clearly depicted, although without a height. Roy said of this map that *"it is rather to be considered as a magnificent military sketch than as a very accurate map."* However it was undoubtedly more accurate than anything yet produced.

Over the next century many Estate and County maps were produced, of varying scales and quality.

The next major cartographic development was the survey of Inverness-shire CLI (151), a 6":1 mile map, published by the Ordnance Survey in 1875. This was the first map to delineate the complex form of Ben Nevis, although unlike its English counterparts, did not include contouring. This map was revised in 1899 to include the recently constructed 'pony track' and observatory and republished in 1902.

During the late nineteen fifties the Ordnance Survey embarked upon a resurvey of the upland areas of Scotland, based upon aerial photography and in 1967 published a new and detailed 1:10,560 map, NN17SE, of Ben Nevis with twenty five foot interval contouring. Rumour has it that the surveyor responsible for the ground completion of this sheet became totally lost in thick cloud on the summit plateau, eventually descending the mountain on the wrong side and returning to base only just in time to prevent the launch of a full scale rescue party!

All subsequent smaller scale mapping has been based on NN17SE and it seems certain that it will remain the definitive map of the forseeable future although its conversion from 1:10,560 to the metric scale of 1:10,000 is a possibility.

TRIANGULATION AND PILLAR MAINTENANCE

The prominent white concrete Ordnance Survey pillar situated on the summit plateau of Ben Nevis, just to the south of the cliff edge, (code named PP323) is part of a network of similar pillars spread throughout the country. Contrary to popular opinion these pillars are not necessarily sited on the highest point of a mountain (although they often are) but are positioned to allow intervisibility with surrounding pillars. They exist to allow the instrumental observation of a rigid framework of triangles, braced quadrilaterals and polygons, known as triangulation, which forms the skeleton upon which the mapping of the country is based. This geodetic framework is related, via astronomical observation, to latitude and longitude, thus ensuring cartographic sympathy between adjacent countries.

William Roy had proposed a systematic triangulation of Britain in the eighteenth century but his desire was not fulfilled until much later, being published as the 'Principal

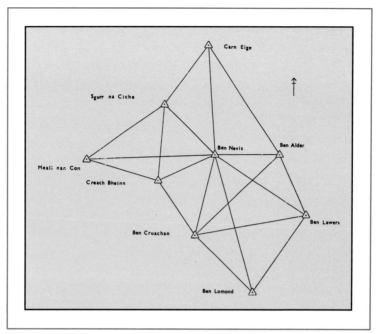

Fig. 6   Triangulation figure for Ben Nevis

Triangulation' in 1858.

The triangulation pillar in its present form, was erected in August 1936 upon the site of an earlier triangulation station. PP323 is unusual, if not unique, in that it was built on the top of a man made cairn and not on 'living rock' as is the normal practice. However a flat, three metre wide, concrete platform was laid over the cairn and the foundation of the pillar extended well into its body and as such was considered stable and permanent.

Despite the choice of May when weather is likely to be at its clearest for long-range triangulation observations, it took senior observers and their helpers 22 nights to clear the station. Senior observers Bert Smith and Bernard Willis had agreed to take turns with each other on the Tavistock theodolite, but the strain of climbing up and down so often proved such a strain they decided to take alternate spells on top.

Much of the time was spent in the tent with the Primus going in a temperature of 26 degrees Fahrenheit. Their first camp pitched on the snow in mist had to be moved in the first clearing, when they found they were dangerously close to the lip of the cornice overhanging the cliffs. Nevis proved to be one of the most exactingly rigorous stations of the whole Primary triangulation, completed in the remarkable space of seven Field Seasons. Begun in 1936 and suspended on the outbreak of war, it was resumed in 1949 and completed in 1951.

Inevitably the ravages of the elements and the passage of countless thousands of feet have caused considerable damage to both cairn and pillar over the years.

The first major repair work undertaken was in 1959 when two tons of material were lifted, by helicopter, to the plateau. Serious undermining of the concrete platform, threatening the stability of the pillar, was made good by the use of pit prop type timbers and stone infill.

Despite continued maintenance, by 1971 the removal of stone and thirty five years exposure to the mountain's hostile climate had caused slight pillar movement and further cairn deterioration. In 1972 the cairn was again repaired and a new pillar cast and erected.

Maintaining the triangulation pillar on Britain's highest mountain is an ongoing process but one that is essential, not only as a matter of prestige but to retain an occupiable station for inevitable cartographic and scientific use in the future.

DEPICTION OF RELIEF

The relatively small scale of early mapping precluded a detailed survey of the complex form of Ben Nevis. Initially a very symbolic, hand drawn, hill denoted its approximate location. Early attempts to show its actual mountain form used brush strokes of grey wash (P. Sandby) or hachures (W. Johnson), often to great effect if not accuracy. (Hachures are short lines to indicate steepness of slope by their closeness).

Not until 1870 were surveyors called upon to map out the steep and complicated rock features of the great north eastern precipice of Ben Nevis, which must have presented a difficult not to say dangerous undertaking. At this time the Ordnance Survey was still a military concern and visions of the commanding officer ordering his troops to measure distances over impossible terrain spring to mind! However it can reasonably be assumed that the surprisingly accurate depiction achieved of the major gullies and ridges on this 1:10,560 map was due more to the surveyor's eye and artistic talent than to the quality of his surveying equipment or the selflessness of his men! An attractive hand etched rock system was used, most effectively, to depict cliffs on this map, its presentation being an 'art form' quite unique to each individual area. (see map, this Appendix, and the front endpapers.)

The use of aerial photography, in the mid twentieth century, revolutionised the survey of precipitous relief features and heralded an era of mapping excellence. The precise contouring derived from stereo photography was far superior to anything that had or could be achieved by ground methods. Although some may lament the passing of the cartographer's artistic skills the clarity and accuracy of relief depiction on current Ordnance Survey 1:10560 and 1:25,000 mapping is beyond criticism. Not only can all the mountain features be clearly located but the trained eye may even identify climbing routes in the comfort of his own home!

On small scale mapping, as an addition to contours, layer tinting (Bartholomew 1:1,000,000) and hill shading (O.S. 1":1 mile Tourist Map) have been used for relief enhancement. In fact various combinations of hachuring, hill shading, layer tinting and contouring have been used over the years often creating stunning three dimensional visual effects.

PLACE NAMES

The history of Ben Nevis mapping throws light not only on the development of topographic data depiction but also on the evolution of place and feature names. Ironically, perhaps, the change in spelling and usage over the centuries can frequently be attributed to cartographic misrepresentation. The early surveyors, rarely being Gaelic speakers or scholars, commonly transcribed phonetic versions of place names, sometimes at great variance to the pure ethnic version, which have subsequently become the accepted form.

The Gaelic root of Ben Nevis itself is open to considerable conjecture having appeared on mapping in a variety of forms. Likewise Coire Leis and Allt a'Mhuilinn have undergone numerous changes in spelling although, unlike their parent mountain, have remained close to their Gaelic roots.

The earliest recognisable cartographic references to the name are Bin Novesh in c.1595 (T. Pont) and Bin Neves in c.1640 (R. Gordon). In the 18th Century a variety of versions occurred from Ben Nevish (M. Armstrong) to Ben Nivis (R. Campbell), with the first appearance of Ben Nevis (W. Roy) in c.1750. With the exception of Bein Nevis in 1830 (W. Johnson), in the nineteenth and twentieth Centuries the version of Ben Nevis seems to have been widely accepted.

The incorrect application of feature names has occasionally occurred, most strikingly perhaps, Castle Ridge is positioned at the head of Number Four Gully on the first edition of O.S. 1:10,560 mapping, over seven hundred and fifty metres south of its true location! Even more remarkably this error has been perpetrated on the current 1:10,560 map although on the 1:25,000 edition of 1980 it has at last found its true location!

On the 1902 1:10,560 map only two rock feature names are shown, Tower Ridge and Castle Ridge, whereas the 1967 edition contains a dozen. The criteria for their inclusion seems a trifle inconsistent in that The Castle is named yet The Comb isn't, the vast and accessible Observatory Gully isn't named yet curiously Point Five Gully, definitely a pure climbing route, is.

Although the forces of erosion will inexorably if slowly alter the topography of Ben Nevis it seems likely that its name and the names of its myriad features have now entered into a long period of stability.

HEIGHTING

Scottish hill heights are a subject of great sensitivity and often controversy. The desire to establish a 'true' height value is inevitably at odds with an equally strong desire to maintain the status quo. This applies to Ben Nevis perhaps more than any other Scottish peak.

'A New and Correct Map of Scotland or North Britain' published in 1794, in two sheets, boldly announced, *'Ben Nivis — 4370 feet High — The Highest Mountain in Great Britain'*. This map, at a scale of 7.5 miles:1", was an updated version of a 1782 map and bears the name of an unknown cartographer Lt. R. Campbell. How this surprisingly good height value was calculated remains unclear and the assertion following it is equally surprising as at the time many authorities believed Britain's highest mountain to lie in the Cairngorms.

Between the publication of the 6" map in 1875 and the publication of the results of post war triangulation and levelling in 1964 a remarkable cartographic consistency reigned, the height of Ben Nevis being universally accepted at 4406 feet. The new value announced of 4418 feet caused much comment and confusion but in fact this value was to the flush bracket (No.81595), a brass levelling plate low down on the face of the pillar, and not to ground level. As the pillar is built upon a cairn 9.5 feet high the true ground level height is actually 4408.5 feet. This figure when converted gives a value, to the nearest metre, of 1344 metres and this height now appears on all current mapping.

Thus the calculated height difference between the nineteenth and twentieth century observations was slightly under one metre, surely a great compliment to the expertise of the early Ordnance Survey cartographers.

Ben Nevis is indisputably Britain's highest mountain at 1344 metres and barring some major reactivation of the Great Glen fault, seems certain to maintain its status. As mapping technology becomes more sophisticated it will become possible to height the mountain with even greater precision. To the traditionalist however this is of no consequence; the height of Ben Nevis is and always will be 4406 feet!

Bibliography

1. The Early Maps of Scotland. Vol.I. Royal Scottish Geographical Society.
2. Harley, J.B. 'Ordnance Survey — A Descriptive Manual'. (H.M.S.O.:Oxford, 1975)
3. The Mitchell Library Map Collection (Glasgow).
4. The National Map Library of Scotland (Edinburgh).

APPENDIX D
THE NATURAL HISTORY OF BEN NEVIS

FLORA

As the Ice Age drew to a close and bare ground gradually became exposed, so plants began to colonise the land. The first plants to move in were Arctic and Alpine types, such as may be seen at present adjacent to glaciers and snowfields. The plant cover was much as seen on Ben Nevis today, above a height of about 2,400 feet, or just above the CIC Hut, being an abundance of low-growing, cushion-like perennial forms. The low-growing habit resists drought; in addition the leaves of alpines are usually very small, with a coating of wax or perhaps a thick, leathery epidermis. The root system has to be well-developed, often more so than the visible part of the plant, while most alpines also possess an underground stem or rhizome in which food can be stored in the summer. With the arrival of milder weather, though before water absorption may be possible, such plants can begin growing almost immediately, therefore making use of the short growing season.

Such alpines may be found growing on the margins of the smaller streams, perhaps where a spring provides more reliable water, alpines such as the Yellow Mountain Saxifrage (Saxifraga aizoides), clusters of which may be mixed with denser white-flowered Mossy Saxifrage (Saxifraga hypnoides). The shady spots on rock faces may harbour such rosette forms as the Starry Saxifrage (Saxifraga stellaris), its short main stock crowned by a rosette of egg-shaped leaves. Each rosette sends up a flowering shoot topped by a panicle of small, white flowers, each one conspicuously star-shaped. The Starry Saxifrage can attain considerable elevation.

More rarely, on the rock faces will be found the Alpine Saxifrage (Saxifraga nivalis). Its thick leaves are well adapted to conserve water, while it has four to twelve fairly large, white flowers. In early summer the drier rocks may exhibit sheets of the evergreen, purple-flowered Purple Saxifrage (Saxifraga oppositifolia), one of our most beautiful alpine flowers. It may be seen flowering on Nevis about May, when much of the snow may have cleared. The leaves of the Purple Saxifrage possess an interesting mechanism for drought control. Water pores are found at the apex of each leaf. The tissue around this pore can secrete chalk, supplied by the roots. Water leaving this pore will contain some dissolved chalk, which on a day of high evaporation will soon leave sufficient chalk to block the pore and thereby reduce water loss. At night, when evaporative losses are reduced, escaping water will dissolve this chalk barrier, permitting transpiration again. Even on rocks containing little or no chalk, the roots of this plant can selectively obtain sufficient minerals to continue this protective mechanism.

Accompanying the Purple Saxifrage may be found the Moss Campion (Silene acaulis), a typical Cushion Plant, with a proportionally much larger root system. Throughout the short summer the woody rhizome of this plant, and others like it, will be storing energy. In the four short months on Nevis in which average temperatures will be above freezing, these plants must go through the entire reproductive cycle.

The Cerastium family is represented on Ben Nevis by the Starwort Mouse-ear (*Cerastium cerastioides*), while another hairy-leaved plant is the Alpine Lady's Mantle (*Alchemilla alpina*), which has its stems and leaves covered with shining, silver hairs as a protection against excess water loss. The Scottish Sibbaldia (*Sibbaldia procumbens*) is a perennial forming a low growth well adapted for long periods under snow. Its small hairy leaves are, of course, to guard against drought. The flowers do not produce nectar and are probably usually self-fertilised.

Another plant which can coat a fair area of ground is the Dwarf Willow (*Salix herbacea*), sometimes known as 'the smallest tree in the world'. Its roots dive deep in this plant, while its very small leaves conserve moisture. The catkins are very short with very few flowers.

Of immense importance to climbers, but rarely noticed until the rocks are wet, are the algae, whose thin film on the rocks becomes very slimy when wet. And then there are the lichens, whose natural history fills books and occupies the lives of researchers full time. The algae and lichens are best left to the expert, but some introductory words can be said. The green algae (phylum *Chlorophyta*) are mostly small, simple plants, from which the land plants are believed to have evolved. Many are single celled, though others consist of thin sheets of cells.

The lichens arouse much interest. These strange plants have evolved through the combination, in the same tissue mass, of an alga and a fungus. The fungus, an *Ascomycete* or *Basidiomycete,* forms a dense mat of interwoven hyphae (a mass of long thread-like structures, which contain many nuclei unseparated by cell walls). Within this mat the algae grow. The relationship is a symbiotic one, as the fungus obtains its organic food from the algae, which in turn obtains dissolved salts and water which the fungus has extracted from the rock. Most of the algae and fungi are incapable of living independently, but together form a tough combination, one which can survive environmental conditions hostile in the extreme. The various patterns and colours formed by the lichens are beautifully subtle, though the andesite of Ben Nevis is not nearly so good a substrate as say the easily eroded mica schists of the Southern and Central Highlands.

The lichens have two especially interesting uses, despite their simplicity and small size. One is a use which dates back to prehistory, as a source of natural dyes. Their colours are mostly in the yellow to brown range, though some purples and reds are also available in some areas. The other use is the more contemporary one of being a pollution index, as they are very sensitive to atmospheric sulphur dioxide amongst other pollutants. Some work has been done on the effect of the pulp mill on local lichens. Generally, the western seaboard of Scotland will be a safe haven for the lichens, as here the atmosphere is almost free from pollution.

Another modest group of plants which must be mentioned in the passing are the numerous grasses, sedges and rushes. The Glaucous Meadow-grass (*Poa glauca*) is a slightly creeping plant with smooth, narrow leaves, sometimes of a bluish-green colour. Another species, the Wavy Meadow-grass *(Poa flexuosa),* is closely related to the Alpine Meadow-grass, though very hard to find. The Alpine Cat's-tail *(Phleum alpinum)* is to be found on wet, rocky ledges, as is the Alpine Fox-tail *(Alopecurus alpinus).* All of the above are real Alpine grasses, only to be found on the flanks of the high hills. The success of the grasses can be explained by their prolific seed production, their perennial habit, and their production of runners and offsets, by which the plants reproduce themselves.

The Sedge Family *(Cyperaceae)* belong mainly to the genus *Carex,* containing over 75 British Species. The Sedges have their flowers united into shapely conical or cylindrical spikes. The flowers are pollinated by the wind, no nectar being produced. The Stiff Sedge, *(Carex bigelowii),* is to be found on Nevis, as well as on most of the other high hills. It is barely six inches high, with flat and very rigid leaves. Besides the grasses and sedges there are the wood-rushes, represented on Ben Nevis by the Curved Wood-rush *(Luzula arcuata).* Its leaves are almost cylindrical with its flowers found in a panicle of small clusters.

As we approach the summit rocks of Nevis there appear the various mosses. These show two growth forms; the tightly packed, upright stems which form dense cushions, and the flattened, creeping sort. Like the lichens, this is not the place to go into these beautiful plants in detail. Also like the lichens, these plants are adapted to withstand conditions of drought.

Finally, for the plant world, Lochan Meall an t-Suidhe has various aquatic plants, such as the Water Awl-wort *(Subularia aquatica).* This interesting little plant may be seen in summer as a soft green carpet on the bottom of shallow parts of the lochan. It is unusual for a mountain plant in being an annual, the seed starting to germinate as soon as the temperature of the water rises sufficiently in the early summer. The leaves rise above the surface of the water, while from the middle of the leaves rises a short, naked stalk which gives rise to a raceme of small white flowers.

The Water Lobelia *(Lobelia dortmanna),* is a common species, found around the shores of many a Highland loch, including Lochan Meall an t-Suidhe. It usually forms a carpet of green leaves beneath the surface of the water. The rootstock is topped with a tuft of bright green leaves, formed into two hollow tubes placed side-by-side. This structure allows the plant to withstand the strong wave action often caused by wind. Its flower is a bright blue.

This list of plants to be found on Ben Nevis is by no means exhaustive; we have not, for example, gone into the bog flora, nor the wooded areas lower down the hill. Readers will have no difficulty in finding a suitable reading list as a starter, though there is no substitute for a tour with an expert. The rocks of Ben Nevis may not be as rich in plants as hills nearby, but the eagle eye can still find much to interest from the plant kingdom.

FAUNA

In the autumn the hare moults into a new brown coat. The white coat then begins to appear, perhaps as early as October. The change to white is usually complete by about late

November. A sudden thaw in mid-winter can result in an embarrassed looking hare, stark white against a dark background. In the snow, and unmoving, a passing climber is unlikely to notice. Tracks of hare criss-crossing with those of the fox are more often seen than the animals who make them.

Stoats *(Mustela erminea)* and Weasels *(Mustela nivalis)* were well known to the observatory staff. Likewise, the common Rat *(Rattus norvegicus)* and Mouse *(Mus musculus)*, who were unwelcome occupants of the summit observatory. A humourous sighting of a large mammal was that of the Badger *(Meles meles)* who fell down Green Gully in the early 1970's. The animal rolled down to the bottom of the gully, shook the snow off its coat, and gamely tried to climb back up again.

The Field or Short-tailed vole *(Microtus agrestis)* is relatively common, below the cliffs and sometimes on top of the hill. It is a grass-eater notable for explosive rises in population, reaching a peak density about every four years, and suddenly collapsing then building up again. Shrews, *(Sorex araneus)*, much smaller and darker than voles, were commonly caught by the observatory cat.

The Golden Eagle *(Aquila chrysaetos)* gets mention as a common sight on the Nevis cliffs in the 1936 guide book. It is a less likely sight today, though the author has seen it above upper Glen Nevis. Perhaps the most interesting bird of Ben Nevis is the Snow Bunting *(Plectrophenax nivalis)*. This hardy sparrow-sized bird with the white wings is a true singer. Harold Raeburn describes his pleasure at hearing its song, (see Chapter 4 for this reference), a short, far-carrying musical phrase. Undoubted it breeds on Nevis some years, nesting usually in a rock niche or among the stones. In winter snow buntings may be met with on the summit, even in bad weather, or around the CIC Hut, which a pair adopted in the snowy winter of 1985/86.

A family of Ravens *(Corvus corax)* is usually present on Ben Nevis, their locality differing from year to year. Its aerial acrobatics have drawn applause from many a spectator, while its throaty croak is part of the mountain sound. The Ptarmigan *(Lagopus mutus)* is occasionally seen, though not often enough, and the author was delighted to see a pair in winter on top of the First Platform. It is the only mountain bird that moults three times a year, turning white in winter.

Other small birds to be looked out for on Ben Nevis are the ubiquitous Meadow Pipit *(Anthus pratensis)*, which arrive in Spring, followed by the Wheatear *(Oenanthe oenanthe)*, which nests in convenient holes in the ground. The Ring Ouzel *(Turdus torquatus)* occurs on the lower slopes, a blackbird with a white collar, while the Wren *(Troglodytes troglodytes)* and the Dipper *(Cinclus cinclus)* may be spotted near the streams, on occasion moving upstream and underwater, head down looking for food.

The observant, and expert ornithologist, will no doubt spot other species of birds on Ben Nevis, though the above short list probably includes most of the birds that have been seen on the hillside above the tree line.

Untouched by this section so far are the insects, many of which are blown up by winds, sometimes to land in great numbers on the snow, where snow buntings find them. Also not mentioned so far are the amphibians. Small frogs are quite common on the lower slopes, the common frog *(Rana temporaria)* spawning in the Highlands to a height of over 1,500 feet. Lizards and snakes may be found too, on the lower slopes, with the Common or Viviparous Lizard *(Lacerta vivipara)* and the Adder *(Vipera berus),* its diamond markings distinguishing it from the Grass snake. Again, as with the birds, the patient and experienced observer will see far more than the casual walker or climber.

Bibliography

1. Clapham, A.R., Tutin, T.G. and Warburg, E.F. 'Flora of the British Isles'. 2nd Edition. (C.U.P.:Cambridge, 1962).
2. Darling, F.F. and Boyd, J.M. 'The Highlands and Islands'. New Naturalist Series (Collins:London, 1969).
3. Fitter, R.S.R., Fitter, A., and Blamey, M. 'The wild flowers of Britain and Northern Europe'. (Collins: London, 1974).
4. Fletcher, H.R. 'Exploration of the Scottish Flora'. Trans. Bot. Soc. Edinb. 38, 30-47, 1959.
5. Holden, A.E. 'Plant life in the Scottish Highlands'. (Oliver & Boyd: Edinburgh, 1952).
6. Peterson, R., Mountfort, G., and Hollom, P.A.D. 'Birds of Britain and Europe'. (Collins:London & Glasgow, 1974).
7. MacNally, L. 'Highland Year'. (Pan Books: London, 1972).

Note: (Ge.) = German, (Am.) = American, (Fr.) = French. Words italicised in an entry are defined fully elsewhere in the glossary.

Abseil. (Ge.) To descend rapidly by sliding down a *rope*. Useful method of retreat from a *route* when caught by bad weather or difficulties. Usually done using two ropes tied together for extra length, the climber sliding down both ropes which are hanging from a *belay* point such as a *peg* or rock spike, the ropes being pulled down once a safe *stance* has been gained. A friction device is normally used to control the rate of descent, e.g. a *Figure of eight*. Abseiling is a potentially dangerous technique and many good mountaineers have been killed while doing it. Many modern hard rock climbs are now inspected and cleaned by abseil and *jumar* before being attempted.

Aid Climbing. (Am.) See *Artificial Climbing*.

Alpine line. A thin climbing *rope, hawser-laid*. Known as No.1 rope, with a circumference of 0.625 inch and formerly used for abseil loops. Now replaced for that purpose by nylon *tape*.

Anorak. Originally an Inuit (Eskimo) garment, a wind-proof outer pulled over one's head. Now a generic name for a multitude of (usually) waterproof jackets. Most are made of nylon and have a full-length front zip and a hood. Modern nylons may be employed which permit water vapour to pass through while maintaining the waterproof ability. The most useful anorak is of thigh-length; when worn with nylon overtrousers complete protection may be attained.

Arête. (Fr.) The narrow crest of a *ridge,* usually giving spectacular walking, e.g. the Carn Mor Dearg arête. Sometimes also applied on a smaller scale to a rock feature on a *buttress,* when it may be at a steeper angle.

Artificial climbing. Climbing which relies heavily or completely on *pegs, nuts, slings* and so on for overcoming a difficult section, perhaps overhanging, on a rock or ice face. Basically, *pegs* or *nuts* are inserted in cracks and using *étriers* hanging from these a climber moves up from point to point. In winter climbing *ice screws* can be used in the same fashion for very difficult overhanging sections, or to rest from. When no crack exists a *bolt* may be used. Many routes originally climbed using aid have since been climbed free. Controversy exists over the use of aid, more so in the U.K., where a common point of view is that one point of aid on a route is one too much, particularly on a rock climb. Recent advances in *protection* equipment have virtually eliminated the use of *pegs* for *runners* on rock climbs.

Avalanche. (Fr.) The downward movement of a mass of snow, ice or rock (usually the first). Common during or shortly following a heavy snowfall. The entire snow layer may be involved or only a surface layer may slide, such as in a *wind slab* avalanche. Some avalanches are triggered by a climber walking over a slope which is in a dangerous condition. Some, perhaps most, avalanche danger can be predicted. On Nevis the easier *gullies* are especially prone to avalanche, particularly so during a rapid thaw.

Back and foot. Also called backing up. A technique allowing *chimneys* of suitable width to be climbed by placing one's back on one wall and one's feet or knees on the other then moving up by alternately pushing up with the hands on the back wall and moving the feet or knees further up on the facing wall. As a large amount of friction is usually present this technique is more secure than it would appear.

Balaclava. A woollen, nylon or silk head covering especially useful for use in winter climbing. Originates from the Crimean War and dates from 1892. Covers the entire head and neck with an oval opening for the eyes.

Balance move. A climbing move made without the security of a good handhold, the climber relying on balance to reach the next *hold.* On a friction *slab* several such moves may have to be made in sequence, such as found on the Trilleachan Slabs in Glen Etive.

Ball-up. See *Crampon.*

Bearing. Direction to walk in order to reach a given objective, as determined by the use of a *compass* such as a Silva type designed for orienteering. Particularly useful when visibility is limited due to mist or darkness and a descent route must be reached, e.g. from the summit of Nevis to the Carn Mor Dearg arête.

Belay. The technique and necessary equipment employed in fastening a climber to the mountain, commonly one climber being belayed while the other climber is moving. A whole range of belays is possible, both on rock and on ice. Normally, a nylon *tape sling* is placed round the best available rock *flake* or spike, the climber then being firmly attached to the *sling* by tying in the main rope to a *karabiner.* Failing a natural belay point a *peg* or *nut* may be used, or in a situation with poor belays a combination of the above. In winter *ice screws* or a *Dead Man* may be used. Origin the nautical term meaning to coil a running rope round a cleat so as to secure it. See also *Runner.*

Belay Plate. A small metal device designed to allow a belaying climber to safely hold the *rope* using friction and not muscle power. The original belay plate was designed by Fritz Sticht. Most models of plate are disc-shaped and have two slots, through which ropes of 9mm or 11mm diameter can pass. The ropes can be easily fed through these slots for normal movement, or quickly held by friction in the event of a fall. They must be used in conjunction with a *screw gate karabiner* for security. Before belay plates came into use the belaying climber passed the ropes behind his or her waist, giving the rope furthest from the active climber a turn round the wrist for additional friction. A weak or suddenly surprised belayer could lose control of the rope following a leader fall, with disastrous consequences.

Bergschrund. (Ge.) A crevasse formed where a snow slope abruptly changes its angle. More commonly formed in Scotland where a snow slope abuts against a rock wall and is then found in late winter as a deep gap between the snow and the rock. More common in the Alps but small specimens are found on Ben Nevis and other major Scottish mountains.

Bivouac. (Fr.) The spending of a night in the open on a mountain. In Britain this will usually be involuntary, as the result of sudden weather deterioration, too late a start, unexpected difficulties, or plain old-fashioned incompetence. In the Alps a bivouac is often planned, either to permit an early start, or on a long route or a descent. Underestimating the length and difficulty of a route such as Tower Ridge is very common. Winter climbers should be equipped for such an eventuality however, and commonly carry a *bivvy bag,* which may be a simple strong poly bag into which they can shelter, perhaps in conjunction with the digging of a *snow hole*. There are also more robust *bivvy bags,* made from strong nylon, and *Space Blankets,* nylon sheets backed with aluminium to reflect heat back to a sheltering climber. A bivouac, particularly in winter, can be very serious and is to be avoided when at all possible, e.g. by climbing on in torchlight if the weather permits. A special risk associated with winter climbing in Scotland is bad conditions on a summit plateau, e.g. following an ascent of a climb on Nevis. On the summit of Nevis an emergency shelter has been built for such an event, along with two less useful shelters on Carn Dearg and in Coire Leis. The latter is usually buried in winter, while the Carn Dearg shelter can be difficult to find and is, in any case, in close proximity to the top of the descent route via No.4 Gully.

Bivvy Bag. See *Bivouac.*

Bolts. Metal expansion bolts inserted into a pre-drilled hole in an otherwise blank rock wall, thereby allowing a *belay, runner,* or aid point to be used where otherwise none would be found. Their use is a matter of controversy in the U.K. especially, as their use allows any rock to be attempted.

Boots. Footwear for climbing, usually specialised towards walking, winter climbing, or rock climbing, and until recently dominated by leather material. Ankle support to some degree is preferred by most climbers for rough walking. For winter climbing the need is for stiff soles and good ankle support, to allow the use of *crampons*. Winter boots have recently been revolutionised by the introduction of plastic and nylon double boots, a soft leather inner being covered by a hard shell soled in the well-known *Vibram* pattern. Rock-climbing boots require a smooth, high-friction rubber sole with lateral support for using small holds with the edge of the soles, but bending longitudinally so as to allow sloping friction holds to be used.

Bowline. A *knot* commonly used by climbers for attaching the main rope to their *harness*.

Bridging. The technique used to climb a wide *chimney*. The climber places left hand and foot on one wall and right hand and foot on the other wall. Bridging can be used for progress even when no *holds* exist, using friction alone to maintain position. Bridging can also be done in winter using *crampons*.

Brocken spectre. (Ge.) An optical phenomenon seen in mountains when the climber is at about cloud level and a low angle of sunlight is present. The climber's shadow can then be seen thrown on to a backdrop of cloud and can be enormously magnified. Often associated with a coloured halo called a glory appearing to be formed around the shadow's head. Named from the Brocken Mountains of Germany.

Buttress. A defined mass of rock protruding from the side of a mountain, often with flanking *gullies*. If the buttress is long and narrow it may be termed a *ridge*. Good examples are Carn Dearg Buttress and Observatory Buttress.

Cagoule. (Fr.) Form of nylon *anorak* reaching to about knee-height and with no front zip. Named after a monk's habit. Becoming less common.

Chalk. The use of athlete's chalk in powder form which when dusted on to one's hands enables a better hold when rock climbing. Normally used for harder routes and has caused some controversy due to the temporary eyesore it can leave.

Chimney. A steep break in a rock face, usually wide enough to admit a climber's body though still permitting the side walls to be used for *back and foot* or *bridging*.

Chockstone. i. A stone jammed in a crack, varying from very small to the size of a house. Often provide very good *holds*. The Aberdeen spelling is chokestone. ii. Man-made chockstones or *nuts*. These are found in many shapes and sizes, some pre-fitted with wire or nylon *tapes*. The forerunners of these were machine nuts with drilled-out threads. The art of visually sizing a crack on a climb then placing a secure nut *runner* is part of the fun of climbing. See *Friends*.

Cloud sea. Spectacular weather conditions when only the tops of the mountains protrude through a flat sheet of cloud. A good cloud sea can persist for several days.

Compass. A hand-held navigational aid for mountaineers. The most usual model is based on the Swedish orienteering design by Silva and is marked off in degrees. Often includes several luminous points for night navigation.

Coire. (Gaelic). A feature of glaciated mountains, a scooped-out hollow high on the mountain, usually backed by a *ridge* or plateau and often containing a small lochan. Examples are Coire na Ciste and Coire Leis on Ben Nevis.

Corner. A rock feature, resembling the inside angle of a partly opened book. May have a crack in the angle, allowing it to be climbed, or failing that *bridging* may be necessary. Contrasting feature is an edge, resembling the spine of a partly opened book. Note that earlier writers often used corner when they meant edge.

Cornice. (Fr.) An overhanging curve of snow often formed by the wind at the head of a *gully* or at the side of a *ridge*. Not always obvious from above and hence dangerous to the unwary. Frequent cause of an *avalanche* during a thaw if it collapses. If completely blocking a gully, exit may have to be made by digging a *tunnel*.

Crampons. (Fr.) A metal framework which is fastened to the underside of winter climbing *boots* and consisting usually of 12 downward pointing spikes spaced out round the edge of the boot. The spikes are arranged in pairs along the crampons with the front pair inclined forward at an angle. Crampons permit safe and easy movement over snow and ice where otherwise steps might have to be cut. On steep snow and ice the front points are kicked into the slope, allowing upward movement. Origin probably from agricultural use in the Tyrol, where hay-making on steep ground was made easier by their use. Developed as climbing tools especially by Austro-German mountaineers. In wet snow can *ball-up,* causing a large lump of compacted snow to grow underfoot and cause a fall. This is avoided by repeated tapping of the crampon with an *ice axe,* or by wearing a sheet of plastic between the crampon and the sole of the *boot.* The plastic sheet however, will quickly become abraded, especially on a *mixed route.* Crampons may be hinged between the sole and the heel sections, or rigid. The latter are more convenient for climbing ice as they cause less strain on the leg muscles. Crampons are next to useless and very uncomfortable unless used in conjunction with properly stiffened winter *boots*.

Crux. The most difficult *move* or *pitch* on a *route*. From Latin, a cross.

Dachstein. (Ge.) A woollen mitt extensively used for winter climbing. Austrian made and pre-shrunk, these mitts provide a good grip on snow or ice as well as being warm in cold conditions. Sometimes used with waterproof overmitts for wet or extremely severe conditions. The thumb is provided with its own compartment, the fingers being together in a larger space. This is much warmer than a glove with separate compartments for each finger.

Dead Boy. See *Dead Man.*

Dead Man. An extremely effective *belay* for use in snow. A thin alloy plate, rectangular with one end gently pointed and about one foot square. A strong wire cable connected to its centre is tied on to the climbing *rope* via a *karabiner* and the Dead Man is buried in the snow slope at the correct angle of about 40 degrees to the slope, first having cut a T-shaped slot in the snow. The cable runs down the slope to the belaying climber, who has usually cut a small ledge several feet below the placement site. When properly placed in good snow this snow anchor is one of the most secure belays possible. Smaller versions can be used, these are named *Dead Boys.* They originate from the Antarctic, where flat pieces of plywood buried in snow were used to anchor dog teams.

Déscendeur. (Fr.) A metal device for easier and safer *abseiling.* The most common model is the *Figure of eight.*

Dièdre. (Fr.) See *Corner.*

Dinner plating. The fracturing of ice when struck with an *ice axe,* causing plate-shaped fragments to break off. Can also be caused by the placement of *ice screws.*

Drive in. A modern type of *ice screw* which is thinner than the tubular type, allowing it to be quickly hammered in for rapid *belaying* or *protection.* It is removed by unscrewing it. Like a rock *peg* it has an eye at the head end into which a *karabiner* can be fastened.

Duvet. (Fr.) A warm jacket specially filled with down or a synthetic substitute. Developed for Alpine *bivouacs* and of little use for British climbing due to their bulk and warmth. Suitable for winter camping and general comfort.

Étriers. (Fr.) Miniature steps, usually two or three rungs, used in *artificial climbing.* Most are made from nylon *tape* stitched to form footloops and are used in pairs.

Exposure. i.   The sense of a large drop beneath a climber. Long and steep *routes,* or *pitches* are said to be *exposed.* Adds to the enjoyment of a climb. ii. Layman's term for *hypothermia.* A serious condition caused by a drop in core body temperature, usually caused by a combination of bad weather and fatigue. Poor clothing and cold wet conditions are often contributory causes. Progressive signs can be lethargy, unreasonable behaviour, slurring of words, vision disorders, collapse, unconsciousness. If core temperature continues to drop arrythmia sets in, leading eventually to fibrillation and death. Emergency treatment by immediate shelter from the elements, using a *bivvy bag* or sleeping bag. It may be too late if signs of exposure already exist — experienced mountaineers recognise the weather conditions which lead to this condition and take appropriate avoiding action if possible.

Figure of eight. Popular type of *déscendeur,* with the device attached to the climbing *harness* via the smaller ring and loop of the climbing ropes passing through and round the larger ring.

Friction from the rope passing over a *déscendeur* during an *abseil* can produce much heat to damage a nylon rope, the figure of eight contains sufficient metal to dissipate this heat safely during a long *abseil*.

Flake. A spike or leaf of rock on a rock face, part of the main mass of rock. Some flakes are semi-detached and can move slightly when used as a *hold*. Small flakes must be treated carefully as they can break off. This has caused many accidents, even to experienced climbers.

Free climbing. As opposed to *artificial climbing*. Most British routes are free, in that they contain no moves using *pegs* or *nuts* for direct aid.

Friends. Recently developed *protection*, a spring-loaded set of curved, opposing *chockstones* allowing fixation in parallel-sided or even flared cracks, the device jamming more firmly under load.

Front pointing. Modern technique of climbing ice and snow wearing *crampons* and usually with an *ice hammer* and an *ice axe*. Term arises from the frequent use of the two *front points* on each *crampon*. These are kicked into the snow or ice and then stood on, the climber meanwhile holding on to the two ice tools suitably embedded in the slope at about head height or slightly higher. The ice climber moves in a series of alternating foot and hand moves — the two picks of the ice tools are placed solidly above, then the *crampons* are kicked into a higher position one at a time and stepped up on. The aim is to use the larger leg muscles whenever possible. On very steep or overhanging ice the emphasis switches partly to the arms for support.

Frostbite. Local tissue damage caused by ice crystals forming in and between cells, often to exposed fleshy parts of the body such as fingers, ear lobes, noses etc. Also found in toes particularly when circulation is constricted by over-tight boots or too many socks. First signs are loss of feeling followed by loss of normal colour. Emergency treatment is shelter and gentle rewarming, the return of circulation being associated with pain.

Gaiters. (Fr.) Nylon leg covering worn in winter for protection from snow and cold. Run from just below the knee and cover the tops of the *boots*. Latest models may cover the entire *boot* above the sole. Usually zipped, either on front or at the back.

Glissading. (Fr.) If a snow slope is safe enough, with the right consistency of snow, no complications and a safe finish, it is possible for a ski-like descent to be made using *boots* alone. This is, however, a highly dangerous technique not recommended.

Grading. The classification of a climb according to its difficulty, permitting a climber to judge whether a route is a suitable outing for his or her abilities. Gradings have evolved considerably and in summer now take into account the purely technical difficulty of a *pitch* or even move, and the overall difficulty of a route, which could include its steepness, *protection* and so on. In summer the grades are, beginning with the easiest; Easy, Moderate, Difficult, Very Difficult, Severe, Very Severe, Extremely Severe. The latter grade is also given a number from 1 upwards, depending on difficulty. The harder rock pitches are given technical gradings, such as 5a, 6c and so on. Winter climbs are more difficult to grade due to changing conditions but the Scottish system has become widely used, ranging from Grade I, the easiest, to Grade VI. The latter grade appeared as late as 1979 with the first winter ascent of The Shield Direct.

Groove. A rock feature used loosely to describe an open fault too wide to be a crack and not deep enough to be a *chimney* or *gully*. Often V-shaped. See *Dièdre*.

Gully. The deep chasm between two rock *buttresses*. As this feature is usually formed by the erosion of weaker or shattered rock a certain amount of debris is often associated. Some *gullies* provide good summer routes but most are at their best in winter condition. Ben Nevis in particular has a superb set of hard classic winter *gully* climbs such as Point Five, Zero, the Minus Gullies and so on.

Hammer. Climbing tool designed to drive rock *pegs* in. Standard hammer head at one side with often a short spike at the other to clean out cracks etc. Now rarely carried in British rock climbing due to improved alternative methods of *protection*. In winter it has been replaced by the *Ice Hammer*.

Hand traverse. To climb across a rock face relying mainly on hand *holds*. Normally necessary for short sections only and often strenuous.

Harness. Specialised climbing equipment combining waist belt and leg loops to which the climbing *ropes* are attached. In the event of a fall the load will be distributed around the climber's pelvic girdle, lessening the chance of internal injuries. Most common type is the *Sit harness*. These follow the design originated by Don Whillans. Other types favoured by Continental climbers include Chest Harnesses and Whole Body Harnesses. Harnesses also have built-in loops for attaching equipment to. Made from strong nylon loops. Have evolved from the *waist loop*.

Hawser laid. Older method of *rope* construction. The fibres are twisted into three stands which are then twisted into the rope. Now rarely used, *kernmantel* ropes having taken their place.

Head torch. Battery-powered light designed to attach round a climber's head or *helmet*, allowing night climbing. Most designs are still at the primitive stage and many active mountaineers make their own battery case or use a battery otherwise protected from the damp etc. in conjunction with a commercially made head unit. The use of rechargeable cells is about to expand. A head torch should be part of every mountaineer's standard equipment.

Helmet. Protective headgear worn by mountaineers. The choice is usually between a lighter alpine weight *helmet* made of PBS plastic, or a heavier fibreglass model. The latter often curve down at the sides to afford more protection to the ear regions and lower skull. Helmets have clips for affixing a *Head torch*. Many modern rock climbers do not use helmets. They are probably of more importance in winter, when falling ice is fairly common.

Hoar frost. In freezing conditions ice crystals rapidly grow on exposed surfaces, on occasion to large sizes. Hoar is easily broken off however and is more of an aesthetic delight than a climbing problem.

Hold. A small irregularity of rock which can be used by a climber for progress or rest. May come in any shape or form, from cracks, ripples, crystals, *flakes* and so on. Small holds can be used by the finger tips only while larger one may be grasped by the whole hand. In winter holds may be cut in snow or ice by an *ice axe.*

Holster. Small attachment worn on a *harness* to hold an *ice axe* or *ice hammer.* Similar to that worn by a joiner.

Hypothermia. See *Exposure.*

Ice axe. Designed for climbing and walking over snow and ice. Used for balance, *step-cutting,* and in recent years for *front pointing.* Basic design has a head end with a pick and adze, a shaft of varying length depending on the function of the axe, and a lower end tapering to a spike. There may or may not be an attached sling, depending on the owner's preference. The use of wood for the shaft has almost ceased, being replaced by light-weight alloys of far superior strength. A wooden axe when used for a belay usually snapped following a long *leader* fall. Generally, for walking the axe length is dependent on the user's height, the spike being just short of the floor when held by the head and hung alongside the leg. For climbing the length will be much shorter, perhaps down to 45cm or 50cm, with a rubber covered shaft to provide a good grip. A hole at the lower end of the shaft allows a short length of nylon to be used as an attachment to the *harness,* as a security system.

Ice climbing. See *Front pointing.*

Ice hammer. Climbing tool designed for winter climbing, with a hammer head replacing the standard adze. Normally used in conjunction with an *Ice axe* for *Front pointing.*

Ice dagger. Tool for ice climbing technique formerly more in favour on the Continent than in Britain, and now replaced by *Front pointing.* Consisted of stabbing a short metal spike into the slope with one hand and an axe with the other. Designs differed, some being similar to a V-shaped potato peeler.

Ice screw. Metal device for *belaying* on hard snow, ice or frozen turf. Original designs similar to a cork screw with limited strength. Later design became tubular, with the thread on the outside of the tube. Other common model is the *Drive in.* The tubular models are screwed in and out, preferably using an *Ice axe* as extra leverage in order to conserve strength. Generally, the wider the bore, the stronger the screw. Have made winter climbing much safer.

Jamming. Climbing by inserting one's hand, fingers or foot into a crack, increasing the spread anatomically, and thereby firmly but temporarily providing a hold. Experts can climb *overhangs* by this method. Also useful in winter for *mixed climbing.*

Jug handle. Also known as a Jug or Juggie. The ideal rock *hold,* allowing the whole hand to grasp the feature and support the entire body weight if need be. Usually a good incut ledge on an otherwise smooth rock face.

Jumar. The device or action of climbing a fixed *rope* by means of a mechanical aid. Many models available, in left and right hand pairs. Basically a hinged design allows the jumar to be pushed up a rope but grips the rope firmly when loaded. The upper jumar is normally attached to a climber's *harness,* while the lower jumar is used as a foot loop, the ascending climber jumaring by pushing the jumars up the rope alternately. Useful for crevasse rescue or long *artificial climbs*. Also possible to jumar by using rope loops tied with a *Prusik knot*.

Karabiner. (Ge.) Often called a krab for short. An oval shaped alloy link with a spring-loaded gate on one side. Used extensively in climbing for *belays, runners,* rope attachment etc. For attaching the *ropes* to a *harness* and for other uses where security is vital a *Screw gate karabiner* may be used. In this, a collar can be screwed down, preventing the gate from opening accidentally. The strength of the *karabiner* is obviously of importance, many having ratings of over 3000kg.

Kernmantel. (Ge.) The modern method of rope construction, continuous nylon strands running the length of the rope being covered by a woven sheath of nylon. This type of rope handles better than *Hawser laid,* which it has all but replaced for mountaineering purposes. The construction method allows various colours to be used, aiding in identification, pretty photographs etc.

Knots. Various simple knots are in use by mountaineers for several techniques. The *Bowline* is commonly used to attach the main climbing ropes to the *harness,* a *Prusik* knot can be used as an emergency *Jumar*. Two ropes are joined together using a *Double Fisherman, belays* use a *Figure of eight* knot often, while to form a *tape sling* a *tape* knot is required. Also occurs spontaneously when a rope becomes tangled, usually at an inconvenient moment.

Layback. A strenuous rock climbing technique used for climbing cracks and *flakes*. In (say) a *corner,* the hands grip the nearer edge of the crack, while the feet are placed on the opposite wall, thus setting up opposing forces. The climber then 'walks' up the wall, moving hands up the crack in small steps.

Leader. The first climber on a rope, normally climbing while his *second* belays him. A rope of two equally strong leaders usually make alternate leads, while sometimes one leader will do all the leading on a climb. The consequences of a fall for the leader are naturally more serious than for a *second,* who will have the security of the rope above. There is more fun to be had in leading, however, though some climbers are content to be *second.*

Line. i. The way taken by a *route,* followed by climbers. A good *line* often follows a natural weakness of some type up the mountain, e.g. a *line* of cracks, or a *gully*. ii. Almost obsolescent term. Thin *rope* used for *abseil* or *prusik* loops. (See *Alpine line.*)

Mantelshelf. A move in climbing involving gaining a high *hold* or ledge by first placing the hands on the *hold* then pulling one's body high enough so that a foot can be placed on the *hold.*

Mixed route. In Scottish usage a winter route which includes a variety of climbing, with ice and winter buttress techniques necessary. Alpine term would allow rock climbing as well as snow and ice climbing.

Munro. The original compiler of the list of Scottish mountains over 3000 feet which are also called Munros. Sir Hugh T. Munro was an early member of the SMC. There are about 276 Munros, as well as their lesser tops. Munro died before finalising his list, which has been modified slightly several times as surveying changes indicate new heights. Those who 'collect' the Munros are disparagingly referred to by some climbers as Munro baggers.

Nails. Until the end of the Second World War mountaineers climbed with *boots* whose soles were studded with various designs of metal *nails*. One design of nail was known as the *tricouni*, having three flattened prongs of hard steel which was good on rock or ice. Nails were in use through the 1950's, particularly by the Aberdeen school of climbers, until finally replaced by *Vibrams*.

Nevé. (Fr.) As used by Scottish mountaineers is synonymous with *snow ice*. Snow which has undergone some cycles of thawing and re-freezing and is consequently harder than new snow. Is one of the best materials for winter climbing.

Nuts. See *chockstones*.

Overhang. A mass of rock or ice which leans out past the vertical. May be large or small, climbable or not. The underside of a large overhang, if near horizontal, may be termed a *roof*. Snow overhanging at the top of a *gully* or *ridge* is termed a *cornice*.

P.A.'s. Specialised rock climbing *boots* designed by the French climber Pierre Allain. A close-fitting ankle-high boot with a rubberised cotton upper and a high-friction rubber sole and rand. The sole is smooth and is much more flexible longitudinally, allowing small *holds* to be used with the edge of the *boot*. Many models have followed since the P.A. first appeared in the 1950's.

Peg. Modern term for a *piton*. Metal spike with an eye which is hammered into a crack for use as a *belay* or *runner*. A *karabiner* is normally clipped into the eye along with a *tape sling*. Their use in summer rock climbing in the U.K. has virtually been made redundant by improved alternative equipment, though they are still carried for winter climbing.

Peel. Climbing slang for a fall, to 'peel', as in to peel a fruit.

Pendulum. Unusual climbing technique used to reach part of a face to one side by swinging on the rope. More drastic version of a *tension move* or *tension traverse*.

Pinch grip. A rock *hold* in which the fingers grasp the rock like holding a book by the spine.

Pitch. Section of a route between *belays*. Can be up to about 140 feet long when climbing with the normal 150-foot length of rope. Often longer than the straight distance between two belays, due to *traverses* and other small variations. The hardest *pitch* is called the *crux* pitch.

Piton. (Fr.) See *Peg*.

Powder snow. Unconsolidated snow. When blowing loose about a mountain or falling down a *gully* can cause much discomfort. Does not bear any weight and may have to be brushed off a *hold*.

Protection. The safeguards a *leader* can find on a *pitch* in the form of *runners* utilising *chockstones*, *flakes*, *pegs*, *ice screws* and so on. A *pitch* or *route* is said to be serious when *protection* is scarce or absent.

Prusik. A special *knot* invented by the Austrian climber Prusik. See *Jumar*.

Rib. A projecting spine of rock of varying size. Normally steeper than an *arête*.

Ridge. Large feature on a mountain, normally the crest formed where two faces meet, e.g. Observatory Ridge.

Roof. The horizontal or near horizontal underside of an *overhang.* A small one may be *free-climbed,* larger ones may require *aid.*

Rope. i. A party of climbers connected by a rope. ii. The actual rope used by climbers. Modern rope is made from nylon by the *kernmantel* process. Contemporary British technique is for two 45 metre lengths of rope to be used, each 9mm in diameter. The rope colours are usually different for convenience. Two ropes, as used in the double rope technique, are much preferable over a single rope, particularly in rock climbing, as the placing of ropes alternately through *runners* reduces friction called rope drag. *Kernmantel* is found in sizes of 3mm to 11mm, some climbers using a single rope of the largest size, while the smaller sizes are used mainly for *runners,* often being used with *chockstones.* See *Hawser laid.*

Route. A climb or *line.*

Runner. See *Protection.* Short for 'Running Belay', this is the technique of protecting a *pitch.* Should a *leader* fall, he will hang from the highest runner, thereby shortening the length of his fall. The placement of runners takes experience in order to to find the optimum balance between sufficient protection and over protection. To over protect a pitch wastes time, as well as being of dubious ethics.

Run-out. The amount of *rope* used by a *leader* on a *pitch.* A full run-out uses all available rope and enforces a leader to find a *belay.* One task for the *second* is to inform the leader of the amount of rope left, so that a belay can be found in time.

Scree. Loose rock eroded from a mountain and found in steep slopes below cliffs. Can be very awkward to climb though some afford a rapid if exciting descent. Very dangerous if knocked down a *gully.*

Screw gate. See *Karabiner.*

Second man. The climber at the lower end of the *rope* who follows the *leader* up a *route,* the climbers normally moving one at a time and alternating the lead. In a roped descent positions would be the same, the second man then descending first, protected from above by the leader. The second man has to *belay* the leader, paying out the rope as necessary.

Siege tactics. To climb a *route* over several days, leaving fixed ropes on the route so as to by-pass these pitches on subsequent occasions. An unpopular technique rarely recorded in the U.K., e.g. the first winter ascent of Point Five Gully.

Sit Harness. See *Harness.*

Slab. An inclined sheet of rock, between about 30 and 75 degrees and varying in size from a few feet to many hundreds of feet. The greatest extent of slabs can be found in the Trilleachan Slabs in Glen Etive, where difficult moves may have to made using friction only.

Sling. A short loop of *rope* or *tape,* used for *belays* or *runners.* May be formed by tying a *knot* or be bought prestitched.

Snow hole. At its best a commodious cave dug out of a deep bank of snow and affording shelter from the elements. This is normally impossible in bad weather conditions and in an emergency the best that is available may be a hollow behind a boulder or a shallow trench. A good snow hole requires hours of work by several people using shovels.

Snow ice. See *néve.*

Solo climbing. To climb a *route* alone, with or without a *rope* for protection, or to climb with another but without a rope. Provides much satisfaction, though potentially a high risk practice.

Space blanket. A sheet of nylon backed with aluminium to reflect the heat from a climber's body during an emergency *bivouac.*

Spindrift. Loose snow blowing about a mountain or falling down the rocks or *gullies.* Of great discomfort and may cause a *route* to be abandoned.

Stance. The site, preferably a ledge, of a *belay.* May be a natural ledge, or in winter a small ledge cut out of the snow slope.

Step-cutting. The art of forming hand and foot holds in snow and ice using an *ice axe.* Now mostly superceded by *front pointing.* Step-cutting requires strength and stamina, as on a steep *pitch* steps will have to be cut one-handed above the head. Normally the feet use the same holds as the hands do, two columns of offset steps being cut up the slope. The introduction of *front pointing* has made many of the older hard routes easier, particularly the *gullies,* while the buttress climbs have not changed much in difficulty.

Sticht plate. See *Belay plate.*

Sustained. A *pitch* or *route* is said to be sustained if difficulties are maintained at or about the same level.

Tape. Nylon tubular webbing used for *belays* and *runners.* The webbing is manufactured so as stay flat and can then often be insinuated behind *flakes* where thicker *kernmantel slings* would not fit. Can also be had in non-tubular versions and in different widths.

Temperature inversion. See *Cloud sea.*

Tension move. A technique whereby a climber leans across a holdless face using the rope running behind him for balance. Several such moves would be a *tension traverse.* Rarely required in the U.K.

Thread belay. A very secure belay made by feeding a *sling* behind a natural *chockstone* or small passage way in the rock.

Top rope. To climb a difficult section with assistance from the rope above. Note that it is virtually impossible to be pulled up, but that it is possible to be held, allowing a rest to be had. A method also used for training on short rock outcrops, when assistance will then only be taken if strength or ability fails. On a normal climb, the *second* does not use the rope in this fashion, but climbs unaided.

Tricouni. See *Nails.*

Tunnel. See *Cornice.*

Undercut. See *Overhang.*

Vibrams. Cleated rubber soles widely used for mountaineering *boots.* An Italian invention dating from 1935 and commonly available following the Second World War. *Boots* using the Vibram sole are lighter and warmer than the older *nailed* format, but should be used in conjunction with *crampons* in winter.

Verglas. (Fr.) When rocks wet with rain freeze a thin layer of transparent ice forms, giving a treacherously slippy surface. Impossible to climb when thin. Also forms in cracks and chimneys. Similar to black ice on roads in appearance and effect.

Waist loop. A 20-foot length of hemp, formerly used for connecting a climber to the main *rope.* The loop was wound several times round the climber's waist and tied with a reef *knot.* A bad fall using a waist loop could result in internal injuries, while a prolonged suspension could asphyxiate. Now replaced by the use of a *harness.*

Wall. The steep face of a mountain or *buttress.*

Water ice. A hard and often brittle ice formed from running water, as opposed to ice formed from the thawing and re-freezing of snow. Often blue in colour.

Wedge. A wooden protection device hammered into cracks in the same way as *pegs.* Now replaced by large *pegs.*

White out. A dangerous condition in winter when falling or drifting snow, and/or poor visibility cause the horizon to merge with the ground and the sky. It is then difficult to orientate oneself and very easy to walk over an edge.

Wind-chill. The effect of low temperature is compounded by the heat extracting effect of the wind and the two in combination should be taken into account when considering the weather. Charts are available which compute such combinations.

Wind slab. A dangerous snow condition, when an upper layer of firmer snow is loosely attached to a lower layer. The upper layer can then break away in slabby chunks at a climber's touch, causing an *avalanche.*

Wire. See *Chockstone.*

Note: 'SMC Archives' refers usually to the SMC Library, presently housed in the Music Reference Section of the Public Library, King George V Bridge, Edinburgh. Access to this can be arranged by writing to the SMC Librarian, whose address will be found in the current edition of the Scottish Mountaineering Club Journal. The Club Library is opposite to the NLS, the National Library of Scotland. Other useful sources include the excellent facilities of the Mitchell Library, Glasgow, open to the public, and Glasgow University Library, access by application to the University Librarian. The last two hold complete sets of the Scottish Mountaineering Club Journal, without which any research into Scottish Mountaineering would be a vain attempt. The bibliography given here is far from exhaustive, and other sources were consulted but not referenced. A good starting point for the reader wishing to delve deeper would be W.H. Murray's authoritative 'The Scottish Highlands', published by the Scottish Mountaineering Trust and now undergoing a re-write. The outstanding collection of mountaineering books, of course, is that held by The Alpine Club, London. Access to the latter by writing to The Librarian, The Alpine Club, 74 South Audley Street.

Chapter 1 — Early Travellers

1. Watson, William J. 'The History of the Celtic Place-names of Scotland'. (Edinburgh: Blackwood, 1926.)
2. Mackenzie, W.C. 'Scottish Place Names'. (London: Kegan Paul, Trench, Trubner & Co., 1931.)
3. Johnston, J.B. 'Place Names of Scotland'. (London: John Murray, 1934.)
4. MacMillan, Somerled. 'Bygone Lochaber'. (Printed privately, 1971: Printers K. & R. Davidson, Glasgow.)
5. Blaeu, Johan, 'Le Grand Atlas Ou Cosmographie Blaviane'. (Amsterdam:1663). Facsimile edition in twelve volumes (Amsterdam: Treatium Orbis Terrarum Ltd, 1967).
6. Sir Robert Gordon. Unpublished letters to Sir John Scot of Scotstarvet, NLS, Adv.MS,1719.
7. Cash, C.G. 'The first topographical survey of Scotland'. Scottish Geographical Magazine XVII, 1901, 399-413.
8. Drummond, John. 'Memoirs of Sir Ewen Cameron of Locheill'. (Edinburgh: Abbotsford Club, 1842.)
9. Burt, Edward. 'Letters from a Gentleman in the North of Scotland'. (London: 1754). (Edinburgh: John Donald Publishers Ltd., 1974 — Facsimile reprint of 5th edition, London: s.n., 1818.)
10. Pennant, Thomas. 'A Tour in Scotland, 1769'. (Warrington: Printed by W. Eyres,1774; 3rd edition.)
11. Robertson, James. MS Journals in the NLS (1767 and 1771).
12. Hope, John, 'Letter to William Watson, dated 10 April, 1769'. Philos. Trans. R. Soc., 59, 241-242, 1769.
13. Fletcher, H.R. 'Exploration of the Scottish Flora'. Trans. Bot. Soc. Edin., 38, 30-47, 1959.
14. Williams, John. 'The Natural History of the Mineral Kingdom'. In 2 Vols.(Edinburgh: Bell & Bradfute, 1810, 2nd edition.)
15. Bailey, James. 'Diary of Scottish Tour'. National Library of Scotland.
16. Wilkinson, Thomas. 'Tours to the British Mountains, with the Descriptive Poems of Lowther and Emont Vale'. (London: Taylor & Hessey, 1824.)
17. Aust, Mrs Murray. 'A Companion and Useful Guide to the Beauties of Scotland, and the Hebrides'. (London: 1799, sold by George Nicol.)
18. Garden, William. 'Keats And Ben Nevis'. SMCJ 21, 407-413, 1938.
19. Carr, Sir John. 'Caledonian sketches or a Tour Through Scotland in 1807'. (London: Mathews & Leigh, 1809.)
20. Macculloch, John. 'The Highlands and Western Isles of Scotland'. (London: Longman, Hurst, Rees, Orme, Brown, and Green, 1824.)

21. The New Statistical Account of Scotland. (Edinburgh & London: William Blackwood & Sons, 1845.)

22. Forbes, J.D. 'Travels Through the Alps'. (London: Adam & Charles Black: Revised and annotated by W.A.B. Coolidge, 3rd Edition, 1900.)

23. Professor George Adam Smith. 'Rise And Progress of Mountaineering in Scotland — V. The Works of Professor James D. Forbes'. SMCJ 3, 309-315, 1895.

24. Burton, John Hill. 'The Cairngorm Mountains'. (Edinburgh & London: William Blackwood & Sons, 1864.)

Chapter 2 — The First Climbers

1. Naismith, W.W. 'Early Winter Climbing'. SMCJ 17, 124-132, 1925.

2. Naismith, W.W. Diary of Ascents. Scottish National Library.

3. Lord Mackay. 'Vignettes of Earlier Climbers'. SMCJ 24, 169-180, 1950.

4. Naismith, W.W. 'Notes and Queries'. SMCJ 2, 136, 1892.

5. Naismith, W.W. 'Ben Nevis in 1880 and 1889'. SMCJ 1, 215-221, 1891.

6. Kilgour, W.T. 'Twenty Years on Ben Nevis'. (Paisley: Alexander Gardner, 1905.) Reprinted by The Ernest Press, Glasgow, 1985.

7. Clark, W.I. 'Scottish Mountaineering Club Guide to Ben Nevis'. (Edinburgh: Scottish Mountaineering Club, 1902.)

8. Ramsay, G.G., Professor 'The Formation of the Scottish Mountaineering Club'. SMCJ 4, 73-91, 1896.

9. Whymper, E. 'On the Top of Ben Nevis'. Leisure Hour, September 1894.

10. Logbook of Ben Nevis Observatory, Vol.4, 1891-1894, entry for August 7, 1892. Archives Scottish Meteorological Office, Edinburgh.

11. Alpine Notes — Ben Nevis. Alpine Journal 17, 520-521, 1895.

12. Norman Collie. Obituary Notice. SMCJ 23, 95-97, 1943.

13. Hillary, Richard. 'The Last Enemy'. (London: Macmillan, 1942.)

14. Collie, N. Letter to W. Douglas, 1/1/1894. SMC Archives.

15. Collie, N. Letter to W. Douglas, 27/6/1894. SMC Archives.

16. Collie, N. Letter to W. Douglas, 11/7/1894. SMC Archives.

17. Collie, N. 'Divine Mysteries of the Oromaniacal Quest', by Orlamon Linecus, SMCJ 3, 151-157, 1894.

18. Naismith, W.W. Letter to Douglas (undated). SMC Archives.

19. Collie, N. Letter to W. Douglas, 20/4/1894. SMC Archives.

20. Naismith, W.W. Letter to W. Douglas, 28/9/1894. SMC Archives.

21. Brown, William. 'Ascent of Ben Nevis by The N.E. Buttress'. SMCJ 3, 323-331, 1895.

22. Thomson, Gilbert. Letter to W. Douglas, 27/5/1895. SMC Archives.

23. Notice to Club Members, 1896. Club Scrap Book, NLS.

24. Brown, W. 'Proceedings of the Club'. SMCJ 4, 129-132, 1896.

25. Slingsby, W.C. 'An Easter Holiday in the Scottish Highlands'. The Yorkshire Ramblers' Club Journal. 1, 173-187, 1902.

Chapter 3 — The Observatory

1. Humble, B.H. 'An Epic of Ben Nevis'. Chamber's Journal, January, 1936.

2. 'Opening of the Ben Nevis Observatory — Interesting Ceremony'. ('The Scotsman', Thursday, October 18, 1883.)

3. Observatory Log: Meteorological Office Archives, Edinburgh.

4. Kilgour, W.T. 'Twenty Years on Ben Nevis'. (Paisley: Alexander Gardner, 1905.) Reprinted by The Ernest Press, Glasgow, 1985.

5. Drysdale, Alexander. 'Life at Ben Nevis Observatory'. Unpublished Lecture Notes.
6. Cunningham, C.D. 'Hill Climbing in Scotland'. Alpine Journal, 12, 502-509, 1884.
7. Begg, John S. 'Life And Work at Ben Nevis Observatory'. Cairngorm Club Journal 2, 253-270, 1898. Reprinted in SMC Journals for 1984 and 1985.
8. Rankin, A. 'Note on the number of gales observed at the Ben Nevis Observatory'. Journal of the Scottish Meteorological Society 12, 20-22, 1903.
9. Roy, Marjory G. 'The Ben Nevis Observatory 1883-1904'. (Unpublished.)
10. Wilson, C.T.R. 'Ben Nevis Sixty Years Ago'. In: Weather, 9, 309-311, 1954.
11. Transactions of the Royal Society of Edinburgh Vols. 34, 42, 43, and 44 (Parts 1 & 2).

Other Useful Works

1. Paton, James. 'Ben Nevis Observatory 1883-1904'. Weather, 9, 291-308, 1954.
2. Gatty, Victor H. 'The Glacial Aspect of Ben Nevis'. Geographical Journal 27, 487-492, 1906.
3. Duncan, C.N. and Weston, K.J. 'Ben Nevis Observatory, 1883-1983'. Weather 38, 298-303, 1983.
4. Wragge, Clement. 'Ascending Ben Nevis in Winter'. Chamber's Journal 19, No.957, Saturday, April 29, 1882.
5. Wragge, C.L. 'Resumption of the Ben Nevis Meteorological Observations, 1882'. Symons's Monthly Meteorological Magazine 17, July 1882.
6. Wragge, C.L. 'Ben Nevis Observatory'. Nature, March 22, 1883, pp. 487-491.
7. Omond, R.T. 'Zoological Notes from the Log-Book of the Ben Nevis Observatory'. The Annals of Scottish Natural History, July, 1905.
8. Barton, Jim and Roy, Marjory. 'A Monument to Mountain Meteorology'. New Scientist, 16 June, 1983, pp. 804-805.

Chapter 4 — Raeburn and Company

1. Ling, W.N. 'In Memoriam, Harold Raeburn'. SMCJ, 18, 26-31, 1927.
2. Lord Mackay. 'Vignettes of Earlier Climbers'. SMCJ, 24, 169-180, 1950.
3. Naismith, W.W. 'Letter to W. Douglas, November 17, 1896'. SMC Archives.
4. Clark, W.I. 'Photography in Colour for Mountaineers'. SMCJ 10, 294-306, 1909.
5. Naismith, W.W. 'Ben Nevis, Tower Ridge'. SMCJ, 6, 131, 1901.
6. Ling, W.N. 'A Blizzard on Ben Nevis'. SMCJ 6, 213-217, 1901.
7. Raeburn, H. 'The Observatory Ridge, Ben Nevis'. SMCJ 6, 249-250, 1901.
8. Clark, W.I. 'New Climbs on Ben Nevis'. SMCJ 7, 199-211, 1903.
9. Raeburn, H. 'From Sea to Summit'. SMCJ 7, 194-198, 1903.
10. Raeburn, H. IN: 'Ben Nevis Guide', edited by W.I. Clark. (Edinburgh: SMC, 1903).
11. Raeburn, H. 'A Scottish Ice Climb'. SMCJ 9, 153-158, 1907.
12. Scottish Mountaineering Club Guide to Ben Nevis, edited by H. MacRobert (Edinburgh: SMC, 1919).
13. Macphee, George Graham. 'Climbers' Guide to Ben Nevis'. (Edinburgh: SMC, 1936).
14. Marshall, J.R. 'Climbers' Guide to Ben Nevis'. (Edinburgh: SMC, 1969).
15. Campbell, R.N. 'The First Scottish Ice Climbers'. SMCJ 30, 48-57, 1972.
16. Clark, C.I. 'Thirty Hours on Ben Nevis'. SMCJ 10, 73-81, 1908.
17. MacIntyre, J.H.A. 'Proceedings of The Club'. SMCJ 10, 112-119, 1908.
18. Goggs, F.S. 'Ben Nevis: Observatory Ridge'. SMCJ 15, 310-318, 1920.
19. Pigott, A.S. 'Notes on some Scottish Climbs'. Rucksack Club Journal 4, p.193, 1921.
20. Raeburn, H. 'Mountaineering Art'. (London: T. Fisher Unwin Ltd., 1920).

Chapter 5 — A New Hut, New Clubs
1. Proceedings of the Club — Easter Meet, 1925 — Fort William. SMCJ 17, 206-214, 1925.
2. Lord Mackay. 'Vignettes of Earlier Climbers'. SMCJ 24, 169-180, 1950.
3. Mayland, A. Ernest. 'The Club In Retrospect I. — Its Origins and Growth'. SMCJ 22, 6-13, 1939.
4. Clark, W. Inglis. 'The Charles Inglis Clark Memorial Hut'. SMCJ 18, 325-335.
5. Proceedings of the Club. 'The Official Opening of the Charles Inglis Clark Memorial Hut'. SMCJ 18, 365-369, 1929.
6. Richardson, R.T. 'The C.I.C. Hut — Jubilee Celebrations'. SMCJ 31, 342-344, 1979.
7. C.I.C. Log Book, 1971-1980. SMC Archives.
8. Rutherford, R.N. 'Five Nights in the Scottish Hut'. SMCJ 17, 117-122, 1925.
9. Hutchison, A.G. 'The Formation of the JMCS (i) The Beginning of the JMCS'. SMCJ 30, 309-310, 1975.
10. Anon. 'Those J.M.C.S. Bus Meets'. Letters to the Editor. SMCJ 27, 153-156, 1961.

Chapter 6 — The 1930's
1. Dutton, G.J. 'J.H.B. Bell as Editor'. SMCJ 31, 85-88, 1977.
2. Small, A.C.D. 'J.H.B. Bell as Companion'. SMCJ 31, 83-84, 1977.
3. Murray, W.H. 'J.H.B. Bell as Climber'. SMCJ 31, 80-82, 1977.
4. CIC Hut Log Book, Vol.1. November 12, 1928 – July 5, 1949. SMC Archives.
5. Macphee, G. Graham. 'Twelve Days in the Hut'. SMCJ 19, 229-237, 1931.
6. McLeod, Rev. George. 'Proceedings of the Club'. SMCJ 19, 348, 1932.
7. Borthwick, A.C. 'Epic Story Behind The Ben Nevis Tragedy'. Glasgow Weekly Herald, April 7, 1934.
8. Bell, J.H.B. 'A Ben Nevis Constellation of Climbs'. SMCJ 22, 367-376, 1941.
9. Wedderburn, E.A.M. 'A Climb on Ben Nevis'. SMCJ 20, 233-237, 1934.
10. Williams, G.C. 'Days on Ben Nevis'. SMCJ 20, 394-400, 1935.
11. Macphee, G. Graham. 'Ben Nevis Guide Book'. (Scottish Mountaineering Club: Edinburgh: Douglas & Foulis, 1936).
12. Bell, J.H.B. 'Log Book — Vol. 4'.
13. Bell, J.H.B. 'New Climbs — Zero Gully, Ben Nevis'. SMCJ 21, 200-201, 1937.
14. Murray, W.H. 'The C.I.C. Hut — 1930's'. SMCJ 31, 334-336, 1979.
15. Bell, J.H.B. 'The West Face of Observatory Ridge — Ben Nevis'. SMCJ 21, 352-354, 1938.
16. Macphee, G. Graham. 'Scottish Mountaineering and its Relation to Mountaineering Abroad. II — Remarks on Snow and Ice Conditions'. SMCJ 21, 85-92, 1936.
17. MacKenzie, W.M. 'Fourteen Hours on the Observatory Ridge'. SMCJ 21, 337-338, 1938.
18. Stangle, F.G. 'New Climbs — Comb Gully, Ben Nevis'. SMCJ 22, 65-66, 1939.

Chapter 7 — A Constellation of Climbs
1. Bell, J.H.B. 'A Ben Nevis Constellation of Climbs'. SMCJ 22, 367-376, 1941.
2. CIC Hut Log Book, Vol.1. November 12, 1928 – July 5, 1949. SMC Archives.
3. Ritchie, Graham S. 'Third on the Rope'. SMCJ 25, 137-142, 1953.
4. 'New Climbs and Notes — Ben Nevis; No.2 Gully'. SMCJ 23, 109-110, 1943.
5. Dow, J.A.T. Personal communication.
6. Kellett, B.P. 'Recent Rock Climbs on Ben Nevis'. SMCJ 23, 139-152, 1944
7. Kellett, B.P. 'A Record of Ben Nevis Climbs'. SMCJ 23, 333-340, 1946.
8. Langmuir, Eric D.G. 'Nothing Venture'. Cambridge Mountaineering, 1955, 18-21.
9. 'Scotland 1955 — Ben Nevis'. Cambridge Mountaineering, 1956, 61-65.
10. Stead, A.C. and Marshall, J.R. 'Rock and Ice Climbs in Lochaber and Badenoch'. (Edinburgh: Scottish Mountaineering Club, 1981).

11. Bell, J.H.B. 'Climbing Log, Vol.6, p.41, September 1944'.

12. Bell, J.H.B. 'Scottish Climbing Clubs: A Survey. I'. SMCJ 23, 252-260, 1945.

13. Carsten, H.A. 'The Crack'. Wayfarer's Journal No.8, 1947, pp.44-47.

14. Smith, R. 'Twenty-four Hours'. Edinburgh University M.C. Journal, 1957. (Reprinted in SMCJ, 29, 341-346, 1971).

15. Peascod, W. 'The Journey After Dawn'. An Autobiography. (Cicerone Press, 1985).

16. Murray, W.H. 'Mountaineering in Scotland'. (London: J.M. Dent & Sons Ltd, 1947).

17. Bell, J.H.B. 'A Progress in Mountaineering'. (Edinburgh & London: Oliver & Boyd, 1950).

Chapter 8 — Renaissance

1. Don Whillans and Alick Ormerod. 'Don Whillans: Portrait of a Mountaineer'. (London: Heinemann, 1971).

2. Downes, R.O. & O'Hara, M.J. 'Scotland 1956'. Cambridge Mountaineering, 1957.

3. O'Hara, Mike. Personal communication, 1985.

4. Marshall, J.R. 'The Initiation'. SMCJ 33, 1-3, 1984.

5. Vigano, Charlie. 'The Creagh Dhu'. Rocksport, April/May 1972, p.9.

6. Maden, B.E.H. 'Shirtsleeves on Ben Nevis'. Climbers' Club Journal 1958, 192-197.

7. Stead, A.C. and Marshall, J.R. 'Rock and Ice Climbs in Lochaber and Badenoch'. (Edinburgh: Scottish Mountaineering Club, 1981).

8. Williams, G.C. 'Days on Ben Nevis'. SMCJ 26, 394-400, 1935.

9. Patey, T.W. 'The Zero Gully Affair'. SMCJ 26, 205-216, 1958.

10. Haston, Dougal. 'In High Places'. (London: Cassell, 1972).

11. Brown, Richard. Letter dated September 30, 1955, to Ross Higgins. SMC Archives.

12. Grieve, John. 'Nowhere To Fall But Off'. SMCJ 32, 246-250, 1982.

Chapter Nine — The Pinnacle

1. Shaw, Robin. 'The Siege of Point Five'. Glasgow University M.C. Journal, No.4, February 1959, pp.5-8.

2. Clough, Ian. 'Point Five, A Ben Nevis Saga'. SMCJ 26, 335-342, 1959.

3. Clough, Ian. 'Letter to Tom Patey, October 1962'. SMC Archives.

4. Holt, R.K. 'The Orion Face of Ben Nevis'. Edinburgh University M.C. Journal, 1958-1959, 7-10.

5. Crocket, K.V. 'Hadrian's Wall'. SMCJ 30, 147-151, 1972.

6. Haston, Dougal. 'In High Places'. (Cassell: London, 1972).

7. Marshall, J.R. 'JMCS Dinner Speech', Bridge of Orchy, October 1984.

8. Smith, Robin. 'The Bat And The Wicked'. SMCJ 27, 12-20, 1960.

9. Perrin, Jim. 'The Ice Climbers'. In: 'On And Off The Rocks'. (Gollancz: London, 1986).

10. Smith, Robin. 'The Old Man And The Mountains'. Edinburgh University Mountaineering Club Journal 1961.

11. Marshall, J.R. 'Garde de Glace' (The Ascent of Gardyloo Buttress). SMCJ 27, 115-117, 1961.

12. Crocket, K.V. 'Winter Dreams — Gardyloo'. SMCJ 31, 5-7, 1976.

13. Marshall, J.R. 'The Orion Face'. SMCJ 28, 112-115, 1961.

14. Crocket, K.V. 'Winter Dreams — Orion'. SMCJ 31, 3-5, 1976.

15. Haston, Dougal. 'Nightshift in Zero'. E.U.M.C. Journal, 1960-61.

Chapter 10 — Of Whisky, Foot-Races & Cars, & Aluminium — Useful Bibliography

1. House, Jack. 'The Romance of Long John'. (1982: Long John International Limited).

2. Smith, Alexander. 'A Summer in Skye'. (2nd Edition: Edinburgh: W.P. Nimmo & Co., 1885).

3. Halcrow, William Thomson. 'The Lochaber Water-Power Scheme'. Minutes of Proceedings of the Institution of Civil Engineers, 231, Part I, 31-106, 1930-31.

4. 'The Lochaber Water Power Scheme'. Supplement to The Scots Magazine, New Series, Vol.XI, No.6, pp.401-404, September 1929.
5. Paton, T.A.L. and Brown, Guthrie J. 'Power from Water'. (London: Leonard Hill, 1960).
6. Howat, Patrick. 'The Lochaber Narrow Gauge Railway'. (Huddersfield: Narrow Gauge Railway Society: 1980).
7. 'Aluminium in The Highlands'. (The British Aluminium Company Ltd, 1978).
8. Steel, Charles. 'The Ben Nevis Race'. (Printed by Bennett & Thomson, Dumbarton: 1956).

Chapter 11 — Consolidation
1. Tennent, Norman. 'The Primitive Approach'. SMCJ 27, 228-233, 1962.
2. Fulton, Ian. 'Torro'. Glasgow University M.C. Journal, 1970.
3. Marshall, J.R. 'Minus Three in Summer'. SMCJ 28, 87-89, 1965.
4. Robertson, B.W. 'A Climb Called King Kong'. SMCJ 28, 103-108, 1965.
5. Bathgate, D. 'The First Ascent of The Curtain'. SMCJ 28, 108-111, 1965.
6. Marshall, J.R. 'In The Groove'. SMCJ 29, 378-382, 1971.
7. Campbell, R.N. 'Bringing Up Father'. Edinburgh University M.C. Journal, 1969, 48-52.
8. Clough, Ian. 'Guide to Winter Climbs — Ben Nevis and Glencoe'. (Cicerone Press, 1969).

Chapter 12 — Revolution
1. Chouinard, Yvon. 'Salsipuedes'. SMCJ 30, 20, 1972.
2. Carrington, Robert. 'Carn Dearg Commentary'. Mountain 46, 26-37, November/December 1975.
3. Campbell, R.N. 'Ben Nevis Notes'. SMCJ 30, 185, 1973.
4. Crocket, K.V. 'Smith's Route, Gardyloo Buttress'. In: Cold Climbs (Ken Wilson, Dave Alcock & John Barry eds., London: Diadem Books, 1983). pp.75-77.
5. Crocket, K.V. 'Minus One Gully'. In: Cold Climbs, pp.41-43.
6. Stead, Colin. 'One Below The Belt'. SMCJ 30, 221-223, 1974.
7. Quinn, Neil. 'Hadrian's Wall Direct'. SMCJ 30, 224-226, 1974.
8. Rouse, Alan. 'Route 2, Carn Dearg'. In: Cold Climbs, pp.102-105.
9. Anderson, R. 'Personal communication, January 1985'.
10. Christie, J. 'C.I.C. Logbook, January 1985'.

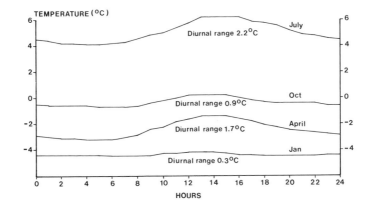

AVERAGE HOURLY TEMPERATURES 1884 - 1903

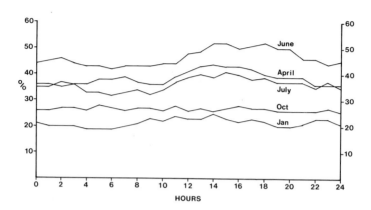

SUMMIT CLEAR OF FOG OR MIST AS PERCENTAGE OF POSSIBLE 1884-1903

AVERAGE MONTHLY RAINFALL TOTALS IN MM. 1885-1903

	JAN	FEB	MAR	APL	MAY	JUN	JUL	AUG	SEP	OCT	NOV	DEC	YEAR
Average	465	344	386	215	201	191	274	339	400	392	390	484	4083

Table 1

AVERAGE DAILY HOURS OF SUNSHINE IN EACH MONTH
Year average : 2 hours per day (16% of possible)

	JAN	FEB	MAR	APL	MAY	JUN	JUL	AUG	SEP	OCT	NOV	DEC
Average	0.7	1.4	1.8	2.7	3.7	4.3	2.7	1.8	2.1	1.3	0.9	0.7
% of poss.	10	16	15	19	23	22	16	13	16	13	11	9

Table 2

HOURS WITH WINDSPEED EXCEEDING 43 KNOTS 1884-1896

	JAN	FEB	MAR	APL	MAY	JUN	JUL	AUG	SEP	OCT	NOV	DEC	YEAR
Totals	640	489	336	301	115	101	48	116	118	233	526	382	3405
% of poss.	6.6	5.6	3.5	3.2	1.2	1.1	0.5	1.2	1.3	2.4	5.6	3.9	3.0

Table 3

MONTHLY TEMPERATURES (°C)

	JAN	FEB	MAR	APL	MAY	JUN	JUL	AUG	SEP	OCT	NOV	DEC
Average	-4.4	-4.6	-4.4	-2.4	0.6	4.3	5.0	4.7	3.3	-0.3	-1.7	-3.8
Stand. Dev.	1.7	1.7	1.3	1.4	2.0	1.6	1.4	1.4	1.4	1.6	1.1	1.3

Table 4